The Early Medieval in South India

The Early Medieval in South India

Kesavan Veluthat

OXFORD
UNIVERSITY PRESS

OXFORD
UNIVERSITY PRESS

YMCA Library Building, Jai Singh Road, New Delhi 110 001

Oxford University Press is a department of the University of Oxford. It furthers the University's objective of excellence in research, scholarship, and education by publishing worldwide in

Oxford New York
Auckland Cape Town Dar es Salaam Hong Kong Karachi Kuala Lumpur Madrid Melbourne Mexico City Nairobi New Delhi Shanghai Taipei Toronto

With offices in
Argentina Austria Brazil Chile Czech Republic France Greece Guatemala Hungary Italy Japan Poland Portugal Singapore South Korea Switzerland Thailand Turkey Ukraine Vietnam

Oxford is a registered trademark of Oxford University Press in the UK and in certain other countries

Published in India
by Oxford University Press, New Delhi

First published 2009

ISBN-13: 978-0-19-569663-9
ISBN-10: 0-19-569663-8

Typeset in Nalandgaramond 10/12.9
by Le Studio Graphique, Gurgaon 122 001
Printed in India at Pauls Press, New Delhi 110020
Published by Oxford University Press
YMCA Library Building, Jai Singh Road, New Delhi 110 001

For

Professor R. Champakalakshmi

Contents

Preface ix
Acknowledgements xi

Introduction 1

PART I
Tamiḻakam

1. Into the 'Medieval'—and out of It 19
2. The Temple in Medieval South India 61
3. Land Rights and Social Stratification 83
4. Labour Rent and Produce Rent 100
5. *Nāḍu* in the Socio-political Structure 109

PART II
Medieval Kerala

6. The *Kēraḷōlpatti* as History 129
7. Epigraphy in the Historiography of Kerala 147
8. Literacy and Communication in Pre-modern Kerala 168
9. The King as Lord and Overlord 183
10. A Capital City as a Sacred Centre 229

11. Medieval Kerala: State and Society 249

12. Landlordism in Medieval Kerala 277

13. Evolution of a Regional Identity 295

PART III

In the Neighbourhood:
Early Medieval Karnataka

14. *Vēḷevāḷi* in Karnataka 315

15. Landed Magnates as State Agents 325

Index 333

Preface

The articles included in this collection were written over the past two decades. The occasion on, and provocation under, which they were written was different in nearly every case. The necessary discipline and coherence expected of a tightly written monograph, therefore, will be looked for in vain in this collection. Even the elementary uniformity in many matters expected of research papers may be missing in them. Read together, however, they will hopefully give a picture of the way in which the 'early medieval' is constituted in the history of the deep south.

All linear histories are necessarily periodized. When history, a new form of knowledge for any part of the world in the modern period, reached India, it was naturally a periodized history. Many, however, find themselves ill at ease with the old tripartite division. One of the more convenient units is the 'early medieval'. There are compelling reasons to identify an intelligible period like this in the context of south India as well, for we see a broad pattern here. The details include the transformation of an economy characterized by cattle-keeping and subsistence agriculture into one of wet rice cultivation and a considerable surplus; replacement of simple exchange with the instituted process of trade and the subsequent development of urbanism; transmutation of a relatively undifferentiated society into one divided sharply into castes and the consequent 'casteization' and peasantization of tribes; acceptance of an organized religion with its ideas and institutions suited to the new economic and social order; the formation of the state with a *kṣatriya*-ized monarchy presiding over it; and a large number of other attendant developments.

There is considerable difference between these phenomena in the context of the south and the pattern obtaining in the north, a major difference being the earlier graduation of the north to a state society where it even got elaborated and refined as an 'empire'. This shows that there have been multiple transitions there. In the case of south India, however, things proceeded on different lines. The phase immediately preceding what I have chosen to call the 'early medieval' was in no way comparable to its counterpart in the north; but comparison becomes possible when it comes to broad patterns and even in details. Detailed studies will bring out the patterns, of which the essays presented here are a modest beginning.

The author hopes that the essays included in this collection will give a picture of how one can make an alternative reading of early medieval south Indian history. This is particularly relevant against the background of the historiographical scene of south India: the conventional picture represented by the writings of Nilakanta Sastri, the much publicized alternative offered by Burton Stein, the systematic analysis of data in the writings of Y. Subbarayalu and Noboru Karashima and the refreshing questions raised by James Heitzman and Leslie Orr. Added to it is the relatively new ground in relation to the history of Kerala. The defense of the present volume, therefore, is that it presents a reading of the history of south India different from what is available now: it will hopefully interest the informed scholar and the inquisitive student as well as the lay reader.

I have benefited immensely from my long association with M.G.S. Narayanan. He was responsible for initiating me into this field and I owe him a debt of gratitude. R. Champakalakshmi has borne with me all through. B. Surendra Rao, my colleague, read the first draft of all these articles. His suggestions and criticisms have helped me to refine them. So also, Raghava Varier and Rajan Gurukkal have helped me in refining my tools of enquiry by criticizing and commenting on them. I thank each one of them, assuring them that the countless defects are in spite of them. Manu helped me with the proofs and the index. Parvathi, as always, excused my absences silently and Krishnan, Narayanan and Nilakanthan encouraged me in various ways. The editors of Oxford University Press would never leave me unless I put this volume together and attended to the details of the execution. How do I thank all of them adequately?

KESAVAN VELUTHAT

Acknowledgements

The author and the publisher wish to gratefully acknowledge the following for granting permission to reproduce the following articles:

Indian History Congress for

'Into the "Medieval" and out of It', first published as 'Into the 'Medieval'—and out of It: Early South India in Transition', Presidential Address, Section II: Medieval Indian History, *Proceedings of the Indian History Congress* (Bangalore, 1997), pp. 166–205.

'Labour Rent and Produce Rent', first published as 'Labour Rent and Produce Rent: Reflections on the Revenue System Under the Cholas (AD 850–1279)', *Proceedings of the Indian History Congress* (Dharwar, 1988), pp. 138–44.

'Literacy and Communication in Pre-modern Kerala', first published as 'Storage and Retrieval of Information: Literacy and Communication in Pre-modern Kerala', in Amiya Kumar Bagchi, Dipankar Sinha and Barnita Bagchi, eds, *Webs of History: Information, Communication and Technology from Early to Post-colonial India* (Delhi, 2005), pp. 67–82.

'*Vēḷevāḷi* in Karnataka', first published as 'The Nature and Significance of the Institution of Vēḷevāḷi in Karnataka in Historical Perspective (AD 800–1300)', *Proceedings of the Indian History Congress* (Calcutta, 1989), pp. 151–9.

'Landed Magnates as State Agents', first published as 'Landed Magnates as State Agents: The Gāvuḍas Under the Hoysaḷas in Karnataka', *Proceedings of the Indian History Congress* (Gorakhpur, 1990), pp. 322–8.

The Editor, *Journal of South Indian History*, University of Calicut, for

'The Temple in Medieval South India', first published as 'Patronage and Reciprocation: The Temple in Medieval South India', *Journal of South Indian History*, vol. 1, no. 1, 2003, pp. 7–30.

Janaki Prakashan, Patna, for

'Land Rights and Social Stratification', first published as 'The Structure of Land Rights and Social Stratification in Early Medieval South India', in Vijay Kumar Thakur and Ashok Anshouman, eds, *Peasants in Indian History* (Patna, 1996), pp. 312–30.

K.N. Ganesh for

'The *Kēraḷōlpatti* as History' first published as 'The *Kēraḷōlpatti* as History: A Note on Pre-colonial Traditions of Historical Writing in India', in K.N. Ganesh, ed., *Culture and Modernity: Historical Explorations* (Calicut, 2004), pp. 19–38.

The Director, Ecole Française d'Extrême Orient, Pondichéry, and the Director, Institut Français de Pondichéry, for

'A Capital City as a Sacred Centre', first published as 'Mahōdayapuram-Koṭuṅṅalūr: A Capital City as a Sacred Centre', in Jean-Luc Chevillard and Eva Wilden, eds, *South Indian Horizons: Felicitation Volume for François Gros on the Occasion of His 70th Birthday* (Pondicherry, 2004), pp. 471–85.

The Asiatic Society, Kolkata, for

'Landlordism in Medieval Kerala', paper first presented as 'Landlordism in Medieval Kerala: Its Origin and Development', at the D.C. Sircar Centenary Seminar, Asiatic Society, Kolkata, November 2007.

Aligarh Historians Society, Aligarh, for

'Evolution of a Regional Identity', first published as 'Evolution of a Regional Identity: Kerala in India', in Irfan Habib, ed., *India: Studies in the History of an Idea* (Aligarh, 2004), pp. 82–97.

Centre for Studies in Civizations, Delhi, for

'Medieval Kerala: State and Society', first published in J.S. Grewal, ed., *The State and Society in Medieval India*, vol. VII, pt I of *History of Science, Philosophy and Culture in Indian Civilization*, General Editor D.P. Chattopadhyaya (Delhi, 2005), pp. 177–94.

In the case of the remaining chapters, the author himself holds the copyright.

Introduction

Historiography of south India, like history itself, presents a case of uneven development. While certain sub-regions within this macro-region, such as the Tamil-speaking regions of the Kaveri Delta, have been subjected to highly refined and sophisticated critical evaluation, certain other regions, like Kerala, have just started to wake up. There is copious material available and equally rich empirical work done in case of Karnataka; but the interpretive richness achieved by other regions does not inform the writing of history in relation to that region. The essays that follow, being concerned with all the three regions mentioned, are apt to raise responses as varied in the respective regions. What I have done in these essays is to follow one particular line of argument, irrespective of the historiographical background of the subject of study. This can raise questions even about the relevance of the exercise in the context of one or the other region; it may be seen as repetitious or foolhardy, depending on the point of reference.

In fact, a question about even the intelligibility of the unit of study, namely, south India, can raise itself. As mentioned above, the spatial spread taken up in these essays is characterized by uneven development from very early times: the archaeological and literary records from these regions make this amply clear. While a part of Karnataka arguably graduated to state society from the turn of the Christian era, regions like Kerala had to wait until the fag end of the first millennium for that experience, and that too in a tenuous manner. This situation leads to the question whether there could be uniform digits of periodization in the case of such a 'south India', or whether there can be such an intelligible unit of historical study at all. If the answer is not in the affirmative, which it certainly cannot be, how can there be a medieval south India? I presume in this 'Introduction' to present an apology for this book in the face of these and similar questions.

In his 'Preface' to *The Making of Early Medieval India*, B.D. Chattopadhyaya wrote about a decade and a half ago:

> Early medieval India has long remained a much maligned period of Indian history both among those who possess a passing acquaintance with India's past and with specialists. The Indian history to be found within most textbooks is still redolent with 'dark ages' and 'periods of crisis' in much the same measure as 'golden ages'. Characteristics generally associated with early middle age have burdened this period and dressed it up as one of the key 'dark ages' of Indian history. The value judgments of historians on personalities, as on periods of history, are carried over as axioms in historiography; early medieval India has not been able to shake off axiomatic pronouncements upon it; this despite the fact that recent researches look at the period from many more angles and have succeeded, to a very substantial measure, in rescuing this epoch out of its dismal maze of dynastic genealogies, chronological charts and chronicles of military success and failure.

The scene is pleasantly different now. Thanks to the solid researches on early medieval Indian history in the post-Independence period, not the least of which is by Chattopadhyaya himself and his disciples, there is not only greater clarity in the issues debated but also serious interest in the subject. Debates around, for example, problems such as Indian feudalism, urban decay, *kaliyuga,* the nature of the state and so on have raised the study of early medieval Indian history to greater heights: it is no longer an account of a 'dark age' with its 'dismal maze of dynastic genealogies, chronological charts and chronicles of military success and failure'. Nor do historians of early medieval India feel any less respectable than those dealing with the 'golden ages' on account of the period they have chosen to study. What is presented as the early medieval in Indian history, it is now recognized, was extremely crucial in the formation of what constituted the distinctive features of Indian civilization. This also denies any foundational qualities to any one or more of its constituents. Eschatological assumptions give way to patterns of denouements and streams joining through the course are taken with an importance equal to what are perceived as fountainheads. Ideas of the 'central' and the 'peripheral', the 'global' and the 'local', are increasingly losing their relevance, not just because it is fashionable in the post-modern conditions.

Naturally, a major beneficiary in the deal has been regional history. This may sound like a contradiction: what is the relevance of making a distinction between the regional and the global in a context when all notions of centrality are taken as suspect? In reality, however, it has to be seen differently. One of the ways in which what was perceived as 'global' has lost its centrality is by this very process of the 'regional' coming of age, as it were. The fact that one of the factors identified as characterizing the early medieval in Indian history is this maturing of the regional may be an accident; but it cannot be ignored in the present context. This is not the only way in which south Indian history acquires importance. In terms of richness, this is one region in Indian historiography where a phenomenal amount of work, both quantitatively and qualitatively, has been done. This richness and variety are due to the work of historians of several generations, employing different strategies, raising new questions, and offering refreshing answers. The assumptions in the writing of one generation may not be acceptable to others; but given the fact that knowledge is cumulative, the considerable amount of clarity achieved in the field cannot be denied.

This clarity has made a new look at the early medieval in Indian history possible. The tripartite periodization of Indian history, handed down by colonial historiography and used by historians of different ideological persuasions and for different purposes, has been effectively called into question. The categories by which a change is perceived have changed. Dynastic change is no longer nearly as effective as other factors such as transformations in the processes and structures in economy, society and polity in explaining epochal changes. Wrongly perceived notions about change in the religion of the rulers are not accepted any more as necessitating an understanding of the entire structure as having undergone a total change. Alternatively, a number of features such as expansion of agriculture in a big way, social differentiation leading to the creation of a hierarchy, transformation of tribes into peasants/castes, emergence of trade as an instituted process involving notions of pricing and profit in place of old exchange systems based on needs and reciprocity and, above all, the authentic arrival of the institution of the state have all been identified as the distinctive markers of the early medieval. Some details of this formation in relation to northern India have been worked out. There is, however, some lack of clarity in case of south India in this respect. What the present volume presumes is to place together the results of a few enquiries related to these problems in south Indian history. It is hoped that these essays will provoke the readers to raise at least some of the nagging questions regarding the constituents and causality of the early medieval in south India.

The existing lack of clarity, however, does not mean a dearth of information or lack of interpretative exercises—both are rich and varied. One factor enabling this richness and variety in the interpretations is the copious nature of the sources. Epigraphy did not need a Champollion or a Prinsep here: Tamil and other south Indian scripts were still in use, if in modified forms and in a limited circle, and it did not take a breakthrough to read inscriptions in the south Indian languages. So also, much of the literary archives was still alive—mostly as liturgical material in temples and marginally as cud for the scholiasts to chew. What these literary sources could not yield was precisely the 'dynastic genealogies, chronological charts and chronicles of military success and failure' as literature of the court was slower to come out of oblivion. Devotional literature had been accepted as canonical; and their liturgical character precluded historical analysis. Even when they were taken up for 'secular' studies, what was achieved was at best a literary and philosophical appreciation. The 'Bhakti Movement' of south India had to wait for the historian's analysis, despite the availability of rich sources. As the more 'secular' texts of the court were still coming to light, they were giving out names of the rulers and their dynasties which the inscriptions were talking about. A defensible chronology and broad outlines of political history were available by 1920s; administration, social life, economic activities, cultural expressions, and so on, came to be studied immediately and a somewhat comprehensive treatment was available by the middle of the 1930s.

The contribution of K.A. Nilakanta Sastri in this field was so influential that the framework he adopted was accepted in the writing of history even in areas in south India about which the great master did not write. Rich quantitative additions of information were made by a number of stalwarts; but the influence of the great scholar was so profound that his model resisted any change. It was only by the 1970s that there was a change in the scenario: Burton Stein shook the edifice of the historiography of Tamil south India violently. Statistical analysis of the epigraphical data and a systematic rethinking of the patterns that the inscriptions and texts presented resulted in considerable re-examination of the existing picture, particularly in relation to the Tamil-speaking region. Historiography in Kerala, which started off along the lines of Nilakanta Sastri in the 1950s, did not acquire this conventional quality as a historical materialist intervention in the form of the writings of M.G.S. Narayanan and his students came not long after the take-off. Karnataka, however, remained where it was, except that in relation to the period of the Vijayanagara Empire, there has been a lot of systematic work and some fresh insight available.

The essays presented here are the product of this historiographical conjuncture. They presume to ask a few questions about the constituent elements of the early medieval in south Indian history. Was there an 'early medieval' distinct from the preceding 'early historical' formation in south India? When did it appear? What were the processes involved in this transition? Is it possible to causally explain the processes and structures characterizing the early medieval in south India? Taking up instances from the deep south, but also taking an occasional peep into the neighbouring Karnataka, these essays, written as they were under different provocations and for different purposes, try to answer these questions in a small way. What constitutes the early medieval acquires significance as the digits of periodization are crucial in the understanding of historiography.

One of the major markers of the early medieval in south Indian history was the temple dedicated to one of the two Āgamaic deities, Śiva or Viṣṇu. The syncretic cults of these deities is the result of a process through which elements of the folk cults and practices were incorporated into the classical traditions of Vedic-Hindu religion. In the earliest historical period in south India, documented elaborately in what is known as the Sangam literature, one does not come across a society in which this religious system had gained acceptance. In that period, which scholars are inclined to bring down to fourth or even fifth century AD, a congeries of cults and practices obtained, where deities appropriate to the landscape and forms of sustenance were worshipped at a personal level. There were no institutions like the temple. The very strong presence of the Brāhmaṇa, with his Vedic sacrifices and even Āgamaic ideas, is hard to miss there; but sprawling Brāhmaṇa settlements with vast areas of agricultural land under their command and the temple as the pivot around which they functioned are not visible in that period. By the seventh-eighth centuries, a complex phenomenon develops in this region with several aspects. These included opening of the fertile river valleys for agricultural purposes, covering of the landscape by a network of big and small Brāhmaṇa settlements, studding of the territory with a large number of temples commanding vast extents of land as their property and all the entailing privileges and, of course, burgeoning of monarchy which anticipated the Cōḻa state in the centuries to come. These developments were extremely complex and, to a great extent, interrelated—particularly the creation of agrarian corporations, emergence of the Brāhmaṇa settlements and rise of the temples. Even at the risk of over-simplification, one may identify these three—the agrarian corporations, the Brāhmaṇa settlements and the temples—as synonymous.

In a joint study of the temple made by M.G.S. Narayanan and the present writer about three decades ago, we had examined the role of the institution within the framework of historical materialism. Serving as an agency for easier and more efficient extraction of surplus from the peasants in the agrarian economy, the temple helped in the extension of agriculture in the tribal areas and the consolidation of the landlord domination. In the course of such extension, it accelerated the process of the disintegration of tribal society and its reorganization as a caste society in which the temple served as an integrating factor linking the high and low in its service and drawing towards itself as clients the different castes and sub-castes. Such integrative role paved the way for the Brāhmaṇa-inspired and Brāhmaṇa-supported state power in the regional monarchies of south India. The temple put the stamp of legitimacy on the new polity and this in turn guaranteed state patronage for the temple. In this process, the Brāhmaṇical *varṇāśrama* ideology strengthened its grip on society. One of its weapons was the Bhakti Movement of which the temple served as an institutional base. In course of time, the prosperous temple, which was a landed magnate from the beginning, also developed into a storehouse of gold and silver and precious jewels as well as the regular place of assembly for the rural, Brāhmaṇical, elite. This produced the need for exclusiveness and protection leading eventually to the development of the temple to fortress-like proportions with several circles of streets within streets, bazaars and armed forces. Finally the temple acted as the agent for developing, consolidating, transmitting and conserving the legacy of high culture.

In a way, thus, the temple represents the early medieval in south India—an institution that had ramifications which touched almost all the aspects of human life. It could be looked upon as representative of a new formation that has come into existence.

Closely related to the temple, which was all-embracing in its reach, was the agrarian expansion that took place in this period. Both the process and its impact were phenomenal. Inscriptions recording grant of land or other decisions concerning agriculture start making their appearance by the seventh century and go on increasing phenomenally in the next couple of centuries. The importance of this cannot be overemphasized. Records show that south India in the early historical period was characterized by a subsistence economy. In the absence of production of any surplus ('a process, not an event') worth the name, there was no unequal distribution of it; nor did it form the basis of social differentiation. When, however, agriculture expanded in a way records of the succeeding period show, in its train followed production of surplus, its differential distribution and the consequent stratification in society. In other words, the undifferentiated tribes of an earlier period were transformed into peasants organized in a hierarchical manner depending on the share of surplus that each was able to command, and identified as so many castes. The structure of land rights and social stratification, thus, provides another good index to understanding the early medieval in the history of south India as distinct from the preceding period. It is this stratified society that has been functioning in its relation with the temple.

Surplus also meant its siphoning out. Labour, over and above what is necessary for its own reproduction and maintenance, is surplus labour. It is by making use of such surplus labour that large-scale activities of production—whether in agriculture or in industry—are carried out. Such surplus labour is extracted from the labourer in two forms: either as labour itself or as the fruits of that labour, what Karl Marx calls labour rent and produce rent respectively. In the records of south India in the period that we consider, there is evidence of the extraction of surplus in both these forms. It is seen that as the incidence of produce rent increases, that of labour rent decreases—a pattern that has been noted by Marx in volume three of *Capital.* Going beyond an indicator of the nature of social formation in this period, this character of the surplus is also crucial in showing the unmistakable presence of the state in early medieval south India. Plunder and prestations formed the basis of earlier regimes of power in south India and now it comes to be graduated as revenue collected from the primary producer and transferred to the state at fixed intervals on an impersonal basis. This makes the early medieval phase in south Indian history once again distinct from an earlier period.

The presence of the state, as opposed to so many stateless polities in an earlier period, then, is another marker of the early medieval in south India—in whatever way we characterize that state. As state is about the exercise of power, the nodes of such exercise and its agency are crucial in the understanding of the state. The state identified a large number of local magnates and enlisted them in its service in early medieval south India. These included individuals and even corporate bodies. The *nāṭu* units in this era had such a major role. However, the importance of these bodies went beyond being simple building blocks of the political edifice under the Cōḻas or other polities; they were units of socio-economic organization. Spontaneously evolved as agrarian sub-regions following the opening up of river valleys and spread of agriculture in south India, these corporations were an identifying feature of the early medieval.

If some of the major features defining the character of the early medieval in south India can be identified in this way, several questions about the transition to that period will raise themselves. When did these features show themselves up? What were the forces behind a transition from one formation to another? What were the processes through which it went in order to finally settle with the identifiable early medieval features? There is sufficient clarity about many periods and formations in Indian history both in Marxist and other historiography; but there are very few 'transition debates' in Indian history, and fewer in the context of south India. Scholars in the past had largely depended on very tenuous evidence of a 'Kaḷabhra interregnum' to explain the end of what was described as the 'Sangam Period' in the history of south India. The Kaḷabhras were thought to have been patrons of Jainism and Buddhism and were also presented as 'ubiquitous enemies of civilization' although they were so totally elusive in evidence! For others the Kaḷabhras represented marauders from upland Karnataka, standing in opposition to the emerging peasantry of the Tamil plains. Another fashion tried to look at the reference to the Kaḷabhras in one record as reminding the pathological fear of the Kali age in the Purāṇic accounts and thus argued that this represented a social crisis on the eve of a transition from one age to the other. The first essay presented in this collection interrogates evidence of these and proposes an alternative thesis about the processes and causality of the transition from the early historical formation to the early medieval in the history of south India.

The essays presented in the next section, dealing with medieval Kerala in a broad manner, seek to test these general patterns about south India as a whole within the limited region of the west coast of the deep south. To be sure, there are clearly distinguishable specificities in the case of Kerala which marks this region out from the rest of south India. The experience on the west coast in the southern end of the peninsula had no exact parallels, even if they cannot be described as unique in any sense. This will amply support a case for a distinct early medieval in this part of south India. In fact, that experience can serve as a case study in the processes and structures that define the early medieval in south India. This is one reason for our including a larger number of studies on Kerala in this collection than about the rest of south India.

The territory of the present-day state of Kerala on the west coast formed part of the larger socio-cultural unit called Tamiḻakam in the early historical period. The expansion of agriculture in the river valleys and the establishment of Brāhmaṇa settlements with control of much of the agrarian land were instrumental in a series of changes including the establishment of a stratified society on *jāti* lines, the acceptance of temple-based Purāṇic Hinduism and, above all, the formation of state presided over by a Brāhmaṇa-influenced monarchy. A consciously created self-image of Kerala becomes visible in the records of this period, which indicates that the west coast in the deep south had been successfully weaned away from the old Tamiḻakam. The name Kerala, a Prakrit-Sanskrit variant of the Tamil name of the ruling house of the Cērals, is used exclusively in the sense of a lineage, as in *Kēraḷavaṃśa, Kēraḷakula*, etc. Gradually, the expression comes to denote a territorial identity as in *Kēraḷaviṣaya, Kēraḷakṣmā*, etc. This can be dated from the establishment of the Cēra kingdom of Mahōdayapuram around the beginning of the ninth century. This was more than just another event; it marks the beginning of a new era in the history of Kerala, as indeed does the emergence of the new state under the Pallavas or Pāṇḍyas, in relation to those respective regions in south India. A highly differentiated economy and society, with extra-kin labour, production of surplus and its distribution and notions of pricing and profit in exchange, came to replace the older one by the time the new state, as for example the Cēra kingdom of Mahōdayapuram on the west coast, was established in south India. A characteristic feature of the state that came into existence by this period, under the Pallavas, Pāṇḍyas, Cēras and Cōḻas, is the highly Kṣatriya-ized monarchy which presided over them, answering in every detail to the model available in the *kāvya-śāstra-nāṭaka* literature in Sanskrit. In case of Kerala, there were further differences from its counterparts elsewhere in south India.

The introduction of the Brāhmaṇical element with the Paraśurāma tradition seems to be the starting point of the distinctiveness of Kerala and its departure from the rest of Tamiḻakam. The Brāhmaṇical claim, that it was Paraśurāma who created *their* land and donated it to *them*, is seen all over the western seaboard in India. In the case of the south, it is the strip of land from Gokarna to Kanyakumari which is identified as the land retrieved by Paraśurāma. Gradually, even this unit disintegrates, as the land between Perumpuḻa (in Kasaragod district) and Kanyakumari is defined as actually the Malanāṭu within the Paraśurāma-*kṣētra*. This newly defined unit was earlier part of Tamiḻakam, but there is a conscious, if implicit, rejection of this affiliation in the changed context. The historical tradition of this new formation does not cherish details concerning the earlier Cēra rulers and their exploits contained in early Tamil songs such as the *Patiṟṟuppattu* any more. For instance, a Malayalam narrative called *Kēraḷōlpatti*, concerned with the history of Kerala, is totally silent about this aspect of the past. We take this narrative for some detailed discussion in this collection, as it was a major means by which the self-image of Kerala was constructed. The clearly defined identity that Kerala had acquired in the Perumāḷ era continued in nearly all its detail. In fact, this period looked upon itself as a continuation of the earlier period whereas the earlier one was conscious of the break that it represented. These differences, and the factors behind it, are a matter recognized by the authors of this period. For instance, a medieval *Maṇipravāḷam* text speaks of the speciality of the land on account of its fertility, also a gift of Paraśurāma: 'the rainy season, under orders of Paraśurāma, comes here with such frequency as if to breastfeed her children'. In the *Śukasandēśa*, the messenger of love, on his way from Ramesvaram to Guṇakā in Kerala carrying the message to the separated heroine, is introduced to the land when he is to cross the Western Ghats: 'Now you can see the *brahmakṣatra* land which testifies to the might of Paraśurāma's arms. This country, rich in pepper and betel vines growing on tall coconut and areca palms, is celebrated as Kerala'. It is here that one sees a conscious attempt at defining Kerala and its language, creating a self-image, as it were. M.R. Raghava Varier has made a brilliant analysis of a medieval text, *Līlātilakam*, a manual of the grammar, prosody and poetics of *Maṇipravāḷam*, a 'union of *bhāṣa* and Sanskrit', where *bhāṣa* stands for Malayalam. This, or any other contemporary text from Kerala, does not call Malayalam by that name, it being used for the first time outside Kerala in the fifteenth century Telugu work, *Śrībhīmēśvarapurāṇamu* of Śrīnātha.

It is the different aspects of this early medieval Kerala that we seek to study in the second section, beginning with the historiography of the land, both as handed down to us by tradition and as taken up by modern scholars. It has long been maintained that Kerala, like other parts of India, lacked in a tradition of historical writing. We take up an examination of a traditional narrative, the *Kēraḷōlpatti*, which is a narrative of history which tells the story of Kerala right from the creation of the land. I argue that it exhibits a sense of history inasmuch as there is in it, to use a famous statement of Romila Thapar defining a sense of history, 'a consciousness of past events, which events are relevant to a particular society, seen in a chronological framework and expressed in a form which meets the needs of that society'. Which of the past events were thought to be more relevant than others will also show the interests and concerns of society and explain, at least partly, the choice of the form for expressing them. The discussion will also show that history was used here as elsewhere as 'a handmaid of authority'.

There are two essays on the epigraphy of Kerala in this volume. One is on the way in which modern historians have used inscriptions in the reconstruction of history and the other tries to look at how the medium of storing and retrieving information went on changing, taking up the case of inscriptions as one such media in the early medieval society of Kerala. The next four essays are on features of the early medieval/ medieval period in the history of Kerala. It may be useful to situate them within the historiographical context of Kerala.

Even in the middle of the twentieth century, history had not quite come of age as a disciplined enquiry in Kerala, the work of scholars like William Logan, K.P. Padmanabha Menon and K.V. Krishna Ayyar notwithstanding. It was not yet possible to distinguish between a mythologically recovered past and a scientifically reconstructed one. When Elamkulam P.N. Kunjan Pillai, a professor of Malayalam, pieced together information available in inscriptions and literature, a major shift in the way history was written had effected. Pillai was given to nationalist effusions and his eagerness to create a Garden of Eden of the past also led him to look for the Fall and its causes. He drew the picture of an egalitarian society which gave way to the dominance of the Nampūtiri Brāhmaṇas in economy, society and culture resulting in an all-round decadence. This earned him a lot of criticism of a casteist variety which he did not actually deserve. In any case, the broad outlines of political history and much of the history of economic and social processes that emerged were to stay. It was on these foundations that M.G.S. Narayanan worked out a definitive and exhaustive history of Kerala in the ninth, tenth and eleventh centuries—the authentic early medieval in the history of Kerala. Following the work of Narayanan, a few other scholars have enriched the field, which has to be seen as the essential background to these studies.

One of the major questions that can be raised about the early medieval is about the nature of the state. In fact, this has been the concern of many historians who have worked on the early medieval period of Indian history, north or south. There are many models to grapple with—a centralized empire, a feudal state, an integrative polity, an early state, and so on. The essay on the king as lord and overlord participates in this debate and tries to lay bare the details of the early medieval political system in Kerala with a view to finding out meaningful patterns there. That a definite answer regarding the nature of the state is not finally given is true; but there is an attempt to achieve clarity in the matter of details even in this search for elusive answers. If the reader finds the essay too eclectic, the excuse lies in the fact that it is an attempt to question hitherto available answers rather than to answer hitherto available questions. It is claimed that a consistent pattern regarding the state at various levels is available there.

Closely linked to the state and its nature is the capital city. In our study of Mahōdayapuram, the capital city of the Cēra kingdom of Kerala in the early medieval period, we have been able to show that the city owed its origin to its location at the mouth of a river as an entrepôt of transmarine trade. When, in the changed circumstances of the drying up of Roman trade and the opening of the river valleys for purposes of rice cultivation, the area came to be surrounded by sprawling agrarian settlements owned by Brāhmaṇa groups and symbolized by temples, this city continued to be important for a different reason. A sacred nature got attached to it, due partly to the presence of the temples there and, more importantly to the sacred character of the monarchy presiding over the city and the territory around it. Even after the disappearance of that monarchy, the city survived along with the ṇostalgia for the old capital although more of it was in the form of a centre of pilgrimage. The patterns of urban growth and urban decay seen here may be used in the debates on those subjects; but the intention here is not to participate in them.

One of the major subjects of interest to historians on the early medieval is the problem of the emergence of a structured relationship in the field of agriculture—what has been described as landlordism. In fact, one of the major debates regarding the 'early medieval' in Indian history is centring on the question whether such relationships could be described as feudalism or plain landlordism. In the case of Kerala, answers to the question of origin and development of landlordism also led to casteist criticisms against the first serious attempt made by a historian. Elamkulam Kunjan Pillai's work, based on a transparent analysis of the sources as it was, was still beset with problems. He explained the process as resulting from the conditions emerging from a war between the Cōḻas and Cēras that lasted for a century: when able-bodied men were busy fighting, the capricious Brāhmaṇas appropriated their land and women. M.G.S. Narayanan showed that the logic in this construction was unacceptable and that the evidence of a 'Hundred Years' War' was not forthcoming. However, although he effectively demolished the caprice-conspiracy theory, he did not propose an alternative explanation for the emergence of landlordism except in a general way. We make a modest attempt to answer this question using the inscriptions of the later Ceras and the palm leaf records of a later period.

These studies in relation to the Tamil- and Malayalam-speaking regions prompted the author to go into questions regarding the neighbouring Karnataka, particularly when he was required to teach certain aspects of the history of that region. Some of the similarities were striking. For instance, the institution of what M.G.S. Narayanan has called 'companions of honour', the band of trusted bodyguards of the ruler in early medieval south India, is present with equal prominence in the records of Karnataka and has been written about profusely. Historians of Karnataka had taken the groups known in Kannada records as *vēḷevāḷi, leṅka, garuḍa, tuḻilāḷgaḷ,* and so on for something unique to that part of the country. Our examination of the evidence within the context of the rest of south India shows that this formed part of a larger pattern—a pattern that lent the early medieval in south India its character. So also, the practice of recognizing landed magnates by the state and enlisting them in the service of the state is something that an earlier study of ours had laid bare. The *gāvuḍa*s or *gāvuṇḍa*s, who were described by historians of Karnataka earlier as village 'headmen', belonged exactly to this category. This realization, together with the one in relation to *vēḷevāḷi,* also leads us to ask the question if there is more to it than mere similarities in a couple of institutions. It is here that historians look for patterns; the pattern that one sees in the early medieval in relation to other parts of south India becomes valid in the case of Karnataka as well. True, further studies are necessary to bear this out in other respects.

This is what we see from these studies. There are compelling reasons to identify an intelligible early medieval period in south India as we see a broad pattern here. The details of this pattern include

1. transformation of an economy characterized by cattle-keeping and subsistence agriculture into one of wet rice cultivation and a considerable surplus,
2. replacement of simple exchange with the instituted process of trade and the subsequent development of urbanism,
3. transmutation of a relatively undifferentiated society into one divided sharply into castes and the consequent 'casteization' and peasantization of tribes,
4. acceptance of an organized religion with its ideas and institutions suited to the new economic and social order,
5. the emergence of the state to suit the newly evolved social order, and
6. a large number of other attendant developments, including the defining of the regional as, for instance, in the case of Kerala or Karnataka.

Even though the coherence necessary for a monograph devoted to a single theme may not be present here on account of the fact that these are essays written at various points in time and in response to different demands, it is still hoped that they bring out a case for an early medieval in south India.

Apart from making this important statement that there was an early medieval in the history of south India and defining its features, these essays may also be seen as differing, historiographically, from some of the assumptions in the received wisdom. The picture that is available in the canonical texts, represented by Nilakanta Sastri's monumental work regarding the presence of a centralized, bureaucratic structure in the Cōḻa Empire, is questioned in later writings. The alternatives—the segmentary state and the feudal formation—too have their limitation as has been demonstrated by many writings including by the present author. How then can the early medieval be characterized? I am getting increasingly convinced that the experience was too complex to lend itself to any single characterization. With the features outlined above, it is hoped that the early medieval would make sense as an intelligible period of historical study in south India, whether or not it fits into the patterns that are familiar in the context of other societies—be it medieval European, modern African, or anything else. Perhaps the early medieval south Indian formation will stand on its own feet.

Part I

Tamil̲akam

1

Into the 'Medieval'—and out of It*

The present essay embodies the results of an attempt to examine the process of transition from the 'ancient' to the 'medieval' in the history of the deep south of India. To look for a 'medieval' in the history of south India will mean rejecting the facile but pernicious equation 'Medieval = Muslim' in Indian history.[1]

Ironical as it is, this also happens to be my first paper to be read in this section of the Congress. My own limited reading and research have been largely in the now disputed territory lying between the 'ancient' and the 'medieval' in Indian history and, with no decent reason, I used to submit my papers to the other section. Nearly being hijacked into the 'medieval', now I am told that I belong here, not there! Standing in this twilight zone between the two periods and being claimed by both, I presume here to look for the passages from the one to the other in the case of the history of the deep south where I am more at home. This would involve reviewing the existing periodization with its rationale and labels as well as looking at deviations in the historical processes which, together, could be taken to suggest a transition from one period to another.

Periodization in history, particularly a tripartite division, is not an innocent exercise, undertaken 'for the sake of convenience'. On the face of it, it presents itself as a habit. Looked at more closely, it can be seen to be intensely ideological. First of all, it assumes a Eurocentrism in the context of world history. To accept it is to accept a hegemony, at least tacitly.[2] Behind the conventional tripartition in the context of

* First published as 'Into the "Medieval"—and out of It: Early South India in Transition', Presidential Address, Section II: Medieval Indian History, *Proceedings of the Indian History Congress* (Bangalore, 1997), pp. 166–205.

India also lurks the danger of a communal ideology with the 'Muslim period', which is said to have followed the 'Hindu period', being presented as either 'bad' or 'good'.[3] Even a more 'secular' tripartition, when applied uniformly to the subcontinent as a whole, might be used to historicize, positively or negatively, the domination of certain parts of the country by certain other parts. So also, the paradigm of the mode of production, in spite of its excellent analytical potential, has come to fit snugly into the tripartite scheme, with its Slavery-Feudalism-Capitalism/Colonialism sequence for the three historical periods.[4] Attempts have been made to locate this sequence in Indian history with varying results. Among the more creative debates that ensued has been the one around 'Indian Feudalism'.[5] A by-product of the debate is a readiness to look for an 'early medieval' at the fag end of the 'ancient' period of Indian history.[6]

The problem of periodization is highly complex. Addressing oneself to it, one comes across certain in-built disadvantages. Apart from falling into one or the other ideological trap, there is also difficulty in treating long-term processes across periods. At the same time, to ignore changes in the processes and structures over long periods will be self-defeating. The historian, by knowing what he is looking for, can come to terms with these two. Allowing for sufficient flexibility, and recognizing that one's parameters can be different from those of others, he can try and locate clearly identifiable formations and then isolate the forces which brought about a transition from the one to the other. Identifying periods and labelling them should follow. It is an axiom here that the historian's ideological position, taken consciously or otherwise, has a major role to play in the entire process.

The problem is worse confounded in the case of south India, as 'medieval' was never defined there in any clear fashion. There was no 'Muslim period' to correspond with the 'medieval' there. The larger scheme followed for 'Indian history' accommodated the peninsula rather uncomfortably. Where does the 'medieval' begin there? What brings it about? What are the ways in which it is different from the preceding, 'ancient', period? According to the Constitution of the Indian History Congress, ancient Indian history is 'upto AD 1200 for Northern India and AD 1300 for Southern India'.[7] This does not obviously follow any serious consideration: at best a generous allowance is made for a century of relative backwardness to south India by the condescending big brother! Even outside, there is a lack of clarity when adjectives like 'ancient' and 'medieval' are used freely. For instance, the Hoysaḷas who ruled in Karnataka from the eleventh century belonged to a 'medieval Indian royal family'[8] while their Tamil contemporaries, the Cōḻas, flourished in a period described still as 'ancient'.[9] Moreover, even those who take the Hoysaḷas as 'medieval' never discuss in what way life and conditions in their period differed from the earlier periods of, say, the 'ancient' Gaṅgas or Kadambas or Cāḷukyas or Rāṣṭrakūṭas so that a transition can be located there. In other words, digits of periodization in south Indian history have been cruder than those in relation to 'Indian history'. Not even a change in the religion of the rulers is observed there! There are no spectacular conquests; nor are dynastic changes dramatic and noisy enough to proclaim the exit of one period and the entry of another. Therefore, one will have to look for changes of a different nature, those which affected economy and society, politics and culture in a decisive way and brought into existence a totally new formation after dissolving the earlier one. And, such an examination can be even more meaningful if it brings to bear on it a consideration of the causality involved in such changes.

A tripartite division is unacceptable in the context of the history of the deep south, comprising the modern states of Kerala, Pondicherry and Tamil Nadu, what is described as Tamiḻakam in the early sources. A casual look at what our Constitution defines as its ancient period, stretching from the beginning to AD fourteenth century, will demonstrate this. This period covers, if not also the whole of prehistory and protohistory, the early historical period represented by the early Tamil anthologies, the period of what historians have described as the 'Kaḷabhra interregnum', the establishment of the first monarchical states, the period of the Bhakti literature and the elaboration and refinement of the monarchical state under the Cōḻas and their decline and disappearance. If a single period can subsume such disparate conditions covering several millennia, then periodization loses its significance: one can as well dispense with periodization altogether and tag the six centuries or so that followed to the same 'period'. If, on the other hand, the historian is interested in changes at various levels of human affairs, then it will be useful and necessary to look at this long span of time as consisting of various formations.

There are two aspects of the problem which the present paper concerns itself with. In the first place, it seeks to locate an 'early historical' phase in south Indian history, a clearly identifiable formation which came into existence closely following its pre- and proto-historic periods. Received historiographical tradition calls this period 'the Sangam Age'. It is appreciated differently in recent years. Second, we try to identify the next definite phase in the historical process, with structures, ideas and institutions which are entirely different from what obtained under the preceding formation. This is the period represented by the first monarchical states culminating in the Cōḻa Empire, with its impressive and durable political institutions as well as the spectacular mementoes which it left behind. We then seek to raise the question relating to the process of transition from the one formation to the other. In this rather long passage could be located what has been described as the 'Kaḷabhra interregnum', the later 'Sangam' texts including the twin epics, the rise and growth of huge agrarian corporations, the emergence of the temple, the Bhakti Movement, the domination of Brāhmaṇical institutions and the conditions for the establishment of the monarchical states under the Pallavas and Pāṇḍyas. We attempt to find out the forces that led to the break-up of the earlier formation and brought about the new one. Abusing the license offered by this chair, one may also venture to make a statement or two regarding the causalities involved, even though there is the risk of oversimplifying an extremely complex process. The question of labels could be taken up here.

The early historical period of the deep south, which followed the prehistoric period, witnessed the emergence, maturing and dissolution of a clearly identifiable social formation. It was more or less coterminous with the beginning of the Iron Age in this part of the country.[10] Iron itself appears to have, as it were, arrived in south India without a preceding Copper/Bronze Age or a Chalcolithic Age. While the implications of this jump are very serious, we do not take it up as it is beyond our scope in this paper. Historians assign a variety of sources to this period: the megaliths and their furniture; the hero stones; the Tamil Brāhmi cave labels; the early Tamil anthologies (the 'Sangam texts'); punch-marked coins, references in the *Arthaśāstra* and in Aśōkan edicts and an occasional sherd of the Northern Black Polished Ware; Greco-Roman accounts and the archaeology and numismatics of Roman presence and so on. An impression of a glorious civilization, which lasted for a few centuries with no substantial change, is created by historians from V. Kanakasabhai to N. Subramanyan.[11] That historiography has been also responsible for looking at this civilization as representing the 'classical' period of south Indian history, which rubbed shoulders with the Roman Empire with which it had extensive trade relations. Recent writings, however, do not entertain such a conceit. The work of scholars such as K. Kailasapathi, K. Sivathambi, Kamil Zvelebil, George L. Hart III, R. Champakalakshmi, M.G.S. Narayanan, Rajan Gurukkal and others has made a more realistic appreciation of the sources, placing them within a perspective derived from a combined use of the social sciences.[12] Our understanding of the social formation there is indebted to the work of these scholars.

The period of about a thousand years or more represented by the above categories of sources is not any more looked upon as a single, unchanging, entity. On the other hand, it has been more profitably considered as representing the various stages in the biography of a social formation—its emergence, maturing and dissolution. This period was characterized by different forms of production, different ways in which man sought to relate himself to nature in his struggle for livelihood. One of these forms, however, tended to dominate. That world is best represented in the early anthologies of the Tamil literature known as the 'Sangam' literature. Considered formerly as constituting a single corpus of literature, these texts are now recognized as composed over a vast period of more than a millennium and belonging to different strata. They are essentially bardic compositions exhibiting the traits of oral poetry.[13] They were selected, thematically arranged, and brought together at a much later date in a highly disciplined manner. It was probably at this point in time that a text of grammar and poetics was composed. The rigour involved in the collection and the unity and discipline of the grammatical work and later traditions were among the factors responsible for identifying all these songs as belonging to one corpus and their period as relatively short, representing a single, undifferentiated period in history. It is now recognized that of the various groups of anthologies known as *Eṭṭuttokai*, *Pattuppāṭṭu* and *Patineṇkīḻkkaṇakku*, six anthologies of the first, excluding *Kalittokai* and *Paripāṭal*, are the earliest.[14] They use an interesting floral symbolism in the nomenclature of what is called *tiṇai*s, and this is standardized and theorized in the later work of poetics. Each of these *tiṇai*s signifies primarily a poetic situation and context in the literature and its poetics, representing generally particular expressions of war and love. Of the *tiṇai*s a grouping of five is of particular interest to the historian. These five *tiṇai*s represent a division of the physiographic region of the Tamil-speaking world into five different eco-zones.[15] Thus the five *tiṇai*s of *Kuṟiñci* (hills and forests), *Mullai* (pastures and thickets), *Marutam* (riparian plains), *Pālai* (parched lands) and *Neytal* (coastal tracts) represented clearly distinguishable geographical zones. People who lived in these zones lived an appropriate life close to nature: the hunters and gatherers of *Kuṟiñci* worshipped Cēyōn, the war god; the pastoralists of the *Mullai* had their bucolic god in Māyōn; the plough agriculturists of *Marutam* prayed to Vēntan, the rain-god; the fierce robbers and fighters of *Pālai* propitiated the blood-thirsty Koṟṟavai, and the fishermen of the *Neytal* knelt before Kaṭalōn, the sea god. It goes without saying that the greatest potential for development was enjoyed by the *Marutam* plains. This was the potential on account of the fertility of the soil and the availability of water, holding out the prospect of a veritable agrarian revolution. Labour employed for production was largely kin-based and so were all the relations. *Kuṭi*s or households and *ūr* or clan settlements were the units of social organization. This division into different *tiṇai*s did not, to be sure, involve any watertight division of any kind: transitional situations indicating merger or overlap of more than one tiṇai are spoken of in what is called *tiṇaimayakku*.[16] The picture available is of a society in which people pursued their livelihood by following different ways of production. In transitional situations, ways more than one obtained at the same time in the same place. As to the relations of production in these different eco-zones, the information is clear: the principle of organization was kinship. This is visible in situations of pastoralism and agriculture. In fishing too, we have evidence of descent groups not only participating in production processes but also handing down skills of the trade from generation to generation within the same descent groups. In such a system of production, distribution of surplus to the various factors of production is irrelevant. In any case, production was largely for subsistence and hardly for surplus.[17]

The picture provided by archaeology, too, is complementary. In the megalithic horizon,[18] which corresponds to this literature both chronologically and culturally, human settlements are sparsely distributed. Sites throwing up evidence of settled agriculture, if few and far between, are nonetheless noticed with continuous occupation from Neolithic levels.[19] Iron is indeed present, but the implements show a marked bias to hunting and fighting, to the point of a near-total exclusion of iron technology in agriculture.[20] Artefacts such as pottery, terracotta, beads, semiprecious stones, bronze objects, etc. besides the iron implements, point to the level of craft production which had a place in the economy. But it is questionable if there was any concern with surplus even here, for such exchange as we have was not, as might be conventionally understood, a disposal of the surplus. The supplementary sidelight provided by the Tamil Brāhmi cave labels illumines the picture further[21]: they speak of certain varieties of traders who sold gold, cotton clothes, (? iron) ploughshare, salt, sugar and liquor, etc. There is a solitary reference to a goldsmith. One of the records refers to, 'the men of the *nigama*'. The reference to the *nigama* and the fact that most of these labels are associated with Jain and Buddhist monks may indicate a northern origin for at least a section of the traders. It is not without significance that the term used for trader in these documents is *vāṇikan*, derived from Sanskrit *vaṇik*. The location of the find spots of these inscriptions is itself revealing: they lie on major routes within the Tamil country. In the anthologies, too, we have references to exchanges of the products of different *tiṇais*. That literature also makes occasional references to *cāttu* (? Sanskrit *sārtha*), translated as 'caravans'. Uṟaiyūr Iḷamponvāṇikanār and Madurai Aruvaivāṇikan Iḷavēṭṭanār are described by historians as 'specialized traders' in gold and textiles respectively although they figure in the literature as poets who composed songs.[22] In any case, trade, oriented towards profit, is hard to come by. What can at best be seen is exchange based on need and reciprocity.[23] Gift and redistribution were the other forms of exchange,[24] but even there the basis was either reciprocity or patronage—not value or profit.

The Roman presence—attested by the Tamil songs, Greco-Roman accounts, archaeology of Roman settlements themselves and innumerable hoards of Roman coins—tells a similar story.[25] This was taken in the past to show that south India had reached a high degree of civilization, to have had trade with the Roman world on equal terms. That historiography waxed eloquent about the numerous ports, marts and emporia on the south Indian coast. Hadn't the draining away of all the gold from Roman treasury sent a chill of consternation down the spine of every responsible Roman citizen? Wasn't it on account of this trade in 'oriental luxuries' whose balance was heavily in favour of south India? In discussing evidence of Roman trade, it is important to bear in mind the fact that, in the items exported, there is a conspicuous absence of the only possible surplus product of the most productive regions of south India, namely, rice. So also, there is no indication that items imported were fit for consumption. For what was exported included pepper, ginger, cardamom, cloves and similar spices; faunal articles such as animal hides, ivory, apes and peacocks; wild wood articles such as aloe, sandal and teak; precious stones like beryl and pearl and some cotton fabrics.[26] Gold and silver coins constituted the chief items of import, besides some copper, tin and arsenic.[27] Significantly, a major share of the Roman coins discovered from south India come from hoards and very few from occupational levels.[28] Most of these are yet fresh from the mint, showing no wear and tear. Some of them also have a hole at the edge, indicating their having been used as ornaments such as in necklaces or as pendants. This shows clearly that the Roman coins were not used as a medium of exchange, but as primitive valuables used for their socio-technic or ideotechnic value.[29] This points, once again, to a situation where ideas of price and profit do not make much sense from the Indian point of view, although what the Roman traders were paying was the price of the commodities they bought as it was a veritable spice trade for them.[30] So also the ports and centres of exchange in the interior could be shown as urban centres; but they were rather enclaves brought into existence by what has been described as stimulus from outside and not any organic development from within.[31]

Thus, the economy and society are shown as being characterized by subsistence production, redistribution, reciprocity and patronage. The literature of the period elaborates this further. The copious accounts of war, where the concern was plunder and cattle-lifting, illustrate the general ethos of society.[32] The hero par excellence was the warrior-hero and the poets are never tired of extolling his heroism in different ways.[33] The innumerable hero-stones as well as references to the elaborate procedure of raising and worshipping them in the literature are further evidence of the general ethos of war and the cult of the warrior-hero.[34] Redistribution of the booty captured in war and the communal feasts following the plundering raids are brought out vividly in the texts, the latter often approximating to potlatch-like destruction.[35] This went a long way in claiming prestige and status to the hero who went to war, and his kinsmen basked in the reflected glory. Side by side, we also see a number of bards and minstrels, known as *pāṇas*, sometimes with members of their families, singing the praise of the hero in the numerous poems of love and war contained in the anthologies. These bards and minstrels moved from one centre to another and were rewarded amply by the heroes with gifts. The munificence of the hero was often the subject matter of the songs, and they earned their composers further gifts from the patrons. This cycle, too, formed part of the process of legitimation, apart from the redistributive and potlatch-like exercises mentioned above. What emerged was the somewhat contradictory notion of a chief in the relatively acephalic societies, apart from the heads of the households or the elders of clan settlements.

We come across a number of such chiefs in the literature. Where it was possible, the chief led plundering raids into the rich rice-producing *Marutam* plains and sought to control them. These raids and the booty which they brought enhanced the resources of those chiefs. They could now give more gifts, organize more of potlatch-like ceremonies. This was a definite advantage which those chiefs who lived in the proximity of the riparian plains had over the others farther afield. Such chiefs, naturally, got greater legitimacy, commensurate to the more generous gifts they were able to give and the more elaborate feasts and other communal gatherings they were able to organize. Claims staked on the rice-producing plains in the form of occasional raids got graduated as regular control once this potential was realized.

Control of the riparian plains meant control of the rivers. These were arteries, as it were, which connected the hills and forests to the sea. It was largely at the mouths of these rivers that the ports frequented by the Roman traders lay. It was possibly through these rivers that the hill-products, which formed the bulk of the merchandize, flowed to the ports. Thus, those chiefs who were privileged enough to have control over the *Marutam* plains and their produce also had control over the precious items brought in by the Roman traders. The primitive valuables of ideotechnic value which they were now able to flaunt and occasionally give away as gifts enhanced their prestige and legitimacy as never before. This relative superiority, gained by the twin advantage of controlling the rice-producing plains and the transmarine trade, set them apart from the less fortunate chiefs. Thus we see the distinction made in the literature between two kinds of chiefs as *vēntar* and *vēḷir*. These were the Cēra, Cōḻa and the Pāṇḍya constituting the *mūvēntar*, often translated as the 'three crowned kings', and several of the *vēḷ*s known as the *kuṟunilamannar* or the lesser 'kings'. The relatively insignificant distinctions of detail apart, the organization and functioning of these chiefs were similar. Kinship, agnatic and affinal, formed the major principle of organization while reciprocity and patronage formed the basis of redistribution. Mobilization of resource was largely through plundering raids. No regular mechanism of appropriating surplus as tax can be identified there, nor does one come across any agency that can be considered even distantly as carrying out functions associated normally with the state, not to speak of a bureaucracy. Such 'urban centres' as we come across are presented as resulting from 'external stimuli' and not as products of an organic development from within. No trace of what could be described as monumental architecture has come down to us. There certainly is evidence of literacy, but how far it was used for purposes of communication is very questionable.[36] Its exotic character in the context of south India is hard to miss. In any case, there is nothing which presents itself as an 'administrative document', showing the presence of the state through these records. Again, even though the general ethos of society was centred on war and the cult of the warrior hero, nothing which can approximate to an organized military arm of a state is visible in the songs. Ferocious fighters do figure as individuals; and they attach themselves occasionally to this chief or that, or a caravan which needed defense from a plundering raid. In short, there is nothing, whether in literature, epigraphy or archaeology, which points to the institution of state in that society.

However, it was not a seamless world, sealed off from any influence from outside. Right from the days of the Mauryan empire, there is evidence of its contact with the Gaṅga Valley.[37] South India was getting exposed to ideas and institutions which had their origin in the north Indian plains. Evidence of this can be seen in the artefacts brought in by the traders from the north. These included, apart from the punch-marked coins and other material objects, faiths such as Jainism and Buddhism.[38] Their prevalence is attested by the Cave Label inscriptions and the poems of a later date.[39] Another element from the north, though not introduced through the agency of trade in any direct manner, was the Brāhmaṇical one.[40] A number of poets who composed the songs were themselves Brāhmaṇas. At least in one case, a Brāhmaṇa poet says that he had stepped into the shoes of the *Pāṇa* bard.[41] And, the Brāhmaṇa poets could be more effective in their new role, as they were veterans equipped with the panegyric genres such as the *gāthā*, *nārāśamsī*, *ākhyāna*, etc. of the Vedic type and the *itihāsa-purāṇa* tradition which developed later.[42] There are also cases where the Brāhmaṇas cajoled the chiefs into performing Vedic sacrifices.[43] At least a beginning towards accepting the hegemony of the Vedic-Śāstraic-Purāṇic ideology can be seen in this literature, giving the lie to the argument in favour of a 'pure Tamil' character to the literature and the society which produced it.[44] There is even the claim that the chiefs got the *Mahābhārata* translated into Tamil.[45] Although the name of the poet to whose credit it goes is available to us, the text of the Tamil *Mahābhārata*, if it existed, has not come down to us. There are also attempts in the songs to seek linkages between the chiefs on the one side and the epic heroes on the other, assuming thereby a close familiarity with the heroes and themes. In fact, apart from the bardic songs themselves and the potlatch-like feasts, a new means of legitimacy was now available to the chiefs. The sacrifices and what adumbrated court poetry were available in return for the patronage extended to the Brāhmaṇas.

If this is the picture, which I hope I have not caricatured, that we get about the early historical period of south India, the one that we have about the next distinct phase in the history of south India is almost entirely different. The passage from the one to the other is not as clearly illuminated as what are obtaining at either of its ends. Therefore, what the historian can do is to try and extrapolate the information from both sides with a view to constructing a meaningful picture of what lay between them.

By the seventh century, the historical scene becomes brighter once again. Profuse light is shed from various angles. A notable feature, however, is the entirely different nature of the sources in both form and content. Inscriptions, in their thousands, form the chief category of sources now. Literature, too, is another important category, but it is not any more the oral compositions of the wandering minstrels; it is the literature of the court and the temple, with all its stereotypical character. There are other expressions of the high culture, which include monumental architecture of stupendous proportions. It will be a truism to say that this sudden emergence of newer and richer sources, entirely different in form and content from those of an earlier period, is indicative of a transformation that society had gone through.

When one goes deeper into the sources and examines the world represented by them more closely, the transformation will be brought home more clearly. The inscriptions themselves, for instance, demonstrate this in numerous ways. The epigraphs record largely royal charters or proceedings of local bodies of various descriptions with the somewhat pompous statement that both the medium and the message were intended to last 'as long as the moon and the stars endure'. Both announce the presence of the state in an unmistakable manner, the royal charters directly and the resolutions of local bodies in an oblique way. They are concerned with the grant of land or other arrangements related to the utilization of land. Thus they show the importance that agriculture had come to acquire in the economy. They also tell us how far the distribution of agrarian surplus had led to differentiation, bringing about a division of society into distinct, and mutually antagonistic, classes. There are also records related to urban centres and trade, artisans and their activities and so on, all going to show the sea change that had overtaken economy and society by the time these records begin to make their appearance.

Of these the single most striking factor is perhaps the phenomenal expansion that agriculture had registered. One comes across numerous agrarian settlements in the period. In fact, a process which characterizes this period is the steady growth and expansion of such settlements in both number and scope. Although we come across the existence of agrarian settlements in a very sporadic way even in the earlier period, they are too few and far between to have been of any serious consequence to economy and society as a whole. On the contrary, the ones which came up in the period after the seventh century proved crucial. However, there is one problem in studying these settlements, a problem caused by the nature of the inscriptions themselves. These records are mainly from or related to the temples and the information we have is largely one-sided and biased heavily in favour of the Brāhmaṇical institutions.[46] This picture need not be taken to represent the reality; groups invisible in historical records cannot be taken as non-existent; their partial visibility is a function of the nature and interests of the records themselves rather than a commentary on their importance. Even in the heavily one-sided documents, we do get information regarding the numerous non-Brāhmaṇa peasant settlements known as *veḷḷānvagai* villages. Thus an examination of a couple of records from the Big Temple at Tanjavur and another from

Gaṅgaikkoṇḍacōḻapuram has helped demonstrating the character of such settlements.[47] The *veḷḷānvagai* villages, it has been shown, contained in them habitation sites, cremation grounds, sources of drinking water, irrigation channels, cultivated fields, pasture lands, etc. The residential areas, on closer look, present the following: the quarters of the landholders (*ūr-nattam* or *ūr-irukkai*), that of the cultivators (*kuḍi-irukkai*), that of the artisans (*kammāṇaccēri*), that of the *īḻavas* (? toddy-tappers) (*īḻaccēri*) and that of the agricultural labourers (*paṟaiccēri*). This demonstrates the existence of at least five strata in society distinguishable even at a physical plane. Of these, those who owned land, referred to as the *kāṇiyuḍaiyār*, show themselves up in such records as are available for the non-*brahmadēya*, *veḷḷānvagai*, villages.[48] Since they are mentioned as residing in the quarters known as *ūr-irukkai* or *ūr-nattam*, it follows that they were largely identified with the *ūr*. This helps in the identification of the composition of the corporate body of the *veḷḷānvagai* villages known as the *ūr*, *ūrār* or *ūrōm*. It has been shown that membership of this body varied from one to twenty-nine.[49] A large majority of them had about ten members on an average. It has been calculated that individual members held land in extent ranging from two to ten *vēlis*. The process of individual landowners acquiring more and more land, and larger number of private landowners coming into existence, is registered by documents showing the steady expansion of agriculture.[50] This led, naturally, to an increased importance of these peasant proprietors and their corporate bodies.

As I stated earlier, the information regarding the organization and functioning of the corporate bodies of the *veḷḷānvagai* villages is far less copious than that we get about the Brāhmaṇa villages, in spite of the former being probably more numerous. This is quite natural on account of the character of our records. However, it is clear that such bodies of the *veḷḷānvagai* villages were constituted by the landholders in the villages. There were not too many other restrictive qualifications such as the ones which obtained in the Brāhmaṇa villages. This body known as the *ūr*, the *ūrār* or the *ūrōm* acted as a corporate entity and concerned itself with the management of landed property in various ways, namely, sale and purchase of land, gift of land, assessment and collection of tax, exemption of dues, etc.[51] It is the landowners who had any business in such bodies and there are even explicit statements to the effect that only the members of the *ūr* paid tax and also conversely that only those who paid tax were members of the *ūr*.

However, a body which is seen more prominently in the records is that of the *nāḍu*.[52] This expression was used to indicate both a grouping of several villages and the assembly of its spokesmen. The *nāḍu* is shown as a spontaneous grouping of several *ūr* villages. All the constituent villages were homogeneous, none having had any special privilege. The assembly of the *nāḍu*, also known as *nāṭṭār*, was likewise constituted by the members of the *ūr* assembly. There is no indication in the records that any one member had any special privilege in the assembly; there was no 'chief' or 'president'. Historians in the past had taken these as administrative divisions of the Pāṇḍya or the Pallava or the Cōḻa government.[53] On the other hand, Burton Stein takes these units as the foci of power in the medieval south Indian social and political organization.[54] An examination of evidence inspires confidence in neither. They appear to have been spontaneously evolved groupings of the peasant proprietors, looking after problems of agriculture such as irrigation or donation of land when the state recognized and incorporated them.[55] They were identified as so many agents to carry out the function of the state such as the assessment and collection of revenue. The penetrating analysis of James Heitzman[56] has brought this out effectively and shown that the pattern seen in the process of this incorporation is exactly in conformity with the pattern in the fortunes of the Cōḻa state: the more successful the attempts at centralization, the more subdued these local units and vice versa.

If the historian is handicapped by a paucity of sources in relation to the *veḷḷānvagai* villages, it is a profusion of information regarding the *brahmadēya* villages that confronts him.[57] This is not, as I said earlier, to be taken to mean that the latter had any priority in terms of number. But priority they did enjoy as they represented what could be described as a more progressive force in society. The fact that it is from the Brāhmaṇical villages that we have the largest number of inscriptions, including those which throw light on the non-Brāhmaṇa villages, shows not only a higher level of literacy for those groups but also a concern they had to record their decisions for future reference and in 'a more or less permanent form';[58] 'the inscriptions on temple walls served the purpose of a public registration office by conserving a trustworthy record of sales, mortgages and other forms of transfers of property rights in village-lands'.[59] This concern itself is significant. Besides, the records show a more evolved nature of the relations of production in those villages and consequently a more stratified society with both divisions and antagonism among the sections articulated in a clearer manner.

The Brāhmaṇa villages functioned as corporations of landowners who were not only Brāhmaṇas by birth but also required to be accomplished in their educational qualifications, with the knowledge of Vēdas, Śāstras, etc.[60] The organization of the corporate bodies such as the *sabhā* and the *mahāsabhā* or their sub-committees such as the *pariṣad*, the *vāriyam*, etc. followed the prescriptions of the *Dharmaśāstras*.[61] So did their proceedings and the actions taken to follow up the decisions. The solidarity of the group is brought out by the ruthless discipline, bordering on the masochistic, with which decisions were enforced on individual members; more than a concern with 'justice', it is the instinct of self-preservation that is seen most strikingly in these exercises.[62] The importance of such self-discipline is appreciated best when it is borne in mind that these bodies were enclaves of an exotic minority surrounded by a majority with local roots and moorings. They acquired control over vast tracts of land and with them the minds of people and standardized the pattern of social differentiation.

The grants they received, of which there is increasing evidence from the eighth century onwards, created superior rights over land and its earlier occupants; or else the grantees were allowed to evict them or extinguish the existing rights of the earlier occupants and assign them fresh rights.[63] This section does not show itself up in the vast majority of the grants of the Pallavas which may suggest that the land that was granted in most cases was relatively unsettled.[64] These early charters from the seventh century present the beginnings of a structured relationship in the matter of land rights. We have at least three tiers indicated by the records: the state at the top with its rights to collect surplus as tax and enjoying at least a theoretical final right over land, the intermediary Brāhmaṇical groups with the newly created superior rights over land, and the tenant-cultivators at the bottom. The groups at the bottom were not themselves undifferentiated.[65] In the Pāṇḍyan territory in a slightly later period, the picture is clearer.[66] The grants of land, mostly to Brāhmaṇas and their temples but occasionally also a Jain centre, confer two kinds of rights: the *kārāṇmai* and the *mīyāṭci* which were the right to cultivate and the supervisory right respectively, echoing the expression '*karṣayataḥ karṣāpayataśca*' in similar contexts in the records from north India in the post-Gupta period.[67] Below these two shades, there appears to have been *kuṭimai* or occupancy right and at the bottom were labourers who were attached to the soil and transferred along with the superior rights over it. In the Cēra kingdom on the west coast, too, we have a comparable situation.[68] Land was 'owned' variously by the ruler as part of his private estate and by the local chiefs. But what is most visible in the records is that held by Brāhmaṇical groups as their own property (*brahmasvam*) and as the property of the temple (*dēvasvam*). Below these owning groups were the tenants (*kārāḷar*) and the occupants (*kuṭiyāḷar*) and at the bottom, the labourers (*aṭiyāḷar*). In some cases where land is mentioned explicitly as granted on service tenure, there were those groups too, enjoying a superior right over the labourers. This pattern repeats itself even in the case of a trading organization which possessed land.

It is in the case of the Cōḻa country that the picture is clearest both on account of the fabulously rich data we have from that country and the systematic analysis which they are subjected to.[69] The complex structure of agrarian relations is brought out by these: the king at the top and different kinds of hierarchies below him. On the one side, there were the large number of *nāḍu* groups which were themselves congeries of the numerous peasant settlements known as the *ūr*, with the magnates who possessed land and the hierarchy which came to be established below them. On the other side, either directly below the king or the chiefs were the numerous eleemosynary tenures such as *brahmadēyam*, *dēvadānam*, *paḷḷiccandam*, *śālābhōgam*, *kaṇimuṟṟūṭṭu* and *veṭṭāpēṟu*. Even in these, the tenurial pattern was not different; the tenants (*kārāḷa*), the occupants (*kuṭi*) and the labourers (*paṟaiya*) placed one below the other in that order.

If the world of primary economic activity, namely agriculture, is shown to have undergone such phenomenal changes, the case of trade was not any different either. It has been shown that in the wake of the agrarian developments that were taking place under the Pallavas and Pāṇḍyas and which continued under the Cōḻas, trade and urbanization became more elaborate and complex and showed signs of being structurally different.[70] It is not any more the exchange, based on need and reciprocity, of natural products for primitive valuables; it was trade in finished goods, as an instituted process with clear notions of pricing and profit and other forces of market operating. Well-organized groups of merchants of both native and foreign origin are met with in the records together with elaborate details of their activities and organization.[71] Trading centres acquire a certain degree of autonomy and are controlled by corporations of traders. The role of the state and its symbiotic relations with the trading corporations are brought out clearly by the records and the recent analyses of those records. An interesting case is recorded by the Syrian Christian Copper Plates (AD 849), which were granted by the chief of Vēṇād, a chief who acknowledged the overlordship of the Cēra ruler.[72] There was what appears to be a fort and a guard of this fort is mentioned in the record. Goods reached the marketplace both by land and water. The record mentions privileges conferred on the trading groups called *Añcuvaṇṇam* and *Maṇigrāmam* in relation to the market town. I quote from the record at some length:

> They are exempted from the one-sixtieth duty at the time of entrance and at the time of sale. Slave-tax shall not be realised for the slaves purchased by them. They shall pay eight *Kasu* per carriage at the time of entrance and at the time of departure, and four *Kasu* per boat at the time of entrance and departure. Taxable articles shall be taxed in consultation with them. His majesty's business in anything like the fixation of the price of articles shall be conducted in association with them. The *Ancuvannam* and *Manikkiramam* shall keep the duty collected each day after affixing the seal. When any land within the four gates of the fort is obstructed and leased out to tenants, the one-tenth share of the sovereign shall go to the prince and the one-tenth share of the lord shall go to *Ancuvannam* and *Manikkiramam* .... If they have any grievance they are authorised to redress the grievance even by obstructing the payment of duty and weighing fee. The *Ancuvannam* and *Manikkiramam* ... shall themselves enquire into the offences committed by their people. That which is done jointly by these two heads alone shall be valid. In the case of the *Varakkol* and *Pancakkanti* ... *Maruvan Sapir Iso* shall keep the measure and hand over the measuring fee to the church.[73]

These statements are enough to drive home how elaborate and streamlined the process was when compared to the earlier period. Such records are not isolated: a number of such corporations flourished, and in a number of centres in south India.[74] Their activities go a long way in the process of urbanization, *nagaram* being the word used to indicate both a trading corporation and a town.[75] Equally significant is the fact that separate caste groups emerge with trade and artisanal activities as their profession. That the *vaiśya* category was absent in this part of the country has been pointed out as an aberration and sought to be explained away in various ways by historians.[76] What is more important than the *vaiśya* label are the putative functions of the groups, with agriculture, pastoral activities and trade being taken up by distinct caste groups in society.[77]

In fact, the institution of caste itself was a characteristic feature of the changed scenario. Doubts about the very existence of caste in south India in the period of the Cōḻas have been expressed by scholars who have, doubtless, examined the inscriptions.[78] This conclusion is unwarranted. One sees not only the Brāhmaṇas, Veḷḷāḷas and Śeṭṭis, who accounted for the prominent groups but also a number of others which included major sections of the semitribal groups that were getting transformed into peasants and other occupational groups. Interestingly, even the legal myth of *saṅkīrṇajāti* is invoked, in several cases, to define the caste status of newly consolidating occupational groups such as masons, weavers, etc.[79] Again, at least from the time of the Cōḻas, there are references to the existence of the well-known vertical division of castes into 'right hand' and 'left hand' sections.[80] Whatever the origin of caste system, the way in which it functioned in south India followed the Brāhmaṇical norms and, with the principle of *varṇāśramadharma* as the rationalization, the institution gave the stratified society a standard appearance. In any case, the fact that society was divided into distinct sections with a clearly defined hierarchy is unmistakable in the records. This is a marked deviation from the picture represented by the early Tamil anthologies, where social differentiation, if not altogether unknown, had not got entrenched and *jāti* had not congealed itself as an institution.

A closely related aspect is religion and its expression. If the cult of the hero and of the deities of the respective landscapes formed what could be described as religion in the earlier phase, both were relegated to the background in the period that followed.[81] Its place was taken increasingly by the worship of the Āgamaic deities such as Śiva, Viṣṇu and those who are identified as their kith and kin. This subsumed the old folk deities, with Māyōn being identified as Kṛṣṇa, one of the *avatāra*s of Viṣṇu, Cēyōn as Skanda-Kārtikēya, a son of Śiva and *Koṟṟavai*, variously as one of the female gods of the Āgamaic pantheon.[82] Another feature which was strikingly absent in the earlier period and which came into existence in this period, dominating the new landscape in every possible way, was the temple.[83] The importance of this institution not only in the religious history but also in economy, society, politics, culture and other aspects of human life can be hardly exaggerated.

Such a formation, with relatively advanced means of production; considerable agrarian surplus and its differential distribution leading to relations of production going well beyond kinship ties and bringing about distinct and mutually antagonistic classes; the instituted process of trade and the urban networks replacing the exchange of natural products for primitive valuables and the isolated urban enclaves; a hierarchically oriented society where clannish loyalties had broken down and caste identities had solidified; and an overarching ideology which subsumed and legitimized all these, was ready to receive the state, as it were, on its arrival.

What announces this arrival in the most unequivocal way is the unmistakable presence of the sovereign. A carefully constructed self-image of royalty is available in the royalist literature including the *praśastis*.[84] Several aspects went into the making of this self-image—origin myths, dynastic traditions, genealogies, etc. through which the dynasty to which the ruler belonged sought legitimation as well as the presentation of the individual king as a *Kṣatriya*, a *cakravartin*, a warrior-hero, a protector and fountain-head of all *dharma*, a munificent donor, a divine figure, of an attractive mien and a patron of arts and culture. These aspects make, generally, a deliberate attempt to seek linkages with the well-known *Kṣatriya* lineages celebrated in the *itihāsas* and *Purāṇas*, an attempt which had begun in a small way in the earlier period itself. But there is an effort to underplay the local, south Indian, origin of these dynasties; the traditions concerning them in the early anthologies is not something in which the new court poets take delight in. The other aspects such as the numerous ways in which the *Kṣatriya* caste status was claimed, the attempt to emulate the ideal of the *cakravartin*, and the projection of the ruler as a war-hero are important. They not only make comparisons with the well-known heroes from the *kāvyas*, *śāstras* and *nāṭakas* in Sanskrit but also present the king as powerful, which power is used for military and police functions. Military functions included both defence and aggrandizement of territory while police function was concerned with punishing the erring and protecting the worthy. Protection meant protection of the ideal social and moral order, that is, the *varṇāśramadharma*, which covered the interests of the owning classes. The positive role of the sovereign in social and economic change is brought out by his donor image, especially in relation to land. Again, the divinization of monarchy invokes a religious symbolism in an attempt to legitimize political power. That the sources of this symbolism are derived from the Brāhmaṇical, Āgamaic, practices and lore, and not from the cults of the earlier period, is significant. Thus, the image of the king presented in the texts is not merely of a political figure; he had significant social and cultural roles to play as well. He was as much an organizer, a symbol of unity within the new structure, as he was the pillar of the state.

State did not just mean the king. Various nodes of power existed, deriving their power either from a delegation or from other sources which, however, were integrated into the system by the superordinate authority of the state. These nodes included a large number of what could be described as political chiefs controlling a certain territory within the kingdom, numerous officials who carried out the functions of the state, groups which had power and authority in the localities, and so on. An important feature of the political structure of south India which emerges by the seventh century and which gets clearly established by the ninth is the presence of a large number of political chiefs (the 'feudatories' of an earlier fashion of south Indian historiography[85]). They begin to acknowledge the overlordship of a monarch. These chiefs may have included descendants of the *vēḷ*s or *kuṟunilamannar* of the earlier period; a few such as the Adigamāns, the chiefs of Koḍumbāḷūr, the Āys and others can be clearly shown as such. They continue to live in the old world of cattle raids and hero-worship as the numerous hero stone inscriptions from the Dharmapuri and South Arcot districts demonstrate.[86] What is new, however, is the fact that these records are dated in the regnal years of the Pallava rulers and that at least some of them speak of a territorial control they had acquired (as indicated by the expression *in=nāḍu=pāviya*).[87] Even a three-tiered relationship is brought out by a couple of records with the Pallavas at the top, the Gaṅgas in the middle, and the Adigamāns at the bottom.[88] The records are more numerous and the picture, clearer by the time we come to the eighth century. The chiefs' acknowledgement of the Pallava overlordship is articulated more clearly; and the Pallava claims in their *praśasti*s complement the picture.[89]

In the case of the Cēra kingdom on the west coast, too, there is information regarding a similar, but more evolved, pattern.[90] There were chiefs such as the Āys and Mūṣikas who continued from an earlier period; there were also others who figure in the records of this period for the first time. A few were hereditary chiefs while a few others owed their position to a nomination by the Cēra rulers. A few claimed the *Kṣatriya* status but many are clearly of what later came to be known as the *Nāyar* caste. At least one of them was a Brāhmaṇa. Records bring out the numerous ways in which these chiefs recognized the superordinate authority of the Cēra ruler. Their inscriptions are dated in the regnal years of the Cēra king. Many documents speak of the share of the king and the share of the chief in the localities. Military obligations, to which we shall refer presently, are redeemed by the chiefs on numerous occasions. The chiefs assembled at the court of the Cēra sovereign in situations of emergency[91] and at least in one case, that court was held at the headquarters of one of the chiefs.[92]

One sees three clear stages in the fortunes of these chiefs under the Cōḻas.[93] Till the close of the tenth century, the situation was comparable to that under the Pallavas in an earlier period. For about another century, there is, as they say, a deafening silence in the records about the chiefs in the localities. Members of these chiefly houses, however, do appear in the documents as officials of the state and in regions away from their home territory. They begin to reappear by the end of the eleventh century and assert with a vengeance in the next. Mutual quarrels, and pacts settling them, increase.[94] Their relative independence is indicated by an autonomous 'protection of territory' (*pāḍi kāval*)[95] which they engage in and the progressive shaking off of the Cōḻa yoke by the end of the twelfth century.

The role of these chiefs is very crucial for the understanding of the nature of the state in this period. The process by which these chiefs, whether they represented a continuation from the old world or a new emergence following the agrarian expansion and potentials of resource mobilization, were incorporated into the newly evolved states presided over by the newly developed monarchies is suggested by the records. Most inscriptions of the chiefs are dated in the regnal years of the Pallava, Cēra, or Cōḻa overlords, thus indicating a superordinate authority which the latter had over the former. There are suggestions of the overlords and the chiefs sharing the revenue from the territories of the chiefs.[96] In fact, there are even instances where the overlord intervenes in the reduction of the revenue dues in the chiefly territories.[97] That the chiefs were required to pay tributes is indicated by references in literary texts.[98] We also come across the pattern of matrimonial relations involving the cultivation of a network in which ties of mutual dependence were strengthened further. This also went to ensure the superior position of the house of the overlord.

What is most significant is, however, the military obligation of which we have weighty evidence. Perhaps the most illustrative cases are provided by instances involving the Cēras with their subordinate chiefs on the one side and their Cōḻa overlord on the other. The Cēras and Cōḻas were close allies in the ninth century when they conferred certain privileges and honours jointly on a Kadamba-Gaṅga chief, Vikki Aṇṇan by name.[99] A few years later, we see the Cēras reconciling themselves to a subordinate position. A number of Malayāḷi soldiers, stated to be hailing from the chiefly houses of Kerala, are fighting on the Cōḻa side against the Rāṣṭrakūṭas in the famous battle of Takkōḷam.[100] Perhaps as a preparation for this, the Cēras go to the extent of forcing one of their subordinate chiefs, the Mūṣikas, whose loyalty to the Cōḻas was held in suspicion, to accept the ultimate suzerainty of the Cōḻas along with the hand of a Cōḻa princess in marriage.[101] Subsequently, the Mūṣikas fight for the Cōḻas. Interestingly, the tables are turned in a matter of less than a century: the Cōḻas no longer take kindly to the Cēras and, naturally, we have the chiefs of Kerala, including the Mūṣikas, fighting against the Cōḻas in the late tenth and early eleventh centuries.[102]

One of the chief features of a state society is 'government'. The governmental functions in the newly emerged monarchies is another aspect which can clarify the nature of the state. A lot of dust has been kicked up by the debate over the picture of 'the superior executive strength' on account of 'a highly organized and thoroughly efficient bureaucracy' which was both 'numerous and powerful' on the one side[103] and that of a total lack of anything that carried out any governmental work on the other.[104] Truth, for a change, may yet remain in the middle! This is not a compromise formula; that is what recent analyses of records show. They present evidence of the existence of a large number of landed magnates in the localities and also the process of their growth in both number and importance by the tenth and eleventh centuries—a picture which is in tune with that of the expansion of agriculture and the consolidation of individual property in land.[105] These magnates sported high-sounding titles such as *uḍaiyān, kiḻān, vēḷān, mūvēndavēḷān, araiyan*, etc. and, in most cases, these titles were prefixed by the name or title of a ruler.[106] It is stated explicitly in one record that what the person held was a title conferred on him (*paṭṭam kaṭṭina peyar*).[107] Thus we see a process by which the landed magnates in the localities, who were growing in importance, being identified, recognized and enlisted by the state. This process is shown to be in operation in other parts of south India as well.[108] It was such magnates with impressive titles who were pressed into the service of the state as its agents to carry out the administrative functions of the state.[109] The large number of officials who figure in the documents in various capacities, all over the area covered by the Cōḻa rule at its height in the eleventh century, are drawn largely from this category; a few who hail from the chiefly houses, but far afield from their home territory, too, are found there. These functionaries, who represented the influential sections of society, are described as the 'king's men' looking after 'his business'.[110] That the whole affair was impersonal is brought out also by the instances of promotion, demotion and transfers from one 'department' to another as well as from one region to another.[111]

Another significant aspect of the working of the government in south India in this period is the heavy use it had made of the corporate groups of the landlords, both Brāhmaṇa and non-Brāhmaṇa, as well as traders. In fact, this use was so pervasive that historians in the past have taken these groups as 'local bodies' forming the smallest units in the 'administrative system'.[112] Our own understanding is that they too acted as agents of the state in matters of the assessment, collection and remittance of revenue and also as dispensers of justice, besides looking after their own business of agriculture or trade as the case may be.[113] What was happening was that the community corporations which had evolved in the localities were, like so many individual magnates, recognized and co-opted to the state system. The beginning of this process of incorporation could be seen when the pastoral-agricultural bodies in the Toṇḍaimaṇḍalam region in northern Tamil Nadu, known as the *kōṭṭam*, were integrated into the state system by the Pallavas,[114] and its elaboration and refinement could be found in the Cōḻa country when bodies such as the *nāḍu*, *nagaram* and *sabhā* functioned as full-fledged organs of the state.[115] The first phase of this process may compare with the way in which the political chiefs were incorporated into the system with varying results or individual landed magnates were made use of by the state with consummate success.

A good pointer to the nature of the state is its resource base and the mobilization of the surplus. When 'revenue system' is looked at in this way, much of the smoke that has risen from the debate concerning the revenue system will be blown away. Nilakanta Sastri overdraws the picture by taking the myriad terms referring to levies as forming the revenue system in a very literal way;[116] the summary rejection of any revenue collected by the state, in the writings of Burton Stein, goes to the other extreme.[117] However, a closer look at the situation, following systematic analyses of the data, has resulted in a clearer picture.[118] It can be seen that a revenue system did exist which assessed and collected taxes from the territories covered by the political authority of the state. This constituted the way in which the surplus produced was pumped out of the producer. At the same time only a few of the hundreds of 'revenue' terms are seen to occur more than once in the records. Those terms which do occur throughout the period of the Cōḻa rule and all over the territory covered by that state hold the key to understanding the nature of the way in which surplus reached the state. Of these, the most important were the levies charged on land.[119] This was an obligation (*kaḍamai*), an annual payment (*āṭṭaikkōl*) and a fee for protection (*rakṣābhōga*)[120]—terms which clarify the nature of these dues which went beyond an occasional tribute or prestation. A whole 'department' of land revenue can be identified in the records, which gets ramified by the time we come to the climacteric of the Cōḻa state under Rājarāja I and his immediate successors.[121] There was no single, uniform, rate of taxation applicable to the entire territory: rates varied from as low as one-tenth to as high as half of the total produce.[122] Another significant aspect we notice is the prevalence of the exaction of what could be described as labour rent and this being gradually replaced by a produce rent in later times.[123] On the whole, the analyses of the revenue system show a high degree of regularity, periodicity and impersonal character in the resource mobilized by the state. This, it may be recalled, is in marked contrast to the situation obtaining in the earlier period which represented a world whose resources were formed by the booty captured in plundering raids and the occasional tributes that the tribal chiefs were able to command.

In the matter of the military, too, we are caught between two opposing historiographical positions. While Nilakanta Sastri and his followers wax eloquent about the 'numerous regiments' of the army 'spread over the country' 'in the form of local garrisons' and 'in cantonments' as well as a navy consisting of 'numberless ships',[124] Burton Stein dismisses any coercive power of the ruler, identifying such evidence as he sees as of the localities and caste groups.[125] We have to resort to the 'compromise formula' once again! It is true that the picture of the impressive armed and naval wings of the military is certainly exaggerated. On the other hand, it is shown that each of the political chiefs (the 'feudatories') had a trusted band of 'Companions of Honour' around him, taking up police duties in times of peace and acting as soldiers in times of war.[126] This pattern is repeated in the capitals of the Cēra, Pāṇḍya, or Cōḻa monarchs, larger in scale, stronger in number and wider in scope.[127] Even in the case of other parts of south India such as Karnataka under the Rāṣṭrakūṭas and Hoysaḷas, this pattern is shown to have been valid.[128] These bands, known as the 'Hundred' and the 'Thousand' organizations in Kerala, the *Tennavan Āpattudavigal* in the Pāṇḍyan kingdom, the *Uḍan Ceṉṟa Paḍai Vīrar* and the *Vēḷaikkārar* of the Cōḻa country and the *Vēḷevāḷi* and *Vēḷevaḍica* of the Kannada records, taking an oath to lay down life for the honour of the master, constituted the core of the military arm. They approximate more to feudal levies, nonetheless regular. There are also references to horse riders, elephant-riders, archers and such other specialists. This core was supplemented by mercenaries recruited from among peasants and artisans. The references to various *nāṭṭuppaḍai*s and the *Kaikkōḷapperumbaḍai* can be explained in this way. So also, the *vēḷaikkārar* described to belong to the *valaṅgai* and *iḍaṅgai* divisions can be taken as those recruited from among the peasant and artisan castes respectively. There are at least four *sēnāpati*s in the Cōḻa records sporting the title *uḍaiyān*, showing that prominent landholders in the localities were assigned high military offices as well. There are a few Brāhmaṇas figuring as *sēnāpati*s. They too were landholders, but they were probably also products of Brāhmaṇical institutions of education such as the *śālai* and *ghaṭikai* whose curriculum included military training as well. Thus, to deny any coercive power which the centre had will be wrong. The picture that we have of the military organization conforms to the general pattern of a polity with varying nodes of power; but it does point to a marked transformation from the earlier situation of tribal war-bands pouncing upon the cattle of others and marauding the agrarian plains, indulging in looting and arson.

The political form which thus came into existence is eminently qualified for the description of state. It was in every way the expression of the new social formation, which had come up on the ruins of the old. Its ideological apparatus of legitimation, too, conformed to the new situation. In speaking about the self-image of royalty, we have seen the sources of this validation.[129] Further statements of the power of the ruler can be seen by the elaborate claims about the military expeditions and, of course, success, which the rulers are always credited with.[130] The way in which even iconography and architecture, apart from whole genres of court poetry, were used for this purpose is phenomenal.[131] How the concept of sovereignty is elaborated in the different sculptures and how the sovereignty of the divine is transported into the temporal plane is an interesting study.[132] So also, how monumental architecture, starting from its very size, proclaimed the greatness of the builders is very significant as witness the example of the Bṛhadiśvara Temple at Tanjavur: it was the house of 'Rājarājēśvaram Uḍaiyār' built by 'Uḍaiyār Rājarājadēvar'[133]—a mere transposition of the substantive as the adjective covers the entire distance from the sacred to the profane! Such monuments are unequivocal statements of the power and resources of the builder; they have to be understood as more than a mere 'system-maintaining mechanism of a weakly organized polity'[134] or as one of the means of extending a ritual hegemony.[135] Munificent endowments formed another aspect of this attempt at validation: Rājendra Cōḻa's Karantai Plates record the creation of a new settlement of as many as 1080 Brāhmaṇas.[136] The way in which a certain ideology was made use of for the legitimation of a hegemony is crucial here. It is important to realize that this hegemony was far from ritual. It was *real political hegemony*.

Thus we have two formations, entirely different from each other, on either end of what has been conventionally described as the 'ancient period' of the history of south India. It goes without saying that no meaningful scheme of periodization can treat these two as parts of the same period. We believe that there is a definite case for identifying two distinct periods there, the one coming to a close by the third or fourth century and the other emerging by the seventh or eighth century of the Christian era. The three or four centuries that lay between the two may be considered as the passage representing the transition from the one to the other. This process of transition, and the factors responsible for it, can be understood with clarity if the passage itself is examined closely. What obtains there would explain its causality and its effects.

There are mainly two ways in which the centuries following the 'age of the Sangam' have been looked at by historians. One of them regards it as 'a long historical night'. 'We know little of the period of more than three centuries that followed', says Nilakanta Sastri.[137] Using the 'peepholes' provided by epigraphy and literature, he sees that a mysterious and ubiquitous enemy of civilization, the evil rulers called Kaḷabhras, had come and upset the established political order which was restored only by their defeat at the hands of the Pāṇḍyas and Pallavas as well as the Cāḷukyas of Badami. He admits that 'of the Kaḷabhras we have as yet no definite knowledge';[138] but from such information as could be pieced together from a Buddhist text, a late Tamil grammatical text and the Vēḷvikuḍi Plates, he regards the Kaḷabhras to have uprooted and kept in confinement the rulers of Tamiḻakam such as Cēra, Cōḻa and Pāṇḍya and abrogated *brahmadēya* rights. 'There was no love lost between these interlopers and the people of the lands they overran', he declares.[139] Elsewhere he writes that 'the Kaḷavar-Kaḷabhras were a widespread tribe whose large-scale defection to the heretical faiths [Jainism and Buddhism] resulted in a political and social upset lasting over some generations.'[140] But the 'Kaḷabhra interregnum' was not entirely unproductive. Sastri writes:

> This dark period marked by the ascendancy of Buddhism and probably also Jainism, was characterised also by great literary activity in Tamil. Most of the works grouped under the head *The Eighteen Minor Works* were written during this period as also the *Śilappadikāram* and *Maṇimēkalai* and other works. Many of the authors were votaries of the 'heretical' sects.[141]

There is another way in which these centuries are looked at—there was no disjunction at all and there was a slow, gradual development of society and culture during this period.[142] Interestingly, even this line cannot do without the Kaḷabhras or the notion that what went before the seventh century was still a 'mysterious period'. Nearly every detail of the other fashion regarding the 'Kaḷabhra interregnum' is accepted here but it is seen as marking 'a point where non-peasant people made their strongest bid to control some, at least, of the lowland peasant population; ... this onslaught appears to have been the culmination of a long period of non-peasant, armed resistance to the expansion of peasant society'.[143] Nothing, however, in the scanty evidence of Kaḷabhra presence in the sources of doubtful authenticity supports this picture of a 'long period' of armed struggle between the peasants and non-peasants in which the latter, represented by the Kaḷabhras, ultimately emerged successful.

Historians have not quite given up chasing the Loch Ness Monster. In an attempt to look for evidence of a crisis which might have led to the dissolution of the earlier mode of production, brought about by the intensification of contradictions 'to a point where the economy could not function in its fundamental form', Rajan Gurukkal has turned to the Kaḷabhras.[144] In references to them in the epigraphs of the later periods are seen 'pointers' to a kind of 'total crisis'. 'It *seems*', writes Gurukkal, 'that the Kaḷabhras held *probably* a sort of predatory control over Tamiḻakam for some time after *suspending its ruling lineages.* The period also witnessed the in-flow of numerous groups of Buddhists and Jains to the land' (emphases added). We are taken to the following certainty from these probabilities: 'It is significant that the *main targets* of the Kaḷabhras were the landed households of the Brāhmaṇas. The early copper plates of the Pallavas and Pāṇḍyas *allude* to the dislocation of Brāhmaṇa households and their gift lands. *Many* of the *ēkabhōgabrahmadēyas* lost their privileges and *the brahmanas had to flee in the wake of aggression.* The *general chaos* reminded the landed Brāhmaṇas of the evils of the *Kali* age' (emphases added). Gurukkal refers to the influential papers of R.S. Sharma and B.N.S. Yadava on the Kali age as social crisis and argues that 'the thoughts are quite relevant to the questions of transition from ancient to medieval in south Indian history also'. This adds one more dimension to the problem of the Kaḷabhras by equating it with the tension associated with Kali Age and looking at it as basic to a transitional process in Tamil history.

This calls for looking at the evidence once again.[145] As I suggested earlier, the picture of a Kaḷabhra presence in the Tamil country rests on evidence of doubtful validity. A Buddhist work speaks of the patronage its author had from Kaḷabhra Accuta Vikkānta. A much later Jain writer on Tamil grammar speaks of the patronage he had from the Kaḷabhra who had imprisoned the Cēra, Cōḻa and Pāṇḍya. As for evidence in epigraphy, it is even more dubious. In the formulaic descriptions of universal conquests, different Pallava rulers are credited with subjugating the Cōḻas, Kēraḷas, Pāṇḍyas, Maḻavas, Simhaḷas, Bāṇas, Āndhras, Saindhavas, Kadambas, Tuḷus, Koṅkaṇas and Kaḷabhras.[146] The solitary reference in a Pāṇḍyan inscription is to the claim of a Brāhmaṇa, seeking the grant of a village to him, that the village belonged formerly to his ancestors as granted by Palyāga Muduguḍumi Peruvaḻudi, the Pāṇḍyan king and that the Kaḷabhras had abrogated the grant.[147] The evidence of the 'general chaos' reminding 'the evils of the Kali age' is limited to the formulae by which individual rulers are described to have put an end to the evils of Kali and established dharma.[148] These statements are a far cry from the pathological fear of the Kali age in the Purāṇic literature. It is clear, therefore, that the evidence of the presence of the Kaḷabhras and the ground to equate the period of their dominance as indicating a general crisis do not support the overdrawn pictures we have in the writings of historians from Srinivasa Aiyangar to Rajan Gurukkal. When evidence is not at peace with theory, it is the former that the historian should go to, however alluring the latter may be.

How, then, can one characterize the passage? Extrapolating from what is known on either side and using such evidence as are available, one can still seek to fill the gap, however tentatively. We have seen that forces capable of dissolving a whole formation and bringing about a new one were present even towards the close of the earlier historical period. These included the importance that plough agriculture was gaining in the riparian plains and the Brāhmaṇical element that was introduced into society and culture. The warriors who took part in the plundering raids for the chiefs start insisting that they would settle for nothing less than fertile paddy fields in return for their services.[149] Brāhmaṇas who work as priests and officials in sacrifices are granted land on a large scale.[150] The didactic texts attributed to the last phase of what is called the Sangam Age extoll the virtues of agriculture as opposed to plunder and almost simultaneously underline the superiority of the ethics of the Brāhmaṇical Śāstraic texts.[151] It is in this context that the significance of that 'outstanding epigraphical discovery'[152] of the Pūlāṅkuṟicci inscriptions is brought home. They record the creation of *brahmadēyas* with superior rights over cultivating tenants (*kārāḷa*) and earlier occupants (*kuṭi*). The process is shown to have begun at least from AD fifth century. Thus we have, on the one side, the picture of an agrarian expansion and, on the other, that of the creation of a class of non-cultivating Brāhmaṇa landholders placed above the peasantry. The latter, in all probability, worked as a major catalyst, for the grants of cultivable land to them assumed a labour force outside kinship. This proved to be the thin end of the wedge[153] which brought about the eventual erosion of the earlier system of production and distribution based on kinship, reciprocity and patronage and the evolution of a new system based on the differential distribution of surplus. Needless to say, the process was slow, uneven and extremely complex.[154]

The new elements in society and culture that show themselves up in this period reflect and legitimize this new system. For one thing, we have the emergence and solidification of the institution of *jāti*. The change in religion, represented by the worship of Āgamaic deities consecrated in temples, is another factor. But more important than all these is the emergence of what has been described as the Bhakti Movement in south India.

Elements of devotion to personalized gods of the Āgamaic tradition have been identified in the texts which formed part of the later strata of the 'Sangam literature' such as the *Kalittokai* and *Paripāṭal*.[155] But their north Indian, Brāhmaṇical, character is hard to miss. In a joint study of the movement which M.G.S. Narayanan and I had undertaken, we have argued that the movement represented an ideology which sought to reflect and legitimize the emerging socio-political order.[156] It is possible to imagine that the Bhakti Movement developed as an unpremeditated by-product of the new Brāhmaṇical agrarian settlements centred on temples, partly as a means of fulfilling their mission and partly as an antithesis. This antithetical aspect, represented by the elements of dissent and protest in the early phase of its development, however, gave way to the ideology which would dominate society in the new milieu. It is significant that the movement is not only centred on the temple but also a projection of the cult represented by that institution.[157] The trajectory of the development of the movement, from Vēṅkaṭam and Kāñci, through the Cōḻa and Pāṇḍya countries to the west coast, also charts the trajectory of the growth of temples and the agrarian expansion it represented. As this expansion was at the root of a series of developments in economy, society and polity, the Bhakti Movement is to be seen as organically related to them. The acrimony involved in the disputations between Jainism and Śaivism, evidence of which is available in literature and epigraphy,[158] and the success of the latter, can be shown as indicating the triumph of the agrarian order which the latter represented. So also, the patronage that the Movement got from rulers such as Mahēndravarman, Neḍumāṟan, Kōcceṅgaṇān, Cēramān Perumāḷ and Kulaśēkhara shows how this ideology was made use of by them in consolidating their position and gaining legitimacy for the new formation presided over by the monarchies which they represented.[159] Even in a later period, when the Cōḻa state was established in a most authoritative manner, it used in a big way the literature and institutions associated with the temples as props.[160] In short, the Bhakti Movement can be seen as representing the transition, at an ideological plane, from one formation to another in this part of the country.[161]

If it is accepted that the complex developments of the rise of agrarian corporations, the proliferation of Brāhmaṇical settlements and their control of economy and society through the institution of the temple, the religious ideology it represented and the fulfilment of the whole process in preparing for the formation and firm establishment of the state represents a transition from one specific period to another, then the question raises itself as to how to characterize and label the periods. A tripartite division of the whole historical period in this part of the country is not acceptable for the simple reason that there would be certainly more than three parts there. In such a situation, 'medieval' becomes a meaningless term to describe the period which followed the earliest historical period. By thus getting out of the tripartite scheme in general and the 'medieval' in particular, the tyranny of labels, as Romila Thapar has put it in another context,[162] can be avoided. Providing alternative labels would, of course, mean providing for alternative tyrannies. And it would also involve considering the entire history, not just the earlier part of it. Such a project is evidently too ambitious for the scope of this paper. For the two periods considered here, it can be tentatively suggested that the former represented a period of chiefdom-level organizations and the latter, of a state society. These labels are likely to invite the criticism that they are related to the superstructural aspects of the political. But it is they that present themselves in the records in a most visible fashion. If the historical method of going from the known to the unknown is accepted, then what is visible can provide pointers to what are beneath and beyond it.

ACKNOWLEDGEMENTS

I thank B. Surendra Rao and M.G.S. Narayanan for discussing an earlier draft of this address. I have benefitted immensely from their suggestions and criticism. If this version is not quite an improvement, it is in spite of them!

NOTES AND REFERENCES

1. The tenancity of the historiographical tradition which has handed down this legacy is surprising. It catches, unawares, even those very historians who have been at the forefront of rejecting this legacy altogether. See, for an example, the following statement occurring in a 'Marxist interpretation': 'The Ghorian conquests of northern India, leading to the establishment of the Delhi Sultanate (1206–1526), may be said to mark the true beginning of the medieval period in India'. Irfan Habib, *Essays in Indian History: Towards a Marxist Perception* (New Delhi, 1997), p. 80.
2. The idea of the Middle Age was invented in the context of European historical writing to celebrate the splendours of classical antiquity on the one side and its modern revival on the other. It began with the humanist outlook of the Renaissance itself and was popularized by historians of the Enlightenment. It is usually accepted that the terms 'ancient', 'medieval' and 'modern' were invented by Pousin of Friege in his book *Feodium* (1639) and advocated by Christopher Cellarius or Keller (1634–1701) of the University of Halle. Arthur Marwick, *The Nature of History* (London, 1975), p. 169. The ideological hegemony of the West in this scheme of periodization serves to 'overestimate the role of the West in world history and underestimate both qualitatively and quantitatively the place of non-European peoples in human development'. Such a scheme of periodization becomes 'an integral part of the intellectual apparatus of imperialism'. 'To the vast majority of mankind, the events regarded so decisive—such as the fall of the Roman Empire, the capture of Byzantium—mean little. The choice of these events also emphasizes the history of political superstructures, of states—a preference that is not without ulterior motives'. Jean Chesnaux, *Pasts and Futures or What is History For?* (London, 1978), pp. 63–7, esp. p. 64.
3. For an effective rejection, Romila Thapar, Harbans Mukhia and Bipan Chandra, *Communalism in the Writing of Indian History* (Delhi, 1972).
4. The 'ancient' period is characterized by the slave mode of production, the 'medieval' by the feudal and the 'modern' by the capitalist. For a brilliant attempt in the context of India, where the colonial takes the place of the capitalist, see Habib, *Essays in Indian History*, pp. 8–9.

5. For a summary of the debate, Vijay Kumar Thakur, *Historiography of Indian Feudalism* (Patna, 1989).
6. Even this Congress had a separate section for the 'early medieval', which is given up now. *Proceedings of* the *Indian History Congress* (hereinafter *PIHC*), 13th Session (Nagpur, 1950); 14th session (Jaipur, 1951). However, the 'early medieval' there corresponded to the period of the Sultanate of Delhi. For a thoroughgoing discussion of the 'early medieval' and its constituents and causality in the context of much of northern India, B.D. Chattopadhyaya, *The Making of Early Medieval India* (Delhi, 1994).
7. *Indian History Congress Association Constitution* [as last amended at the 52nd Session (1991–2), Delhi], Section 7. Ancient India, *PIHC* (Delhi, 1992), p. 1116.
8. J.D.M. Derrett, *The Hoysalas: A Medieval Indian Royal Family* (Madras, 1957).
9. K.A. Nilakanta Sastri, *The Cōḷas* (2nd edition, Madras, 1955, 1975), passim.
10. Evidence of and literature on the Iron Age in south India are reviewed in Clarence Maloney, 'Archaeology in South India: Accomplishments and Prospects', in Burton Stein, ed., *Essays on South India* (New Delhi, 1975) and Rajan Gurukkal, 'The Beginnings of the Historic Period: The Tamil South (Up to the End of the AD Fifth Century)', in Romila Thapar, ed., *Recent Perspectives of Early Indian History* (London, 1995).
11. The discovery and publication of the 'Sangam' literature by the turn of the present century was a great event. Historical studies began with V. Kanakasabhai, *The Tamils Eighteen Hundred Years Ago* (Madras, 1904). It was followed by many celebratory exercises. One of the latest and more serious in the series is N. Subramanyan, *Sangam Polity* (revised edition, Madurai,1980).
12. K. Kailasapathi, *Tamil Heroic Poetry* (London, 1968); K. Sivathambi, 'Early South Indian Society and Economy: The Tinai Concept', *Social Scientist*, vol. 29, 1974; Kamil Zvelebil, *The Smile of Murugan* (Leiden, 1973); George L. Hart III, *The Poems of Ancient Tamil: Their Milieu and Their Sanskrit Counterparts* (Berkeley, 1975); George L. Hart, 'Ancient Tamil Literature: Its Scholarly Past and Future' in Stein, ed., *Essays on South India*; R. Champakalakshmi, 'Archaeology and Tamil Literary Tradition', *Purātattva*, vol. VIII, 1975–6; R. Champakalakshmi, *Trade, Ideology and Urbanization: South India 300 BC to AD 1300* (Delhi, 1996); M.G.S. Narayanan, 'The Mauryan Problem in Sangam Works in Historical Perspective', *Journal of Indian History*, vol. 53, no. 2, 1975; M.G.S. Narayanan, 'The Vedic, Puranic, Sastraic Elements in Tamil Sangam Society and Culture', *PIHC* (Aligarh, 1975); M.G.S. Narayanan, 'Cattle Raiders of the Sangam Age', *PIHC* (Bhubaneswar, 1977); M.G.S. Narayanan, 'The Warrior Settlements of the Sangam Age', *PIHC* (Kurukshetra, 1982); M.G.S. Narayanan, 'Peasants in Early Tamilakam',

in H.V. Sreenivasamurthi, B. Surendra Rao, Kesavan Veluthat and S.A. Bari, eds, *Essays on Indian History and Culture: Felicitation Volume to Professor B. Sheik Ali* (New Delhi, 1990); J.A. Marr, *The Eight Anthologies: A Study in Early Tamil* (Madras, 1987); Rajan Gurukkal, 'Aspects of Early Iron Age Economy', *PIHC* (Bodh Gaya, 1981); Rajan Gurukkal, 'Forms of Production and Forces of Change in Ancient Tamil Society', *Studies in History*, new series, vol. 5, no. 2, 1989; Rajan Gurukkal, 'Early Social Formation of South India and its Transitional Processes', in Sreenivasamurthi, *et al.*, eds, *Essays on Indian History*; Rajan Gurukkal, 'Towards a New Discourse: Discursive Processes in Early South India', in R. Champakalakshmi and S. Gopal, eds, *Tradition, Dissent and Ideology: Essays in Honour of Romila Thapar* (Delhi, 1996).

13. Kailasapathi, *Tamil Heroic Poetry.*
14. Zvelebil, *The Smile of Murugan*; Gurukkal, 'Towards a New Discourse'.
15. Sivathambi, 'Early South Indian Society'.
16. This was taken formerly as 'confusion by poets of the native habits of different regions': N. Subramanyan, *Pre-Pallavan Tamil Index* (Madras, 1990), p. 430 s.v. *Tiṇai Mayakku.* For a different interpretation, Gurukkal, 'Early Social Formation'.
17. Gurukkal, 'Early Social Formation'. It is important to remember that surplus had no relevance in such a society and that surplus 'is in any case not an event but a process'. Romila Thapar, *From Lineage to State* (Bombay, 1984), p. 77.
18. B.K. Gururaja Rao, *Megalithic Culture of South India* (Mysore, 1972); A. Sundara, *Early Chamber Tombs of South India* (Delhi, 1975); L.S. Leshnik, *South Indian 'Megalithic' Burials: The Pandukal Complex* (Wiesbaden, 1974). It will be rewarding to read these with Champakalakshmi, 'Archaeology and Tamil Literary Tradition'.
19. Paiyampalli is a good case in point. *Indian Archaeology: A Review* (1964–5), pp. 22–3; (1967–8), pp. 26–30.
20. Gururaja Rao, *Megalithic Culture*; Sundara, *Early Chamber Tombs.*
21. T.V. Mahalingam, *Early South Indian Palaeography* (rpt, Madras, 1974); Iravatham Mahadevan, 'Corpus of the Tamil Brahmi Inscriptions', in R. Nagaswami, ed., *Seminar on Inscriptions* (Madras, 1966); T.V. Mahalingam, *Tamil Brahmi Inscriptions* (Madras, 1970). For an insightful analysis, Rajan Gurukkal, 'Writing and its Uses in the Ancient Tamil Country', *Studies in History*, vol. 12, no. 1, new series (1996) pp. 67–81.
22. Gurukkal, 'Early Social Formations', p. 21, n. 18. For more such names and useful details, Champakalakshmi, *Trade, Ideology and Urbanization*, p. 107.
23. Ibid.
24. Narayanan, 'Cattle Raiders'; Gurukkal, 'Early Social Formations'.

25. Champakalakshmi, *Trade, Ideology and Urbanization*, pp. 175–202; Romila Thapar, 'Black Gold: South Asia and the Roman Maritime Trade', *South Asia: Journal of the South Asian Studies Association*, University of New England, ? New South Wales, Armidale, 1992, vol. XV, no. 2 (new series); Vimala Begley and Richard Daniel de Puma, eds, *Rome and India: The Ancient Sea Trade* (Madison, 1992).
26. Champakalakshmi, *Trade, Ideology and Urbanization.*
27. Ibid.
28. There are twenty-seven hoards, thirty-seven stray or surface finds and only two occurrences from occupational levels. Ibid., Appendix B, pp. 158–74.
29. Ibid., pp. 25–36.
30. Thapar, 'Black Gold', pp. 13–14. She suspects that the hoards of Roman coins represented protection money to ensure safe passage of goods from one coast to another.
31. Champakalakshmi, *Trade, Ideology and Urbanization*, pp. 97–174.
32. Narayanan, 'Cattle Raiders'; Gurukkal, 'Towards a New Discourse'.
33. Gurukkal, 'Towards a New Discourse'. He speaks of 'about thirty-five enunciative codes ... which may be grouped ... into five clusters of closely related meanings: those extolling individual heroism; the family tradition and heritage of heroes; the virtues of raids and plunder; the collective passion of the communities for raid; and the act of gift-giving.'
34. Narayanan, 'Peasants', p. 30; Subramanyan, *Sangam Polity*, chapter VI, pp. 126–86.
35. Narayanan, 'Cattle Raiders', Subramanyan, *Pre-Pallavan Tamil Index*, p. 129 s.v. *uṇḍāṭṭu.* These details may be profitably read with the insight provided by Romila Thapar, *From Lineage to State*, chapter II, esp. pp. 31–3.
36. Gurukkal, 'Writing and its Uses'.
37. Naryanan, 'The Mauryan Problem'.
38. K.A. Nilakanta Sastri, *A History of South India* (Madras, 1966), pp. 143–5; R. Champakalakshmi, 'Buddhism in Tamilakam: Patterns of Patronage', paper presented at the International Seminar on Tamil Buddhism, Institute of Asian Studies, Madras, 1992.
39. Above, n. 21. Also, Sastri, *loc. cit.*
40. For the unmistakable Brāhmaṇa presence in the 'Sangam' literature, N. Subramanyan, *Sangam Polity*, pp. 274–90; T.V. Kuppuswami, *Brahmanas and Brahmanism in Sangam Literature* (Madurai, 1978) quoted in Narayanan, 'Peasants'.
41. Narayanan, 'Peasants', p. 33.
42. Ibid.
43. Ibid., p. 33 and n. 76 on p. 43.
44. Narayanan, 'The Vedic, Puranic, Sastraic'.
45. Subramanyan, *Pre-Pallavan Tamil Index*, p. 600, S.V. Perundēvanār. He is described to have 'sung the Bhārata'.

46. M.G.S. Narayanan, review article on Noboru Karashima, *South Indian History and Society*, in *Tamil Civilization*, vol. 3, no. 1, 1985, pp. 61, 68–9.
47. Noboru Karashima, *South Indian History and Society: Studies from Inscriptions AD 850–1800* (Delhi, 1984), pp. 40–55.
48. Ibid.
49. Y. Subbarayalu, 'The Place of Ūr in the Economic and Social History of Early Tamilnadu', paper presented at a seminar on south Indian History organized by Indian Council of Historical Research, Madras University, February 1977.
50. This is demonstrated by the increase in the number of landholders mentioned in the inscriptions as brought out by Karashima, *South Indian History*; Y. Subbarayalu, 'Transfer of Land in Kaveri Valley', *PIHC* (Calicut, 1976), etc.
51. Above, n. 49.
52. For a discussion, Kesavan Veluthat, 'The Role of Nāḍu in the Socio-Political Structure of South India (*c.* AD 600–1200)' in Sreenivasamurthi, *et al.*, eds, *Essays on Indian History*, pp. 85–100. Chapter 5 below.
53. Historians in the past had taken *nāḍu* as an administrative unit of the kingdoms and empires of south India. Sastri, *The Cōḷas*, pp. 465, 503–4; T.V. Mahalingam, *South Indian Polity* (Madras, 1975), p. 369. It was the penetrating research of Y. Subbarayalu, although initiated within the same framework, that brought about a change in this notion. Y. Subbarayalu, *Political Geography of the Chola Country* (Madras, 1973).
54. Basing himself on Subbarayalu, Burton Stein offered a radically different explanation of the role and functions of the *nāḍus* where he looked at them as so many peasant micro-regions and thus the foci of power in medieval south India. Burton Stein, *Peasant State and Society in Medieval South India* (Delhi, 1980), pp. 90–140; 270 ff.
55. My own view is what is taken up here. Kesavan Veluthat, *The Political Structure of Early Medieval South India* (Delhi, 1993), pp. 177–95.
56. James Heitzman, 'State Formation in South India, 850–1280', *Indian Economic and Social History Review*, vol. XXIV, no. 1, March 1987, pp. 35–61.
57. In the somewhat lengthy chapter (XVIII) on 'Local Government', Sastri (*The Cōḷas*, pp. 486–519) devotes a little more than a quarter of a page to the *ūr* (p. 492), about one-third of a page to the nagaram and about two pages to the *nāḍu* (pp. 503–5), the remaining portion being generally concerned with the *brahmadēya* villages. This predicament, forced by the nature of the sources, has brought to Sastri a lot of unearned and uninformed criticism.
58. Sastri, *The Cōḷas*, p. 6.
59. Ibid., and n. 11 on p. 15.
60. This is brought out most clearly by inscriptions from Mānūr in the Pāṇḍyan country, Uttaramērūr in the Cōḻa country and Airāṇikkaḷam

in Kerala. For a review of the literature and the sources, Kesavan Veluthat, 'The *Sabhā* and *Pariṣad* in Early Medieval South India: Correlation of Epigraphic and Dharmaśāstraic Evidence', *Tamil Civilization*, vol. III, nos 2 and 3, 1985, pp. 75–82.

61. Ibid.
62. The instance of interpreting a particular reference from the inscriptions of Kerala will be revealing here. A large number of records refer to an agreement of Mūḻikkaḷam, one of the prominent Brāhmaṇa settlements. The agreement was followed as a precedent in a large number of other places and laid down severe punishments to those who violated the decisions of the bodies. Elamkulam Kunjan Pillai took this as measures to protect the interests of the tenants. *Janmisampradāyam Kēraḷattil* (Kottayam, 1959), p. 74. M.G.S. Narayanan, however, has shown that the function of this and other similar agreements was the protection of the corporate interest of the Brāhamaṇical bodies. *The Perumals of Kerala: Political and Social Conditions of Kerala under the Cera Perumals of Makotai (c. AD 800–1124)*, (Calicut, 1996), pp. 114–20.
63. For a brilliant discussion, R. Tirumalai, *Land Grants and Agrarian Reactions in Cola and Pandya Times* (Madras, 1987), pp. 93–8.
64. Of the thirty copper plates of the Pallavas granting land included in T.N. Subramanyan, ed., *Thirty Pallava Copper Plates* (Madras, 1966), only three (p. 29, l.53; p. 166, l.107 and p. 187, ll.20–21) speak of the earlier occupants. Veluthat, *Political Structure*, p. 224.
65. Veluthat, *Political Structure*, pp. 224–5.
66. For a review of the sources and the literature as well as an excellent analysis of the structure of land rights in the Pāṇḍyan kingdom, Rajan Gurukkal, 'The Agrarian System and Socio-Political Organization under the Early Pāṇḍyas, *c.* AD 600–1000', unpublished PhD Thesis, Jawaharlal Nehru University (New Delhi, 1984), esp. pp. 109–25.
67. The extension of the same structure, even in phraseology, is indicative of the sources of this tradition. The institutions and ideas represented by the *Dharmaśāstras* point generally to a northern origin.
68. Narayanan, *Perumals of Kerala*, pp. 174–8.
69. There is rich data on and an impressive literature around, the situation in the Cōḻa country. For a review, Dharma Kumar, 'Private Property in Asia? The Case of Medieval South India', *Comparative Studies in History and Society*, vol. 27, no. 2, April 1985 and Kesavan Veluthat, 'The Structure of Landrights in Early Medieval South India', in Vijay Kumar Thakur and Ashok Anshouman, eds, *Peasants in Indian History* (Patna, 1996). Chapter 3 below.
70. Champakalakshmi, *Trade, Ideology and Urbanization*, pp. 203–310.
71. Ibid., pp. 311–30.
72. *Travancore Archaeological Series* (hereafter *TAS*), vol. II, part I, no. 9, pp. 60–85. I have followed the text and translation of M.G.S. Narayanan, *Cultural Symbiosis in Kerala* (Trivandrum, 1972), pp. 31–7; 54–9; 86–94.

73. Ibid., p. 93.
74. Above, n. 71.
75. Kenneth Hall, *Trade and Statecraft in the Age of the Colas* (Delhi, 1980).
76. E.g., Suvira Jaiswal, 'Caste in the Socio-Economic Framework of Early India', Presidential Address, *PIHC*, Ancient India Section (Bhubaneswar, 1977), p. 30.
77. Habib, *Essays in Indian History*, p. 128, wonders how the peasants could be described as Śūdras rather than Vaiśyas.
78. B. Suresh, 'Historical and Cultural Geography and Ethnology of South India with Special Reference to Cōḻa Inscriptions', unpublished PhD Thesis, Deccan College (Poona, 1965), p. 315, quoted in Stein, *Peasant State*, p. 103.
79. J.D.M. Derrett, 'Two Inscriptions Concerning the Status of Kammalas and the Application of *Dharmaśāstra*', *Professor K.A. Nilakanta Sastri 80th Birthday Felicitation Volume* (Madras, 1971); Veluthat, *Political Structure*, pp. 236–7.
80. Arjun Appadurai, 'Right and Left Hand Castes in South India', *The Indian Economic and Social History Review*, vol. XI, nos 2 and 3, 1974, pp. 216–60.
81. Gurukkal, 'Towards a New Discourse'.
82. K.A. Nilakanta Sastri, *The Development of Religion in South India* (Calcutta, 1963). For the growth of Vaiṣṇavism and Śaivism, respectively, S. Krishnaswami Aiyangar, *The History of Vaishnavism in South India* (Madras, 1920); C.V. Narayana Ayyar, *Origin and Early History of Saivism in South India* (Madras, 1920).
83. Burton Stein, ed., *The South Indian Temples* (Delhi, 1977).
84. Veluthat, *Political Structure*, pp. 29–69.
85. K.A. Nilakanta Sastri, *The Pandyan Kingdom* (London, 1929), pp. 74–5; *The Cōḷas*, pp. 126–8, 187–9, 259–60, 347–8, 372–5, 400–8, 429–32; T.V. Mahalingam, *South Indian Polity*, pp. 321–8; M.S. Govindaswamy, *The Role of Feudatories in Pallava History* (Annamalainagar, 1975). M.S. Govindaswamy, *The Role of Feudatories in Later Chola History* (Annamalainagar, 1979); M. Arokiaswamy, *The Kongu Country* (Madras, 1956); V. Balambal, *Feudatories of South India 800–1070 AD* (Allahabad, 1978). The information they provide is copious; but the feudal jargon is used without any rigour.
86. Veluthat, *Political Structure*, p. 109 and n. 11 on p. 131.
87. Ibid., and n. 13 on p. 131.
88. Ibid., pp. 109–11 and nn. 14–28.
89. Ibid., p. 110.
90. Narayanan, *Perumals of Kerala*, pp. 90–105.
91. 'Jewish Copper Plates of Bhaskara Ravi Varman', in Narayanan, *Cultural Symbiosis*, pp. 79–81.
92. *TAS*, vol. V, no. 13, pp. 40–6.

93. Veluthat, *Political Structure*, pp. 121–6.
94. Ibid., p. 127.
95. Ibid., p. 126.
96. Ibid., p. 129.
97. *TAS*, vol. V, no. 12, pp. 37–40.
98. Veluthat, *Political Structure*, p. 129.
99. *South Indian Inscriptions* (hereafter *SII*), vol. III, p. 89; Narayanan, *Perumals of Kerala*, pp. 25, 44.
100. Ibid., pp. 44–9.
101. Ibid., p. 46.
102. C. Girija, 'The Mūṣikavamśakāvya: A Study', unpublished MPhil Dissertation, Mangalore University, 1990.
103. Sastri, *The Cōḷas*, pp. 461 f.
104. Burton Stein, 'The State and Agrarian Order in Medieval South India', in Burton Stein ed., *Essays on South India* (Delhi, 1975); Stein, *Peasant State*.
105. Noboru Karashima, Y. Subbarayalu and Toru Matsui have undertaken a computer-aided analysis of personal names figuring in Cōḻa inscriptions. *A Concordance of Personal Names in Cola Inscriptions* (Madurai, 1978), 3 vols. Our analysis is based on this. Veluthat, *Political Structure*, pp. 78–99.
106. Ibid.
107. *SI*, vol. III, no. 147; Veluthat, *Political Structure*, p. 82.
108. Kesavan Veluthat, 'Landed Magnates as State Agents: The Gāvuḍas under the Hoysaḷas in Karnataka', *PIHC* (Gorakhpur, 1989). Reproduced in Bhairabi Prasad Sahu, ed., *Land System and Rural Society in Early India* (Delhi, 1997), pp. 322–8. Chapter 15 below.
109. Veluthat, *Political Structure*, pp. 78–99.
110. Ibid., pp. 97–8.
111. Ibid., pp. 95–7.
112. Above, n. 57.
113. Veluthat, *Political Structure*, pp. 168–220.
114. R. Champakalakshmi, 'Introduction', *Studies in History*, vol. IV, no. 2, July–December 1982, pp. 164–5.
115. Veluthat, *Political Structure*, pp. 168–220.
116. Sastri, *The Cōḷas*, chapter XIX: 'Taxation and Finance', pp. 520–45.
117. Above, n. 104.
118. Karashima, *South Indian History and Society*, pp. 69–130; P. Shanmugam, *The Revenue System of the Colas*, 850–1279 (Madras, 1987).
119. Ibid., A systematic survey of land was undertaken before assessing revenue: Shanmugam, *The Revenue System*, pp. 67–79.
120. Narayanan, *Perumals of Kerala*, pp. 134–5.
121. Shanmugam, *The Revenue System*, pp. 121–38.
122. Ibid., pp. 80–91; Tirumalai, *Land Grants*, p. 172.

123. Kesavan Veluthat, 'Labour Rent and Produce Rent: Reflections on the Revenue System of the Colas', *PIHC* (Dharwar, 1988). Chapter 4 below.
124. Sastri, *The Cōḷas*, pp. 453–60.
125. Stein, 'State and Agrarian Order', pp. 75–6; Stein, *Peasant State*, pp. 256–7, etc.
126. M.G.S. Narayanan, *Reinterpretations* in *South Indian History* (Trivandrum, 1977), pp. 99–112.
127. Veluthat, *Political Structure*, pp. 154–7. The discussion below follows this work of ours.
128. Kesavan Veluthat, 'The Nature and Significance of the Institution of Vēḷevali in Karnataka', *PIHC* (Calcutta, 1990). Chapter 14 below.
129. Above, n. 84.
130. The *praśastis* of the rulers and the later *meykkīrtis* are such accounts.
131. Champakalakshmi, *Trade, Ideology and Urbanization*, pp. 424–41. She takes up Tanjavur, but similar examination of other expressions of art and architecture will be rewarding.
132. R. Champakalakshmi, 'The Sovereignty of the Divine: The Vaiṣṇava Pantheon and Temporal Power in South India', in Sreenivasamurthi, *et al.*, eds., *Essays on Indian History*.
133. Veluthat, *Political Structure*, p. 58.
134. This expression is used by George W. Spencer, 'Religious Networks and Royal Influence in Eleventh Century South India', *Journal of the Economic and Social History of the Orient*, vol. XII, no. 1, 1969, pp. 42–56.
135. Stein, *Peasant State*, pp. 331–43.
136. K.G. Krishnan, ed., *Karandai Tamil Sangam Plates of Rajendrachola* (New Delhi, 1984). Stein uses this and other similar records to prove his point of ritual hegemony. Stein, *Peasant State*, pp. 343–61.
137. Sastri, *History of South India*, p. 144.
138. Ibid.
139. Ibid.
140. K.A. Nilakanta Sastri, *Culture and History of The Tamils* (Calcutta, 1965), p. 19 quoted in Stein, *Peasant State*, p. 77.
141. Sastri, *History of South India*, p. 145.
142. Stein, *Peasant State*, p. 65.
143. Ibid., p. 77.
144. Rajan Gurukkal, 'Non-Brāhmaṇa Resistance to the Expansion of Brahmadēyas: The Early Pāṇḍya Experience', *PIHC* (Annamalainagar, 1994), pp. 181–4; Rajan Gurukkal, 'Early Social Formation of South India', in *Essays on Indian History*; Rajan Gurukkal, *The Kerala Temple and Early Medieval Agrarian System* (Sukapuram, 1992), p. 27. The quotations here are from the book mentioned last.

    The association that Gurukkal sees here with Kaliyuga has lured a number of scholars. D.N. Jha, ed., *Feudal Social Formations in Early India* (Delhi, 1987), 'Introduction', p. 92. B.P. Sahu takes a more sober position. 'Conception of Kali Age in Early India: A Regional Perspective', *Trends in Social Science Research*, vol. 4, no. 1, June 1997, pp. 31–2.

145. The sources are reviewed in Sastri, *The Cōḷas*, pp. 101–2 and P.T. Srinivasa Aiyangar, *Tamil Studies; or Essays in the History of the Tamil People, Language, Religion and Literature* (Madras, 1914), pp. 435–7.

146. Thus, Narasimhavarman is stated in the Kūram plates to have defeated 'Cōḻa, Kēraḷa, Kaḷabhra and Pāṇḍya': Subramanyan, ed., *Thirty Pallava Copper Plates*, p. 47, l.15; Avanisimha is described in the Kāśākkuḍi Plates to have defeated 'Maḻavas, Kaḷabhras, Cōḻas, Pāṇḍyas, Simhaḷas and Kēraḷas': ibid., p. 161, ll.51–2; Nandivarman is said in the Pullūr Copper Plates to have forced the kings of 'Kēraḷa, Cōḻa, Pāṇḍya, Māḷava, Kaḷabhra, Bāṇa, Āndhra, Saindhava, Gaṅga and Kadamba' to pay obeisance to him: ibid., p. 186, ll.8–10; he is celebrated in the Pattattalmangalam Plates as being waited upon by 'Vallabha, Kaḷabhra; Kēraḷa, Pāṇḍya, Cōḻa, Tulu, Koṅkana and others': ibid., p. 241, ll.17–18. Again praśastis of the Cāḷukyas of Badami include Kaḷabhras among those whom they had defeated in their *digvijayas* in the same manner; so they were not opposed to the Tamils alone! Thus, the Kaḷabhras figure in the Pallava and Cāḷukya records as one of the *et ceteras* defeated by different Pallava and Cāḷukya rulers, making it difficult to pin them down to space and time. That they are in the company of Cēra, Cōḻa and Pāṇḍya mocks at the statements that the Kaḷabhras had 'imprisoned' (Sastri, *The Cōḷas*) or 'suspended' (Gurukkal, *The Kerala Temple*) the Tamil rulers.

147. Tamil Varalāṟṟuk Kaḻagam, ed., *Pāṇḍyar Ceppēṭukaḷ Pattu* (Madras, 1967), p. 22, l.40.

148. See, for instance, *kalibalamardana*, *TPCP*, p. 127, l.29; *Calitakalimalaprōllasatkīrti*, ibid., p. 186, l.3; *kaliśāsana*, ibid., p. 254, l.21; *kaliyugadōṣāvasannadharmōddharaṇanityasannaddha*, p. 286, ll.12–13; p. 299, l.10; p. 311, ll.12–3; etc. Neḍuñjaḍaiyan, the donor of the Vēḷvikudi Plates, is described as *kalippagai*: above, n. 147, p. 28, l.100. Gurukkal quotes a Vaigai bed inscription of Cēndan Arikesari, who claims that he had 'surmounted (*sic*) the *Kali* through *mahādānas: mahādanaṅkaḷāl kali kaṭintu*': *The Kerala Temple*, p. 27, n. 3. The only link which relates the Kaḷabhras with Kaliyuga is the epithet of Kaḷabhra as *Kali araśan*! Above, n. 147. And, that is translated rightly to mean 'evil king'.

149. Narayanan, 'Warrior Settlements', *PIHC* (Kurukshetra, 1982).

150. Narayanan, 'Peasants', p. 28, n. 20 on p. 40. A large number of instances where land is said to be gifted to Brāhmaṇas are given here.

151. Gurukkal, 'Towards a New Discourse'.

152. R. Nagaswami, 'An Outstanding Epigraphical Discovery in Tamilnadu', *Proceedings of the Fifth International Conference Seminar on Tamil*

Studies, Madurai, 1981. I am indebted to M.R. Raghava Varier for allowing me to use his transcription of the record.

153. M.G.S. Narayanan proposes a 'wedge hypothesis' where the newly introduced Brāhmaṇical element is described as a wedge driven between the chiefs on the one side and the 'traditional Tamil society of the tribal-pastoral-agrarian type' on the other. 'Peasants', p. 35. We take this further and argue that the grant of land to Brāhmaṇas necessitated the use of non-kin labour and that this was responsible for the ultimate break-up of the old formation. *Cf.* Thapar, *From Lineage to State*, p. 36.
154. Here I reject explicitly the disjunctive character of the transition, whether explained in the conventional terms of a 'Kaḷabhra intenegnum' or in the more recent terms of a 'crisis' as seen in some of the literature reviewed above, pp. 45–7
155. R. Champakalakshmi, 'From Devotion and Dissent to Dominance: The Bhakti of the Tamil Alvars and Nayanars', in Champakalakshmi and Gopal, eds, pp. 135–63.
156. M.G.S. Narayanan and Kesavan Veluthat, 'The Bhakti Movement in South India', in S.C. Malik, ed., *Indian Movements: Some Aspects of Dissent, Protest and Reform* (Simla, 1978), pp. 33–66.
157. Kesavan Veluthat, 'The Temple-base of the Bhakti Movement in South India', *PIHC* (Waltair, 1979).
158. R. Champakalakshmi, 'Religious Conflict in the Tamil Country: A Reapprisal of Epigraphic Evidence', *Journal of the Epigraphical Society of India*, vol. 5, 1978.
159. Kesavan Veluthat, 'The Socio-political Background of Kulaśēkhara Aḻvār's Bhakti', *PIHC* (Bhubaneswar, 1977).
160. R. Champakalakshmi, 'Patikam Pāṭuvār: Ritual Singing as a Means of Communication in Early Medieval South India', *Studies in History*, new series, vol. X, no. 2, July–December, 1994.
161. Gurukkal, 'Towards a New Discourse', Champakalakshmi, 'From Devotion and Dissent to Dominance'.
162. Romila Thapar, 'The Tyranny of Labels', Text of the Zakir Hussain Memorial Lecture, 1996, in *Social Scientist*, vol. 24, nos 9–10, September–October 1996, pp. 3–23.

2

The Temple in Medieval South India*

Matters related to religion, art, and the like, even when they are studied for their own interest, are of extreme importance to the historian and the social scientist, because they involve considerable amount of patronage and, as nothing comes free, there is also the expectation of reciprocity along with patronage. The relationship between the patron and the client is mutual. In order to understand this interdependence, the historian will have to go beyond what is visible in the sources and interrogate them in ways which would bring out the factors that led to the patronage and the ways in which the clients reciprocated.

I will take up for discussion a problem related to the deep south of India, namely, the present day states of Kerala, Pondicherry, and Tamil Nadu in the period between the AD seventh and twelfth centuries. Stated briefly, my purpose is to show that the temple as a religious institution was patronized by the state as well as other owning groups in various ways and that this patronage was not entirely without its rcturn. Thc patronage helped the patrons to use the symbols of that religion for their benefit. The exercise of power in the particular socio-political formation was achieved primarily through the use of the symbols of the Āgamaic Hindu religion, which was propagated through the aggressive Bhakti Movement and its institutional expression, the temples. As this religion got firmly established and became part of the consciousness of those sections of society to which an appeal was

* First published as 'Patronage and Reciprocation: The Temple in Medieval South India', *Journal of South Indian History*, vol. 1, no. 1, 2003, pp. 7–30. This paper draws heavily on two of my earlier papers presented elsewhere: one in the University of Hyderabad and another in the Postgraduate Department of History of the Government College, Thrissur. I had also tested these ideas in the Sankara-Parvathi Lecture I gave at the Madras University in March 2000.

made, its symbols came in handy in a bid for achieving some sort of ideological domination with great profit. This political use of religion included, in the first place, the use of its symbols for purposes of political mobilization and then, using them as metaphors of power. Finally, we also see that religious institutions start functioning as the state itself in a surrogate way.

One of the more important aspects of the religious history of early medieval south India is the emergence of the temple dedicated to one of the two Āgamaic deities, Śaiva, or Vaiṣṇava. The syncretic cult of these deities is itself the result of a process through which elements of the folk cults and practices were incorporated into the classical traditions of Vedic-Hindu religion. In the earliest historical period in south India, documented elaborately in what is known as the Sangam literature, one does not come across a society in which this religious system had gained acceptance.[1] In that period, which scholars are inclined to bring down to AD fourth or even fifth century, a congeries of cults and practices obtained[2], occasionally sprinkled with Vedic-Śāstraic-Purāṇic ideas[3], but not standardized in a recognizable form or reduced into an institutional framework. The very strong presence of the Brāhmaṇa, with his Vedic sacrifices and even Āgamaic ideas, is hard to miss there; but sprawling Brāhmaṇa settlements with vast areas of agricultural land under their command and the temple as the pivot around which they functioned had not yet taken shape in that period. Perhaps it was this element, which necessitated extra-kin labour, that brought about a transition from one formation to another in this part of the country in the period that followed immediately.

By the time we reach the seventh-eighth centuries, the picture is altered significantly. A complex phenomenon develops in this region with several interrelated aspects. Among the more important ones of these were the opening up of the fertile river valleys for agriculture, the covering of the landscape by a network of big and small Brāhmaṇa settlements, the studding of the territory with a large number of temples commanding vast extents of land as their property and all the entailing privileges and, of course, the burgeoning of monarchy which anticipated the Cōḷa state in the centuries to come. To be sure, these developments were extremely complex and, to a great extent, interrelated—particularly the creation of vast agrarian corporations, the emergence of the Brāhmaṇa settlements, and the rise of the temples. In fact, one may even risk oversimplification by identifying these three—the agrarian corporations, the Brāhmaṇa settlements, and the temples—as synonymous. One has to take them in their totality if one is trying to understand the complex relations between religion and politics and the way in which aspects of patronage and reciprocity operated there.

The Āgamaic variety of Brāhmaṇical religion, thus, struck deep roots in south India by the seventh or eighth century of the Christian era, that is, by the period when the monarchical state had established itself in south India. The agency for this penetration was the brahman groups that had infiltrated into this part of the country in the early historical period, evidence of which is available even in the earliest strata of Tamil literature. Although they began as practitioners of the Vedic religion, it is the Āgamaic and Purāṇic variety of religion that they had propagated in south India in a big way. In fact, the Brāhmaṇical factor has been shown as the thin end of a wedge, which led to the ultimate break-up of the early social formation characterized by chiefdom-level organizations and the emergence of a state society in south India.[4] Gaining the confidence of the chiefs and cajoling them, the Brāhmaṇas received major grants of land as *brahmadēyas* and *dēvadānas* and other privileges and established themselves as a considerable force in society and economy. In fact, this proliferation of Brāhmaṇa settlements and the consequent rise of temples as their nucleus have been presented as having brought about a veritable revolution in south India in the age of the Pallavas and Pāṇḍyas, which saw its fulfilment in the age of the Cēras and Cōḻas. In a joint paper which M.G.S. Narayanan and I have written on the socio-economic role of the temples in south India, we have summarized the way in which the temple behaved in the following manner:[5]

1. The temple served as an agency for easier and more efficient extraction of surplus from the peasants in the agrarian economy and this contributed to the extension of agriculture in the tribal areas and the consolidation of the landlord domination.
2. In the course of such extension, the temple accelerated the process of the disintegration of tribal society and its reorganization as a caste society.
3. In the newly formed caste society, the temple served as an integrating factor linking the high and low in its service

and drawing towards itself as clients the different castes and sub-castes.

4. Such integrated role paved the way for the Brāhmaṇa-inspired and Brāhmaṇa-supported state power in the regional monarchies of south India. The temple put its imprimatur of legitimacy on the new polity and this in turn guaranteed state patronage for the temple.
5. In this process, the Brāhmaṇical *varṇāśrama* ideology strengthened its grip on society, its latest weapon being the Bhakti Movement for which the temple served as an institutional base.
6. In course of time, the prosperous temple, which was a landed magnate from the beginning, also developed into a storehouse of gold and silver and precious jewels as well as the regular place of assembly for the rural elite.
7. This produced the need for exclusiveness and protection leading eventually to the development of the temple to fortress like proportions with several circles of streets within streets, bazaars and armed forces.
8. Finally the temple acted as the agent for developing, consolidating, transmitting and conserving the legacy of culture.

Naturally, the temple represented a most revolutionary and forward-looking force in south India and all those who were related to it in many complex ways accepted the religion it represented. The temple, with its strong ideological weapon in the Bhakti Movement, was able to register the victory of what can be called the Hindu Brāhmaṇical religion. This succeeded in gaining the victory of the agrarian order in south India bringing about differentiation of society with infinite gradations in a caste hierarchy that it entailed. This social order found its normative definition in the textual prescriptions or *varṇāśramadharma.* The upper classes consisting largely of the owning groups in society accepted this ideology. But what was more important was that this ideology should be extended to other sections of society. We have argued elsewhere that the Bhakti Movement in south India, which was in reality a temple movement, was coeval with the rise and fulfilment of the temple.[6] It reflected the newly emerging social order and legitimized it comprehensively. Thus, the temple was an institution whose potential was realized by the monarchs of south India as early as the period of the origin of the monarchical state in this part of the country represented by the Pallava kingdom.

In speaking about patronage and reciprocity in the context of temples in medieval south India, it is important to remember that the temple received its patronage from many quarters: royalty, political chiefs, landlords of all varieties, trading groups—in short, all those who were of any consequence in society. This patronage included gifts of substantial resources including land and gold, protection of those resources and those who managed them as well as the premises, and other kinds of services. Naturally, all these groups also benefited immensely from this patronage. To be sure, one does not mean that there was something of a calculated business deal; but the reciprocity involved in the patronage should not be lost sight of. To put it briefly, the ways in which the temple reciprocated the patronage it received from the rulers, whether the bigger 'monarchs' or the minor chiefs, included considerable legitimacy to the ruler and the support of the more important sections of society. Where it was the landlord class that patronized the temple, it ensured a more peaceful integration of the agrarian order as the peasants and those lower sections of society had started accepting the ideological hegemony of the temple. The traders and artisans, too, benefited from their relation with the temple as the temple was a major consumer and as the temple provided an occasion and a centre for the coordination of their activities.

All this was possible because the temple was at this point in time synonymous with Brāhmaṇical groups owning vast extents of land. This land was known as *dēvadānam* ('a gift to the god') and *brahmadēyam* ('a gift to Brāhmaṇas')—*dēvasvam* ('god's property') and *brahmasvam* ('Brāhmaṇa's property') respectively in Kerala. By the efficient management of this huge resource, such as clearing land and the management of irrigation, they could effectively promote and manage wealth; they could also wean away the royalty, the social groups and the market from the tribal background of an earlier period. Patronage of temple thus meant patronage of the powerful Brāhmaṇical groups.

It is against this background that we can examine how symbols of this religion were made use of for achieving ideological domination in society by the ruling classes in general and for seeking legitimacy for the ruler himself in particular. The opening up of the river valleys for agriculture had brought about a major social change and historians have looked upon this as one of the significant factors behind state formation here. Starting from Toṇḍaimaṇḍalam or the Pallava country in northern Tamil Nadu, this expansion of agriculture led to the formation of clear-cut divisions in society and this process extended further south to include the territories of the Pāṇḍya and to south-west to those of the Cēra in the centuries that followed. By the ninth century, the Kāvēri Valley itself becomes the core region of a new kind of monarchical state. In other words, social change resulting from agrarian expansion reflected itself in the newly emerging political institutions with its gradual expansion southward, to find its culmination and fulfilment in the Cōḻa country.

It is significant that an identical trajectory is followed in the spread of the Bhakti Movement.[7] The early Āḻvārs and Nāyanārs are connected with Toṇḍaimaṇḍalam; they sing about temples in that region such as Vēṅkaṭam or other temples like those in Kāñci. By the time we come to the last of these culture-heroes, they start singing about temples in the Pāṇḍyan and Cēra countries, and the maximum number of temples sung about by them is in the Cōḻa country on either side of the Kāvēri. Thus, the Bhakti Movement has been demonstrated to have had direct links with the expansion of agriculture and the formation of the state based on it.

It is interesting that among the patrons of the Bhakti Movement in the early days we have the names of rulers belonging to the newly established dynasties. The great Appar had Mahēndravarman Pallava as his patron; the story goes that he was instrumental in the latter's conversion to Śaivism from Jainism whereupon a Jaina monastery was pulled down to construct a Śiva temple.[8] Neḍumāṟan, a Pāṇḍya king, is likewise believed to have been converted to Śaivism from Jainism under the influence of his minister Kulaiciṟai Nāyanār and this occasion was promptly celebrated by the impalement of 8000 Jains.[9] A Cōḻa, Kōcceṅgaṇān, identified by scholars as the grandfather of Vijayālaya[10], was a Śaiva Nāyanār and so was Cēramān Perumāḷ, identified as the founder of the Cēra kingdom of Mahōdayapuram. Kulaśēkhara Āḻvār, one of the leaders of the Vaiṣṇava Bhakti Movement, was a ruler of the Cēra dynasty.[11] In the early days of these monarchies, it is probable, the rulers found the support of these movements quite handy and useful. The movement itself, in its turn, derived much benefit from royal patronage, especially in making use of state power for winning their conflicts with rival creeds in a physical way. This mutual support between the Bhakti Movement and the newly established monarchies is significant.

Even at the deeper levels of society, the Bhakti Movement had a major role to play. As the temple gained in popularity with the Bhakti Movement, the services in the temple and the jargon of bhakti came to reflect a particular kind of social organization. For instance, the deity in the temple was accorded full royal status, with no detail in the attendant paraphernalia wanting. Thus *uḍaiyār* or *perumāḷ* meant both the king and the deity, *kōil* meant both the temple and the palace and the day-to-day routine of services in the temple followed, to the last detail, the services in the palace.[12] However, although the terminology used in all these cases pertained to royalty, it was equally applicable to any major landed magnate or local chief. For, in the political structure obtaining in south India at that time, every chief or landlord looked like a 'king' in his own way. In fact, the plurality and coexistence of a large number of deities, arranged sometimes in positions of precedence, reflected eminently a political structure with the plurality and coexistence of a large number of lords and magnates arranged in a hierarchical order with codes of precedence and with strong ties of dependence.[13]

If the deity was thus equated with the lord, the devotee was equated with the vassal. The devotee addressed the deity habitually as *uḍaiyār* or *tambirān* (lord) while he described his own position as that of *aḍiyār* (serf). Statements identifying oneself as 'the servant of the servant of the servant' or 'devotee of the devotee of the devotee' of the deity reflects the typical feudal pyramid, where, barring the apex and the base, each at every point was a lord for his immediate vassal and a vassal for his immediate suzerain with ties of allegiance and dependence. By the time we come to Sundaramūrtti, perhaps the last of the Nāyanārs, the Brāhmaṇical character of the movement and its institutional base, the temple, is underlined by the opening verse of his *Tiruttoṇḍar Purāṇam* where he claims himself to be the 'slave of the slaves of the Brāhmaṇas of Tillai'.[14]

This reflection of the existing social order and the recreation of a parallel world of authority in the realm of religion went a long way in legitimizing the polity that came to be established in this period. Through creating an illusion of cutting across caste lines, what the Bhakti Movement really achieved was to ensure the acceptance of caste and its ideology, which expressed the nature of differentiation, by all sections of society. The stories of Nantanār who was a Paṟaiya and Tiruppāṇa Āḻvār who was a Pāṇa apparently showed that even people belonging to those lowly castes could reach the highest rung in bhakti hierarchy; but its real purpose was to show where, as a rule, the ordinary Paṟaiya or Pāṇa belonged.[15] The existing social structure and the power structure, thus, got the necessary sanction and validation from the temple-based religion of Āgamaic/Purāṇic Hinduism, eminently spread by the Bhakti Movement.

Once these religious ideas got acceptance in society and validated the existing power-structure, that the symbols derived from them should be made use of in seeking legitimacy for the ruler himself is only natural. But before taking up this problem, it is necessary to look at the broad outlines of polity over which the ruler was presiding. By the time of the firm establishment of the Pallavas in Kāñci, it is shown that a new form of state had arrived, as it were, in south India, following the model of kingship prescribed in the *śāstra-kāvya-nāṭaka* literature in Sanskrit.[16] This form of state found its further refinement and elaboration in the other monarchies of the Pāṇḍya, Cēra and Cōḻa. According to their model, the ruler had to be a Kṣatriya par excellence, for the rules of *varṇāśramadharma*, which were accepted as the norm of social organization, demanded a Kṣatriya as the ruler. In fact, an elaborate self-image of the monarch was constructed in the expressions of the ideologues in the court, the contours of which were sharpened by elements drawn from various sources.[17] Among the various aspects of this self-image was an attempt to attribute divinity to the king.[18] This was, by no means, a novel aspect as we see it in northern India in the context of the Gupta empire or even before. In fact, most of the details of this in south India were borrowed from a northern Indian source, thereby showing once again that the model of kingship in south India in the period of the Pallavas and after was derived largely from northern India. However, in the particular context of the socio-religious history of south India, this element of divinity, which added another dimension to the image or royalty, had a special significance.

In attempting to equate royalty with divinity, the divine figures chosen are, significantly, gods of the Āgamaic/Purāṇic Hinduism. In the context of the gaining popularity of this religion with the temple as its institutional base and the Bhakti Movement as its ideological weapon, its gods, naturally, had greater appeal than the ones worshipped in south India in an earlier period. Similarly, since the entire scheme was within the category of *varṇāśramadharma*, it was necessary to accommodate even the gods with whom the newly 'Kṣatriyaized' rulers were equated into the pattern of the Purāṇic texts. Hence the significance of this attempt at divinizing monarchy. At the same time, it has to be borne in mind that this should not be confused with the 'divine right' theory of kingship.[19] The equation of the king with one of the gods was achieved by various means. It is well known that the dynasties of south India such as the Pāṇḍyas, Cēras and Cōḻas had an autochthonous origin; they figure prominently in what is called the Sangam literature. But by the time we come to our period, they were already identified as belonging to the Candravamśa or the Sūryavamśa of the Purāṇic fame. Thus the Pāṇḍyas are stated to belong to the Candravamśa and the Cēras and Cōḻas, to the Sūryavamśa.[20] In the case of the Pallavas, they are said to belong to a category of *brahma-kṣatra*,[21] although there are faint claims to Candravamśa origins also.[22] Curious genealogies are invented in all cases, often at variance with the accounts of the Candravamśa or Sūryavamśa as they figure in the Purāṇas. The origin is invariably traced in all cases to Brahmā, not as the Creator but as the very lineal ancestor of all these dynasties. Even Brahmā is presented as residing in the lotus of Viṣṇu's navel. Purāṇic and divine figures such as Rāma, Kṛṣṇa and Arjuna are introduced at various points in the genealogy so that the king is presented as a descendant of these figures as well.

Then there were the numerous traditions in which each of these dynasties participated, by which a divine status was claimed for the dynasts. There are a large number of exclusive traditions which the Pāṇḍyas, for example, claimed for themselves which include participation in the Mahābhārata war, sharing throne with Indra, acting as messengers to gods, negotiating peace with Rāvaṇa, etc.[23] These, through the Purāṇic associations invoked, accorded a certain amount of divinity to those who participated in these traditions. Comparable traditions are cherished by the Cōḻas: they claim that the famous Śibi who is well known for his kindness and Manu himself, the ruthless law-giver, were among their ancestors.[24] The origin myth of the Cōḻa dynasty as given in the Kanyākumāri inscriptions of Vīrarājēndra, by its close resemblance with the Mārīca story, suggests that it might well have been taken from one of the Purāṇas.[25] In the case of the Pallavas, the ancestry is traced through sages such as Bhṛgu, Aṅgiras, Bharadvāja, Atri, Śamyu, Drōṇa, Aśvatthāman[26]—another instance of using popular religious symbols for claiming a special status for the members of the dynasty.

If the above instances show how whole dynasties were accorded a divine status, there are instances by which individual kings were attributed divine qualities. This was achieved through employing various figures of speech such as the *doubles entendres*, simile, metaphor, etc. Whole verses in contemporary court poetry employ the double entendre, one meaning applicable to the king and another to a god. Thus the opening verse of the astronomical treatise called the *Laghu Bhāskarīya vyākhā* would yield meanings both in praise of Śiva and the patron of the poet, Sthāṇu Ravi Kulaśēkhara of Kerala.[27] The closing verse of what is called the Huzur Office Plates of the Āy king Karunataṭakkan, who was a local chief in former south Travancore, can be taken to be an invocation of Viṣṇu as well as the ruler.[28] Such instances of the use of the double entendre can be multiplied.

A ruler is described in a particular set of terms that echo attributes of a particular deity or Purāṇic hero for a specific achievement. Narasimhavarman's victory over Vātāpi (the Cāḷukya capital) is almost always a feat which made him comparable with Sage Agastya who liquidated Vātāpi (the demon).[29] The alleged victory of the Cēra king Kulaśēkhara over Mallaimānagar is described in such terms that he is treated as Mallāri (Viṣṇu).[30] The Cōḻa king Rājēndra is described as comparable to Śiva for his capture of Kerala, the land created by none less than Paraśurāma.[31] Such examples, which are numerous, show how a specific feat of the king was taken as demonstrating his identity with one of the gods or Purāṇic figures, perhaps unmindful of the uncomfortable questions which may be thrown up in the process.

More numerous are the use of figures of speech such as the simile or the metaphor, or a particular adjective so that the attributes of a deity or a Purāṇic hero are shown in the ruler, too. The Vēḷvikuḍi Plates speak of the bewilderment of the Pallava ruler at the sight of Pāṇḍya Māṟavarman, at a loss to explain whether the latter was 'a human, a demon, Śiva, the supreme being (Para Pūruṣa = Viṣṇu), or Indra'.[32] The same record speaks of Jaṭilavarman as equal to the son of Śiva (Harasūnukalpa).[33] Another Pāṇḍyan record contained in the Śrīvaramaṅgalam Plates likens the birth of Jaṭilavarman, who was equal to Indra, to the birth of Budha from the Moon, of Pradyumna from Viṣṇu, of Subrahmaṇya from Śiva.[34] Speaking about Śrīvānavan Mahādēvi, the wife of Parāntaka Viranarayana, the larger Sinnamanur

Plates say that she was what Śrī was to Śrīnivāsa and Paulōmi to Indra.[35] There are many more such examples.

The titles that the rulers adopted or were conferred on had in many cases the purpose of suggesting the qualities of the gods or Purāṇic figures. Mahēndravarman Pallava had Puruṣōttama, Mahēndra, Vidhi, Sthāṇu, etc., among his numerous titles.[36] The earliest known copper plate record of the Cēras describes the Perumāḷ as Rājaśēkhara;[37] Cōḻa Parāntaka called himself Śrīnilaya;[38] Pāṇḍya Māṟavarman was Śrīvallabha[39]; and so on. The last mentioned titles are further significant because they open the doors to a whole world where the king is presented as the husband of the goddesses of prosperity and of earth.[40] This is a recurring theme in the records of most south Indian dynasties. The ruler thus appropriates the clear attributes of Viṣṇu of being both Śrīpati and Bhūpati. It is these which are presented in the sharp and brief beginnings of the *meykkīrtti* of Rājarāja: *Tirumagaḷ pōla Perunilaccelviyun tanakkē urimai pūṇḍamai manakkoḷa.*[41] The same idea is repeated, *ad nauseum*, in the *meykkīrtti*s of the later Cōḻas and the Pāṇḍyas of what Nilakanta Sastri calls the 'Second Empire'.

At very concrete levels also, there were attempts at 'divinizing' the king. The Cōḻas started the practice of consecrating images of the kings in temples and thus making them objects of worship. A large number of such 'portrait' images of the Cōḻa kings have come down to us.[42] Rulers of later dynasties in south India repeat this. Another way was naming temples after the ruler who had them endowed. In most cases, the deity himself was known by a name or a title of the ruler, the most striking example being that of the Great Temple of Tanjavur. Especially noteworthy is the way in which 'Uḍaiyār Śrī Rājarājadēvar' boasted of the temple he built for 'Śrī Rājarājēśvaram Uḍaiyār'.[43] Closely related to this aspect is that of building what is described as sepulchral temples or *paḷḷippaḍai*s. This has been shown as allied with the cult of Dēva-rāja in Southeast Asia.[44] Temples were constructed over the mortal remains of kings, princes, and princesses. This practice obtained among the Cōḻas in south India. The Ādityēśvara temple at Toṇḍamānāḍ was a *paḷḷippaḍai* erected by Parāntaka I over the remains of his father; the Ariñjigai-īśvara at Mēlpāḍi commemorated Ariñjaya who died at Āṟṟūr; the Pañcavanmahādēvīśvara at Rāmanāthankōil, etc. are among the most conspicuous examples of such sepulchral temples.[45] It is reported that human bones were discovered from underneath the *sanctum sanctora* of several temples when their renovation was undertaken.[46] However, this practice appears to have lost its popularity shortly afterwards and was, in fact, looked upon with great disapproval as the attempt to erase the word *paḷḷippaḍai* in the inscription at Rāmanāthankōil shows.[47]

The above instances show how an attempt was made to equate the king with a deity or at least with a Purāṇic hero. As stated above, it was not a new invention in this part of the country and followed only the models obtaining in an earlier period in northern India. This finds standardization in the textbooks of social conduct and statecraft, too. Incidentally, this north Indian source of inspiration for this particular aspect, as also some others, of the image of royalty projected in the royalist expressions points also to the agency through which that inspiration may have reached this part of the country.

What was the function of this attempt, expressed in various ways, to attribute divinity to the king in the particular context of south India? It does not require any major argument to show that it was one of the means to seek legitimation for the ruler by making use of certain symbols of a religious system, which had already gained early acceptance among the people. The historical context in which this attempt was made in south India is very significant and is worth recapitulating even at the risk of repetition. We have seen that the beginning of our period was characterized by, among other things, (a) a total reorientation of society on caste lines accepting the paradigm of *varṇāśramadharma* as the organizing principle and with the Āgamaic-Purāṇic-bhakti religion as the expression of its religious ideology and (b) the formation of a new kind of monarchical state. Both were somewhat revolutionary in character. As the religious ideology had gained acceptance among at least those sections of society with which the ruling classes had to come to terms, the idiom of its symbols suited them to validate their position. In other words, religious idioms provided the necessary legitimacy for the newly emerging power structure and the monarch within it.

There is another way in which the historian can look at the use of religion in the service of politics: this can be done by seeing the temple in its political aspect. We can consider two kinds of temples, viz. what have been described as the 'royal' temples and the temples that grew up as centres of agrarian corporations and Brāhmaṇa settlements, the latter with claims to a richer religious tradition behind them.[48] They too had, to be sure, considerable patronage from royalty in most case;

but their *raison d'être* lay outside state patronage. The former, on the other hand, were not only patronized by royalty but also meant by their builders to be a *statement* of state power. A good case in point will be the Bṛhadīśvara temple at Tanjavur.

It is important that Tanjavur was not one of the centres celebrated by the Bhakti saints of the Śaivites; nor is there any tradition, even in the *Sthalapurāṇa*, linking that place or the temple there with one of the Nāyanārs. It was the nucleus of a collection of agrarian villages at a relatively high ground on the Kāvēri, where the river begins to fan out into its system of distributaries. What we hear about the place for the first time is that it was under the control of the Muttaraiyar chief, from whom Vijayālaya Cōḻa is said to have captured it.[49] We are told, in a mood of historicizing the Cōḻa control of the place, that he built a temple for Goddess Niṣumbhasūdinī there.[50] The capture of Tanjavur, in any case, brought a vast resource base, the Kāvēri Delta, under the control of the Cōḻas. By making that place the base of his operations and the ceremonial centre of the state, Rājarāja was not only able to control the resources very strategically but also made the statement of his power loud and clear, audible to all the important magnates of the territory he was controlling. The project was undertaken relatively late in his life, probably after all his military expeditions were complete.[51] He was by then heading a powerful and somewhat centralized state most authoritatively, and the statement he made about that state was very bold and unequivocal. The temple was far from a 'system-maintaining mechanism of a weakly organized polity', which is the way George W. Spencer understands it.[52]

This statement had two aspects about it: what is directly conveyed and what is symbolic or metaphorical. The number of royal inscriptions present on the walls of the temple, which is the 'literal' aspect of the statement, is too well known to bear one more repetition.[53] The range of activities in the temple, the amount of wealth and other resources that were mobilized in favour of the temple, and such other details which bring out the importance of the institution require no repetition either. The stupendous nature of the structure, too, has been adequately written about. The *vimāna* itself was a metaphor for the structure of the state presided over by Rājarāja—a pyramidal structure with a heavy top. Its conception as Dakṣiṇamēru (the southern Mēru, Mēru being the mythological axis or the earth), surrounded by shrines of the guardian deities of the four cardinal directions and the four corners, is the first step in identifying the temple with the cosmos itself.[54] The chief deity is Dakṣiṇamēru-viṭaṅkar, also called Śrī Rājarājēśvaram-uḍaiyār. We have seen above how, by a sleight of words, as it were, *Śrī Rājarājēśvaram-uḍaiyār*, the deity, is equated with *Uḍaiyār Śrī Rājarāja-dēvar.*[55] Thus the temple-cosmos identification goes to the level of the identification of the temple as the territory and the god as king, where what he presides over is the entire cosmos.[56] The sacred and the secular blend so perfectly here. This is also seen in the architectural plan and the sculptural and other artistic details.

The most frequently occurring theme in the sculpture of the temple is that of the Tripurāntaka. This theme makes its appearance in the sculpture of Cōḻa temples for the first time in the age of Rājarāja and in the environs of Tanjavur. There are about thirty representations of this theme in the temple.[57] Scholars have interpreted this in various ways. There is a fresco in Chamber 11, which recaptures the details of the mythological story in all its magnificence. It tells us how Śiva destroyed the *puras* of the three demons and reduced them to a state of servitude. Brahmā was Śiva's charioteer in this battle and the four Vedas were the wheels of his chariot. Agni was his arrow and Mount Mandara, his bow. Nearly all gods played a supportive and subordinate role in the battle. Even Viṣṇu is presented in such a role when he, in the guise of Māyāmōha, is represented as attempting to delude the demons. Śiva destroyed the three *puras* ('towns') in the battle and took the demons as his servants, two of them as his *dvārapālas* ('doorkeepers') and the third, his drummer.[58] R. Champakalakshmi has argued that 'By using this myth and the iconographic form in the temple's art in a dominant position and in the narrative paintings, Rājarāja achieved his aim of consolidating Śaivism and subordinating other faiths.'[59] While we do not deny that the consolidation of Śaivism and subordination of other faiths may well have been among the agenda of Rājarāja, the political message there should not be lost sight of. She does take the massiveness of the *dvārapāla* images to show the power of the king; but not in the context of discussing the Tripurāntaka theme.[60] K.R. Srinivasan had earlier appreciated the political message by saying that Tripurāntaka was Rājarāja's favourite choice as the Śaiva counterpart of the Cakravartin ideal.[61] C. Sivaramamurthi had, as early as 1955, used this to emphasize the warrior aspect of Tripurāntaka and the Cōḻa Rājarāja's choice of this form as indicating his prowess as a warrior.[62] Gary J. Schwindler argues that Tripurantaka was Rājarāja's favourite personal deity, *iṣṭadēvatā*, and that he used its unique iconographic symbology to restore the honour and dignity of his lineage, damaged at Takkōḷam. For him, it is evidence of the king's conscious assimilation of the divine and royal roles.[63]

Does the political significance of this theme, repeated over and over again, go beyond what has been suggested by these interpretations? Does it allude to the way in which Rājarāja reorganized the Cōḻa polity by rolling the juggernaut of the state over the locality chiefs (described as 'feudatories' by historians) and attempting to centralize the administration of the empire? It is important to remember that these chiefs had exercised considerable power in their territories in the pre-Rājarāja period. We do not hear about them any more in the age of Rājarāja and immediately thereafter. They were wiped off as political chiefs by Rājarāja and what we notice is that they function under him as the functionaries of the state (the 'bureaucracy' of conventional historiography), that too in areas far removed from the home territories of these chiefs.[64] Here Rājarāja is himself Tripurāntaka, rendering the 'demons' homeless but taking them into his personal service. By stressing on the power of those whom he subjugated, as witness the massiveness of the *dvārapāla*s in the temple, what is really shown is the still greater power of the monarch who subjugated and drafted them into his system, an effective commentary on his own power. Thus Tripurāntaka forms an icon of Rājarāja's imperial power and position in every way. It may not be irrelevant that in the same chamber where the Tripurāntaka fresco figures is a fresco depicting Śiva as Rāvaṇānugrahamūrtti.

Caṇḍēśvara, described as the *mūlabhṛtya* (lit., 'basic servant') of Śiva, is consecrated in a big way in this temple and in a bigger way in the Gaṅgaikkoṇḍacōḻapuram temple. This is not without its significance. The *mūlabhṛtya*s are of great importance in the military-political structure of early medieval south India. It is shown that the *mūlabhṛtya*s, the 'Companions of Honour' of the kings, constituted the core of the military establishment there.[65] Their role in the Pāṇḍya, Cēra and Cōḻa states is adequately appreciated.[66] In the case of the Cōḻa state, where Rājarāja and his immediate successors had taken the military strength of the empire to its logical perfection, it is only appropriate that the *mūlabhṛtya* should have been given the kind of importance in the ritual and iconographic schemes of the great royal temples. Taken along with the message and implications of the Tripurāntaka icon, this acquires great significance. Thus, Champakalakshmi is right in her observation that 'the iconographic programme of Tanjavur was indeed the political iconography of Rājarāja....'[67]

There are many other aspects in relation to the institution of the temple, which lent itself to a political use, if in a different way. Some of them are seen more clearly in the temples in the countryside. They had more or less a spontaneous development, beginning as somewhat humble shrines. As pointed out earlier, they formed the nucleus round which Brāhmaṇa settlements came up. The temples came to be managed by corporations of those who formed these settlements or their more notable representatives. These corporations were synonymous with the managerial bodies of the agrarian settlements around them, controlling landed wealth on behalf of both the temple and themselves. The temples and the corporations that managed them came to possess command over enormous land. This meant controlling major chunks of population. In a period when vast sections of tribal population were getting transformed as peasants and drawn into caste society, this position of the temple was crucial.

This position which the temple enjoyed made it possible for it also to wield enormous political power in the locality in which it functioned. This is visible in the clearest fashion in the Cēra kingdom in Kerala, were monarchical state was perhaps the weakest in south India. The local groups enjoyed vast powers in the political structure obtaining there. The only important local group, apart from the *nagaram* (trading corporation) in a couple of records, was the Brāhmaṇical corporation of noncultivating intermediaries organized around the temple. These bodies came to enjoy immense powers in the matter of fiscal, judicial and political administration, that is, in functions that are thought to be of the state. Its beginning can be noticed in the period of the Cēra kingdom. A lengthy copper plate record, or more correctly an incomplete collection of records in copper plates, known as the Tiruvalla Copper Plates or the Huzur Office Plates, documents the process of this development elaborately.[68] I have made a somewhat detailed study of the development of the Tiruvalla settlement on an earlier occasion, bringing out the growth of a temple-centred Brāhmaṇa settlement in space and range of activities.[69] However, a few more details may be relevant here.

There are many statements in the Tiruvalla Copper Plates which show that the temple was assigned, or else arrogated to it, many functions which are usually regarded as of the state. References to the temple collecting the revenue, which would have been normally due to the various nodes of state power, are many in the records. A very significant case is that of the grant of a village by Iravi Cirikaṇṭan, the chief of Veṇpolināṭu. Kuṭavūr, the granted 'village', is described as *of* the donor (*tannuṭaiya*), and when it was granted to the temple of Tiruvalla, 'all the eighteen taxes and the market [duties]' were also given away. The representative of the manager of the temple committee was authorized to collect 360 *paṟai*s of paddy, this being the equivalent of eighteen *kaḻañju* (unit of weight, used in place of a coin) of gold, the *rakṣābhoga* (land tax) of that village, from the chief himself. In the event of a failure to make timely payment of such dues, the chief was required to pay the original due in gold even if the fault was not his. At the end of the details of the provisions is a very interesting prescription: the temple committee shall take the *rakṣābhoga*, protecting [the settlement] from the wrath of the king and the *sāmanta* (feudatory). Those members of the *sabhā*, who are opposed to this arrangement, shall forfeit their rights including their membership of the *sabhā*.[70] That the same statement, apparently in relation to the same endowment, is repeated elsewhere in the same document[71] may be a scribal error. If it is not, it is an extremely important repetition, bringing out the importance of this endowment and the conditions attached to it.

What does this assignment signify? It is now well known that fiscal assignments were typical of the land grants in what is called 'Indian feudalism'. The temple committee is assigned all taxes from the village and placed in a position where it can redress the grievances caused by even the king and the *sāmanta*s. For those who were concerned, here was the temple committee presenting itself as the very state. This is not a solitary case where the temple and its managerial body arrogated the functions of the state, so far as revenue and judicial administration was concerned. Speaking about a particular expense, the record says elsewhere that it was to be met from the 'tax' (*vari*) due to Ōṭanāṭu.[72] There are several other cases where such assignment of 'taxes' from the *nāṭu* units and the lesser ones such as *ūr* and *vāḻkkai* is seen in the record.[73]

As in the case of revenue administration, so in judicial administration as well, we see the temple exercising state power. There is a very interesting case where it is stated that, in the event of any member of the managerial committee standing in the way of performing a particular service for which an endowment is made, he would be deemed to have killed his father and married his mother.[74] Even those who took his side would be treated in the same way. They would lose their caste and the committee was allowed to add their land and the sites of their houses to the properties of the God of Tiruvalla. Elsewhere, Māḷuvakkōn, the chief of Kīḻmalaināṭu, assigns some land to the temple. The trustees of the temple were authorized to attach the property of the village (in which the grant was made) in the event of default of the prompt payment of dues. It is absolutely important that this agreement, where the chief has to look on helplessly as the temple attaches his property, is attested by the Six Hundred, the chief's 'companions of honour' together with his other representatives.[75] The temple not only looks after judicial administration, but it does it over the head of the actual political authority, that is, the local chief. In another case, it is stated that those who were required to supply the stipulated amount of oil to the temple should pay, in the event of their failure to do it, a fine of 50 *kaḻañju* of gold to the *Perumāḷ* or the king, 25 to the *sabhā* of the temple and 10 to the local chief.[76] This, incidentally, gives an idea of the relative position of the various nodes of power in the hierarchy. The temple was clearly above the local chiefs and it represented the state in its visible form. This is not to be confused with some kind of theocracy or with what are called 'temple states'; it was a case of the temple wielding the power of the state. This is apart from the obvious fact that the temple was co-opted as an agent of the state for purposes of the administration in the Cēra kingdom.[77]

What I have tried to argue is that the temple played a role in medieval south India going far beyond a mere 'religious institution'. It had functions of a social, economic, political and cultural nature and they were interrelated in a most complex way. It is only when one is able to appreciate it in its entirety that one will be able to grasp the complexity and also to see how there was a rush to patronize the temple, which has to be understood as prompted by more than piety. And, naturally, the patronage was more than reciprocated.

NOTES AND REFERENCES

1. The validity of treating this period as a single entity on the basis of an imagined unity of what has been called the 'Sangam literature', believed

to constitute a single corpus, is now questioned. Poems traditionally included in that corpus are demonstrated to have been composed during a wide span of about a millennium starting from at least the beginning of the third century BC. Nor do those poems represent a single form of society, there being evidence of different levels of social and economic development. As such, to try and seek a uniform 'religion' there is not likely to yield encouraging results.

2. For a discussion, K.A. Nilakanta Sastri, *The Sangam Age: Its Cults and Cultures* (Madras, 1972).
3. M.G.S. Narayanan, 'The Vedic-Sastraic-Puranic Elements in the Sangam Literature', *Proceedings of the Indian History Congress* (hereafter *PIHC*) (Aligarh, 1975).
4. Kesavan Veluthat, 'Into the Medieval—and Out of It: Early South India in Transition', Presidential Address, *PIHC*, Section II, Medieval Indian History (Bangalore, 1997). Chapter 1 above. See also R. Champakalakshmi, 'Introduction', *Studies in History*, vol. IV, no. 2, 1982.
5. M.G.S. Narayanan and Kesavan Veluthat, 'The Temple in South India', paper read at the Symposium on the Socio-economic Role of Religious Institutions in India in the Indian History Congress, Magadh University (Bodhgaya, 1981).
6. M.G.S. Narayanan and Kesavan Veluthat, 'The Bhakti Movement in South India', in S.C. Malik, ed., *Indian Movements: Some Aspects of Dissent and Protest* (Simla, 1978), pp. 33–66.
7. Kesavan Veluthat, 'The Temple-base of the Bhakti Movement in South India', *PIHC* (Waltair, 1979).
8. *Periyapurāṇam*, 'Tirunāvukkaraśar Purāṇam'.
9. Ibid., Kulacciṟaiyar Purāṇam; Niṉṟaśīr Neḍumāṟar Purāṇam; Maṅgaiyārkkaraśiyār Purāṇam.
10. R. Champakalakshmi, 'Religious Conflict in the Tamil Country: A Reappraisal of Epigraphic Evidence', paper presented at the 4th session of the Epigraphical Society of India (Madras, 1978).
11. For the identity of Cēramān Perumāḷ Nāyanār, M.G.S. Narayanan, 'Political and Social Conditions of Kerala under the Kulasekhara Empire', unpublished PhD Thesis, University of Kerala (Trivandrum, 1972), chapters on 'Chronology', 'Religion and Religious Systems'. So also, Kulaśēkhara Āḻvār is identified as Ceramān Perumāḷ's immediate successor: Ibid.
12. Narayanan and Veluthat, 'The Bhakti Movement', pp. 51–2.
13. Ibid., p. 51.
14. 'Tiruttoṇḍar Purāṇam', in K. Subramaniam, ed., *Periya Purāṇam* (Srivaikuntam, 1974), p. 58, line 1
15. Above, n. 11.
16. Kesavan Veluthat, *The Political Structure of Early Medieval South India* (Delhi, 1993).
17. Ibid., chapter 2, 'The Self-Image of Royalty'.

18. Ibid.; Kesavan Veluthat, 'Royalty and Divinity: Legitimisation of Monarchical Power in South India', *PIHC* (Hyderabad, 1978).
19. R.S. Sharma, *Aspects of Political Ideas and Institutions in Ancient India*, 3rd edn (Delhi, 1999), pp. 301 and 312.
20. Veluthat, *Political Structure*, Veluthat, 'The Self-Image of Royalty'.
21. Ibid.
22. Ibid.
23. Ibid.
24. K.A. Nilakanta Sastri, *The Cōḷas*, 2nd edn (Madras, 1955), p. 7.
25. George W. Spencer, 'Heirs Apparent: Fiction and Function in Chola Mythical Genealogies', *Indian Economic and Social History Review*, vol. XXI, no. 4, 1984.
26. T.N. Subrahmanyan, ed., *Thirty Pallava Copper Plates* (Madras, 1966).
27. P.K. Narayana Pillai, ed., *Laghubhāskarīya* (Trivandrum, 1969), verse1.
28. *Travancore Archaeological Series* (hereafter *TAS*), vol. I, no. 16.
29. Udayēndiram Plates, *Thirty Pallava,* p. 126, l.27.
30. *Cf.* T.A. Gopinatha Rao, *History of Srivaishnavas* (Madras, 1923), p. 22. To be sure, A.S. Ramanatha Aiyar doubts this interpretation. *TAS*, vol. V, p. 108.
31. Tiruvālaṅgāḍu Plates, *South Indian Inscriptions* (hereafter *SII*), vol. III, pt 3, pp. 382–439.
32. Vēḷvikuḍi Plates, *Pāṇḍyar Ceppēḍukaḷ Pattu*, p. 21, ll.21–3.
33. Ibid., l.25.
34. Srivaramangalam Plates, *Pāṇḍyar Ceppēḍukaḷ Pattu*, p. 57, ll.16–19.
35. Larger Sinnamanur Plates, *Pāṇḍyar Ceppēḍukaḷ Pattu*, p. 149, ll.28–9.
36. For the titles of Mahendravarman, Michael Lockwood, 'The Birudas of Mahendravarman', Third Annual Session of the Epigraphical Society of India, Udupi, 1977.
37. M.G.S. Narayanan, 'Index to Cera Inscriptions', a companion volume to his 'Political and Social Conditions of Kerala under the Kulasekhara Empire c. AD 800–1124', unpublished PhD Thesis, University of Kerala, 1972, no. A.1. The dissertation is now available in book form. *The Perumals of Kerala: Political and Social Conditions of Kerala under the Cera Perumals of Makotai (c. AD 800–1124)*, (Calicut, 1996). Unfortunately, this very useful reference material which formed part of the original dissertation is left out in the book.
38. *TAS*, vol. III, no. I, p. 142, l.289.
39. K.A. Nilakanta Sastri, *The Pandyan Kingdom* (London, 1929).
40. J.G. de Casparis, 'Inscriptions and South Asian Dynastic Traditions', in R.J. Moore (ed.), *Tradition and Politics in South Asia* (New Delhi, 1979).
41. Sastri, *The Cōḷas*, p. 170.
42. Ibid., p. 453.
43. R. Nagaswami, ed., *Tañjaipperuvuḍaiyār Kōil Kalveṭṭugaḷ* (Madras, 1972). I am indebted to Y. Subbarayalu for drawing my attention to this important statement.

44. Sastri, *The Cōḷas*, pp. 452–3; K.A.N. Sastri, *South India and Southeast Asia* (Mysore, 1972), pp. 149–71; I.W. Mabbett, 'Devaraja', *Journal of South Eastern History*, vol. X, no. 2, September 1969, pp. 200–23.
45. Sastri, *The Cōḷas*, p. 453.
46. Ibid., also n. 24 above.
47. Annual Reports of (South Indian) Epigraphy, 1927, vol. II, p. 13, quoted in Sastri, *The Cōḷas*, p. 453, n. 25.
48. The religious heritage of such temples is clear from the example of the temples known as the Tiruppatis, sacred to the Vaiṣṇavas. Of the Malaināṭṭut-Tiruppatis or those in Kerala, most were also centres of the early Brāhmaṇa settlements. For details, Kesavan Veluthat, *Brahman Settlements in Kerala: Historical Studies* (Calicut, 1978), chapter on 'Original Settlements'. This heritage was not available to the 'royal temples', whether Śaiva or Vaiṣṇava.
49. Sastri, *The Cōḷas* (Madras, 1955, 1975), pp. 110–12.
50. E.g., The Tiruvālaṅgāḍu Plates of Rajendra I. *SII*, vol. III, no. 205.
51. It is important to note that most inscriptions on the walls of the temple are of Rajaraja, that too of his 29th year (AD 1014), which also happens to be his last known year. *SII*, vol. II. Was he a proverbial 'old man in a hurry?'
52. George W. Spencer, 'Religious Networks and Royal Influence in Eleventh Century South India', *Journal of the Economic and Social History of the Orient*, 1969, vol. XII, no. 1.
53. The corpus of inscriptions from the Big Temple of Tanjavur, the bulk of which are of Rajaraja, is remarkable. *SII*, vol. II.
54. For the cosmic symbolism of the temple, R. Champakalakshmi, *Trade, Ideology and Urbanization: South India 300 BC to AD 1300* (Delhi, 1996), pp. 426–7. Architectural and sculptural details are available in S.R. Balasubrahmanyam, *Middle Cola Temples* (Faridabad, 1975), chapter 2, and K.R. Srinivasan, 'The Peruvudaiyar (Brihadisvara) Temple of Tanjavur: A Study', in *Indian Archaeological Heritage*, Shri K.V. Soundararajan Festschrift (Delhi, 1991), vol. II.
55. See n. 43 above.
56. Champakalakshmi, *Trade, Ideology and Urbanization.*
57. Gary J. Schwindler, 'Speculations on the Theme of Siva as Tripurantaka as it Appears in the Reign of Rajaraja I in the Tanjavur Area, *c.* AD 1000', *Ars Orientalis*, 1987 (pub. 1989), vol. XVII, pp. 163–78. For a treatment of the Tripurāntaka episode in the Big temple of Tanjavur, D. Dayalan, 'Hymns of the Nayanmars and the Tripurantaka Episode in Big Temple, Tanjavur', in *Indian Archaeological Heritage*, vol. I, pp. 445–8.
58. Champakalakshmi, *Trade Ideology, and Urbanization*, p. 431.
59. She looks at the size and volume of the *dvārapāla* figures as 'metaphor in stone for power'. Ibid., p. 428.
60. Ibid.
61. Quoted in Ibid.

62. C. Sivaramamurti, *Royal Conquests and Cultural Migration in South India* (Calcutta, 1955), p. 29.
63. Schwindler, 'Speculations',
64. Veluthat, *Political Structure*, chapter on 'The Role of the Chiefs', esp. pp. 121–4. It may be noted that the *dvārapālas* of Śiva, as worshipped in temples, are Śūlapāṇi ('the wielder of the lance') and Paraśupāṇi ('the wielder of the axe'), both indicating military power.
65. M.G.S. Narayanan, 'The Companions of Honour', in *Reinterpretations of South Indian History* (Trivandrum, 1977).
66. Veluthat, *Political Structure*, pp. 151–7.
67. Champakalakshmi, *Trade*, p. 432.
68. *TAS*, vol. II, no. III, pp. 131–207.
69. Veluthat, *Brahman Settlements*, pp. 39–51.
70. *TAS*, vol. II, no. III, ll.329–45.
71. Ibid., ll.469–79.
72. Ibid., ll.170–1.
73. For the administrative units under the Cēra kingdom of Mahodayapuram, Narayanan, *Perumals of Kerala*, chapters on 'Divisions of the Kingdom' and 'Police and Revenue'.
74. These are not to be taken as mere imprecations with appeal of a moral and ethical variety. For the real implications of the invocation of the *mahāpātakas* in the early medieval south Indian context, M.G.S. Narayanan, 'Socio-economic Implications of the Concept of Mahapatakas in the Feudal Society of South India', *PIHC* (Calicut, 1976).
75. *TAS*, vol. II, no. III, ll. 354–60.
76. Ibid., ll. 370–80.
77. For the temple and its managerial committee functioning as the agents of the state, Narayanan, *Perumals of Kerala*, chapters on 'Police and Revenue' and 'Local Bodies'; Veluthat, *Brahman Settlements*, pp. 52–67.

3

Land Rights and Social Stratification*

Historians in the past have generally tended to view society in early medieval south India as generally smooth and free from any contradictions. In fact, K.A. Nilakanta Sastri would go as far as to glorify the 'political spirit of the time ... [which] aimed at securing the harmony of classes, rather than their equality'[1], and the 'healthy society ... which was free from the glaring economic oppression of one class by another'.[2] He seldom recognized the contradiction between these statements on the one side and the rich empirical data he has marshalled in his own writings about the class distinctions and contradictions on the other. The situation is not any better in the case of later studies by Appadorai, Minakshi and Mahalingam.[3] In Appadorai's work, which is on the economic conditions of southern India in the first half of the second millennium AD, one would naturally expect a picture of class differentiation and contradiction, but in vain.

Recent American scholarship, which starts with the avowed purpose of offering a corrective to the kind of historiography represented by Nilakanta Sastri, hardly makes the position different. For instance, Burton Stein in his major work on peasant state and society in medieval south India characterizes society in the Pallava and the succeeding Cōḻa ages as organized into a large number of peasant localities and cultures.[4] Naturally, one would look for a picture of the structured relationship within such a highly developed peasant society, especially as this work is the extension and fulfilment of a scathing attack on the historiography represented by Nilakanta Sastri and his disciples, which appeared as a 'prolegemenon' a few years

* First published as 'The Structure of Land Rights and Social Stratification in Early Medieval South India', in Vijay Kumar Thakur and Ashok Anshouman, eds, *Peasants in Indian History* (Patna, 1996), pp. 312–30.

earlier.[5] But the whole work is professedly about 'peasants without lords'.[6] Perhaps Stein is right in characterizing his own work as 'somewhat perverse in theoretical and historiographical senses!'[7] Actually, Stein is unabashedly indifferent to the rich data on the differentiation within the peasantry in making the assumption of a world of peasants without lords. He seems to push under the carpet the subject nature of a major chunk of peasantry while describing the relationship between the Brāhmaṇas and the peasants as an alliance. True, it was one of co-operation if we take the Gandhian idea that in every situation of oppression there has to be the co-operation of the oppressed! The conception of an undifferentiated monolithic peasantry obviously springs from perverse theoretical position and a total indifference to data. However, there is a happy development in recent years represented by the works of a few Asian scholars, Noboru Karashima, M.G.S. Narayanan, Y. Subbarayalu, D.N. Jha, R. Champakalakshmi and Rajan Gurukkal among them.[8] This is not to say that every one of them shares the same frame of reference and the same set of assumptions; on the contrary, their theoretical positions and tools of analysis vary considerably. Every one of them is conversant with the primary sources and has also his/her own philosophy of history, which makes it a happy feature for south Indian historiography.

The copper plate records of the Pallavas and the Pāṇḍyas in the seventh and eighth centuries AD provide information on the various shades of rights on land and concomitantly the position of different sections in society depending upon the nature of right that one enjoyed on a particular piece of land. Most of the Pallava copper plates record the grant of land to Brāhmaṇas. Inevitably they are related to the creation and transfer of certain superior rights over land. This is expressed in the case of a few Pallava records by the expression *kuṭi nīkki*,[9] which means, literally, removing the earlier occupants. The same idea is conveyed by another expression *mun-peṟṟārai māṟṟi*[10] found in a couple of other Pallava records. Both these signify that the recipients of the land were at liberty to evict the earlier occupants of the land and settle it with new occupants of their own choice. R. Tirumalai has argued that these expressions need not signify the eviction of the earlier occupants in a physical sense.[11] On the other hand, he suggests that it may indicate the extinction of the existing rights of the occupants over the land which was granted. L.B. Alayev, on the other hand, seeks to explain the expression *kuṭi nīkki* as 'except *kuṭi*', that is, when a piece of land was alienated the *kuṭis* would not form part of it.[12] It is significant that apart from the handful of records speaking of land with earlier occupants—whether they were physically removed or their earlier rights were extinguished or they were not touched at all is another question—the vast majority of Pallava charters do not speak about the fate of the earlier settlers. This would suggest that what was granted to Brāhmaṇas was relatively unsettled land where all the rights were given to the donees.

The land grants of the Pallavas, therefore, indicate the beginnings of a structured relationship in the matter of land rights. In many cases there is no mention at all of the earlier occupants on the land indicating thereby that the donees were granted unsettled land. Here it is clear that what was granted was to be enjoyed by the donees, with the right to get the land cultivated with the help of tenants if they would. In the other records, which do speak of the pre-existing occupants, it is by making it possible for the donees to get it cultivated by the earlier occupants, in whatever way the expression *kuṭi nīkki* is interpreted. Even here the situation is as if there was the state at the top enjoying an overall suzerainty and final right over the land and the occupant-tenant at the bottom who cultivated the land with one stratum of intermediary, that is, the donees of the grant, in between. On them were conferred not only the right to get the land cultivated and its rights enjoyed but also other fiscal and administrative rights such as the collection of numerous imposts and the maintenance of law and order.[13]

As we come to a slightly later situation obtaining in the Pāṇḍyan kingdom, we have a clearer picture of a more evolved system of land rights, thanks to the excellent study of the agrarian system and socio-political organization under the early Pāṇḍyas undertaken by Rajan Gurukkal.[14] Most land grants of the Pāṇḍyas are concerned with the creation or maintenance of *brahmadēya*, *dēvadāna* or *paḷḷiccantam*. They speak of the conferment of two kinds of rights: the *mīyāṭci* and the *kārāṇmai*. These two expressions indicate, respectively, the superior possessive right and the right to cultivate. The phrase in the Pāṇḍyan records, *kārāṇmai mīyātci uḷḷadaṅga* in the Tamil portions and *kārāṇmai mīyāṭciyutam* in the Sanskrit portions, indicating the right to cultivate the land and/or get it cultivated, is an exact translation of the expression *karṣayataḥ karṣāpayataśca* occurring in the same context in inscriptions from the northern India.[15] Below these two shades of rights there appears to have been a third one, namely, that of occupancy (*kuṭimai*). In a stone inscription from Ambasamudram it is clearly stated that the *mīyāṭci* alone was transferred while the *kārāṇmai* was retained by the earlier tenants of the land.[16] It is explicitly stated in the record that the land in question was to be a *mutal kuṭi nīṅṅā dēvadānam*, a *dēvadānam* where the earlier occupants were not be disturbed. This would show that *kuṭimai*, or occupancy right, differed from *kārāṇmai*. There are expressions such as *āḷaḍaṅga* (literally 'including the men') found in the grants indicating the transfer of agrestic labourers also along with the land. This is a clear evidence of labour tied to soil, in the same way as we have in the Sanskrit charters from northern India expressed by the phrase *dhanajanasahitā*.[17] In the Pāṇḍyan records, therefore, one can see the further evolution of land rights into the next stage. In certain records from the Pāṇḍyan kingdom the expressions *mērpāti* and *kīḻpāti*, literally the 'upper share' and the 'lower share', are used in the place of *mīyāṭci* and *kārāṇmai* respectively.[18] This, incidentally, would dispel the misunderstanding created by Stein with regard to the expressions *mēlvāram* and *kīḻvāram* in the Cōḻa records.[19] This discussion of the land rights in the Pāṇḍyan records helps in the reconstruction of the structured relationship with various shades of tenurial rights. With the help of a diagram, Rajan Gurukkal has demonstrated this hierarchy with the *kuṭi*s (occupants) on the bottom of the scale and the king at the top and a graded hierarchy of intermediaries placed between the two. This class of intermediaries consisted of, according to Gurukkal, the chiefs, the *nāḍu*s, the *ūr*s and the *dēvadāna*s or the *brahmadēya*s as the case may be who had the *mīyāṭci* rights, and the *kārāḷar*s (the cultivating tenants) in that descending order.[20]

The situation in the Cēra kingdom was comparable. M.G.S. Narayanan's research into various aspects of the history of Kerala in this period has brought out a detailed picture of the structured relations in land obtaining in the early medieval Cēra kingdom.[21] In a study of the traditional land system in Kerala undertaken by Narayanan and the present writer, the following representation is given with the help of a diagram.[22] The Perumāḷ or the king was at the top. He had his own land known as *cērikkal* (something of a demesne) in which there were the *kārāḷar* or tenants and the *kuṭiyāḷar* or the occupants. Below the *kārāḷar* were the labourers attached to land known as the *aṭiyāḷar*. A portion of the *cērikkal* land may have been granted as *virutti* or service tenure to religious and secular functionaries but the pattern of *kārāḷar-kuṭiyāḷar-aṭiyāḷar* hierarchy remained the same in such cases also. In other areas where the local chieftains obtained, even they had the *cērikkal* land and had granted *virutti* tenures carrying with it the same pattern of subject peasantry. In certain cases between the *kārāḷar-kuṭiyāḷar-aṭiyāḷar* peasantry on the one side and the local chief or the king himself on the other, there was another tier, viz. the significant group of intermediaries in the Brāhmaṇa settlements owing right over land as either *brahmasvam* (Brāhmaṇa's property) and *dēvasvam* (god's property) and marginally the trading groups in the *nagarams*. Thus we get the picture of a stratified peasantry which was itself subjected to several shades of superior rights. Although the number of records available in the case of the Cēra kingdom is too limited to make any precise generalization, the picture of land relations obtaining there presents a slightly more complex and presumably more evolved structure than what we found in the Pallava and Pāṇḍya situations. However, there is a major difference in Kerala as we do not come across the strong non-Brāhmaṇa peasant proprietors who characterize the agrarian structure of the rest of south India.

Coming to the situation in the Cōḻa country, we are in a much better position on account of the vast amount of evidence and the varied literature on the subject. Long before Nilakanta Sastri had published his studies on the Cōḻa history, K.M. Gupta had completed his work on the land system in south India between 800 and 1200 AD.[23] Starting from Gupta till the most recent publication of R. Tirumalai on land grants and agrarian relations/reactions in Cōḻa and Pāṇḍya times, a vast body of literature has grown around this topic. Among them the most significant ones either for the new light they shed or for the refreshing questions they raise are those by D.N. Jha,[24] Y. Subbarayalu,[25] N. Karashima,[26] Dharma Kumar,[27] and R. Tirumalai.[28]

The systematic analysis of epigraphic material undertaken by Noboru Karashima presents a pattern of the evolution of tenurial rights on land. In the studies of earlier historians and those who followed their frame of reference it is the land relations in the *brahmadēya* type of villages that had received greater attention. Karashima takes up the question in relation to the non-*brahmadēya* villages also.[29] This is important in two respects. For one thing, since the non-*brahmadēya* villages were more ancient than the *brahmadēya* villages, they have a greater significance in a study of the historical development of tenurial rights over land. Second, as we have seen, since the non-*brahmadēya* villages far out-numbered the *brahmadēyas*, the basic determinant of the social relations will have to be looked for in the relations of production in such villages. In a comparative study of the nature of landed property in a non-*brahmadēya* village and a *brahmadēya* with the help of nine inscriptions from the former and twenty-one from the latter, Karashima argues that private property was not as well developed as it was in the *brahmadēya* villages.[30] Land was held in common by the community in the non-*brahmadēya* villages. In the case of the *brahmadēya* villages there was individual landholding and the land-holders and the cultivators were separate entities there. This would suggest that in the beginning of the Cōḻa rule individual holdings of land by non-Brāhmaṇa peasant proprietors were not fully developed. This is supported by further studies made by Karashima and Subbarayalu.[31] In a quantified analysis of details available in the 260 Cōḻa inscriptions registering the sale of land, Subbarayalu has brought out the increasing proportion non-Brāhmaṇa individuals selling land in the four periods of Cōḻa rule in a 1.5 : 4.2 : 7.7 : 37 ratio in percentage. This would show that, in the earlier periods of Cōḻa rule, individual landholding was not common in the non-Brāhmaṇa villages while it became increasingly prevalent in the later years of Cōḻa rule.

In fact, this strong section of non-Brāhmaṇa landed magnates is represented in the Cōḻa records. With the help of the now classic *Concordance of the Names in Cola Inscriptions*, it has been shown that about 20 per cent of the entire population figuring in Cōḻa records bear a name or title signifying the possession of a village, for example, *uḍaiyān, kiḻān, kiḻavan*. This, obviously, means 'possession' of some land in the village. It has been shown that the frequency of such titles goes on increasing as Cōḻa rule progresses, a pattern which conforms to the findings of Subbarayalu in relation to increase in the private ownership of land. This is true of similar titles such as *vēḷān, mūvēnta-veḷān, araiyan*, and the like, all sported by landed magnates in the Cōḻa country. It has been shown that these landed magnates were identified by the Cōḻa state and co-opted as its agents.[32]

The fact of individual non-Brāhmaṇa landowners being on an increase in the later periods of the Cōḻa rule is further supported by Karashima's examination of a large number of inscriptions recording the sale or donation of land to the Jambukēśvaram temple in Tiruchirappalli.[33] This has yielded significant information about the growth of huge landed magnates owning in certain cases whole villages. Karashima has brought out, significantly, that patterns of landholding in the same village underwent a transformation of this kind. He seeks to explain this phenomenon in the light of two economic factors:

> First, accumulation of wealth brought by the imperialistic expansion of Cōḻa power during the reigns of Rajaraja I and Rajendra I, which was distributed to the people of the heart of the Cōḻa country, the Lower Kavery Valley. Second, an increase in agricultural productivity was made possible by the introduction of new agricultural techniques such as the construction of dams, the maintenance of water tanks, and channels, etc.[34]

The grant of land on a large scale to secular functionaries of the state on service tenure may have helped in this process. In a further analysis of more inscriptional details, Karashima has laid bare the pattern of some people accumulating large extents of land and becoming big, locally influential, landlords and others losing possession of their land and slipping into the position of tenants and landless cultivators.[35] He has rightly identified in this pattern 'the emergence of a new agrarian order'. Though he is 'still unable to say whether this means the appearance of a feudal system or not, this new agrarian order seems to have brought changes in the relations of many communities belonging to the locality.'[36]

This discussion would dispel any doubts about whether or not there existed private property in land in this period in south India. The weighty evidence presented by Karashima in relation to non-*brahmadēya* villages and non-Brāhmaṇa peasant proprietors has its counterpart in the information concerning individual Brāhmaṇa landowners as well as their corporate bodies such as the *sabhā*, the *pariṣad*, etc. looking after the *brahmadēya* and the *dēvadāna* properties. It is well known that temples had developed into huge landed magnates in this period.[37] In the circumstances, to still support the notion of the Asiatic Mode of Production based on the idea of the absence of private property in land is to close one's eyes towards reality.[38] At the same time, to say that absolute property existed in land will tantamount to ignoring the various shades of rights that different sets of people enjoyed on the same piece of land, a situation that social anthropologists characterize as multiplexity of rights.[39] That would entail consideration of the structured relationship based on land rights as gleaned from the Cōḻa records.

As in the case of land rights existing in the Pāṇḍyan kingdom, records granting land to *brahmadēyas* in the Cōḻa country also speak of land being granted with the rights of both *kārāṇmai* and *mīyāṭci*. As we saw above, these were, respectively, the rights to cultivate the land and to get it cultivated. Another distinction that one notices in land rights, mostly in the case of non-*brahmadēya* villages, is the almost opposing bipolarity of *kārāṇmai* and *veḷḷāmai*. From the contexts in which the expression *veḷḷāmai* occurs, it would appear that this was the right which could be more or less compared with peasant proprietorship. *Veḷḷāmai*, literally that state of being a *veḷḷāḷa*, is interesting as it is presented as a binary opposite of *kārāṇmai*, literally the state of being a *kārāḷa*.[40] However, the facts of the existence of peasant proprietors and of the increase in the strength and number of such peasant proprietors are beyond dispute.

Again, *kārāṇmai* is seen to be of two different kinds in the situation in the Cōḻa country as elsewhere in the Tamil-speaking region. These are expressed by the phrases *kuṭi nīkki* and *kuṭi nīṅṅā*. In the latter case, the *kuṭi nīṅṅā*, the previous settlers were not to be disturbed. Burton Stein has strangely translated the expression *kuti ningaya* to mean an arrangement where 'the previous cultivators are said to have been removed from the land and village at the time of being granted'.[41] R. Tirumalai has shown that even in the *kuṭi nīkki* tenure there was not necessarily a physical eviction of the earlier occupants involved but only a renewal of the terms of occupancy rights.[42] However, this form of tenure may have meant a greater latitude to the new class of intermediaries placed above them, for it is only natural that demands should be enhanced at the time of the renewal of the terms. The same argument is made by Dharma Kumar in her separate study of Cōḻa property rights.[43] In any case, they represented the primary producer with a right over land.

Another element that we come across in the records relating to agrarian relations is the agrestic labour. Given the nature of our records concerned with the upper classes, details about the agrestic labourers are hard to come by. In a masterly analysis of documents pertaining to the villages granted to the Bṛhadīśvara Temple in Tanjavur by Rājarāja I and those granted to the Gaṅgaikkoṇḍacōḻapuram by Vīrarājēndra, it has been shown that in the former list, where 40 villages are involved, 19 of them had a *paṟaiccēri* (separate residential quarters of the *paṟaiyas* who were the agrestic labourers) each and in the latter list involving seven villages there was one, apart from the residential quarters of other communities and occupational groups.[44] Many records speak of the transfer of land together with the labourers attached to it (*āḷaḍaṅga*).[45] If one can go by the indications in the records, which are heavily biased in favour of the upper sections in society, it would appear that these labourers who present themselves to have had a bonded nature occupied the lowest rung in the hierarchy of land rights. By all indications it was these sections who were made use of in redeeming the obligation to pay the service rent, namely *veṭṭi*.

The following structural representation of the complex relationship obtaining in the world of agrarian relations may be made by summarizing our discussion of the nature of land rights in the Cōḻa country. The king was at the top of the hierarchy with his right, which was exercised occasionally, to appropriate the title to grant land both settled and unsettled and also to create superior rights over it.[46] There were different kinds of hierarchies below him. On the one side there were the large number of *nāḍu* groups which were themselves congeries of peasant villages known as the *ūrs*. Each of these villages had a number of magnates who had a share in the arable land there. To begin with they shared common property in the village, but as time progressed individual peasant proprietors also emerged. Most of them had their land cultivated by labourers attached to their land but it is probable that, in certain cases between them and the labourers, there was another tier of sub-tenants. In another hierarchy below the king were the local chiefs. Either below every chief or directly under the king were the huge landed magnates who came to sport bombastic titles and functioned as the state's agents in the Cōḻa political structure. Below these magnates were their tenants, below them the occupants and still below them the agrestic labourers. Again, directly below either the king or one of the chiefs were the different kinds of eleemosynary villages such as the *brahmadēya*, the *dēvadāna*, the *paḷḷiccandam*, the *śālābhōgam*, the *kaṇimuṟṟūṭṭu* and the *veṭṭāppēṟu*. Even in these the tenurial pattern was the same—the *kārāḷas* (tenants), the *kuṭis* (occupants) and the paṟaiyas placed one below the other.

This structured relationship of land rights in early medieval south India, beginning to emerge in a rudimentary form under the Pallavas and getting elaborated by the time we come to the Cōḻa state, is seen extending specially to cover the whole of south India. This compares well with the picture of land rights in early medieval north India as outlined by R.S. Sharma.[47] Again, this strikes a favourable comparison with the situation in medieval Europe,

The tenant who—from father to son, as a rule—ploughs the land and gathers in the crop; his immediate lord, to whom he pays dues and who, in certain circumstances, can resume possession of the land, the lord of the lord, and so on, right up the feudal scale—how many persons there are who can say, each with as much justification as the other, 'That is my field!'[48]

Though one can no longer cling to the idea of the absence of private property in land as the protagonists of the Asiatic Mode of Production would,[49] one cannot be very assertive about the existence of absolute proprietorship over land as Dharma Kumar has tended to suggest in a recent study.[50]

Burton Stein describes this society as a peasant society. His conception is shown to have been taken from economists, sociologists, and anthropologists of varying ideological positions such as Chayanov, Eric Wolf, Marshall Sahlins and Theodore Shanin.[51] He completely misses the subject nature of peasantry. The burden of his theoretical assumptions constrains him to stretch the evidences to such an extent as to force him identify an alliance between the Brāhmaṇas and peasants.[52] In reality, however, the case was far from being such an unchanging monolith. We have seen that varying shades of relationships existed between the Brāhmaṇas (themselves not an undifferentiated lot) on the one hand and the different levels of peasantry on the other, varying at different points of time. But stratification within peasantry is one thing which Stein does not recognize at all. As pointed out by D.N. Jha, to speak of massive peasant support to Brāhmaṇas one will have to ignore the solid evidence that comes out of the entire corpus of published Cōḻa inscriptions, which are largely concerned with arrangements about land; there are only seven identifiable cases of *veḷḷāḷa* peasants granting lands to Brāhmaṇas.[53] The picture that we have seen above is that of a structured relationship where the landowning class, both Brāhmaṇa and *veḷḷāḷa*, occupied the upper stratum exploiting the surplus in agricultural produce by cultivating tenants and agricultural labourers.

Such a structured society with a graded hierarchy of infinite variations in status based on the extent of control over the means of production found its expression in the *jāti* formula. Based on the near total absence of caste designations for those other than Brāhmaṇas named in the temple records of the Cōḻas, B. Suresh has argued that 'the caste system had not yet set'.[54] This confusion is comparable to a similar one in the case of Cēra records from Kerala where, again based on the absence of caste suffixes, Elamkulam P.N. Kunjan Pillai argued that several temple committee members were non-Brāhmaṇas.[55] In the latter case, the researches of M.G.S. Narayanan and the present writer have shown that this is a clear misunderstanding.[56] Even in the case of the Cōḻa country, Subbarayalu has shown that a large number of occupational groups identified in so many words as belonging to different castes make their appearance in the records.[57]

This *jāti* formula, which articulated social stratification, had the contact of each caste with the Brāhmaṇa as the point of reference in fixing the social and ritual status, the assumption there being that the Brāhmaṇas constituted the highest caste. But in reality we see that the *veḷḷāḷa* caste, which is identified significantly as of the Śūdra *varṇa*, is seen to be enjoying an almost equal status with the Brāhmaṇa caste on account of the control of land they had. For instance, in making important decisions concerning land-revenue and allied matters, these two groups are always mentioned together in a premier position. An inscription from Uttaramērūr, recording a decision of the *sabhā* relating to fines to be collected from different castes, gives the following order: Brāhmaṇa, Śiva-Brāhmaṇa, *kaṇakkar*, *veḷḷāḷa* and others.[58] The equal prominence given to Brāhmaṇa and *veḷḷāḷa* is brought out by a couple of records from Mannārguḍi,[59] one dated AD 1118 and the other AD 1239. However, the fixing of the ritual status was always with reference to the contact with the Brāhmaṇas. An inscription of Rājarāja I, dated AD 1002, orders that the landholdings of the members of all castes below the Brāhmaṇas (*Brāhmaṇarkku kīḻpaṭṭa jātikaḷil*) should be sold away in the particular Brāhmaṇa village.[60] This reference certainly includes the *veḷḷāḷas* also, for they were the most prominent landholders.

There is a major lacuna in our sources that we do not get a true picture of the caste hierarchy because, given their concerns, the inscriptions in the temples do not identify the large number of persons mentioned in them by their castes. This is only natural considering the purpose of those records. Thus while the statistical method may be very systematic, in view of the above difficulty in relation to the sources there is the likelihood that one is misled by the results of such analyses. For instance, Y. Subbarayalu has calculated that in the Cōḻa inscriptions the highest frequency of caste obtains in the case of the cattle-keepers or *maṉṟāḍis* (228/663) while the Brāhmaṇas (110/663), the *veḷḷāḷas* (76/663), and others occupy a much lower position.[61] If one were to go blindly after such analyses, the conclusion might be that the cattle-keepers were more than twice as important as the Brāhmaṇas and three times as the *veḷḷāḷas*! But when it is realized that a large number of temple inscriptions are concerned with the endowment of livestock for the maintenance of 'perpetual lamps', the role of a large number of individual cattle-keepers entrusted with the upkeep of such animals in the inscriptions can be appreciated. It is not as if pastoralism was thrice as strong as agriculture! However, even this methodology is far superior to the kind of impressionistic, speculative argument of Suresh and Kunjan Pillai mentioned above.

We have seen that the Brāhmaṇas occupied the highest position in the *jāti* hierarchy. This is only natural. For one thing, *jāti* was a Brāhmaṇical paradigm at least in the historical context in south India. Second, they were not only among the most powerful in terms of economic resources but also as the custodians of religious ideas and institutions centring around the temples which were themselves huge landed magnates. Second to the Brāhmaṇas in the ritual status were the *veḷḷāḷas* who, on account of their land control, occupied an equally influential position in society. Irfan Habib has marvelled that the *veḷḷāḷa* peasants were not accorded the Vaiśya status.[62] This is not necessary. By the period of our study, the *varṇa* principle had become at best a mere theoretical construct irrespective of the question whether or not it ever had any real significance as a representation of social stratification even in northern India. Second, the Vaiśyas, like the Kṣatriyas, even as a category, have not migrated in numbers to south India, and hence one cannot expect a network of the group representing the Vaiśya *varṇa* there such as it was in northern India. Thus it is natural that these peasants of all grades were designated to the residual category of the Śūdras. At the same time not all of them were subjected to the kind of disabilities that the Śūdras in northern India had been[63] for the obvious reason that the *veḷḷāḷa* peasantry constituted a major force as the owners of the means of production. In fact, many of them were granted the status of *satśūdras*, a curious category by the standards of the *varṇa*. This is evidence enough to show that although social stratification expressed itself in the jāti formula, the determinant factor was not caste nor the various shades of connection with the priestly class. On the contrary, it was the control of the means of production in the case of both agriculture and trade that decided the status. This would call into question Romila Thapar's assertion that 'what was immutable in Indian society was ... caste'.[64]

In accommodating the semi-tribal population that was getting transformed into peasants, and other occupational groups into so many *jātis*, the model that was followed was the one prescribed by the *Dharmaśāstras*, viz. that of the *saṅkīrṇajātis*. This allowed for the infinite variations in the graded hierarchy of ritual and social status. Thus we have the different artisan groups being identified as various *saṅkīrṇajātis*. There are also cases of the same artisanal group being given different *jāti* statuses on different occasions, showing thereby that there was nothing rigid about it except the principle. Once this principle was accepted the tribes living in the twilight zones were brought under it and assigned to particular castes. The Paḷḷi, the Curutimān, the Kaḷḷar, the Maṟavar, etc. from the tenth century AD onwards, start getting known as so many castes.[65]

Irfan Habib has raised an important question, 'given the structure of the caste system, who were its chief beneficiaries?'.[66] The truistic answer, that it was the Brāhmaṇas, has been often given by historians including Kosambi and sociologists like Dumont. However, Habib has tried to look at the economic consequences of caste in a different way,

> By its repression of the menial castes, it cheapened labour available for agriculture. At the village level, by providing especially for the services of hereditary village artisans and servants, it reduced the necessary expense on the tools, goods and services that the peasant needed. By thus reducing the portion of agriculture needed for the peasant's subsistence, it enlarged the surplus product, out of which the revenues of the ruling class came. At the same time through hereditary skill-transmission, caste cheapened artisan-products, and thus reduced wage-costs generally. The primary economic consequence of the caste system was, then, a substantial enlargement of the income of the ruling class from both agriculture and crafts.[67]

Thus, within the existing social formation, the standardization of stratification through the *jāti* formula became very handy for the upper classes in society for whom this social institution had a tremendous significance in terms of their interest of the maximization of revenue. This is, however, not to suggest that a crude application of such a calculated material interest was adopted by the powers that be. On the contrary, the acceptance of this formula of social stratification by all sections of society was achieved by subtler means. This took the form of religious ideology which went a long way in validating the stratified social order.[68]

NOTES AND REFERENCES

1. K.A. Nilakanta Sastri, *The Cōḻas* (Madras, 1975), p. 508.
2. Ibid.
3. A. Appadorai, *Economic Conditions in Southern India (1000–1500 AD)* (Madras, 1936); C. Minakshi, *Administration and Social Life under the Pallavas* (Madras, 1938); T.V. Mahalingam, *South Indian Polity* (Madras, 1955).
4. Burton Stein, *Peasant State and Society in Medieval South India* (Delhi, 1980).
5. Burton Stein, 'The State and Agrarian Order in Medieval South India: A Historiographical Critique', in Burton Stein (ed.), *Essays on South India* (Delhi, 1975).
6. Stein, *Peasant State and Society*, 'Preface'.
7. Ibid.
8. See R. Champakalakshmi, 'Peasant State and Society in Medieval South India: A Review Article', *Indian Economic and Social History Review*, vol. XVIII, nos 3–4; Rajan Gurukkal, 'The Agrarian System and Socio-Political Organisation under the Early Pandyas *c*. AD 600–1000', unpublished PhD Thesis, Jawaharlal Nehru University (New Delhi, 1984); D.N. Jha, *Studies in Early Indian Economic History* (Delhi, 1980); D.N. Jha, 'Relevance of "Peasant State and Society" to Pallava–Chola Times', *Indian Historical Review*, vol. VIII, nos 1–2, pp. 74–94; Noboru Karashima, *South Indian History and Society: Studies from Inscriptions AD 859–1800* (Delhi, 1984); M.G.S. Narayanan, *The Perumals of Kerala: Political and Social Conditions of Kerala under the Cera Perumals of Makotai (c. AD 800–1124)*, (Calicut, 1996); Y. Subbarayalu, 'The State in Medieval South India', unpublished PhD Thesis, Madurai Kamaraj University (Madurai, 1976).
9. T.N. Subrahmanyan (ed.), *Thirty Pallava Copper Plates* (Madras, 1966), p. 29, l.53; p. 166, l.107; p. 187, ll.20–1.
10. Ibid., p. 166, l.106; p. 187, l.20.
11. R. Tirumalai, *Land Grants and Agrarian Relations in Cola and Pandya Times* (Madras, 1987), pp. 93–8.
12. L.B. Alayev, 'An Interpretation of Terms Dealing with Land and Revenue (Rent) Rights in South Indian Inscriptions (AD 900–1300)', paper presented at the Workshop on 'Socio-Economic Terms in Ancient and Medieval Indian Inscriptions', organized by Indian Council of Historical Research (Mysore, 1989).
13. Subrahmanyan (ed.), *Thirty Pallava*. See also C. Minakshi, *Administration and Social Life*, but she does not appreciate the significance of such alienation.

14. Gurukkal, 'The Agrarian System', pp. 109–25.
15. *Cf.* D.D. Kosambi, *An Introduction to the Study of Indian History* (Bombay, 1956), p. 323.
16. *South Indian Inscriptions*, vol. XIV, no. 95.
17. *Cf.* D.C. Sircar, *Indian Epigraphical Glossary* (Delhi, 1966).
18. Gurukkal, 'The Agrarian System', p. 113, note 2.
19. See Stein, *Peasant State and Society*, pp. 167–8.
20. Gurukkal, 'The Agrarian System', p. 135, diagram.
21. Narayanan, *Perumals of Kerala*. Chapter on 'Economic Conditions' under Land Tenures.
22. M.G.S. Narayanan, 'The Traditional Land System of Kerala: Problems of Change and Perspective', paper presented to the Logan Centenary Seminar on Land Reforms in Kerala (Calicut, 1981) (unpublished).
23. K.M. Gupta, 'The Land System of South India between about 800 and 1200 AD' (Lahore, 1933) (completed as a PhD Thesis in 1926, London University).
24. Jha, *Studies in Early Indian Economic History*.
25. Subbarayalu, 'The State in Medieval'.
26. Karashima, *South Indian History*.
27. Dharma Kumar, 'Private Property in Asia? The Case of Medieval South India', *Comparative Studies in Society and History*, vol. 27, no. 2.
28. Tirumalai, *Land Grants*.
29. Karashima, *South Indian History*, pp. 1–35.
30. Ibid., p. 12.
31. Ibid., pp. 15–35; Y. Subbarayalu, 'Quantification of Inscriptional Data with Special Reference to the Study of Property Rights in Medieval Tamilnadu', paper presented at the Symposium on 'Quantitative Methods in Indian Historiography' organized by the Indian History Congress (Dharwad, 1988) (unpublished).
32. For a fuller discussion on how landed magnates were identified as state agents in the Cōḻa country, see Kesavan Veluthat, *The Political Structure of Early Medieval South India* (New Delhi, 1993), chapter III 'The King and His Men'; also, Kesavan Veluthat, 'Landed Magnates as State Agents: The Gavudas under the Hoysalas in Karnataka', *Proceedings of the Indian History Congress* (Gorakhpur, 1989), Chapter 15 below, for testing the model in the context of medieval Karnataka.
33. Karashima, *South Indian History*, chapter II.
34. Ibid., p. 20.
35. Ibid., pp. 26–7.
36. Ibid., p. 31.
37. Jha, *Studies in Early Indian*, pp. 74–89.
38. This is what Kathleen Gough does in 'Modes of Production in Southern India', *Economic and Political Weekly*, Annual Number, February 1980.
39. Kumar, 'Private Property'.

40. *Kārāḷa* is generally translated as peasant, tenant, etc. the etymology being not clear. Is it possible to derive it from Sanskrit *karṣaka*? In that case, he would be a cultivating tenant which indeed he appears to have been. *Kār* in the Dravidian languages signifies black and *veḷ* is white. Could therefore *veḷḷāḷa* be treated as the opposite of *kārāḷa*, that is, a peasant proprietor? In any case, *veḷḷāḷa* was one.
41. Stein, *Peasant State*, p. 168, note 74.
42. Tirumalai, *Land Grants*, pp. 93–8.
43. Kumar, 'Private Property'.
44. Karashima, *South Indian History*, pp. 44–5; Chart 1.
45. This is a common feature in the Pāṇḍya, Cēra, and Cōḻa records.
46. For a fuller discussion, see Kesavan Veluthat, *The Political Structure of Early Medieval South India* (Delhi, 1993), chapter III.
47. R.S. Sharma, *Indian Feudalism* (Delhi, 1980).
48. Marc Bloch, *Feudal Society* (tr. L.A. Manyon), vol. II (London, 1961), p. 116.
49. Gough, 'Modes of Production'.
50. Kumar, 'Private Property'.
51. Jha, 'Relevance of "Peasant State and Society"', pp. 74–5.
52. Stein, *Peasant State*, chapters II and III.
53. Jha, *Studies in Early Indian*, pp. 78–9.
54. B. Suresh, 'Historical and Cultural Geography and Ethnology of South India (with special reference of Chola Inscriptions)', unpublished PhD Thesis, Deccan College (Poona, 1965).
55. P.N. Kunjan Pillai, *Janmisampradayam Keralattil* (Kottayam, 1959), pp. 18–50.
56. Narayanan, *Perumals of Kerala*, chapters on 'Police and Revenue' and 'Social Systems'; Kesavan Veluthat, 'Aryan Brahman Settlements of Ancient Kerala', unpublished MA Dissertation, Calicut University (Calicut, 1974), Appendix II.
57. Subbarayalu, *The State*, p. 86 (Table).
58. *Epigraphia Indica*, vol. XXII, no. 33.
59. *South Indian Inscriptions*, vol. VI, no. 57; nos 48, 50, 58.
60. Ibid., vol. V, no. 1409.
61. Subbarayalu, *The State*, p. 86.
62. Irfan Habib, 'The Peasant in Indian History' (General President's Address), *Proceedings of the Indian History Congress* (Kurukshetra, 1982).
63. For the disabilities which the Śūdras in northern India were subjected to, see R.S. Sharma, *Sudras in Ancient India* (Delhi, 1980).
64. *A History of India*, vol. I (Harmondsworth, 1968), p. 77. Thapar takes a position different from D.D. Kosambi, *An Introduction*, pp. 313–14.
65. For a list of the different jātis, see Subbarayalu, *The State*, pp. 84–111.
66. Irfan Habib, *Interpreting Indian History* (Shillong [n.d.]), p. 19.
67. Ibid., p. 20.

68. M.G.S. Narayanan and Kesavan Veluthat, 'The Bhakti Movement in South India' in S.C. Malik (ed.), *Dissent, Protest, and Reform in Indian Civilization* (Simla, 1978), have argued that the bhakti movement in south India was an attempt to standardize and legitimize this kind of a social stratification, the upper sections providing the necessary ideological bulwark.

4

Labour Rent and Produce Rent*

The Cōḻa state has been presented by historians in the past as a top-heavy structure with an efficient bureaucracy and a wide tax-base. Among the arguments to support the conception of wide base of revenue have been the reference to a series of functionaries identified as forming part of an elaborate 'land revenue department' and the occurrence of more than 400 terms denoting 'taxes'.[1] However, in the literature on these two aspects there is no clarity as to the exact nature of either the 'department' or the 'taxes'. Prefacing his discussion of the 'Department of land revenue', for instance, Nilakanta Sastri says: 'The exact functions of the different grades of officials named are not easy to define.'[2] Again, he is not explicit whether the revenues accrued from the several hundred 'taxes' went entirely to the state or not.[3] Nor is there a clear understanding of how such exactions could be characterized. The situation, unfortunately, is much worse in the writings of those who followed Sastri: Appadorai and Mahalingam, by injudiciously mixing up evidences from Tamil inscriptions and Sanskrit texts, arrive at a highly idealized picture.[4] A definite statement about the nature of the revenue or the role of the state is looked for in vain there.

Recently, Burton Stein has sought to correct the conjectural nature in the understanding of the revenue system contained in what he has called the 'conventional historiography' represented by Nilakanta Sastri and his followers;[5] but even there, he has not gone far beyond substituting one kind of impressionistic speculation for another. What is done in this essay is to make use of the results of a systematic analysis

* First published as 'Labour Rent and Produce Rent: Reflections on the Revenue System Under the Cholas (AD 850–1279)', *Proceedings of the Indian History Congress* (Dharwar, 1988), pp. 138–44.

of the copious data in the inscriptions in an attempt to explain certain aspects of the revenue system under the Cōḻas. We have sought here to characterize some of the more frequently obtaining terms denoting levies. This would help not only in understanding the exact nature of such exactions but also in throwing light on the socio-economic formation. We make use of the computational analysis of the rich data made available to us by the by now classic studies of Noboru Karashima, Y. Subbarayalu, B. Sitaraman and P. Shanmugham, undertaken jointly and severally.[6]

I

Historians starting from Nilakanta Sastri have, as stated above, identified an elaborate 'land revenue department' in the records of the Cōḻas, known as the *puṟavuvari-tiṇaikkaḷam.*[7] References to this 'department' begin to occur from the reign of Uttama Cōḻa.[8] It grew into an elaborate establishment with several sections, each under a hierarchy of officers. It was after the reign of Rajaraja I that it came to be known as *puṟavuvari-tiṇaikkaḷam.* The expression *tiṇaikkalam* gets replaced by *śrīkaraṇa* in the reign of Kulōttuṅga II. In the case of areas covered by the rule of the so-called feudatories also, there are references to *tiṇai*, *tiṇaikkaḷam*, and the like evidently the same as *puṟavuvari-tiṇaikkaḷam.*[9]

As stated above, this 'department' in the king's government under the Cōḻas acquired its elaborate character, with the hierarchy of officers from the reign of Uttama Cōla. Two of his copper plate grants give us a list of functionaries related to this 'department': *puṟavuvari*, *varippottagam*, *mugaveṭṭi*, *varippottagakkaṇakku*, *variyil-iḍu* and *paṭṭolai* in that order.[10] This hierarchy gets further elaborated by the time of Rājarāja I. Incidentally, this agrees perfectly with the pattern, as we shall see below, of the increase in the documents of the frequently used land revenue terms in the period of and after Rājarāja I.[11] The hierarchy becomes most elaborate by the time of Rajendra II with as many as ten 'officers' on the scale, the additions being *puṟavuvari-tiṇaikkaḷa-kaṇakkar*, *puṟavuvari-tiṇaikkaḷam* and *puṟavuvari-tiṇaikkaḷa-nāyagam*, all in the place of the simple *puṟavuvari* in Uttama's records.[12] From the time of Kulōttuṅga I onwards, however, we see that the number of officers in this 'department' tapers off. In the records of his reign and after, we come across only two officers, *puṟavuvari-śrīkaraṇa-nāyagam* and *mugaveṭṭi*, the others being generally absent.[13] In the records of the successors of Vikrama, a blanket term *variyilār*, evidently an abbreviation of *pu̱ravuvariyilār*, is used to denote the entire 'department'.[14] What is likely is that by this time all the functionaries in this 'department' were referred to by the general term *variyilār* or, alternatively, the differentiation in this 'department' with the graded hierarchy ceased to exist.

An order of hierarchy of officials in this 'department' has been reconstructed from the sequence in which they are mentioned in the documents. This order is significant because the higher offices are generally sections among the landowning groups.[15] Thus, more than 50 per cent of the incumbents of the top four positions in the hierarchy, for instance, bore the title *uḍaiyān* and about 30 per cent, that of *mūvēndavēḷān*.[16] However, there are very few *mūvēndavēḷān*s among the *puṛavu-vari-tiṇaikkaḷa-nāyagam*, which presumably was an office of the higher cadre.[17] But considering the fact that this office came into existence in a period when the frequency of the title *mūvendavēḷān* was decreasing, this can be explained. As we go down on the scale, for instance from *varipottagam* to *mugaveṭṭi*, the proportion of the *uḍaiyān* title-holders goes up to as much as 70 per cent and that of the *mūvēndavēḷān* title-holders goes down to as few as 10 per cent.[18] Further down, there are still fewer *mūvēndavēḷān*s among the lesser officers such as *variyil-iḍu* and *paṭṭōlai* while the number of *uḍaiyān* title-holders is more numerous there.[19] In a similar fashion, it can be noticed that the sporting of a king's name or title along with the name or title of an officer is more in the case of officers in the higher rungs of hierarchy and less at the lower levels.

Impressive and even formidable as the evidence of this 'department' is, there is no instance recording its actual involvement in the matter of either the assessment or the collection of taxes in the localities. References to this 'department', in fact, obtain only in records pertaining to the central establishment of the Cō̱la rule; it was more or less something of a 'revenue secretariat' or 'revenue board' concerned with the keeping of the records in relation to revenue, especially its remission.[20]

II

The myriad revenue terms figuring in the records of the Cō̱las, to be sure, are known to us more in the context of their remission than their actual collection. In most cases, therefore, rather than the *existence* of a particular levy, it was the *possibility* of such a levy, that was exempted. This is suggested by the stock expression '*eppērpaṭṭa*' ('of whatever description') used in the end of the list of immunities, generally in the sense of an '*et cetera*'. In the numerous records of the Cōḻas, many of these revenue terms figure with a negligible frequency, which is an indication of their insignificance for economy and society. The analysis of such terms in the Cōḻa records, undertaken by Karashima and Sitaraman, shows that out of the hundreds of expressions taken to be revenue terms there are only twenty-seven occurring more than ten times;[21] even out of them, sixteen are exclusive to certain regions (that is, thirteen in the Jayaṅgoṇḍacōḻamaṇḍalam region and three in the Cōḻamaṇḍalam region); and only eleven had universal currency in both the Cōḻamaṇḍalam and Jayaṅgoṇḍacōḻamaṇḍalam areas. All this shows that in spite of the occurrence of a large number of expressions described as taxes in the records of the Cōḻas only a few had universal currency throughout the areas and periods covered by the Cōḻa rule.

Among these eleven, seven are taken out for further detailed treatment on account of their frequency above twenty.[22] These expressions are: *antarāyam* (73), *eccōṟu* (85), *kaḍamai* (65), *kuḍimai* (34), *muṭṭaiyāḷ* (21), *taṭṭārpāṭṭam* (27) and *veṭṭi* (107). *Eccōṟu* signified the obligation to feed the functionaries of the state.[23] In one of the Cēra inscriptions, the same thing is denoted in a slightly different form, viz. *iravu-cōṟu*[24] and in the thirteenth century Malayalam Commentary of *Arthaśāstra*, *irannūṇ*,[25] all of which mean the same thing. M.G.S. Narayanan has rightly likened this to the practice of billetting in medieval Europe.[26] *Veṭṭi* is the Tamil form of Sanskrit *viṣṭi* and meant the obligation to render labour services, that is, labour rent. So was *muṭṭaiyāḷ*, which may also have meant the computation of such labour dues either in cash or kind. *Veṭṭi* or *viṣṭi* is the one levy occurring with the highest frequency. It has been rightly understood as *corvée* labour, a kind of rent paid in the form of labour services. In this case, instead of the surplus produce, it is the surplus labour that is extracted from the primary producer and hence the appellation, labour rent, will be more appropriate. These three obligations, namely, *eccōṟu*, *veṭṭi* and *muṭṭaiyāḷ*, therefore, cannot be described as 'taxes'. Again among the other four, *kaḍamai* and *kuḍimai*, which have been shown as the most important items, were both computed and collected in kind, that is, paddy. In fact, Nilakanta Sastri has calculated that *kaḍamai* accounted for 40 per cent of the total produce[27] while R. Tirumalai believes that it was as much as 50 per cent.[28] Therefore, this turns out to be the most important form in which the surplus was extracted from the producer. Rather than describing it as tax, one would characterize it as produce rent par excellence.

Thus we see that the two most important forms of levies, namely *veṭṭi* and *kaḍamai*—the importance of the former on account of its highest frequency of occurrence (107) and that of the latter on account of its proportion to the total produce (40 to 50 per cent)—formed the crux of surplus extraction in the Cōḻa state. The former is clearly what is described as labour rent. Labour rent is the primeval form in which the extraction of surplus value expresses itself.[29] Its next higher form is rent paid in kind.[30]

III

In this context, the pattern of distribution of these two terms in the records over the periods of the Cōḻa rule acquires significance. Karashima and Sitaraman have prepared a table of period-wise distribution of those revenue terms occurring more than ten times in the records.[31] For this purpose, they have divided the entire period covered by the Cōḻa rule into four: Period I from Vijayālaya to the accession of Rājarāja I (AD 846–985); Period II from the accession of Rājarāja I to that of Kulōttuṅga I (985–1070); Period III from the accession of Kulōttuṅga I to that of Kulōttuṅga III (1070–1179), and period IV from the accession of Kulōttuṅga III to the reign of Rājēndra III (1179–1279).[32] The tabulated form of references in relation to *veṭṭi* and *kaḍamai* may be reproduced here:

TABLE 4.1: Distribution of select items of revenue under the Cōḻas

Term	*Total Frequency*	*Period*			
		I	*II*	*III*	*IV*
Veṭṭi	107	46.5	23.0	15.5	22.0
Kaḍamai	65	1.5	5.5	14.5	43.5

Note: Fraction indicates cases the date of which is not sure

Source: Adapted from Karashima, *South Indian History and Society*. See n. 6.

It is seen that the occurrence of *veṭṭi* goes on decreasing as time progresses while that of *kaḍamai* goes on increasing. In other words, the incidence of labour rent is inversely proportional to that of produce rent. This is very significant. In the classical analysis of the genesis of ground rent in the capitalist mode of production, Karl Marx has characterized labour rent as the primeval form of surplus labour. Labour which is over and above what is absolutely essential for the maintenance and reproduction of the labourer himself is directly appropriated by the 'owner' of the means of production. On the other hand, in the case of rent in kind, it is the fruit of such surplus labour that is appropriated from the direct producer, which presupposes 'a higher stage of civilisation'.[33] 'The transformation of labour rent into rent in kind', however, writes Marx, 'changes nothing from the economic standpoint in the nature of ground rent'.[34] The mode of production, therefore, remains the same.

Another significant feature is that *veṭṭi* continues to obtain at a lower frequency. In fact, we have seen that in period IV it is slightly higher than in period III. In other words, labour rent is not completely replaced by produce rent; the former exists even while the latter becomes the dominant form of surplus extraction. Even this is natural, for, according to Marx,

> To whatever extent rent in kind is the prevailing and dominant form of ground rent, it is furthermore always more or less accompanied by survivals of the earlier form, that is, of rent paid directly in labour, corvee-labour, no matter whether the landlord be a private person or the state.[35]

IV

The above examination of two major aspects of the revenue system under the Cōḻas throws light on the character of surplus extraction and the role of state in it. We saw that the impressive evidence of the existence of what has been described in the past as a 'department' of land revenue does not actually tell us anything about its involvement in the assessment and collection of taxes from the actual producers. What this establishment appears to have been concerned with is the maintenance of records related to land revenue. Whatever actual evidence of assessment and collection we have from the localities is in the inscriptions of local bodies or institutions, an instance of the delegation of fiscal rights. This is not to argue for a slender revenue base for the Cōḻa state: the evidence of the *puṟvu-vari-tiṇaikkaḷam* alone cannot support the description of the Cōḻa state as being supported by a wide tax-base.

Similar is the case of the number of 'taxes'. On the basis of the myriad 'revenue' terms found in Cōḻa inscriptions, historians in the past have tended to draw conclusions similar to the one drawn on the basis of an elaborate land revenue 'department'. But a closer examination of these hundreds of terms has shown that only seven of them were really important and even among them, only two accounted for a significant share of the produce. One of them was a labour rent and the other, a produce rent. Significantly, the evidence we have of these two forms of extraction fits exactly into the pattern suggested by Karl Marx. We may conclude by saying that the form which surplus extraction took in south India under the Cōḻas, therefore, may be taken as a good indicator of the mode of production obtaining there: 'The specific economic form, in which unpaid surplus labour is pumped out of direct producers, determines the relationship of rulers and ruled ...'[36]

NOTES AND REFERENCES

1. The nature of the Cōḻa State has been one of the more amply addressed problems in the recent historiography of south India. For a good summary, Y. Subbarayalu, 'The Chola State', *Studies in History*, vol. IV, no. 1 (1982), pp. 265–306. For references to the department of land revenue, K.A. Nilakanta Sastri, *The Cōḻas*, 2nd edn (Madras, 1975), pp. 146–71; T.V. Mahalingam, *South Indian Polity*, 2nd edn (Madras, 1975), pp. 143–6; Subbarayalu, 'The State in Medieval South India', unpublished PhD Thesis, Madurai Kamaraj University, 1976, pp. 143–52. For the ideas of Nilakanta Sastri on taxation, Sastri, *The Cōḻas*, pp. 520–45.
2. Sastri, *The Cōḻas*, p. 469.
3. Ibid., pp. 520–45.
4. A. Appadorai, *Economic Conditions of Southern Indian* AD *l000–1500* (Madras, 1936), vol. II. pp. 661–732; Mahalingam, *South Indian Polity*, pp. 153–99.
5. Burton Stein, *Peasant State and Society in Medieval South India* (Delhi, 1980), pp. 258–64.
6. Most of the results of these works have been brought together in Noboru Karashima, Y. Subbarayalu and Toru Matsui, *A Concordance of the Names in the Cola Inscriptions* (Madurai, 1978); Noboru Karashima, *South Indian History and Society. Studies from Inscription—AD 850–1800* (Delhi, 1984); Subbarayalu, 'The State in Medieval South India', and P. Shanmugham, *The Revenue System of the Cholas* (Madras, 1987) are useful contributions making use of the results of the computational analysis of the inscriptional data.

7. Sastri, *The Cōḻas*, pp. 469–71.
8. The chronological distribution and other details pertaining to the functionaries attached to this department given in this section is compiled with the help of Subbarayalu, *State*, pp. 145–6 and Karashima, Subbarayalu and Matsui, *A Concordance*, under SA 060, SA 061 and SA 062; SB 032, SB 070, SB 071, SB 090, SB 091 0300.
9. Ibid.
10. Ibid.
11. For details, Karashima, *South Indian History and Society*, pp. 72–3, Table 8.
12. *Supra*, n. 8.
13. Ibid.
14. Ibid.
15. The large number of personal names subjected to computer-aided analysis in Karashima, Subbarayalu and Toru Matsui, *A Concordance*, show a very interesting pattern; landowners sport titles such as *uḍaiyan*, *kiḻān*, *āḻvān*, *araiyan*, *mūvēndavēḷān*, etc. It has been shown that the earlier mentioned titles indicate those who are on the lower rungs of this landed 'nobility' while the later mentioned ones indicate the ones of higher ranks. Karashima, *South Indian History*, pp. 55–64. In fact, it has been shown that there is a close correspondence between these titles and the 'offices' of the king's government under the Cōḻas. Subbarayalu, *State*, chapter on 'Title-holders'. This would, incidentally, show that what has been identified as a 'bureaucracy' by historians in the past was in reality that section of the landed nobility enlisted by the state for services. For details, Kesavan Veluthat, *The Political Structure of Early Medieval South India* (Delhi, 1993), chapter on 'The King and His Men'.
16. The data for this analysis is from the literature cited in *supra*, n. 8.
17. Ibid.
18. Ibid.
19. Ibid.
20. Paradoxically, much of the information we have in the records about the levies is in relation to exemption from such payments. Karashima, *South Indian History*, p. 71 and n. 4.
21. Karashima, *South Indian History*, pp. 69–74 and Table 8.
22. Ibid.
23. *Cf.* Subbarayalu, *State*, p. 205.
24. *TAS*, vol. II, no. 9.
25. This is the Malayalam expression for *praṇaya* in the *Arthaśāstra*, which means offering food to functionaries of the State. Sastri, *The Colas*, p. 520.
26. M.G.S. Narayanan, *The Perumals of Kerala* (Calicut, 1996), chapter on 'Police and Revenue'.
27. Sastri, *The Cōḻas*, p. 533.

28. R. Tirumalai, *Land Grants and Agrarian Reactions in Chola and Pandya Times* (Madras, 1987), p. 172.
29. Karl Marx, *Capital*, vol. III (Moscow edn, 1974), p. 790.
30. Karashima, *South Indian History*, pp. 72–3, Table 8.
31. Ibid., p. 71.
32. Adapted from Ibid., pp. 72–3, Table 8.
33. Marx, *Capital*, vol. III, p. 794.
34. Ibid.
35. Ibid.
36. Ibid., p. 795.

5

Nāḍu in the Socio-political Structure*

In recent years there has been a greater emphasis laid on the importance of understanding the nature of the 'basic building blocks' in a polity than in an earlier period when what was taken up for consideration did not go beyond dynastic-political history to which chapters on 'administration' or 'society' or 'economy' were latched on as unconnected appendages. The organic connection between the units of socio-economic organization on the one hand and the real structure of political institutions on the other is a matter which is increasingly appreciated. In the case of south India, this is a phenomenon of recent historiography since the early 1970s. One of such basic units, the role of which has been brought to light in this perspective, is the *nāḍu*, although historians are not unanimous in their characterization of this unit. In this paper, we seek to examine the role of the *nāḍu* in the socio-political structure of south India, in the process of which some of the existing theories of state and society in early medieval south India will have to be challenged and rejected.

The 'basic unit' of social, political and economic organization in the case of the Tamil country was the village, known as the *ūr*, in the colonial and nationalist discourse in Indian historiography.[1] The archetypal village community was identified here and the attending details of this community was also sought to be located in the south Indian context.[2] This is in fact a leitmotif in the writings of Nilakanta Sastri, and those who followed him chronologically were following

* First published as 'The Role of Nadu in the Socio-political Structure of South India (AD c. 600–1200)', in H.V. Sreenivasamurthi, B. Surendra Rao, Kesavan Veluthat and S.A. Bari, eds, *Essays on Indian History and Culture: Felicitation Volume to Professor B. Sheikh Ali* (New Delhi, 1990), pp. 85–98.

him blindly in their assumptions also.[3] In recent years, however, the 'eternal Indian village' appears to have lost its charm. The researches of Y. Subbarayalu, Burton Stein and Noboru Karashima have provided the necessary empirical details and theoretical refinement which has resulted in this dethronement of the village.[4] At the same time, it has led to the consecration of the *nāḍu* as the most important factor in the socio-political structure of south India under the Pāṇḍyas, Pallavas and Cōḻas, the case of the Cēras being slightly different. In this paper we shall take up the situation obtaining in the records of the Cōḻas for detailed discussion and from there proceed to other areas in relation to which we have less information.

The expression *nāḍu* denoted both a locality and a corporate group of the spokesmen of that locality. The *nāḍu*, in the sense of a locality, was a grouping of the *veḷḷānvagai* villages, that is, the agrarian settlements. There is no way to define precisely the boundaries of the territory of a *nāḍu* although statements describing particular villages as belonging to particular *nāḍu*s would help us identify the territory covered by such *nāḍu*s. They had no natural boundaries such as a river. In fact, there were *nāḍu*s lying on either side of a stream or a watercourse, including the Kāvēri in at least one case.[5] This suggests that at least in those cases importance was given to a source of irrigation as central to the locality, a point which supports the idea that the nāḍus formed spontaneous natural groupings of agrarian settlements. Further, the *nāḍu*s were widely disparate in their size, varying from a handful of square miles to a few hundreds and comprising villages varying from one to as many as forty. These facts, together with the lack of uniformity among the *nāḍu*s, suggests strongly against the idea of their being artificial divisions. There are, of course, a few cases of rearrangements of *nāḍu*s by the regrouping of villages among them; but even such cases lack in evidence of governmental interference.[6] The nomenclature of the *nāḍu* also is indicative of this: it mostly followed the name of a village, which was usually a toponym.[7] On the other hand, the *vaḷanāḍu* units, which were contrived by Rājarāja Cōḻa (AD 985–1014) as clearly administrative divisions of an artificial nature, had natural boundaries; they were named after one of the titles of the Cōḻa ruler; and there was less disparity among them in size.[8]

The situation in the other regions of south India also appears to conform to this suggestion. In the Pallava kingdom we come across a locality called *kōṭṭam*, which is at times taken as a unit bigger than the *nāḍu*. But in all other respects, the *kōṭṭam* answered to the *nāḍu*.[9] In that region, the question of artificial units such as the *vaḷanāḍus* does not arise at all under the Pallavas for the simple reason that the latter were administrative units contrived by the Cōḻa imperial government under Rājarāja I and after, by whose time *Toṇḍaimaṇḍalam* or *Jayaṅgoṇḍacōḻamaṇḍalam*, the erstwhile Pallava territory, had been integrated as part of the Cōḻa empire. In the Pāṇḍyan kingdom, too, Rajan Gurukkal has demonstrated that *nāḍus* had similar characteristics as they had in the Cōḻa country, spontaneous groupings of agrarian village communities.[10] Again, like in the Cōḻa country, when units like the *vaḷanāḍus* begin to appear in the tenth century, they are clearly administrative divisions of an artificial nature, with a name or title of one of the Pāṇḍyan rulers or their Cōḻa overlords prefixed to the name of each *vaḷanāḍu*.[11] In the Cēra kingdom, as in many other cases, we do not have the counterparts of the *nāḍu* or *kōṭṭam* units in the rest of south India. We do come across an expression *nāḍu* in terms such as Kōlattunāḍu, Ēṟāḷanāḍu, Vaḷḷuvanāḍu, Veṇāḍu, etc. which stood for territorial divisions; but they denoted whole territories under chiefly rule, answering to the *rāṣtra* in the Deccan and *pāḍi* in the Cōḻa country.[12] The pattern of settlement with a more dispersed character may have been responsible for this variation there; but its implication, in the absence of the aggressive non-Brāhmaṇa peasant localities in the rest of the Tamil country, was far-reaching for the nature of socio-political organization there.

If thus the spontaneous, evolutionary character of the *nāḍu* is appreciated, then the increase in the number of *nāḍu* units as pointed out by Subbarayalu can be understood more meaningfully. He feels that the fact of more and more *nāḍus* being mentioned in the inscriptional records dating from the period after the ninth century is evidence for the proliferation of such *nāḍu* settlements,[13] a statement which is rejected by Burton Stein who believes that it shows 'not a new existence, but a new recognition of Chola overlordship' in these *nāḍus*.[14] But by extending Stein's own logic, this can be questioned: The first mention of anything in a record is as little evidence of its 'new recognition' as it is for its recent origin! What, however, is significant is the spontaneity as well as the evolutionary nature of these units. It was in the more fertile regions that the earlier *nāḍus* are situated while the later ones are met with in the less fertile regions on the fringes of the settled agrarian society, thus presenting the picture of a gradual agrarian expansion. Again, the more densely populated *nāḍus*, which comprised larger numbers of villages, were in the more fertile regions and the more sparsely populated ones, which consisted of smaller numbers of villages, were in the less fertile regions.

Burton Stein assumes that the *nāḍus* existed 'long before' the Cōḻa empire.[15] He believes that the neolithic farming communities in the plains and uplands were the bases of these groups and that by the early centuries of the Christian era, even the *nāḍu* units were crystallized as is clear (to him) from the early Tamil literature. A major confusion has crept in here in respect both of the archaeological and literary evidence. While we do know of the knowledge that people had possessed of agriculture from excavations, for example, at Paiyampalli, there is nothing on record in the neolithic or post-neolithic archaeology in south India to suggest that well-organized farming communities existed there at that time.[16] Again, even though pockets of agrarian settlements can be identified in what is usually called the Sangam literature, the evidence there is far too inconclusive to suggest that the peasant localities in early medieval south India represented a direct, unbroken continuation from the ancient times. The evidence he presents in favour of this argument is based on references to a number of *nāḍus* found in the Tamil literature;[17] he fails to recognize that the twelve dialect zones in the didactic/prescriptive sections which are demonstrably late compositions use the term in the sense of territory, country, etc.,[18] much in the same way as this word is used in Kerala and Karnataka in the medieval period. Thus expressions like Kuṭṭanāḍu, Kuḍanāḍu, Pūḻināḍu, etc. figuring in the Sangam literature, should not be understood in the same way as the *nāḍus* in medieval times in the Cōḻa country in which latter case they were groupings of peasant settlements with a corporate identity. Perhaps by taking this position what Stein wants is to strengthen his argument about the clannish character of these groups; but what he actually does is to succumb to the orientialist assumption of an unchanging India.

As pointed out earlier, most *nāḍus* derived their names from the name of one of the villages within them.[19] But beyond this eponymous aspect, there was nothing special about that village to qualify it as the 'centre' of the *nāḍu*, its 'head-quarters'. 'There is not a single inscription', writes Subbarayalu, 'which would connect even vaguely the activities of the *Nāḍu* assembly with some chief village or the activities of the Government with the same'.[20] There are at least eleven *nāḍus* where the 'chief village' was a *brahmedēya.*[21] It is not possible that a *brahmadēya,* where administrative, fiscal and judicial powers were alienated, could have been created in a place which was an administrative head-quarters. Indeed, centres such as Uṟaiyūr, Paḻaiyāṟai, Tiruvāmūr, Cidambaram and Kāñcīpuram did not have any *brahmadēya* or other free-hold places within them. Burton Stein asserts that the 'name-giving' village was the earliest peasant settlement of a *nāḍu,* its 'inner core', which attracted subordinate settlements around it and thus welded together the peasant group of the locality.[22] This idea of an 'inner core' and an 'outer pulp' (as it were) is not warranted by the evidence of the *nāḍu* which in reality was a homogeneous entity. The eponymous village may have been the earliest settlement in a locality; but there is nothing to suggest that it had a primacy in the *nāḍu* in any other respect.

These *nāḍus,* which are understood by Stein with an inner core in a primary village and subordinate settlements gathered around it, are taken by him as discrete units of ethnic, social and economic organization.[23] In fact, these are looked upon as the atomic aspects of the segmentary organization in medieval south India. Its salient features, according to him, were: (1) restricted marriage and kinship networks, (2) narrow territorial social coalitions beyond kinsmen and (3) locally-based agrarian relationships, political and religious affiliations and loyalties.[24] While the possibility of the *nāṭṭār* being related to one another in an affinal or agnatic way is not denied here, our evidence shows that it was their common interests as prominent landholders that brought them together and gave them their corporate identity and character. The concern with landed property, agriculture and the management of surplus is prime in the documents and even a suggestion of their bonds being based on kinship loyalties is not found there and will have to be based on mere speculation. In fact, the period between the close of what is described as the Sangam age, which is usually put at AD third-fourth centuries, and the beginning of the period of our study, had witnessed the break-up of such loyalties based on kinship and marriage and the emergence of new loyalties based on economic and social differentiation.[25] By the time we come to the ninth-tenth centuries and after, with large extents of land cleared and larger sections of population transformed as peasants, the clannish loyalties had no place in society as a major organizing principle.

Stein appears, in fact, to be begging the question. He writes:[26]

In the absence of effective, continuous, extra-local, non-peasant authority over agrarian relationships and over the distribution of the products of the land, it was only through secure relationships with those local groups which controlled the land that benefits could be obtained by groups without such control.

In a wonderful exercise of circular reasoning, Stein assumes his main thesis of the absence of extra-local, non-peasant authority over the distribution of the products of the land. He makes that his premise on which to base his argument about the territorially segmented character of society, which argument itself is the major premise of the book, the larger purpose of which is to prove the absence of extra-local, non-peasant authority of an effective and continuous nature!

Another factor which Stein regards as important with respect to territorial segmentation in the southern peninsula is the absence of conquests.[27] It is argued that there have not been any major conquests in this region in historical times and hence there was no major change in society. This not only assumes that war and conquests bring about major social changes; but it also ignores the ability of changes in the means and relations of production to lead to such changes. And, surprisingly, Stein legitimizes his whole argument in this matter swearing by Kosambi[28] who would, in actual fact, consider history as the 'presentation ... of successive developments in the means and relations of production'.[29] Again, thinking in circles, Stein concludes that this changelessness was preserved and protected by the segmentary character of society.

Stein makes a distinction among three types of *nāḍus*, although he does not cite any evidence either primary or secondary to support his distinction.[30] The differences related generally to their internal organization and their connection with other localities. There were *nāḍus* which were horizontally divided ('vertically segmented' in Stein's words) with an elaborate hierarchy with political chiefs at the top (of course, below the Cōḻas according to the diagram on p. 135), Brāhmaṇa ritual specialists below them, the dominant peasantry of the *nāḍu* still lower, followed by the lower peasantry and dependents in the next stratum, the artisan-traders further down, and the landless labourers at the bottom. Such *nāḍus* are designated as 'central *nāḍus*', although the term 'central' has admittedly no spatial connotation about it. They obtained in the fertile plains, where agriculture was easiest and most profitable. A second type of *nāḍus* is stated to have been found in those tracts of the lowlands or in the large interior upland above the Tamil plain lacking reliable sources of moisture for extensive irrigated agriculture. For want of the necessary surplus, there were fewer of the hierarchical elements found in the 'central' *nāḍus*. Here society was vertically divided (or, 'horizontally segmented' in Stein's words). Stein makes an important distinction between the 'central' and 'intermediate' *nāḍus*. While the 'central' *nāḍus* were closely linked to a ruling dynasty, for the most part Cōḻa, in the 'intermediate' *nāḍus* the sovereignty of other dynasties was recognized. Further, the Brāhmaṇical institutions were fewer in the 'intermediate' *nāḍus*. Although 'intermediate' *nāḍus* are stated to have been horizontally segmented giving little scope for differentiation, and so on they show hierarchy nonetheless, although on a less elaborate scale than in the 'central' *nāḍus*. He also distinguishes a third type of *nāḍus* in those parts of south India which were least hospitable to sedentary agriculture or even to mixed agricultural and pastoral activities. These were scattered *nāḍu* localities without any differentiation whatsoever. They are designated as the 'peripheral' *nāḍus*, which are stated to have displayed the strongest tribal characteristics.

However, these distinctions are not supported by any kind of evidence in Stein's treatment.[31] It would appear that he is speculating too much here in order to form the premise on which he seeks to base his arguments about the segmentary nature of the Cōḻa state. In reality, evidences we have about the *nāḍu* as a territorial unit and about the *nāṭṭār*as a corporate body are far less exhaustive than would support this kind of classification.

In the conventional literature on the subject the corporate body of the *nāṭṭār*, also known by the term *nāḍu*, is treated as a sort of territorial assembly which functioned in the territorial unit known by the name *nāḍu*. The assembly is either looked at as consisting of the representatives of each of the villages coming together or by the more influential residents of the unit.[32] It is also stated that the assemblies of *brahmedēya*, *paḷḷiccandam*, *kaṇimuṟṟūṭṭu* and *veṭṭāpēṟu* villages and the *nagara* were subject to the administrative control of the *nāḍu*. However, our view of the *nāḍu* differs from these positions. The part played by the *nāḍu* in the administration of the country is not denied; but the view that it was an organ of the government, constituted for the purpose, is explicitly rejected here. In our view, the *nāḍus* were preexisting groupings of the peasant settlements with a spontaneous character and these groupings were identified and made use of by the state under the Pallavas, Pāṇḍyas and Cōḻas for purposes of government from time to time. In the records of the Cēra kingdom, however, this locality group is strikingly absent which may be explained by the totally dissimilar character of the settlement pattern there, where nucleated settlements as they obtained in the Tamil-speaking regions did not obtain and where the settlements were of a dispersed nature.

As stated earlier, the *nāḍu* was a grouping of the *vellānvagai* villages in a locality. This is explicit in a Kīranūr inscription of AD 1310 mentioned above, which speaks of the *ūrōm* of the villages Nāñjil, Peruñcēvūr, Viraikkuḍi, Cunaiyāikkuḍi and Oḍuvūr as 'qualified for the *nāḍu* of Vaḍa-Ciṟuvayil-nāḍu: *nāṭṭukkuc-camainda* = *Nāñcil-ūrkkuc-camainta* = *ūrōmum*, *peruñcēvūr-ūrkkuc-camainta* = *ūrōmum*, etc.[33] A Mannargudi inscription of AD 1239 states that "the *nāṭṭavar* of the *Taniyūr* (generally a *brahmadēya* and less frequently a temple excluded from the jurisdiction of *nāḍu* within the territories of which it was located and constituting practically a *nāḍu* in its own right) Rājadhirājacaturvēdimaṅgalam represented to a gathering of the local *sabhā*s and the *nāṭṭavar* of five other *nāḍu*s that 'they could not carry on their agricultural profession (*veḷḷāmaicceydu-kuḍiyirukka-ppoḻutil-laiyeṉṟu*)' due to the exacting nature of the tax collectors.[34] This also brings out the fact that the *nāṭṭār* consisted of *veḷḷāḷa*s. Further, in all other available cases the signatories to the transactions of the *nāḍu*s belong to the *veḷḷāḷa* community and they in most cases bear the *vēḷān* title.[35]

The *nāḍu* thus being a grouping of agricultural settlements, the *nāṭṭār*, the spokesman of those groupings, had agriculture as their prime concern. It was the *nāṭṭār* who were addressed in the Pallava, Pāṇḍya and Cōḻa copper plates granting land, and it was they who acted on the order by delimiting the boundaries, resettling the occupants and implementing the grant in other ways. This shows the ultimate acquiescence of the *nāṭṭār* to the writ of the king who appears to have reserved the right to create superior rights in land, either by removing earlier occupants or by subjecting them to the new superior rights of the donees.

Among the other functions performed by the *nāṭṭār* we see that they took care of the management of irrigation in many cases.[36] There are a number of cases where the *nāṭṭār* donate landed property, mostly to temples.[37] The *nāṭṭār* also figure as custodians of some charities made by others, in the same way that the *panmāheśvaras* and *śrīvaiṣṇavas* figure in some other records relating to land owned by temples.[38] There are cases, rare though, where the *nāḍus* receive and administer endowments from private individuals by making a remission on the tax on the piece of land donated in lieu of a specified amount of money which they took as a capital deposit.[39] The donations that the *nāḍu* made to temples, etc. are also put under the category of tax-free land which is described as *nāṭṭiṟaiyili*. The *nāḍu* undertook to pay the tax on account of such land to the state.[40] The *nāḍu* appears to have collected a due for defraying the expenses incurred on such acts.[41] Such levies were known as *nāḍāṭci*, *nāṭṭu-viniyōgam* or *nāṭṭu-vyavasthai*. There are also records relating to transactions of temple lands including leasing and sale with the involvement of the *nāṭṭār*.[42]

From the records stating that the *nāḍu* undertook to pay the taxes on lands made tax-free or *nāṭṭiṟaiyili*, it is clear that it was the *nāḍu* which assessed and collected tax on land. There are records which say that the *nāṭṭār* were responsible to pay the tax to the king's agents *kōmaṟṟavar*.[43] These records suggest that the king's agents made regular demands and collections of such dues from the *nāḍus*. There are more cases where it is given to appear as if the spokesmen of the *nāḍus* themselves acted as the agents of the state in many cases.[44] Thus, the *mudaligaḷ* who are clearly royal agents in a record of AD 1267 are 'stated to be the *mudaligaḷ* belonging to the *nāḍu*' (*nāḍu uḍaiya mudaligaḷ*);[45] a Tirumayam inscription describes a *daṇḍanāyakam* as 'of this *nāḍu*' (*in-nāḍ-uḍaiya*)[46] the earliest of this category appears to have been a Tiruvāmāttur record of AD 917 which mentions a certain Cōḻaśikhāmaṇi Pallavaraiyan as one who obtained the local *nāḍu* (*innāḍu-peṟṟa*).[47] It follows that the major landowners of a locality who formed the group known as the *nāḍu* were recognized by the state as its agents for administrative purposes. All this is clear evidence of the king's control over the *nāḍu* units, typical of a feudal political structure in which a local magnate or corporate group as a fictitious individual is recognized as the agent of the state.

There are clearer statements in some other records to show the close link between the groups of the locality called the *nāḍus* on the one hand and the royal government on the other; in fact it would appear that the former was the local expression of the latter.[48] This is clear from the fact that in questions related to land revenue, the chief source of royal revenue, it was the *nāṭṭār* who mattered most. As the *nāṭṭār* were the dominant landowners and hence the chief source of revenue, so also they came in as the most handy groups with whom the royal government could have negotiations over the assessment and settlement of land revenue. Thus, it is a recognition of this commanding position of these groups of landed magnates by the royal government that is expressed in the fact of their being addressed in making a grant of land. Further, expressions such as *nāṭṭup-puṟavu*, *nāṭṭu-vari* and *nāṭṭuk-kaṇakku*, the first two indicating the land revenue account of the *nāḍu* and the revenue account of the *nāḍu* in general respectively, and the third meaning both these accounts collectively as also the person in charge of those accounts,[49] clearly show that the *nāḍu* was the basic revenue unit. The revenue demands and collection from a village were settled in relation to the *nāḍu* locality within which it was situated. When an *ūr* made remissions of tax, corresponding deductions were made in the dues from the *nāḍu* as well.[50] When the dues from a temple were diverted by a king for instituting certain services in that temple, this was caused to be entered in both the *variyilārkaṇakku* (the revenue account of the royal government) and the *nāṭṭukkanakku*,[51] emphasizing the significance of the *nāḍu* as an integral part of the state system albeit with its local autonomy.

Burton Stein asserts that 'no contemporary documents speak of the *nāḍu* in terms the Cōḻa governmental structure or function'.[52] This is simply not the case. The instances examined above are themselves indicative of this function, with the *nāḍu* taking an active part in the revenue administration of the state. We have further evidence of officers or the king's agents concerned with the *nāḍu* and its administration. We have at least three different categories of royal agents: the *nāḍu vagai ceyvār*, the *nāḍu kūṟu ceyvār* and the *nāḍu kaṇkāṇi nāyāgam* or *nāḍu kaṇkāṭci*.

Stein takes them as functionaries of the *nāḍu* itself concerned with the maintenance of accounts and assessment.[53] It has been demonstrated that these were clearly agents of the royal government in the *nāḍu* localities and that they were not employed by the *nāḍu* groups.[54] To maintain that they were the employees of the *nāḍu* groups would imply two things: (a) the existence of specialized administrative staff appointed and maintained by the local groups which would certify to the segmentary nature of the Cōḻa state and (b) the relative lack of penetration of the 'central government' to the localities which would, again, indicate a weak centre in a segmentary state.[55] In reality, however, the evidence we have would not support this position with its implications, much as Stein would have it so. Hence, the idea that the *nāḍu* localities formed 'subordinate foci of power' does not stand the scrutiny of the evidence concerning 'specialized administrative staff'. Closely related to this position taken by Stein is his interpretation of the significance of *madhyasthan* and *madhyasthan-karaṇattān* in the Larger Leiden Plates. This has been rightly questioned by Jha[56] and Ramaswamy.[57] Besides, it has been shown that this term gets increasingly replaced by clearly identifiable royal agents in the post-Rājarāja I period, which detail gets clearly fitted into the pattern of an increasing penetration of royal power in the localities.

On account of the nature of our sources which are highly biased in favour of the temples, these officers are seen in relation to the temples; but one may reasonably believe that they did not exclusively relate to the religious institutions. Their function was not religious in character. An inscription of AD 1116 of Kulōttuṅga I is very interesting in this respect.[58] Here, a *nāḍu kūṟu* settled the affairs of a new *dēvadāna* and arranged for the services out of the income from the land. He did it expressly under the authority of a *tirumugam* (royal order) from the king, of the *ūḷvari* (a duplicate entry made in the tax register) of the *puṟavuvariyār* (an officer of the land revenue department), and of a *kaḍaiyīḍu* (deed of execution) of the *maṇḍalamudaligaḷ*. This is a clear instance of the king's government penetrating into the *nāḍu* through its agents at various levels. These officers were also charged with the work of checking and auditing the accounts of temples in the localities.[59] A *nāḍu vagai* officer is even found to be present in a meeting of the *sabhā* of a *brahmadēya* village.[60] We find the *nāḍu kaṇkāṇi* officers also in a similar role. In a Tiruviḷanguḍi inscription dated AD 1013, a certain Cikāruḍaiyān Tāyan Aḍigaḷ is clearly stated to be in the locality in charge of the *nāḍu kaṇkāṇi nāyagam* office as a subordinate (*kanmi*) of the *sēnāpati*, Muḍikoṇḍacōḻa viḻupparaiyar by name.[61] There are instances of the *nāḍu* officers, both *nāḍu vagai* and *nāḍu kaṇkāṇi nāyagam* being transferred from place to place.[62] Again, instances of the same officer who was in charge of more than one *nāḍu* are also met with.[63] This shows clearly that these officers, though acting in the *nāḍus*, were not part of the corporate group of the *nāṭṭār* and that they were agents of the royal government.

A very important aspect about the *nāṭṭār* as agents of the king's government is brought out by James Heitzman.[64] Heitzman takes up five study areas within Cōḻa state for intensive study of the problem of state formation in south India.[65] Out of these five areas, the Pudukkottai area to the south, which is the most outlying among them and ecologically the least hospitable to rice cultivation, has the largest number of references to the *nāṭṭār* groups in relation to governmental functions, in spite of the fact that this area has yielded fewer inscriptions than the other areas.[66] In the other areas, two, Kumbakonam and Tiruchchirapalli, which have yielded larger number of inscriptions, make fewer references to the *nāṭṭār* groups.[67] In the case of the other two, viz., Tirukkoyilur in south Arcot district and Tirutturaippundi in Tanjavur district, the former was in an intermediary zone under the chiefly rule of the Malaiyamāns and, following the pattern that we have seen elsewhere, the period of Rājarāja and his immediate successors found a greater penetration of the Cōḻa king's government there in the form of the royal functionaries present in the inscriptions.[68] In the case of the latter, which represented the tail-end of the irrigation channels and which has been described by Heitzman as a political backwater, the situation was comparable to that which obtained in the other two areas in the core territories.[69] Again, in the Pudukkottai area, which has the maximum number of references to the *nāṭṭār*, most of these references are noted to be of either of the pre-Rājarāja or post-Virarājēndra periods.[70] This suggests the very important fact that state function in the more outlying areas was carried out by and through the *nāṭṭār* groups as much as it was done directly in the core regions and by the chiefly families in the intermediate regions of Cōḻa political authority and that in the period of Rājarāja and his immediate successors, there was a greater attempt at centralization which aimed at steamrolling the entire territory as a single political system. This finding in relation to the period AD 985–1070 is exactly in the same pattern that we have demonstrated elsewhere[71]: of a greater penetration of state functionaries, a ramified 'revenue department' and a corresponding eclipse of chiefly rule wherever it prevailed. In other words, the evidence we have about the *nāḍu* also conforms to the situation obtaining in relation to other aspects of the governmental structure. This, however, will have to be further elaborated.

Though thus subject to the administrative control of the state's agents, the *nāṭṭār* still were a cohesive group of landowners within a locality. From the large number of records pertaining to the group called *nāḍu* examined by Subbarayalu, there is no evidence to suggest that there was a head, a leader, a president, of this group.[72] It functioned collectively. As in identifying a 'chief village' as an 'inner core' of the *nāḍu* and distinguishing among three types of *nāḍus*, so in attributing a leader to the *nāṭṭār*, Stein is not backed by any evidence. He states:

> The deltaic portion of Chola-mandalam can be designed the central area of the central domain of the Chola segmentary state. It was here that the power of the kings from Rajaraja I to Kulottunga I was concentrated; this was their *nāḍu;* they were the leaders of its *nāṭṭār.*[73]

In reality, however, the evidence we have is far from sufficient to support this position. For one thing, there is nothing on record to show that there was a chief, a president, of the *nāṭṭār* group. Stein grants such a position to the holders of the titles such as *uḍaiyāns*, *araiyans*, *mūvēndavēḷāns*, and the like, always equating them with the so-called feudatories.[74] This, as we have shown elsewhere, is not warranted.[75] They were landed magnates with a different character altogether. In fact, among the very few cases where the personal identity of the members of the *nāḍu* assembly is known, most held one of these titles, many sporting the same title, which, by extending Stein's logic, would suggest that there were too many chiefs in one *nāḍu*. And none of them is described as the chief or presiding member of the group.

If thus there was no chief among the *nāṭṭār*, that will have major implications for the understanding of the nature of state under the Cōḻas. The identity of the Cōḻa rulers as one among the chiefs of the many *nāḍus* as Burton Stein would have it, is lost in favour of a more conservative picture of their being rulers of a monarchical state. Second, in the absence of chiefs in them, the *nāḍus* would no longer answer to the description of being miniature replicas of the political system obtaining in the centre; that is to say, the major argument concerning the segmentary nature of the Cōḻa state is proved to be invalid.

Thus, it would follow from the above examination that although the smallest identifiable peasant community in south India in this period was the *ūr* or the agrarian village, it was not the spokesmen of the *ūr* village that were taken into consideration in the copper plate charters and other records for purposes of land settlements, etc., this recognition being reserved to the larger locality group, viz. the *nāḍu*. These *nāḍu* groups are seen as preexisting groupings of peasant settlements, spontaneously come together. They were recognized by the state in medieval south India under the Pallavas, Pāṇḍyas and Cōḻas as its agents to carry out the royal writ as in the case of the settlement of land, creation of superior right over it, assessment of revenue, and so on. As the state grew and sought to centralize authority and power, the autonomy and aggressiveness of these groups dwindled, and we see direct penetration of the state through its officialdom into areas where the *nāḍu* and its spokesmen, the *nāṭṭār*, functioned as the state agents even in the more peripheral regions of the Cōḻa state. This is a picture which is in conformity with other aspects of polity in south India that we have appreciated elsewhere—a polity with a largely decentralized character, attempting at a certain point in time to achieve a degree of centralization which, however, was foiled by the centrifugal forces of a typically feudal nature.[76] Again, our findings would suggest that the details would not agree with the formulation of a segmentary state with subordinate foci of power functioning as replicas of the centre, with a chief, a head-quarters and a specialized administrative staff repeating at each of such foci.

NOTES AND REFERENCES

1. For a succinct account and a critique, Louis Dumont, 'The Indian Village Community from Munro to Maine', *Contributions to Indian Sociology*, old series, vol. IX, 1966, pp. 67–89.
2. Ever since the discovery and publication of the documents on the history of south India, scholars had started this exercise. The best example is S. Krishnaswami Aiyangar, *Ancient India and South Indian History and Culture* (Poona, 1941) and S.K. Aiyangar, *The Evolution of Hindu Administrative Institutions in South India*, apart from articles by V. Venkayya, H. Krishna Sastri, T.A. Gopinatha Rao and K.V. Subrahmanya Aiyar.
3. K.A. Nilakanta Sastri, *The Cōḻas* (Madras, 1975 edn), pp. 503–4; T.V. Mahalingam, *South Indian Polity* (Madras, 1975 edn), pp. 369; Sastri, *Readings in South Indian History* (Delhi, 1978), pp. 94–105, etc.
4. Y. Subbarayalu, *Political Geography of the Chola Country* (Madras, 1973); Y. Subbarayalu, 'State in Medieval South India', unpublished PhD Thesis (Madurai Kamaraj University, 1976); Y. Subbarayalu, 'The Place of Ur in the Economic and Social History of Early Tamilnadu',

paper presented at a Seminar on South Indian History organized by Indian Council Historical Research (Madras, February 1977); Burton Stein, *Peasant State and Society in Medieval South India* (Delhi, 1980), esp. pp. 90–140; Noboru Karashima, *South Indian History and Society: Studies from Inscriptions* (Delhi, 1984), esp. 'Introduction'.

5. Subbarayalu, *Political Geography*, p. 22 and Map 10.
6. Ibid., pp. 21–5, 28–9.
7. Ibid., p. 31. List of *nāḍus* with village contents in the end of the book, which is not paginated. For a similar situation in the Pāṇḍyan country, Rajan Gurukkal, 'The Agrarian System and Socio-political Organisation the Early Pandyas', unpublished PhD Thesis, Jawaharlal Nehru University (New Delhi, 1984), pp. 105–7.
8. Subbarayalu, *Political Geography*, pp. 56–71.
9. Minakshi, *Administration and Social Life*; Subbarayalu, 'State in Medieval South India', chapter on 'Territory'.
10. Rajan Gurukkal, 'The Agrarian System' pp. 107 ff.
11. Ibid.
12. M.G.S. Narayanan, *The Perumals of Kerala* (Calicut, 1996), chapter on 'Divisions of the Kingdom'.
13. Subbarayalu, *Political Geography*, p. 21.
14. Stein, *Peasant State*, pp. 97–8.
15. Ibid., pp. 99–100.
16. For Paiyampalli, *Indian Archaeology: A Review* (1964–5), pp. 22–3; (1967–8), pp. 26–30.
17. Stein, *Peasant State*, p. 107.
18. Ibid., esp. n. 32.
19. Subbarayalu, *Political Geography*, p. 31.
20. Ibid.
21. Ibid., p. 32.
22. Stein, *Peasant State*, pp. 104–5.
23. Ibid., chapter III, passim.
24. Ibid., p. 101.
25. M.G.S. Narayanan, *Reinterpretations in South Indian History* (Trivandrum, 1977), pp. 1–20.
26. Stein, *Peasant State*, p. 102.
27. Ibid., p. 100.
28. Ibid., n. 19.
29. D.D. Kosambi, *An Introduction to the Study of Indian History*, 2nd edn (Bombay, 1975), p. 1.
30. Stein, *Peasant State*, pp. 134–40.
31. In the entire section in ibid., pp. 134–40, there are only two footnotes, both of them irrelevant to the question of categorization of *nāḍus*!
32. Sastri, *The Cōḻas*, pp. 503–4; Mahalingam, *South Indian Polity*, p. 369.
33. *Inscriptions of Pudukkottai State* (hereafter *IPS*), no. 546.
34. *South Indian Inscriptions* (hereafter *SII*), vol. VI, nos 50 and 58.

35. Noboru Karashima, Y. Subbarayalu and Toru Matsui, *A Concordance of the Names in Cola Inscriptions* (Madurai 1978), 3 vols, under S13210.
36. E.g., *IPS*, no. 28.
37. *SII*, vol. XVII, nos 503, 534, 539, *Annual Reports of Epigraphy* (hereafter *ARE*) 234 of 1924.
38. *SII*, vol. VIII, nos 576, 719; vol. XIII, nos 281 (A), etc.
39. *IPS*, no. 36. This practice of commuting the tax on a piece of land for all time to come and receiving a capital deposit, the interest accrued on which was considered as in lieu of the tax, was known as *iṟai-kāval*, the capital deposit being known as *iṟai-dravyam*: Sastri, *The Cōḻas*, p. 509.
40. For *nāṭṭiṟaiyili* land, Subbarayalu, *Political Geography*, p. 39; for the *nāḍu* paying tax in such instances, *SII*, vol. XVII, no. 549.
41. *SII*, vol. vol. XVII, nos 143, 462, 540, etc.
42. *IPS*, nos 266, 281, 343, 367, 374.
43. *IPS*, nos 196, 375.
44. Thus, fitting into the pattern where the more important landed magnates were identified by the state and made use of as its agents, here also the corporate body is made use of as the state agents. Kesavan Veluthat, *The Political Structure of Early Medieval South India* (Delhi, 1993), chapter III.
45. *IPS*, no. 370, *Nāḍu-uḍaiya= mudaligaḷ* may be literally translated as *mudaligal* who 'possesses' the *nāḍu;* but as in the case of the titles with a village name + *uḍaiyān* pattern, this also has to be identified as a *mudaligaḷ* who possesses some land in the *nāḍu*. Alternatively it can also mean the *mudaligal* of the *nāḍu*.
46. *IPS*, no. 340.
47. *SII*, vol. VIII, no. 739.
48. In fact, in most cases the penetration of the state to the localities was through these bodies, although the role of royal agents themselves was of equal importance. Veluthat, *The Political Structure*.
49. Subbarayalu, *Political Geography*, p. 41.
50. *IPS*, no. 267.
51. *SII*, vol. XVII, nos 135, 143.
52. Stein, *Peasant State and Society*, p. 96.
53. Ibid., p. 111.
54. Veluthat, *The Political Structure*, chapter III.
55. Stein, *Peasant State*, p. 265.
56. D.N. Jha, 'Relevance of Peasant State and Society to Pallava-Cola Times', *Indian Historical Review*, vol. VIII, nos 1 and 2, pp. 83–4.
57. Vijaya Ramaswami, 'Peasant State and Society in Medieval South India, A Review Article', *Studies in History*, vol. IV, no. 2, pp. 310–11.
58. *IPS*, no. 126.
59. *SII*, vol. VII, no. 988.
60. *ARE*, no. 262 of 1912.

61. *IPS*, no. 90.
62. Veluthat, *Political Structure*, chapter III. Also, Subbarayalu, *Political Geography*, p. 44.
63. Subbarayalu, *Political Geography*, p. 44.
64. James Heitzman, 'State Formation in South India, 850–1280', *Indian Economic and Social History Review*, vol. XXIV, no. 1 (March, 1987), pp. 35–61.
65. Map 1 on ibid., p. 40.
66. Table 1 on ibid., p. 41 for the nature of land; n. 47 on p. 53 for the distribution of references to *nāṭṭār*.
67. Ibid., p. 53, n. 47.
68. Ibid., pp. 52–3. For our own treatment, Veluthat, *Political Structure*, chapter IV.
69. Ibid., p. 39.
70. Thirteen references to *nāṭṭār* occur in records prior to 985, seventeen in those after 1178. The time between the accession of Rājarāja I and that of Kulottunga I (985–1070) saw only five references to this group. Ibid., p. 53, n. 49.
71. Veluthat, *Political Structure*, chapters III and IV.
72. Subbarayalu, *Political Geography*, p. 39.
73. Stein, *Peasant State* p. 286.
74. Ibid., pp. 111–17.
75. Veluthat, *Political Structure*, chapter III.
76. Ibid., chapter IX.

PART II

Medieval Kerala

6

The *Kēraḷōlpatti* as History*

The form in which historical consciousness expresses itself varies from society to society, sometimes to such an extent that one society, used to its own particular notions of history, may fail or even refuse to recognize historical consciousness expressed in other forms as pertaining to history at all. In the case of India, writers of the colonial era held that India had neither a consciousness of history nor a sense of the past. They explained this lack variously: the greater concern of India with the spiritual than the material, the changelessness of Indian society, Muslim vandalism, and so on were thought to account for history being a weak point of this otherwise splendid civilization. However, the fact seems to be that, for those scholars brought up in the Rankean tradition of historical writing, any statement that was not authenticated by 'evidence' from 'contemporary sources' was less than history. What was presented as history had also to look like 'what actually happened'. Indian forms of historical writing fell short of these standards. Naturally, India was stated to have 'produced no Herodotus or Thucydides...'—a statement repeated *ad nauseum* by every third-rate textbook of Indian history.

Such refusal to accept Indian forms of historical writing as valid need not be taken as entirely innocent either: it often formed part of a larger project of rejecting a whole knowledge before establishing another in its place. The 'secure and usable past' which the colonial masters had 'invented' for the colony had to pass for, and be used, as the knowledge that would help them establish and maintain control and dominance over the colony. A necessary first step then would be

* First published as 'The *Kēraḷōlpatti* as History: A Note on Pre-colonial Traditions of Historical Writing in India', in K.N. Ganesh, ed., *Culture and Modernity: Historical Explorations* (Calicut, 2004), pp. 19–38.

to repudiate Indian forms of historical writing and knowledge, which they did in a consummate way. It came to be accepted on almost all hands that India was an ahistorical society, lacking in a sense of history and not given to maintaining authentic and accurate records of the past. The manifold specimens of historical writing from any part of the country were variously ridiculed as superstition, legend and nonsense. It will be interesting in this context to look at the instances of historical reconstruction attempted by the colonial masters. In his justly famous *Malabar Manual,* William Logan pooh-poohs the narrative called *Kēraḷōlpatti* as a 'farrago of legendary nonsense'.[1] It is not altogether beside the point that Logan, nonetheless, leans heavily on the statements in the *Kēraḷōlpatti* for his own reconstruction of the history of Kerala. Thus, even while there was a refusal to accept 'native' forms of historical writings as reliable, there was also a tacit acceptance of them, if in an attempt to pin events and personages in them down to points in space and time. What is more important in this case is the publicized rejection of the 'native' tradition than the secretive use to which they were put when it suited those scholars to do so.

In recent years, however, the statement that India was an ahistorical society has been called into question. It has been shown that India did have a sense of history; but the form in which historical consciousness expressed itself in India was not the same as what one finds in the Greco-Roman or Judaeo-Christian or post-Enlightenment traditions of Western historiography. The privileging of these Western traditions is not just a matter of Eurocentrism; it is part of the baggage of colonialism. This baggage and all that it contains are being challenged and rejected effectively in the context of the post-colonial self-understanding of the former colonies. At another level, not only is it doubted whether the expressions of a historical consciousness in the western tradition can be really taken as *the* standard, but it has also been demonstrated that other societies, too, had an equally strong or stronger tradition of historical writing.[2] No society can be really said to be devoid of a sense of history. In fact, it is even persistently argued that pre-modern societies all over the world had a greater sense of history than modern societies.[3]

Since the whole debate veers around the question of an understanding of what a sense of history is, it may be useful to begin by something of a definition. Romila Thapar defines a sense of history as 'a consciousness of past events, which events are relevant to a particular society, seen in a chronological framework and expressed in a form which meets the needs of that society'.[4] There are inadequacies about this view; but the essentials, such as the relevance of particular instances and the choice of the form, are important. If this view is accepted, it can be seen that India too, like most other ancient societies, had a clear sense of history although literature that can be specifically called historical may be lacking there in the earliest periods. Historians have prised out and appreciated veins of history embedded in the Vedic, Buddhist and Jain literatures, not to speak of full-length texts of what could be described as externalized history dating from a later period.[5] The purpose of the present essay is to look at a few expressions of such historical consciousness in narratives from pre-colonial Kerala in an attempt to identify the notions of history which obtained in this part of India. In the course of the discussion the needs of that society, which prompted the preference of certain specific forms to certain others to express that consciousness also will be taken up for examination. I intend to consider specimens which are specifically from Kerala, leaving out songs from the Tamil 'Sangam' or Bhakti literature which are products of a cultural idiom not typically Keralan, although they are heavily historical and extremely relevant to Kerala.

I want to begin by speaking about an absence before I take up the presences for discussion. Typical of south India, or nearly the whole of Indian subcontinent, in the early medieval period is a profusion of what are known as *praśastis*.[6] This genre of literature has been a form in which historical consciousness found its expression in early medieval India. The *praśastis* form largely prefaces to inscriptions recording grant of land and contain, generally, a supposedly historical account of the dynasty of the donor in whose honour they are composed. Usually there is a recitation of the tradition, real or invented, regarding the origin of the dynasty, a somewhat detailed description of the 'career and achievements' of the immediate ancestors of a patron, and then a dwelling at some length on the patron himself.[7] All these items use a particularly manufactured image of the past and, in every case, that image would be used in the validation of the new political forms which came into existence in different regions in the subcontinent in the early medieval period. The *praśasti* begins to make its appearance as a form of expressing historical consciousness from the time of the Guptas (AD fourth century) onwards in early medieval India. It went a long way in legitimizing the new monarchical state and the monarch in it in south India in the period of the Pallavas (AD seventh century) and later.[8]

It is interesting that there is a conspicuous absence of such *praśastis* in Kerala, even while a new state, contemporaneous with and comparable to other early medieval states of the deep south, was very much in existence in the Cēra kingdom of Mahōdayapuram. This enigma cries out for an answer. M.G.S. Narayanan, an acknowledged authority on the history of this kingdom, has suggested that the Cēras had little to boast of in their ancestry since they followed the matrilineal order of succession.[9] This argument does not hold much water because ancestry is ancestry, whatever the system of succession. Any system is as good or as bad as any other, and there is nothing that makes patriliny better than matriliny except under the tutelage of a particular discourse. The one in Kerala, if anything, was in favour of matriliny. In fact, in the *Mūṣikavamśakāvya,* a dynastic chronicle from the northern part of Kerala dating from the period of the Cēra kingdom itself (AD eleventh century), the poet describes elaborately the genealogy and also the fact of matrilineal succession in the chiefly house of Kōlam in the historical period.[10]

An alternative possibility, therefore, is that the form in which Kerala society expressed its consciousness of past events, and the events themselves it chose to record, were different from what obtained elsewhere in south India. The needs of society seem to have been different in this case. It is clear that the state that came into existence in Kerala under the Cēras of Mahōdayapuram was characteristically different from its contemporaries in other parts of south India.[11] For one thing, there was a much heavier Brāhmaṇical presence in the political economy of Kerala—the Brāhmaṇas are presented as the 'power behind the throne' in that kingdom—and, more than the genealogy and status of the ruling house or its claim to legitimacy through a particular origin myth or celebrated ancestors, it was the fact of the subservience of the ruler to the Brāhmaṇa groups that needed emphasis and sanction. The kind of legitimacy that those in power in Kerala wanted to seek was hence different from what it was elsewhere. The *praśasti,* with its concern with the origins and succession of the ruling house, was hardly the tool for this. Naturally, therefore, those sections in Kerala society avoided this form of expressing the consciousness of the past as it failed to meet the specific needs of society. The *praśasti* failed to take roots there.[12] There were, however, other forms of expressing a consciousness of the past.

I shall now turn to the much-maligned *Kēraḷōlpatti* and show it as one such form through which the elite in Kerala chose to express its historical consciousness from time to time. The *Kēraḷōlpatti* is a narrative in somewhat Sanskritized Malayalam prose, giving an account of Kerala's history from the creation of the land by the inevitable Paraśurāma, expressed in the style of Purāṇic exposition. There are many recensions and more copies of this book, at least half a dozen available in print and many more that number in palm leaf manuscripts. In fact, many old houses of landlords and local chieftains had in their collection one or more copies of it, a fact which has interest for us. Even a Tamil translation is available. It is also important that the standard way in which the book ends is by saying that it is the work of Tuñcattu Rāmānujan Eḻuttacchan, the seventeenth-century Malayalam poet who was responsible for popularizing the Purāṇic lore among the non-Brāhmaṇa aristocracy of Kerala through his translations of *Mahābhārata* and *Rāmāyaṇa* in *Kiḷippāṭṭu* metres.

Historians in the past have taken widely varying positions, ranging from describing it as 'a farrago of legendary nonsense' and as 'having attained the rank of authentic history'.[13] Attempts to study it were centred on the question of accepting or rejecting the veracity of statements related to heroes (or villains) and events in this narrative. Thus Paraśurāma or Śaṅkarācārya or Cēramān *Perumāḷ* or the *Paṭamēl Nāyar* or the creation of Brāhmaṇical settlements or the conversion of the last *Perumāḷ* or the partition of Kerala were all variously accepted, rejected, or explained away by those who worked on the history of Kerala using the narrative. In other words, the concern of those scholars was with the *historicity* or otherwise of the narrative, rather than the *historical consciousness* expressed in it or its social function. Thus, they failed to identify or appreciate the narrative as an expression of the sense of history shown by Kerala society.

The *Kēraḷōlpatti* is, to be sure, not to be taken for a work that would satisfy modern sensibilities of chronology, causation and generalization. Its chronology is not absolute, and where there is mention of absolute chronology in terms of the Kali era or the Christian era (as in Hermann Gundert's edition), the dates are hopelessly inaccurate, abounding in anachronisms and impossible correspondences. There are minor confusions in terms of geography as well. It has, naturally, failed to make the grade as 'history' in the assessment of modern historians. However, after scholars of an earlier generation dismissed it as a bundle of legends, there has been an increasing appreciation of the fact that the *Kēraḷōlpatti* is

> not to be rejected outright but to be used with caution. The statements made there should not be accepted at their face value. However, they contain references which supplement and clarify evidence obtained from other sources of information though it reflects interest and prejudice and suffers from interpolation as well as misinterpretation.[14]

This is a great leap forward. In fact, M.G.S. Narayanan has brought out many instances mentioned in the narrative which get attested by other sources, thereby showing the validity and authenticity, if not accuracy, of the statements there. Moreover, there is an attempt to appreciate the social function of the narrative in Narayanan's work, although he does not develop it to the logical conclusion. His exercise, pioneering as it is, remains nevertheless at the level of looking at *Kēraḷōlpatti* yet as a *source* of history, accepting or rejecting the historicity of individual statements contained in it.

My purpose here is to look at the *Kēraḷōlpatti* as a narrative of history which tells the story of Kerala right from the creation of the land. I will argue that it exhibits a sense of history inasmuch as there is in it 'a consciousness of past events, which events are relevant to a particular society, seen in a chronological framework and expressed in a form which meets the needs of that society'. An examination of these events and how they are represented here will clarify the extent of historical consciousness that it exhibits. Which of the past events were thought to be more relevant than others will also show the interests and concerns of society and explain, at least partly, the choice of the form for expressing them. The discussion will show also that history was used here as elsewhere as 'a handmaid of authority'.[15]

Different versions of the *Kēraḷōlpatti* are available. All of them, however, share the same structure with a more or less uniform chronological scheme. It falls into three broad periods, namely 'the Age of Paraśurāma', 'the Age of the *Perumāḷs*' and 'the Age of the *Tampurāns*'.[16] The variations in the different versions are related largely to the third period, that is, the age of the *Tampurāns*, namely the period of the petty locality chieftains in the post-twelth century period of Kerala history. There are also variations in relation to the position that different castes are given in different versions of the

Kēraḷōlpatti, with a clear social purpose where the position of particular castes is sought to be defined as something of a charter of social validation. The details in relation to the earlier periods tally in a broad manner, probably showing a common source of the tradition in those two sections. I have used here the version related to the kingdom of the Zamorins in Calicut.[17] I make cross-references to a few other versions where relevant, particularly to the one related to the *rājā* of Kōlattunāḍ in the north.[18] I confine myself to statements of a political nature, the social aspects being the subject of a separate study.

The *Kēraḷōlpatti* begins with an account of Paraśurāma's creation of Kerala, the land between Gōkarṇa and Kanyākumāri, by raising it from the Arabian Sea with a fling of his axe and settling it by Brāhmaṇas brought from the north in sixty-four *grāmas*, of which thirty-two are in Tuḷunāḍ and thirty-two in present-day Kerala. Scholars in the past have looked upon this as an attempt to explain some mysterious geological phenomenon in terms of a divine intervention. However, it is important to see that this is not a tradition prevalent in Kerala alone. One sees this, at dates earlier than the references pertaining to Kerala, in relation to regions further north on the west coast. In fact, it is seen first in relation to Gujarat. Then it moves down to the Sopara region in Maharashtra, and further south to what is known as the *Sapta-koṅkaṇas* before reaching the Canarese coast. Scholars have noted the moving character of this legend.[19] It has been suggested that a legend migrated from the north to the south along the coast, which is indication that it represented a moving chain of group migration, the migrants carrying with them the tradition that Paraśurāma created *their* land and donated it to *them*. The Brāhmaṇical groups wanted to remember this as an important item in relation to their past, as the control they had in large areas of land received considerable sanction from this memory.

Speaking about the way in which Paraśurāma peopled the land of Kerala after raising it from the sea, the *Kēraḷōlpatti* says that the Brāhmaṇas who were brought and settled in the first instance would not stay; they returned to their original home in Ahicchatra for fear of serpents in the new land. Paraśurāma brings a second wave of Brāhmaṇas from Ahicchatra. In order that they would not be accepted if they returned, he has their hair style and style of clothing changed. He also persuades them to accept matriliny so that he could expiate for his own matricidal sin; but only the house of one village, namely

Payyannūr, would oblige. Paraśurāma also establishes 108 temples each for Śiva and Durgā. He selects 36000 Brāhmaṇas from the different grāmas and confers on them the right to arms (*śastrabhikṣā*), so that they could protect their land themselves.

Following the battle royal between historians who rejected *Kēraḷōlpatti* as legendary nonsense on the one side and those who accepted it as authentic history on the other, there have been attempts of another kind in the historiography of Kerala going on for the past two or three decades now. For instance, the story of the creation of the land by Paraśurāma by raising it from the sea is identified as something that was not exclusive to Kerala, and that it indicated the fact of a long chain of migration along the west coast of peninsular India. All the speculation about the story being an explanation of some geological phenomenon is put to rest, as it should be now applied to other parts of the peninsula. Similarly, all the thirty-two *grāma*s mentioned in the text, except one, have been identified with the help of inscriptions, literature, monuments, and surviving ethnic traditions. The meetings of their committees are now better known from other records, the details of which correspond to the indications in the *Kēraḷōlpatti*. The curious group of fighting Brāhmaṇas, on whom Paraśurāma conferred *śastrabhikṣā*, are identified with the prominent group of what are known as the *cāttirar* or *caṭṭar*. Their organization of the *śālai*, where military training was part of the curriculum, has been studied extensively. Their presence in inscriptions and medieval literature has been a subject of engaging study.

In this context, a comparison of the Paraśurāma tradition obtaining in South Canara and Kerala will be interesting. The story in relation to South Canara is told in the Kannada text, *Grāmapaddhati*.[20] The account of the creation of the land and its donation to the Brāhmaṇas occurs in both regions, but the latter part is not represented in the *Grāmapaddhati* with as much importance as it is in the *Kēraḷōlpatti*. In the *Grāmapaddhati* version, the sage creates Brāhmaṇas from out of fishermen and donates the land to them. Subsequently, as they turn out to be ungrateful to him, he curses them and turns them into untouchables.[21] According to the *Grāmapaddhati*, the Brāhmaṇa settlements in coastal Karnataka are, thus, not survivals of the ones created by Paraśurāma. They date from a much later period, and are established by Mayūravarman Kadamba or even later. Here is the crucial difference between the situations in Kerala and South Canara, and it is a significant indication of the difference in the role of the Brāhmaṇical groups in the two societies. The landed wealth in South Canara was not under the control of the Brāhmaṇical groups as much as it was in Kerala and, therefore, the importance that the Brāhmaṇas of Kerala had in polity and society was not matched by what their counterparts in South Canara had. As it was much greater in the case of Kerala, it would take none less than Paraśurāma to be not only the creator of the land but also the donor to the Brāhmaṇa groups. So also the exceptional importance attached to the arms-bearing Brāhmaṇas called *śastrabrāhmaṇas* or *cāttirar* and their group meetings[22] is another instance of the use of the past in seeking validation for the Brāhmaṇical groups in Kerala society. Paraśurāma establishes a *brahmakṣatra* in Kerala, where Brāhmaṇas looked after the work of the Kṣatriyas, with every arrangement for the welfare of the people, including religion, administration and law. The Brāhmaṇical authority in Kerala was so great that it took a Brāhmaṇical *avatāra* of Viṣṇu, with sufficient Kṣatriya pretensions, to do the job.

In the period that followed, too, it is interesting that the text shows that the Brāhmaṇical groups had played a major role in society and politics. Representatives of the Brāhmaṇical establishment govern the land gifted to them by Paraśurāma as *brahmakṣatra*. In course of time, however, they realized that the business of governance corrupted them, and they themselves decide to a get a Kṣatriya as their ruler. Accordingly, a Kṣatriya and his sister are brought; the brother is anointed king who is made to swear habitual allegiance to them. A monarchical state was established in Kerala. The sister is married to a Brāhmaṇa and it is agreed that the progeny would be Kṣatriya according to the matrilineal system of succession. The descendants of this sister would be the successors to the throne. The conviction that the business of governance is not the Brāhmaṇas' cup of tea and that it belongs to the Kṣatriya is very much in tune with the Brāhmaṇical principles and the theory of *varṇāśramadharma*, which expressed the ideology of the ruling class in early medieval India in general. At the same time, there is no attempt to latch the origin of the dynasty on to one of the reputed Kṣatriya lineages of Purāṇic fame; nor is an origin myth in the tradition typical of the medieval court literature in Sanskrit invented or the heroic deeds of the ruler or his ancestors recited. On the other hand, the progeny of a union between a Brāhmaṇa male and a Kṣatriya female is recognized as Kṣatriya, even at the expense of contradicting the *Śāstra* rules of *sankīrṇajāti,* obviously following the matrilineal system of succession obtaining in Kerala. That the ruler was himself both a Kṣatriya through matrilineal inheritance and the son of a Brāhmaṇa by birth was sanction enough! After this, the kings were enjoined to listen to what the representatives of the Brāhmaṇical establishment would dictate to them through their body of the *Nālu Taḷi,* which acted as a council of the king.

Many details here have lured historians in the past; but, in the absence of what the Rankean tradition of historiography would call 'corroborative evidence', it was not quite possible for any of them to accept or reject these statements, except at the level of assertions and wishful thinking. From the middle of the previous century, however, a number of inscriptions dating from the ninth century onwards have been discovered and published. They have been subjected to a critical study within the discipline of historical method as well. They bear out many statements contained in the *Kēraḷōlpatti.* For instance, Mahōdayapuram or Koṭuṅṅallūr was the capital of Kerala. The members of that dynasty which ruled from there followed matrilineal descent. The ruler was known as the *Perumāḷ.* He was under the habitual tutelage of the Brāhmaṇical establishment. He had a council of advisors called the Nālu Taḷi, every detail of which corresponds in the inscriptions, medieval literature and the *Kēraḷōlpatti.*

A definitive and exhaustive study of the history of the Cēra kingdom of Mahōdayapuram has brought out several interesting details about the nature of polity there. It has effectively brought out the overwhelming importance of the Brāhmaṇas there, who functioned as 'the real power behind the throne'.[23] This position of theirs has been shown owing to the fact that they controlled the best agricultural land in the fertile river valleys of Kerala; and the resultant command they had in economy and society reflected itself in the political structure as well. The polity with such overwhelming importance of the Brāhmaṇical groups in it required a legitimation different from what was used and found successful elsewhere in contemporary south India. Thus, the story of Paraśurāma creating the land and donating it to Brāhmaṇas, the Brāhmaṇas carrying out the governance of the land upon the bidding of Paraśurāma, the Brāhmaṇas themselves creating the ruler in every sense of the term, and the ruler being habitually obedient to them are all motifs which would be extremely useful in this unique means of legitimation. The difference between the Kerala tradition in expressing a sense of the past on the one hand and its Tamil or Kannada counterparts on the other lay in this difference in the composition of the two societies: the predominance of the Brāhmaṇical groups in the former. The *Kēraḷōlpatti* is unique in relation to this period: it is a Brāhmaṇical document par excellence and, as such, records those events of the past which it thought were relevant to the Brāhmaṇical groups of Kerala society. The form that it chose, too, was most suited to the needs of the Brāhmaṇical groups in society.

There are other aspects of the *Kēraḷōlpatti* that are important and relevant in relation to the age of the Perumāḷs, that is, this second chronological phase. The ways in which Nampūtiri heroes like Āḻvāñcēri Tamprākkaḷ[24] or Vāsu Bhaṭṭatiri[25] or, most of all, Śaṅkarācārya[26] are treated are cases in point. Of particular interest is Śaṅkarācārya. If we are to believe the biographies of the great teacher ascribed to his own disciples, he owed hardly anything to Kerala and she had no claims on him to boast about.[27] But, after he became a celebrity, he was shamelessly appropriated and the origin of anything that needed sanction in the Brāhmaṇa-dominated society of Kerala was attributed to him. Thus, the beginning of the Kollam Era, the introduction of the graduated scale of untouchability for different castes, the peculiar codes of conduct for the Brāhmaṇas of Kerala, etc. were all presented as gifts of the great *Advaita* philosopher! The fact that the *Kēraḷōlpatti* is a Brāhmaṇical document aimed at the validation of the Brāhmaṇical groups through a particular use of history is underlined in all these instances. The way in which the arms-bearing Brāhmaṇas who had a major presence in medieval Kerala society and their group meetings [28] is described in the accounts is another instance of the use of the past in seeking validation for those groups which enjoyed and sought to perpetuate status.

The account about the end of the Perumāḷ regime is also interesting. The *Kēraḷōlpatti* says that as the last Perumāḷ overstayed and thus incurred the sin of misappropriating the wealth of the Brāhmaṇas, he wanted to expiate for it. But since it was too serious an offence to be expiated according to the provisions of the four Vedas and six *śāstras*, he decided to accept the fifth Veda. Accordingly, he abdicated the throne, divided the kingdom among his sons and relatives, and left for Mecca after accepting Islam.

Writers from at least the sixteenth century have repeated and commented on this tradition in one way or the other. Suggestions that would support one or the other aspect of the story are there in the sources. They include a sense of guilt which the last *Perumāḻ* had about wronging the Brāhmaṇas, his attempts to atone for it, the chronological sequence of the disappearance of the last Perumāḷ and the appearance of independent rulers in many principalities, the appearance of the first datable mosques in Kerala at the same time, and so on. And nearly all rulers of what could be described as the 'successor states' claimed a gift of the last Perumāḷ at the beginning of their kingdom and dynasty.

The next chronological phase in the *Kēraḷōlpatti* is related to 'the age of *Tampurāns*'.[29] Historically, this corresponds to the period following the end of the Perumāḷ era in AD twelfth century. The character of the narrative suddenly changes in this section in a big way. The role that the Brāhmaṇical groups have to play now is little, if any. It is the newly emerging political power, and the support it had from trading groups, that are highlighted in this section. In Gundert's version, for example, the fortunes of the kingdom of Calicut are taken up. A gift of the last *Perumāḷ* to two Ēṟāṭi brothers is presented as marking the origin of the kingdom: of a strip of useless land and a few equally insignificant symbols of royalty such as a piece of rusted sword and a broken conch. The throne (or any piece of ramshackle furniture that pretended as one) of any ruler in the post-Cēra period was presented as a similar gift from the *Perumāḷ*. Again, when the growth of the kingdom of Calicut is taken up, the military aggrandizement of the Zamorin comes in, unlike in the case of the *Perumāḷ* in an earlier period. The Ēṟāṭi brothers push forward, following the *Perumāḷ*'s leave 'to annexe [territories] by dying and killing'.[30] The support that they got from the trading groups, especially the Muslims, is treated at some length.[31] So also, the various nodes of power in the localities with the Nāyar landed elements occupying a crucial place in the power structure are acknowledged. The medieval festival of *māmākam* is described elaborately, where the Zamorin of Calicut is presented as the veritable sovereign of the whole of Kerala.[32]

As I have suggested above, there are many differences in the nature and content of the narrative from this point on. For one thing, there is the recognition that political power is more a function of military aggrandizement. Second, in a region with few Brāhmaṇical settlements and therefore limited Brāhmaṇical control over agricultural land, the real power behind the throne was different from what it was under the *Perumāḷs*. At the same time, there were a large number of local landed magnates who were incorporated into the political system as so many *sāmanta* 'feudatories', civil and military functionaries of the state in the localities, managers looking after the private estates of the ruler and other members of his family in different parts of the kingdom and other elements of the 'bureaucracy', such as it was.[33] There was also the considerable wealth that trade, particularly Arab, fetched to the port of Calicut. At the same time, the relatively inferior ritual status of the family of the Zamorins was something that they cherished not exactly with pride. Rituals in temples such as the *paṭṭattānam* or the *māmākam* helped somewhat in getting over this disability as also the royal courtly rituals, where the Brāhmaṇas condescended to bless the Zamorin and the junior princes. A historical narrative had to take all these realities into consideration; and the *Kēraḷōlpatti* promptly did it. The down-to-earth political, and to a considerable extent secular, character of the historical narrative is hard to miss in this section of the *Kēraḷōlpatti*.

Interestingly, this section in the Kōlattunāḍ tradition of *Kēraḷōlpatti* follows the period of the *Mūṣikavamśakāvya,* another specimen of historical writing from the same region. The latter is a typical dynastic chronicle and has been written about elaborately by scholars since its discovery.[34] It typically participates in the tradition of historical writing in India known as dynastic chronicles that came up in the post-Gupta period, legitimizing the newly emerging kingdoms in the regions. The function of the *Mūṣikavamśakāvya* too was not different. It is significant that the *Mūṣikavamśakāvya* pertains to a *nāḍu* division that contested, with varying degrees of success, the overlordship of the *Perumāḷs* of Mahōdayapuram. The way in which it related itself to the *Perumāḷs* was different from that of other *nāḍus* in Kerala in this period.[35] Is it possible that, given this proclivity of that *nāḍu* to claim autonomy, it used well known, successful techniques of political validation? One is tempted all the more when one considers that *Udayavarmacaritam,* the first 'historical biography' from Kerala, is related to a king of this house ruling immediately after this period.[36] These two aspects, namely the existence of a separate dynastic chronicle and the fact of the first 'historical biography' in Kerala coming from this region, however, need further elaboration and analysis.

My argument here is that Kerala too had a sense of history, which it expressed in forms that were found most suitable for its needs.

History being generally a record of the activities of socio-political status groups, those who have status at different times find a place in recorded history. Where it was a social group like the Brāhmaṇas which enjoyed power and wielded control of resources, they found themselves in the centre-stage. When in a later period status came to be defined in different terms, an alternative form for expressing historical consciousness is devised. In the earlier sections of the *Kēraḷōlpatti,* one sees what seems to be a larger-than-life picture of the Brāhmaṇical groups. Later on, when political power was in the hands of other groups which had less respect for the Brāhmaṇical groups, the concern of historical writing also gets shifted to those who are at different nodes of power. Hence we see in the *Kēraḷōlpatti* a large number of non-Brāhmaṇa chiefs figuring with prominence in the 'Age of Tampūrans', whether it is in the kingdom of Calicut or of Kōlattunāḍ. As history is basically a charter of validation for status groups in society, there is a greater concern at this later stage with these non-Brāhmaṇa sections as much as there was with the Brāhmaṇical sections in an earlier period. In short, I beg to submit in this preliminary report on a reading of *Kēraḷōlpatti* that Kerala, or India for that matter, was not a society entirely devoid of a sense of the past and that the different forms which that sense of history took to express itself eminently suited the needs of society from time to time.

I do believe that there is a case for taking up all expressions of historical consciousness from the region and subjecting them to analysis within the social and political context in which they were written. Such exercises in relation to different parts of the country will bring out the way in which Indian civilization perceived the past. Apart from giving the lie to the statement that India was an ahistorical society, it will also hopefully throw light on one of the significant systems of knowledge in Indian society and the function that it had to serve.

NOTES AND REFERENCES

1. William Logan, *Malabar Manual,* (Madras, 1887) ed. by P.J. Cherian with detailed studies and notes (Thiruvananthapuram, 2000), chapter III, 'History' esp. pp. 221–44. In spite of this rejection, much of Logan's formulation on the early history of Kerala with AD 825 as a central date hinges on accepting the statements in *Kēraḷōlpatti.* For situating Logan within the historiographical context of colonial India, Kesavan Veluthat, 'Logan's *Malabar.* Text and Context' in Cherian, ed., *Malabar Manual,* pp. xxxvi–xlvii.

2. J.H. Plumb, *Death of the Past* (Harmondsworth, 1973), esp. pp. 17–33.
3. Ibid., esp. pp. 34–50.
4. I borrow this definition from Romila Thapar, 'The Tradition of Historical Writing in Early India' in *Ancient Indian Social History: Some Interpretations* (New Delhi, 1978), p. 268.
5. This geological analogy is proposed by Romila Thapar, 'Society and Historical Consciousness: The *Itihasa-purana* Tradition', in *Interpreting Early India* (New Delhi, 1992), p. 137.
6. For an engaging discussion of 'the early medieval' and the rise of regional states there, B.D. Chattopadhyaya, *The Making of Early Medieval India* (New Delhi, 1994), esp. pp. 17–34 and pp. 183–222. I have taken up this problem, if slightly differently, in my Presidential Address to the Medieval Indian History Section of the Bangalore session of the Indian History Congress. Kesavan Veluthat, 'Into the 'Medieval'and Out of it: Early South India in Transition', *Proceedings of the Indian History Congress* (Bangalore, 1997). Chapter 1 above.
7. For discussions on the *praśastis*, J.G. de Casparis, 'Inscriptions and South Asian Dynastic Traditions', in R.J. Moore, ed., *Tradition and Politics in South Asia* (New Delhi, 1979); George Spencer, 'Heirs Apparent: Fiction and Function in Chola Mythical Genealogies', *Indian Social and Economic History Review,* vol. XXI, no. 4, 1984. I have examined how the *praśastis* were used in the validation of the newly emerging political context of south India in the early medieval period. Kesavan Veluthat, *The Political Structure of Early Medieval South India* (Delhi, 1993), pp. 29–69.
8. For further details about this function of the *praśastis* in early medieval south India, Veluthat, *Political Structure,* pp. 29–69.
9. M.G.S. Narayanan, *Perumals of Kerala: Political and Social Conditions of Kerala under the Cera Perumals of Makotai* (*c.* AD *800–1124*) (Calicut, 1996), p. 85.
10. K. Raghavan Pillai, ed., *The Musikavamsakavya of Atula* (Trivandrum, 1977), *sarga* XI, VV., 62–90, presents a story of a shift from patriliny to matriliny in the succession in that house. Historians in the past, in fact, have taken this as 'historical' and explained it as resulting from the conquest of the Mūṣika territory by the Cēras of Kerala who were followers of the matrilineal system. What is more likely is that the Sanskrit poet explained what to him and his readers would look like an 'aberrant phenomenon'—the case of matriliny in a Kṣatriya house—by means of a mythical incident placed in the twilight of the remote and the recent pasts. In any case, what is important here is that the fact of matriliny being the system of inheritance in that house in the historical period does not stop the court poet from singing the praise of the ancestors of the patron and preparing elaborate genealogies. For a study of the *kāvya*, C. Girija, 'The Mūṣikavamśa Kāvya: A Study', unpublished MPhil Dissertation (Mangalore University, 1990).
11. I have brought out this difference in Veluthat, *Political Structure.*

12. In fact, it will be wrong to believe that Kerala did not know the *praśasti* at all. A copper plate record from Kerala dated AD 1188, contained in the Kollūr Maḍham Plates, describes itself as a reissue of an earlier '*praśasti*'. *Travancore Archaeological Series,* vol. IV, no.7, pp. 22–65. However, it is not a *praśasti* in the strict sense of the term, as none of the elements related to the structure and functions of the *praśasti* is present there. The term is used in the sense of a grant!
13. For the former statement, Logan, n.1 above. The latter statement is of V. Nagam Aiya, *Travancore State Manual* (Trivandrum, 1906), p. 210. Elamkulam P.N. Kunjan Pillai, *Caritrattinte Pascattalattil* (Kottayam, 1961), p. 37 believed that the *Kēraḷōlpatti* contains 'stories concocted by a Nampūtiri on a fine morning with a view to supporting the story of Paraśurāma'.
14. Narayanan, *Perumals of Kerala,* pp. 9–20. Narayanan has established the historicity of many statements contained in the text. Ibid, passim. The present writer followed this line in an attempt to identify the Brāhmaṇa settlements mentioned in Kerala. Kesavan Veluthat, *Brāhmaṇ Settlements in Kerala: Historical Studies* (Calicut University, 1978), pp. 20–38.
15. Plumb, *Death of the Past,* p. 33.
16. Hermann Gundert, ed., *Kēraḷōlpatti (the Origin of Malabar),* (Mangalore, 1868) has, in fact, given these as three sub-headings, probably a contribution of the editor. Although the other versions do not give these sub-headings, the neat division, without overlap, is hard to miss in them. The references below are to the edition of eight works of Gundert brought together with a prefatory study by Scaria Zacharia, *Keralolpathiyum Mattum* (Kottayam, 1992).
17. Ibid.
18. M.R. Raghava Varier, ed., *Keraḷōlpatti Granthavari (the Kolattunad Traditions),* (Calicut University, 1984).
19. Many scholars have studied the Paraśurāma tradition in relation to the west coast. F.E. Pargiter, *Ancient Indian Historical Tradition* (London, 1922), pp. 106 ff.; V.S. Sukhtankar, 'The Bhrugus and the Bharathas', *Annals* of *the Bhandarkar Oriental Research Institute,* vol. XVIII, pp. 1–76; A.D. Pusalkar, 'Paraśurāma and the Konkan', in P.K. Narayana Pillai, ed., *Kerala Studies* (Trivandrum, 1955); B.A. Saletore, *Ancient Karnataka:* vol. I, *History of the Tuluva* (Poona, 1936), pp. 1–30. The work of Saletore is of particular interest to us as he deals with the region neighbouring on the north. A recent study by Pradeep Kant Chaudhary, 'The Cult of Parashuram: the Making of an Avatar', unpublished PhD Thesis (Delhi University, 2001) makes an analysis of the Paraśurāma tradition in its various aspects. Narayanan, *Perumals of Kerala,* has made a brilliant analysis of this in relation to Kerala. See also Veluthat, *Brahman Settlements in Kerala.*
20. There are various versions of the *Grāmapaddhati,* too, like *Kēraḷōlpatti.* For a study, Nagendra E. Rao, 'The Historical Tradition of South Canara

and the Brahmanial Groups: A Study of Gramapaddhati and Sahyadrikhanda', unpublished MPhil dissertation (Mangalore University, 1995). I have used the version *Grāmapaddhati,* ed. by Krishniah Holla (Balanadu, 1924).

21. Kesavan Veluthat, 'Non-Brahmana Protest in Brāhmaṇical Literary expressions: The *Gramapaddhati* from South Canara', an unpublished paper, 1995.
22. Zacharia, ed., *Kerlolpathiyum,* pp. 156–7, 172–5. This group of arms-bearing Brāhmaṇas was an enigma in the history of Kerala. Elamkulam Kunjan Pillai was the first scholar to explain it sensibly. He presented it in the context of education, where Brāhmaṇa boys were given instruction in both the use of arms and in the 'academic' disciplines. M.G.S. Narayanan pursued it further and brought out the significance of the Brāhmaṇa groups in the historical records of Kerala, in the process appreciating the significance of the statements in the *Kēraḷōlpatti.* For details, M.G.S. Narayanan, *Aspects* of *Aryanisation in Kerala* (Trivandrum, 1973), chapter on 'Bachelors of Science'. Following the trail suggested by him, I have sought to explain the existence of the phenomenon all over India, something which earlier writers had missed out. Kesavan Veluthat, 'The Cattas and Bhattas: A New Interpretation', *Proceedings* of *the Indian History Congress* (Aligarh, 1975).
23. Narayanan, *Perumals of Kerala.*
24. Zacharia, ed., *Kerlolpathiyum,* pp. 176, 179–80. Āḻvāñcēri Tampṟākkaḷ is a Brāhmaṇa of great religious merit and spiritual traditions, and is held in high esteem in the Brāhmaṇical establishment in Kerala.
25. Ibid., p. 177. Vāsu Bhaṭṭa was a Brāhmaṇa poet, celebrated for the *yamaka kāvyas* he wrote in Sanskrit
26. Ibid., pp. 182–7.
27. For situating Śaṅkara in the history of Kerala, Narayanan, *Perumals of Kerala,* p. 214 and notes on p. cxxxiii.
28. Above, n. 22. Inscriptions from the period of the Cēra kingdom record the proceedings of the Brāhmaṇical bodies known as *sabhā, ūr, kaṇam,* etc., Narayanan, *Perumals of Kerala,* chapter on 'Local bodies'; Veluthat, *Brahman Settlement,* chapter on 'Organisation and Administration'. There is an elaborate statement in the *Kēraḷōlpatti* as to how the meeting of one of these, the *gaṇa* or *kaṇam,* was to be held.
29. Zacharia, ed., *Kerlolpathiyum,* pp. 193–211. In this section of this version, the Zamorin is invariably referred to as 'our lord'. Interestingly, this version has a Tamil translation of unknown date. T. Chandrasekharan, ed., *Kēraḷadēśa-Varalāṟu* (Madras, 1960). Does it mean that it wanted to appeal to the Tamil elements also? Varier, *Kerlolpatti,* contains two versions of the *Kēraḷōlpatti.* The first is more or less a copy with only minor variations of the 'standard' version which Gundert has edited except for the lack of details in relation to

the Zamorin. The second summarizes the earlier two parts relating to Paraśurāma and the *Perumāḷs* and elaborates on the Kōlattiri, the Rājā of Kōlattunāḍ. The other versions of the *Kēraḷōlpatti,* likewise, elaborate the history of other principalities in this third phase.

30. Zacharia, ed. *Kerlolpathiyum,* p. 191. The accounts of the Zamorin's conquests are contained in pp. 193–9, 201, etc.
31. Ibid., pp. 198–9, 201.
32. Ibid., pp. 201–2.
33. For an account of the state of affairs in the kingdom of Calicut, K.V. Krishna Ayyar, *The Zamorins of Calicut* (Calicut, 1938), esp. pp. 261–96: 'How the Empire Was Governed'. Ayyar wrote long before the history, or even the sources for writing one, of the Cēra kingdom of Mahōdayapuram had been published. There is a later work which gives further details from the documents of the Zamorin's archives. N.M. Nampoothiry, *Samūtiricaritrattile Kāṇappuṟaṅṅaḷ* (Sukapuram, 1987). This book is no better in terms of the methodology and rigour of analysis. There is a brilliant study: V.V. Haridas, 'The King, Court and Culture in Medieval Kerala: The Zamorins of Calicut', unpublished PhD Thesis (Mangalore University).
34. It was T.A. Gopinatha Rao who discovered, and published extracts of, the *kāvya* for the first time. *Travancore Archaeological Series,* vol. II, part ii, pp. 87–113. Many scholars have commented on it. C. Girija, The *Mūṣikavamśa,* gives a summary of these earlier works and an elaborate bibliography.
35. For details of the history of Kōlattunāḍ under the Cēra kingdom, Narayanan, *Perumals of Kerala,* pp. 91–4. For the differences of Kolattunāḍ from other chiefly territories, Veluthat, *The Political Structure,* pp. 113–17. For the *Mushikavamśakāvya* as legitimizing the king and the kingdom, Romila Thapar, 'The Mouse in the Ancestry', in S.D. Joshi, ed., *Amritadhara: Essays in Honour of R.N. Dandekar* (Delhi, 1984).
36. For the significance of historical biography in early medieval India, Romila Thapar, 'Of Biographies and Kings', in Kesavan Veluthat and P.P. Sudhakaran, eds, *Advances in History: Essays in Memory of M.P. Sridharan* (Calicut, 2003), pp. 80–94. Thapar takes up the case of the well-known historical biography, the *Harśacarita.* It will be interesting to consider the situation in Kerala with the help of the insights available here.

7

Epigraphy in the Historiography of Kerala*

In the history of historical writing in modern Kerala, we do not come across any startling epigraphical sensations such as are usually associated with the names of François Champollion, James Prinsep or Michael Ventris. The reason is rather simple. The ancient scripts such as Vaṭṭeḻuttu and Kōleḻuttu, used to write Malayalam, and Grantha, used to write Sanskrit, in this region in the earlier periods, were not quite forgotten even in modern times as they were in use well into the nineteenth century. Documents continued to be executed in Vaṭṭeḻuttu and Kōleḻuttu; and anybody with a justifiable claim to literacy in modern Malayalam script could venture into reading the Grantha script. In spite of this, the reconstruction of the history of Kerala with the help of epigraphical sources is of relatively recent origin. The present essay tries to look at how such sources were used in the writing of the history of Kerala from time to time ever since they were recognized as sources of history and identify the shifts that have taken place in the paradigms and methodologies of doing so. We may take into account the way in which history was constructed at various points in time, placing it within the perspective of contemporary compulsions.

EPIGRAPHY IN TRADITIONAL HISTORIOGRAPHY

The reason for the inscriptions not being used for the reconstruction of history until the nineteenth century lies largely in the differences in

* First published in K.K.N. Kurup ed., *New Dimensions in South Indian Historiography: Essays in Honour of M.R. Raghava Varier* (Calicut, 1996), pp. 126–49.

the ways in which past was perceived by our society and the strategies in which it was sought to be retrieved. In fact, these differences have led to the creation of certain major stereotypes in relation not only to Kerala but to the entire country as a whole. One of the more important stereotypes of this category is represented by the statement that 'ancient India has produced no Herodotus or Thucydides, no Tacitus or Livy' which 'quotation' is a repeated *ad nauseum* in all textbooks of Indian history and Kerala history.

Kerala, like other parts of India, too had a strong sense of the past and a rich tradition of historical writing. The *Patiṟṟuppattu* in Tamil, *Mūṣikavamśa* in Sanskrit, the *Kēraḷōlpatti* in Malayalam, etc. were among the elements which enriched it. The concerns of this tradition were with origins, genealogies, etc. and differed significantly from those of the Greco-Roman and Judaeo-Christian traditions which were at the base of the historiographical traditions of the West. In the latter, particularly after the celebrated 'Berlin Revolution', the 'facts' as paraphrased from the archival sources achieved an unquestionable sanctity. When, towards the end of the eighteenth century, the English East India Company established its political authority over this region, the alien masters came face to face with a society with so unrecognizable a historical tradition. They, whose understanding of history was entirely different from what they saw here, refused to grant the status of history to the 'farrago of legendary nonsense'—to use the words of William Logan describing the *Kēraḷōlpatti*.[1]

HISTORIOGRAPHY AND COLONIALISM

It is also possible that there was a hidden agenda here. For the colonial agents of the Company and the Crown, it was politically important to create a certain kind of knowledge about the colony in such a way as to make their domination easier. One of the most crucial areas of such knowledge was in relation to the past and the Western scholars realized it all too well and cultivated it assiduously. Their brand of history being different from the 'native' ones, it was not at all a hard task for them to present theirs as the superior. The new techniques of historical enquiry that had developed in the West by the close of the eighteenth century lent a certain kind of legitimacy to their claims. An alternative discourse displaced the traditional one. The new one invariably presented the natives as having had no sense of history. This rejection of the tradition of pre-colonial historiography was a necessary first step towards making the subjects accept the knowledge that was created for them by the masters. The master knew better, and the subjects accepted that knowledge uncritically. We do not go into the nature of the knowledge which was so manufactured and retailed and the uses to which it was put. The point here is that an entirely new tradition of historical enquiry with its concerns and methodology different from what existed here came into vogue. In this new tradition every 'fact' was considered as sacred. The authenticity of a fact was supremely important. One of the assumptions, however questionable it may be, of such Rankean tradition of historical writing was that the closer an authority to an event, the more reliable it is for the historian. Such archival tradition became the cornerstone of historical writing.

It was in this context that there was a thorough search for 'contemporary' sources. Given the torrid but humid climate of this part of the country, documents which could be expected to have survived from a remote past were inscriptions on copper plates and stone slabs as other materials such as palm leaves are highly perishable. Naturally enough, scholars began to take interest in the inscriptions as sources of historical reconstruction. A few inscriptions were well known: the so called Syrian Christian Copper Plates and the Jewish Copper Plates.[2] These were documents which flattered the ego of these exotic communities which possessed them and guarded them jealously, occasionally making them available to the foreigners for study. Thus Portuguese and Dutch scholars had tried their hands at these documents even before the establishment of the British rule and the inauguration of a new historiographical tradition here. When missionary activities got strengthened in the nineteenth century, a new dimension was added: the Judaic and Christian traditions of this land were exaggerated out of all proportions. This greatly added to the character of the new knowledge mentioned above. Services of missionaries such as Rev. George Mathen and Rev. Hermann Gundert are very significant in this respect. Rev. Gundert deciphered a couple of records related to the Syrian Christians and another of the Jews and provided a chronological and political framework to these records, apart from interpreting their contents. Scholars like A.C. Burnell proposed further refinement, particularly in the matter of dating. Gundert's interpretations and Burnell's dating formed the basis of the earliest use of epigraphy in the reconstruction of Kerala history.[3]

EPIGRAPHY IN MODERN WRITING

Thus when William Logan, the then Collector of Malabar District, undertook the compilation of the manual of the Malabar District as was required of all the districts under Madras Presidency, he sought to distinguish 'traditionary ancient history' from 'early history from other sources'.[4] For the latter the earliest native documents used were these inscriptions as deciphered and interpreted by Gundert and dated by Burnell. He adopted the following scheme of chronology for the three inscriptions.[5]

(a) The Jewish Copper Plates—End of the seventh or the beginning of eighth century.

(b) The Syrian Christian Copper Plates of Vira Raghava—AD 774.

(c) The Syrian Christian Copper Plates of Sthāṇu Ravi 'Guptan'—AD 824.

Apart from adopting this chronological scheme for 'the petty suzerains who ruled this tract of the country',[6] Logan also discussed at length the many privileges which these communities were granted by means of these documents. But what influenced later historiography most was the chronological frame and the political history based on it. The last of these 'petty suzerains' was identified with the Cēramān *Perumāḷ*, 'whose name is on the lips of every child'.[7] Further, the title 'Guptan', which was wrongly read in the record, was strangely taken as suggesting his being of Mauryan extraction. The date to which the record was ascribed, that is, AD 824, corresponded well with the beginning of the Kollam era in AD 825, which was the date proposed by Logan for the flight of Cēramān *Perumāḷ* to Mecca. All these go to create the impression that Logan was pinning the *Perumāḷ* saga down to a particular point in time, notwithstanding his distaste for the stories in *Kēraḷōlpatti*. Elsewhere he even invoked a tombstone of the *Perumāḷ* reported from Zaphar which was stated to carry an inscription giving the date of his death as equivalent to AD 832 and his name as Abdul Rahiman Samiri, although 'the facts are still to be verified'.[8] In any case, the picture of a Kerala reduced to anarchy, in the absence of even such of the 'petty suzerains' as existed before, is presented for the period of about a thousand years since the second quarter of the ninth century. This was the picture which stayed in the historiography of Kerala for several years to come, in spite of a large number of inscriptions discovered, deciphered, and published in the meantime.

FRESH DISCOVERIES

It may be an accident that the year which saw the publication of Logan's *Malabar* also witnessed the publication of the first annual report of the Department of Epigraphy, Government of Madras.[9] E. Hultzsch, who headed that department, systematized epigraphy in the Presidency. He prepared a decipherment of the Jewish Copper Plates which was freer from errors than the earlier versions. He also combed the Presidency for inscriptions, and a large number of them from the district of Malabar were noticed in the *Annual Reports of South Indian Epigraphy* published by the department. A few of these inscriptions were published in the *South Indian Inscriptions,* particularly volumes V and VII. At the same time, a few records saw the light of the day through the pages of *Epigraphia Indica, Indian Antiquary,* etc. Scholars such as F.W. Ellis, L.A. Cammiade, F. Keilhorn, Robert Sewell, Kukkil Kelu Nair and others either published newly discovered inscriptions or helped in dating and interpreting them. Thus, by the turn of the century, there was a thorough and systematic attempt to widen the data base of inscriptions from Kerala.

As early as 1891, P. Sundaram Pillai had published *Some Early Sovereigns of Travancore,* basing himself mainly on inscriptions.[10] Although it is technically far advanced from the earlier narratives such as Pachu Moothath's *Tiruvithamkur Charitram*[11] or Shungoonny Menon's *History of Tranvancore,*[12] it was not pursued by historians. At the same time, the princely state of Travancore started a Department of Archaeology there, almost on the lines of its predecessor in Madras. Its *Administration Reports* noticed a few inscriptions; but it was only with the launching of the *Travancore Archaeological Series* (hereafter *TAS*) that what was achieved in the Madras Presidency was begun in Travancore. A number of copper plates and stone inscriptions were deciphered and published in the pages of the *TAS,* and a fresh decipherment with detailed discussion of the Syrian Christian Copper Plates of Sthāṇu Ravi was among them.[13] His 'title' Guptan was evidently dismissed as a misreading and by combining the palaeographical logic with synchronism with a Cōḻa king identified with Āditya Cōḻa (which identification, to be sure, was rejected later), this ruler was assigned to the second half of the ninth century AD. Similarly, with the help of the astronomical data yielded by a copper plate record from Tirunelli published by L.A. Cammiade[14] and a triple synchronism, Gopinatha Rao fixed the date of the Jewish Copper Plates to the turn of AD eleventh century[15]—over three centuries later than the date assigned by Burnell for the record. So also the other Syrian Christian record of Vīra Rāghava came to be assigned to either the thirteenth or the fourteenth century[16]—about five centuries later than the date which Burnell had given it. Another significant contribution was the publication of the lengthy record on copper plates from Tiruvalla,[17] which brought out many interesting details about the temple there, the properties it possessed, the range of its activities, etc. In a similar way, the text and translation of a large number of records from different parts of Travancore, together with detailed discussions, were made available to the students of history, language and culture by the hard work of T.A. Gopinatha Rao, K.V. Subrahmanya Iyer and A.S. Ramanatha Iyer, who successively headed the Department of Archaeology in the state of Travancore.[18] R. Vasudeva Pothuval, who edited the last volumes of the *TAS*, merely published the texts of inscriptions which, however, was of great value.[19]

The epigraphical publications of the Governments of Madras and Travancore had made a significant assumption about the language of these inscriptions what with the near-perfection in the matter of decipherment. The language was taken as Tamil or at best a variant of Tamil, its 'western dialect'.[20] Not only was the Tamil script used for transliterating even modern Malayalam records such as the Paliyam Plates of 1663,[21] but incongruencies arising out of it were explained away as grammatical and/or orthographic aberrations.[22] The factors working behind the use of Tamil script in transliteration may have been many such as a preponderance of Tamil elements in the bureaucracies of Madras and Travancore or the abiding influence of Caldwell's *Comparative Grammar of the Dravidian Languages*;[23] in any case, the effect was that it severely circumscribed their readership and also vitiated thinking about the evolution of Malayalam language, even when scholars of such brilliance as A.R. Rajaraja Varma,[24] Ulloor S. Parameswara Iyer,[25] L.V. Ramaswami Iyer[26] and A.C. Sekhar[27] worked on the problem. (Incidentally, all but one of them were Tamil Brāhmaṇas.) The autonomy of Malayalam as a separate language is yet to be worked out.

The inscriptions from different parts of the state of Cochin, too, were being surveyed, noticed and published in the same period. Apart from the sporadic work of the Department of Archaeology in that state, a research institute known as the Rama Varma Research Institute brought out the texts and translations of many inscriptions throughout the state of Cochin through its periodic Bulletins.[28] Besides, they also carried studies based on inscriptions by scholars such as K. Rama Pisharodi and V.K.R. Menon who discussed the implications of the inscriptions for chronology and political history.[29] The lengthy article of A. Govinda Warrier, correlating the evidence of epigraphy with that of the literary text of *Mūṣikavaṁśa,* is a case in point.[30] Such attempts were made in the *Kerala Society Papers*, too, which was being published from Trivandram.[31]

THE CONTINUING BACKWARDNESS

Thus, the first three or four decades of the present century witnessed a hectic search for, and discovery and publication of, epigraphical material bearing on the history of Kerala in British Malabar and the princely states of Travancore and Cochin. However, outside the publications which carried the decipherment and interpretations of these inscriptions, they hardly had any immediate impact. K.P. Padmanabha Menon's monumental works on the *History of Cochin* (in Malayalam, 1912) or *History of Kerala* (in English, completed in 1919) may be charitably described to have been written too soon to have taken notice of these developments. But no such justification offers itself in the case of K.V. Krishna Aiyar's *Zamorins of Calicut*[32] or P.K.S Raja's *Medieval Kerala*.[33] All these books were written within the paradigm of Logan, although in the matter of details there may be differences, mostly of a speculative nature.

This framework, created by Logan and carried forward by later writers, suited the interests of the colonial masters best. Two aspects in relation to Kerala in the pre-modern period stand out clearly in it: (a) the anarchic and chaotic political condition of Kerala and (b) the rather primitive and therefore obnoxious institutions of Kerala. This latter aspect simply lurks behind the rich encomia which Logan pays to the age-old institutions of Malabar,[34] but reading between the lines, we can see how Logan tries to 'orientalize' Malabar in the Saidian sense.[35] In relation to the former, too, the acceptance of the story of Cēramān Perumāḷ partitioning his kingdom and leaving for Mecca was of central importance. That this event was placed early in the ninth century too was significant because the anarchical condition of Kerala, which, it would seem, it took the British to put an end to, was shown as about a millennium old. Padmanabha Menon's or Krishna Aiyar's writings only, if unwittingly, helped to buttress this picture. It was only in the second half of the twentieth century that this paradigm was challenged and rejected by historians.

THE SYNTHESIS OF NEW EVIDENCE

Even while the *TAS* and *Bulletins of the Ramavama Research Institute* were publishing the newly discovered inscriptions, it was being gradually recognized that these records and the different rulers mentioned there probably belonged to a single dynasty. A.S. Ramanatha Iyer attempted to reconstruct a chronological sequence in which these rulers could be placed.[36] This was greatly improved upon by V.K.R. Menon,[37] although the identification of the rulers' dynasty or the capital from which they ruled took some more time. It was Elamkulam P.N. Kunjan Pillai who not only refined the chronology of these rulers further but also established that they belonged to the Cēra dynasty which ruled from Mahōdayapuram, modern Koduṅṅallūr, and showed that they exercised sway over the entire territory of modern Kerala during the ninth through eleventh centuries of the Christian era.[38] He pinned down the date of Sthāṇu Ravi of the Syrian Christian Copper Plates to AD 844–885 with the help of an astronomical work, *Laghu Bhāskarīya Vyākhyā* of Śaṅkaranārāyaṇa.[39] He also fixed the dates of Bhāskara Ravi of the Jewish Copper Plates as between AD 962 and 1020 with the help of an inscription from Perunna and identified two, probably three, rulers of that name.[40] He identified a certain Rāmavarma Kulaśēkhara as the last ruler of this line and assigned him to AD 1089–1102.[41] He also filled the gaps in between and rounded out the outlines of chronology and political history. When he took up the dating of Vīra Rāghava Copper Plates, it was found to fall in the year AD 1225, thus placing it outside the reign of the dynasty to which the other two sets of copper plates belonged.[42]

More important than this chronological outline was the firm rehabilitation of the political history of Kerala within the larger context of south India. For one thing, the idea that Kerala formed a single political unit under what Elamkulam described as the 'Second Cēra Empire' or the 'Kulaśēkhara Empire' threw overboard the earlier picture of anarchy and lawlessness for the period since the beginning of the Kollam era.[43] This had serious implications for the period in which he was writing when the movement for a united Kerala was at its highest. The identification of the dynasty as the Cēra dynasty also linked it with its predecessors in an earlier period and also its contemporaries such as the Pāṇḍyas and Cōḻas in the neigbhouring regions of Tamil Nadu. Relations of the Kerala kingdom with these neighbouring powers such as the Pāṇḍyas and Cōḻas were brought out, thus underscoring the fact that the history of Kerala is in reality part of the history of south India. The details of the relations so reconstructed, however, are problematic. For instance, the Professor failed to realize the unequal statures of the Cēras on the one side and the Cōḻas on the other and posited a protracted war between the two lasting for a century, which he called bombastically as 'the Hundred Years' War'.[44] Much of his understanding of the historical processes in Kerala in the fields of economy, society and polity was based on this premise of a 'Hundred Years' War'. It was also thanks to the work of the Professor that the history of the minor dynasty of the Āys was brought out.[45] Their position as a buffer between the Cēras and the Pāṇḍyas was brought out effectively. So also the fortunes of a large number of chiefs in Kerala in this period too were laid bare by Elamkulam.

The identification of a centralized imperial government in Kerala for about three centuries since the beginning of the Kollam era or a little earlier, in the place of anarchy and confusion, made a revolutionary change in the historiography of Kerala. Consequently, all other elements with which golden ages are made in nationalist historiography were identified, including munificent cultural patronage, particularly of the Sanskritic variety. Śaṅkara, who lived in that area, was presented as the representative of the *geist* of that Golden Age. One of the elements which added to the lustre of the age was the vibrant and autonomous institutions of the local administration. It goes to the credit of Elamkulam that the details of information regarding social and political organization, found scattered in the inscriptions from different parts of the state, were pieced together and a comprehensive picture of these bodies was presented. It is another thing that this picture itself is permeated through and through by a nationalist ideology of which Professor Elamkulam was an unwitting victim. Democratic, representative bodies of *ūrār* or *ūrāḷar* at the level of the village and a *nāṭṭukkūṭṭam* at a higher level were identified. Their functioning corresponded to similar bodies about which nationalist historians such as K.P. Jayaswal, R.K. Mookerjee, R.C. Majumdar and

K.A. Nilakanta Sastri had waxed eloquent. These 'popular' assemblies functioned as a vital unit of the administrative machinery.

Professor Elamkulam also located in these bodies the basic units of economic relations, the inscriptions in relation to them being largely temple inscriptions dealing with the transactions of landed property. In fact, it was Elamkulam who, based on the evidence of the inscriptions, first drew the picture of the agrarian relations in Kerala in this period in a comprehensive manner.[46] The role of the bodies of the *ūrāḷar* and the temples which they managed as veritable landed magnates was brought out effectively in his writings. The gradual growth of individual landlordism, however, was assigned to factors such as the 'Hundred Years' War' and the increasing caprice of the Nampūtiris while Nāyar soldiers were away in the warfront. The unacceptability of this casuality notwithstanding, the credit of examining the process with the help of sources goes to Professor Elamkulam.

As in the case of his work on the rise of the *janmi* system, so also in the case of his work on matriliny in Kerala, Elamkulam worked with a certain ideological preoccupation.[47] It is obvious that he had taken the side of the less fortunate sections of society in his analysis of social and economic history, however incongruent it may be with his nostalgia for a golden age of the Sanskritic variety. In the case of his analysis of matriliny in Kerala, he started with the premise that the earliest mention of the system in the records dated from the thirteenth century. This was a notion created by Padmanabha Menon, who in his famous *Marumakkathayam Committee Report* and the Memoranda attached to it had worked with this assumption.[48] Elamkulam believed that the 'Kulaśēkharas' were patrilineal and that the shift took place somewhere in the twelfth century or slightly earlier. The ubiquitous 'Hundred Years' War' was invoked as a causal explanation for this also. Rarely did he consider that such major shifts in the pattern of descent and inheritance for a whole society cannot be occasioned by events like a war, even if the 'Hundred Years' War' is accepted as historical. The same pattern of a 'Garden of Eden' and a 'Fall' caused by the 'Hundred Years' War' informs the Professor's examination of the *dēvadāsi* system, for the understanding of the details of which, in any case, we are indebted to nobody else.[49] He also paid attention to the development of Malayalam language, on which he brought to bear an integrated understanding of Dravidian linguistics, historical grammar and knowledge of other languages.[50] One of the most important sources of his information was inscriptions. In the matter of at least these three aspects—landlordism, matriliny and the *dēvadāsi* system—Elamkulam followed the lead of epigraphical sources belonging to the period of the 'Kulaśēkhara Empire'.

Elamkulam's writings presented a sharp contrast to the kind of imperialist construction represented by the writings of Logan and those who followed him. We can see all details of nationalist historiography there, if in the form of a Kerala nationalism. The kind of Travancore patriotism, characteristic of the *Tiruvitamkur Caritram* of Pachu Moothath, *History of Travancore* of Shungoonny Menon, *Some Early Sovereigns of Travancore* by Sundaram Pillai, cannot be seen there although Elamkulam too cannot be described as entirely free from that sentiment. What, however, is most significant about him is the expression of clear anti-colonial sentiments. In fact, his eagerness to attribute a democratic and popular character to the local bodies which, in reality, were corporations of property owners belonging to the upper caste, is a good instance of his anti-colonial enthusiasm. His nostalgia for a 'golden age' and the general pattern of historical development where a fall is the central theme are all typical of this nationalist preoccupation. Together with this, his sympathies for the less fortunate sections of society are hard to miss. The past, for him, was a period devoid of caste distinctions and disabilities and those sections of society which later were consigned to the lower rungs of caste hierarchy were, in those wonderful days, of a very high status. It was elaborating on this thesis that he looked at the epigraphical records of the 'Kulaśēkharas' and after. He assumed that members of the local bodies and temple committees were non-Brāhmaṇas (as, on the one hand, their names did not carry either the title Nampūtiri or the suffix Śarman with them and, on the other, these names were spelt in the Dravidian forms). This made him believe in a Brāhmaṇa takeover at a later point in time. He suggested that this took place in the period of uncertainty during and after the 'Hundred Years' War' when almost as if by a law of universal conscription, all adult males of the non-Brāhmaṇa castes were away on the front. The same pattern explains, for him, the licentiousness of the upper castes, the sexuality of the medieval centuries, and a whole lot of other problems.

What made the framework of Elamkulam something of accepted wisdom which tenanted the notions of both specialized student of history and the lay reader for a relatively long time since the publication of his work was the publication of the District Gazetteers, edited by A. Sreedhara Menon.[51] Menon also brought out his influential textbook, *A Survey of Kerala History,* almost simultaneously.[52] Menon exhibited the courage to incorporate the most up-to-date information in his Gazetteers and textbook, rejecting the old stories contained in the Logan–Padmanabha Menon–Velu Pillai construction of Kerala history. To that extent, Menon's achievement is praiseworthy: Elamkulam was taken seriously after he had published his findings. This is exceedingly rare, considering the 'heretical' nature of what Elamkulam wrote. It is not, therefore, surprising that books written in the same vein of Logan and Padmanabha Menon, Krishna Aiyer and P.K.S. Raja continued to appear. The two-volume *History of Kerala* brought out by the Kerala History Association is a typical example of this backwardness, where not only is the information outdated but the approach is vicious for the communalist and casteist implications there.[53] That the works of political activists such as E.M.S. Namboodiripad[54] and K. Damodaran,[55] published after much of the results of Elamkulam's research was available in print, do not take them into account or the sources used there is another matter. Historiography, however, was not exactly enriched by this; nor could this bring about a shift in the paradigm, for theory without empirical strength cannot hold much water.

FURTHER SHIFTS

It was in the early 1970s that another major shift took place in the pattern of the use of epigraphical material in the reconstruction of the history of Kerala. Starting from where Elamkulam had left and initially following the same lines, M.G.S. Narayanan deviated significantly from the course charted by Elamkulam.[56] He achieved this both by using records unknown to Elamkulam and by reinterpreting those which the latter had used in other ways. He effected corrections in the details of the chronology of the Cēras of Mahōdayapuram; he cleared cobwebs about the identity of rulers like Sthāṇu Ravi and Bhāskara Ravi; he saw that the rulers of that dynasty used different titles like Rājaśēkhara, Kulaśēkhara, Vijayarāga, Kēraḷa Kēsari, Manukulāditya, Rājasimha, Raṇāditya, etc. instead of single eponymous title Kulaśēkhara as assumed by Elamkulam. This led to the rejection of the label 'Kulaśēkhara' for the dynasty. He also demonstrated that the political form which that dynasty presided over could by no stretch of imagination be described an 'empire'. 'Kulaśēkhara Empire', therefore, was a misnomer in both ways! This had implications for the understanding of the whole gamut of political and social relations obtaining in this part of the country at that time. The organic connection between the temple-centred agrarian corporations, managed by Brāhmaṇa landlords, and the social organization was clearly brought out by Narayanan. It was these which functioned as the basic building blocks of the political organizations as well. In analysing the processes and structures there, Narayanan brought to bear on the study of the inscriptions in the perspective that was emerging in the historiography of early medieval India particularly after D.D. Kosambi and R.S. Sharma introduced a lot of clarity in the all-India context. In fact, in a couple of later papers, he has tested the applicability of Marc Bloch's definition of the 'fundamental features' of feudalism in the light of evidence from the inscriptions of Kerala.[57] In fact, here he used the results of his own earlier studies of various institutions mentioned in the epigraphical records.

A couple of them deserve special mention. A curious institution known as 'the Hundred Organization' was taken by the earlier historians as denoting 'democratic' 'popular assembles' reminding R.C. Majumdar of the Vedic *sabha* and *samiti* and compelling Elamkulam to identify in them a unit at a level higher than the village, something of a *nāṭṭukkūṭṭam*. By a careful contextual examination of the references to these organizations in inscriptions and by integrating the evidences from other sources and from other parts of India, Narayanan demonstrated that they constituted the bodyguards of the local chiefs, their 'companions of honour'. He also identified their counterparts in the capital, around the person of the Cēra Perumāḷ himself. Further, this institution was demonstrated to have been the expression in a Kerala idiom of similar bodies found in other parts of India dating perhaps from the time of the *Arthaśāstra* itself.[58] Another significant detail of a comparable nature is Narayanan's reinterpretation of the significance of the expression '*Kantaḷūr śālaik-kalamaṟuttaruḷi*' figuring in the *meykkīrtis* of Rājarāja Cōḻa, the debate among epigraphists and historians about the interpretation of which had kicked up a lot of dust. Following the lead provided by Elamkulam with the help of what is known as the Parthivapuram Plates of the Āy ruler Karunantaḍakkan, Narayanan showed that Kāntaḷūr Śālai was an institution offering education.[59] The implications of this, which are rather tremendous, were also brought out. Thus he was able to prove that there was an aggressive, warlike, element in the Brāhmaṇa community here, and traced its history through medieval literature and modern survivals. Both these helped to present the evolution of Kerala society in the context of the developments in the entire subcontinent.[60]

This kind of a presentation provided a viable alternative to the causality of a large number of developments such as the rise of landlordism or the problem of matriliny or the *dēvadāsi* system which, at the hands of Elamkulam, were sought to be explained as a consequence of the 'Hundred Years' War'. Narayanan not only exposed the absurdity of such a causality, which puts down major changes in society and economy to a war, but he also showed that the 'Hundred Years' War' itself was at best imaginary. Placing the relationship between the Cōḻas on the one side and the Cēras on the other in historical perspective and considering the heavily unequal nature of the two parties, he examined the evidence afresh and traced various stages such as the one of cordial friendly relations, the one of Cōḻa invasion of Kerala, the one of Cōḻa overlordship and finally the one of recovery for a short while. In fact, to posit a 'Hundred Years' War' is demonstrated as against evidence and further to say that such a nonexistent thing was at the base of significant socio-economic changes was eminently rejectable. This places the political relations of Kerala with the neighbouring regions in a better perspective.

Another exercise which Narayanan has taken up bringing about a significant shift in the methodology of using inscriptions for Kerala history is the integration of evidence from the inscriptions with that from traditions, both literary and oral. With the help of inscriptions from Kōlattunāḍu, he demonstrated the authenticity of the *Mūṣikavamśakāvya,* identifying rulers in the epigraphs and the temples from which they are discovered, etc. in the text.[61] This helped him to situate the text both spatially and temporally and use the evidence from it more confidently. In fact, the very significant pattern of relations among the Cēdis, Rāṣṭrakūṭas, Cōḻas, Cēras and Mūṣikas is brought out with the help of this text. In a similar way, inscriptions helped him to take traditional accounts more seriously.[62] For instance, he does not either accept chronicles like *Kēraḷōlpatti* as 'having attained the status of history'[63] or reject them as 'a farrago of legendary nonsense'.[64] The story of the creation of the land by Paraśurāma there is traced in the traditions of the rest of the west coast figuring in texts of an earlier date, indicating that this is a tradition which itself moved from north to south along with the community which migrated carrying this tradition with them. The account of the settlement of Brāhmaṇas in Kerala in thirty-two villages is demonstrated to have been supported by inscriptions; and Narayanan has also located many of these settlements in the epigraphical records. Similarly, the reference to a council of the Brāhmaṇas which advised the king at Mahōdayapuram is found to have been endorsed by the inscription. The arms-bearing Brāhmaṇa groups of the *caṭṭa*s, mentioned above, are shown to be present in both these traditions and the inscriptions, apart from the literary texts in Sanskrit and Maṇipravāḷam. So also, fleeting references to the 'Companions of Honour' in the same tradition were located when the bodyguards of the rulers of Mahōdayapuram were referred to as the *Āyiram*. Finally, the statement in the same Brāhmaṇical traditions about the partition of the kingdom and the conversion to Islam of the last Cēramān Perumāḷ was found supported by at least circumstantial evidences. Thus, Narayanan appreciated the fact that traditions such as the *Kēraḷōlpatti* preserved a very clear sense of the past and that the form in which it was expressed suited the needs of the society which created that form. Here we can find the clear rejection of the colonial notions about 'native' attitudes towards the past. On the whole, Narayanan's work turned a new leaf in the historiography of Kerala, particularly with reference to the use of epigraphy.

THE CONTEMPORARY SCENE

Narayanan's work has been carried forward by a few of his students and colleagues including the present writer. Some of them have elaborated on the suggestions made by him; some others have gone into areas outside Narayanan's own. The work of Raghava Varier on Jainism in Kerala,[65] that of K.N. Ganesh on the agrarian system of Vēṇāḍ in the period after the Cēras,[66] that of P.L. Chackochan on the Cultural Geography of Vēṇāḍ from the post-Cēra inscriptions[67] and that of the present writer[68] on the fortunes of the Brāhmaṇa settlements in Kerala in the post-Cēra period may be taken as examples of this category where a lot of empirical details are made available, largely within the same framework. Of greater interest is the work of Rajan

Gurukkal on the medieval Kerala temple,[69] where he analyses epigraphical material with considerable theoretical refinement. His theoretical apparatus is drawn from different disciplines.

There are a few works which have come out in Malayalam in recent years. The works of Raghava Varier on the 'historical dimensions of Keraliteness',[70] and Ganesh's book on 'Kerala's Yesterdays'[71] continue the good work which they have been doing in the field. Varier has also discovered and deciphered a few inscriptions not noticed earlier. They enrich our understanding considerably.

One publication which is likely to have a lasting impact on the historiography of Kerala is the joint book of Raghava Varier and Rajan Gurukkal, namely a history of Kerala from the earliest times to the end of the fifteenth century AD.[72] For the integrated use of archaeology, epigraphy, numismatics, literature, onomastics, and the like, this book may rightly be described as comprehensive. The authors have made use of recent theoretical tools for purposes of the analysis of evidence. Imbalances and inconsistencies notwithstanding, this publication has the potential of inaugurating a new trend in the historiography of Kerala.

The picture is not certainly one of gloom and despair; those who complain about the scarcity of sources and the lack of their use simply close their eyes towards reality. This does not mean that all that has to be done had been done and that there is nothing left for us or the generations to come. Among some of the immediate requirements are:

1. The preparation of a comprehensive bibliography of inscriptions from and on Kerala.[73] This has to include references to both the inscriptions themselves and studies based on them. This will help the researcher immensely.
2. The editing and publication of inscriptions from Kerala in one series, giving the text and translation of all inscriptions discovered so far, either in a chronological or in a geographical order.[74]
3. More systematic analysis of data with the help of a computer or so, with a view to bringing out the frequency, context and other patterns of terms and expressions in the inscriptions. What has been done about Cōḻa or Vijayanagara inscriptions may be followed as a model.[75]

4. A distribution map of inscriptions from Kerala, bringing out the exact location of the findspot. This can be superimposed on other maps showing details of the density of population, geography, crop patterns, etc. which would throw much welcome light on various aspects of the past.[76]
5. Less work has been done in relation to the period following the end of the Cēra rule, particularly in areas outside Vēṇāḍ. There are also new questions to be raised and answered, which of course will be taken care of by future generations of historians.

NOTES AND REFERENCES

1. William Logan, *Malabar*, vol. I (Madras, first published 1887; 1951 edn), p. 244.
2. For a survey of the interest which these documents had evoked, Walter J. Fishcel, 'The Exploration of the Jewish Antiquities of Cochin on the Malabar Coast', *The Cochin Synagogue 400th Anniversary Souvenir* (Cochin, 1968), pp. 126–50; H. Hosten, 'The Magna Carta of the St. Thomas Christians', *Kerala Society Papers*, Series 4, pp. 169–204. For a succinct presentation, M.G.S. Narayanan, *Cultural Symbiosis in Kerala* (Trivandrum, 1972), chapters IV and V.
3. For the early editions of these records, F.W. Ellis, *Madras Journal of Literature and Science*, vol. XIII, no. II, pp. 1–11; A.C. Burnell, *Indian Antiquary*, vol. III, pp. 333–4; E. Hultzsch, *Epigraphia Indica*, vol. III, p. 69; Gundert, *Madras Journal of Literature and Science*, vol. XIII, no. 1, p. 130.
4. Logan, *Malabar*, pp. 221–74.
5. Ibid., p. 266.
6. Ibid.
7. Ibid., pp. 147, 266.
8. Ibid., pp. 196–7.
9. Government Order No. 1462, dt 24-10-1887 publishing the first report of the Superintendent of Epigraphy.
10. P. Sundaram Pillai, *Some Early Sovereigns of Travancore* (rpt., Delhi, 1988).
11. Vaikkathu Pachu Moothath, *Thiruvitamkur Caritram* (1867, rpt., Cochin,1986).
12. P. Shungoonny Menon, *History of Travancore from Earliest Times* (Trivandrum, 1878).
13. *Travancore Archaeological Series* (hereafter *TAS*), vol. II, I, no. 9, pp. 85ff.
14. *Epigraphia Indica*, vol. XVI, p. 343.

15. *TAS*, vol. II, p. 31.
16. The date suggested for this set of plates was AD 1340. Even this date came in for revision later.
17. *TAS*, vol. II, iii, pp. 131–207.
18. *TAS*, vols I–VIII.
19. Ibid., vols IX and X.
20. This was the way in which the language of the inscriptions was described. In fact, even earlier writers including Logan believed that Malayalam can be derived by mixing Tamil with Sanskrit.
21. *TAS*, vol. I, no. IV, 'Paliyam Plates of the 322nd year of the Puduvaippu Era'.
22. Ibid., editor's comments.
23. Robert Caldwell, *A Comparative Grammar of Dravidian Languages* (London, 1856). It was revised in 1857 by Caldwell himself and in 1913 by J.L. Wyatt and T. Ramakrishna Pillai. For an interesting study of how the 'Dravidian' was constructed and its political fall-out, V. Ravindran, 'The Unanticipated Legacy of Robert Caldwell and the Dravidian Movement', *South Indian Studies,* vol. I, no. I, January–June 1996, pp. 83–110.
24. A.R. Rajarajavarma, *Kēraḷa Pāṇinīyam* (Trivandram, 1896). In this work, Varma defined six 'tendencies' in the process of the transformation of Tamil into Malayalam.
25. Ulloor S. Parameswara Iyer, *Kēraḷa Sāhitya Caritram* (Trivandrum, 1953), esp. vol. I.
26. L.V. Ramaswami Iyer, 'The Evolution and Morphology of Malayalam' in *Ramavarma Research Studies,* no. I (Trichur, 1936), pp. 366 ff. He had training in modern linguistics and his studies covered various south Indian languages.
27. A.C. Sekhar, *The Evolution of Malayalam* (Poona, 1953).
28. *Bulletins of the Rama Varma Research Institute* (Trichur).
29. Ibid., passim.
30. A. Govinda Varier, 'Studies in Mushikavamsa', *Bulletin of the Ramavarma Research Institute,* vol. VIII, pp. 9–36 (1940).
31. T.K. Joseph, editor.
32. K.V. Krishna Ayyar, *The Zamorins of Calicut* (Calicut, 1938).
33. P.K.S. Raja, *Medieval Kerala* (Annamalainagar, 1957).
34. Logan, *Malabar* pp. v–vi. For a persuasive study, Satish Gatti, 'The Furniture of Empire': A Study of the Manuals and Gazetteers with Special Reference to Malabar, South Canara and Coorg', unpublished MPhil dissertation (Mangalore University, 1995).
35. Edward Said, *Orientalism* (London, 1978).
36. *TAS*, vol. VII, no. 37, *Bulletin of the Rama Varma Research Institute.*
37. *Bulletin of the Rama Varma Research Institute.*
38. Elamkulam P.N.K. Pillai wrote in Malayalam. His articles, published in periodicals, were later brought together in the form of books. *Cila Kerala Caritra Prasnangal* (Kottayam, 1953); *Kerala Caritrattinte*

Irulatanja Etukal (Kottayam, 1955); *Annatte Keralam* (Kottayam, 1960) etc. are among the more important of them. A few selected articles are available in English translation. Elamkulam P.N.K. Pillai, *Studies in Kerala History* (Kottayam, 1970).

39. P.N.K. Pillai 'Sthanu Raviyute Kalam', in *Kerala Charitrattinte Irulatanja Etukal* (revised edn, Kottayam, 1963), pp. 95–106.
40. P.N.K. Pillai, 'Jutasasanam', *Chila Kerala Charitra Prasnangal,* vol. II, p. 48.
41. This was based on a Kollam Rāmēśvarasvāmin temple inscription, *TAS,* vol. V, i, no. 13, pp. 40–6.
42. P.N.K. Pillai 'Vira Raghava Pattayam' in *Chila Kerala Charitra Prasnangal.*
43. 'Introduction', *Chila Kerala Charitra Prasnangal.* Also, Elamkulam P.N.K. Pillai, *Cherasamrajyam Onpatum Pattum Nattantukalil* (Kottayam, 1961). P.N.K. Pillai *Samskarathinte Nazhikakkallukal* (Kottayam, 1996), 80–90.
44. Ibid. Also, *Chila Kerala Charitra Prasnangal*; P.N.K. Pillai *Janmisampradayam Keralattil* (Kottayam, 1963).
45. Pillai, *Annatte Keralam.*
46. Pillai, *Janmisampradayam Keralattil.*
47. Pillai, 'Marumakkattayam Keralattil' in *Chila Kerala Charitra Prasnangal.*
48. K.P. Padmanabha Menon was a member of the Marumakkattayam Committee. It was in the report of this committee that the first comprehensive study of matriliny in Kerala figured. Menon added greater details in an equally lengthy memorandum to the Report.
49. Besides his works on Kerala history mentioned above, his commentaries on medieval literary texts and studies based on them are useful for this purpose. He commented on *Candrōtsavam, Līlātilakam, Kōkasandēśam* and *Uṇṇunīlisandēśam.*
50. See his *Bhashayum Sahityavum Nattantukalilute* and *Keralabhashayute Vikasaparinamangal.*
51. He published gazetteers of 8 of the then 9 districts of Kerala.
52. A. Sreedhara Menon, *Surrey of Kerala History* (Kottayam, 1972).
53. P.A. Syed Mohammed, ed., *Kerala Charitram,* 2 vols (Ernakulam, 1972).
54. E.M.S. Namboodiripad, *Kerala: Yesterday, Today and Tomorrow* (Trivandrum,1953).
55. K. Damodaran, *Kerala Charitram* (Ernakulam, 1966).
56. M.G.S. Narayanan, 'Political and Social Conditions of Kerala under the Kulasekhara Empire', unpublished PhD Thesis (University of Kerala, Trivandraum, 1972) since published as *The Perumals of Kerala: Political and Social Conditions of Kerala Under the Cera Perumals of Makotai (c. AD 800–1124),* (Calicut, 1996); M.G.S. Narayanan *Cultural Symbiosis in Kerala* (Trivandrum, 1972); *Kerala Charitrattinte Atisthana Silakal* (Calicut, 1972); *Aspects of Aryanisation in Kerala* (Trivandrum, 1973).

57. M.G.S. Narayanan, 'The Feudal Society in Kerala', *Proceedings of the Indian History Congress* (Amritsar, 1985); 'The Cera State' paper presented at Seminar on State in Pre-modern India, Jawaharlal Nehru University (New Delhi, 1989).
58. Narayanan, 'Companions of Honour', in *Aspects of Aryanisation in Kerala*.
59. Narayanan, 'Bachelors of Science' in Narayanan, *Aspects of Aryanization*.
60. The present writer has taken the lead in these two aspects and tried to examine evidence of both these institutions in other parts of the country. For the 'Bachelors of Science', Kesavan Veluthat, 'The *Cattas* and *Bhattas*: A New Interpretation', *Proceedings of the Indian History Congress* (Aligarh, 1975) and for the 'Companions of Honour', 'The Nature and Significance of the Institution of Velevali', *Proceedings of the Indian History Congress* (Calcutta, 1990), Chapter 14 below.
61. M.G.S. Narayanan, 'History from the Mushakavamsakavya', *Proceedings of the All India Oriental Conference* (Jadavpur, 1969).
62. Of particular interest is the way in which he has looked at the traditional accounts regarding the Brāhmaṇa settlements, a king's council called the *nālu taḷi* and the mysterious disappearance of the last Cēraman Perumāḷ. Narayanan, *Perumals of Kerala*.
63. V. Nagam Aiya, *Travancore State Manual* (Trivandrum, 1906), p. 210.
64. Above, n. l.
65. M.R. Raghava Varier, 'Jainism in Kerala' unpublished MPhil dissertation, Jawaharlal Nehru University (New Delhi, 1978).
66. K.N. Ganesh, 'The Agrarian System of Vēṇāṭu in the post-Cēra Period', unpublished PhD Thesis, Jawaharlal Nehru University (New Delhi, 1986).
67. P.L. Chackochan, 'Historical and Cultural Geography of Venadu, Travancore, *c.* AD 1124 to 1729, unpublished PhD Thesis, Deccan College (Pune, 1980).
68. Kesavan Veluthat, *Brahman Settlements in Kerala: Historical Studies* (Calicut, 1978).
69. Rajan Gurukkal, *The Kerala Temple and the Early Medieval Agrarian System* (Sukapuram, 1992).
70. Raghava Varier, *Keraliyata: Charitra Manangaḷ* (Sukapuram, 1989).
71. K.N. Ganesh, *Keralattinte Innalekal* (Trivandrum, 1990).
72. Raghava Varier and Rajan Gurukkal, *Keralacharitram* (Sukapuram, 1991).
73. The topographical list of inscriptions, undertaken by the Indian Council of Historical Research and edited by T.V. Mahalingam, is not comprehensive so far as Kerala is concerned.
74. The re-publication of the *TAS* undertaken by the Department of Cultural Publications, Government of Kerala, is to be commended. However, a series on *Kerala Inscriptions* could be planned and brought out.

75. Noboru Karashima, Y. Subbarayalu and Toru Matsui, *A Concordance of the Names in Cola Inscriptions*, vols 2 (Madurai, 1978); Noboru Karashima, *South Indian History and Society: Studies from Inscriptions* AD 850–1800 (Delhi, 1984); Noboru Karashima; Y. Subbarayalu and P. Shanmugham, *Vijayanagara Rule in Tamil Country as Revealed through a Statistical Study of Revenue Terms in Inscriptions,* 3 vols (Tokyo, 1988); Karashima, *Towards a New Formation* (Delhi, 1991).
76. Thomas Trautmann has made a beginning in this direction in the case of the Tamil country. Noboru Karashima, ed., *From Indus Valley to Mekong Delta* (Madras, 1984).

8

Literacy and Communication in Pre-modern Kerala*

Information technology is not just about microchips, computers and dot-coms; it comprises every aspect of the storage, retrieval, and communication of information—whatever the mode used. The present essay makes an attempt to examine the ways in which pre-modern Kerala stored and communicated information. Although there are more than one type of information and more than one way of storing, retrieving and communicating them, what this article presumes to address is the problem of those varieties of information which can be expressed verbally. Naturally, storage and communication of such information will include what is achieved through the oral and written media. There is an assumption that these two are antagonistic if not mutually exclusive; it is also maintained that orality is shut out with the arrival of literacy. However, this need not be the case. The two have functioned in a symbiotic relationship.[1] Our concern, however, is only with the written forms. Even within this limited concern, aspects of literary communication or other forms of knowledge preserved through varieties of writing are beyond the scope of this essay. It deals exclusively with the inscriptions of early medieval Kerala—their appearance and disappearance, features, functions and implications. However, it tries to ask questions about the way in which these patterns have a relevance for the society which produced them.

* First published as 'Storage and Retrieval of Information: Literacy and Communication in Pre-modern Kerala', in Amiya Kumar Bagchi, Dipankar Sinha and Barnita Bagchi, eds, *Webs of History: Information, Communication and Technology from Early to Post-colonial India* (Delhi, 2005), pp. 67–82.

It is well known that present-day Kerala was an integral part of the socio-cultural unit called Tamiḻakam in the early historical period.[2] Society there has been rightly described as one characterized by an oral tradition, and the literature of that period, known popularly, if erroneously, as 'Sangam literature', was oral poetry. This does not, as suggested above, mean that it was a totally non-literate society. A large number of inscriptions, known as 'Cave Labels', as they are found generally in caves improvised for the shelter of monks, have come down to us from different parts of Tamiḻakam.[3] The language of these short inscriptions is Tamil and they are written in a script derived from Brāhmi adapted to the phonological scheme of the Dravidian tongue. These inscriptions are concerned with Buddhist/Jain groups and have a heavy bias towards trade.[4] It is significant that many of the traders mentioned in these inscriptions have a north Indian connection, if not origin.[5] The use of Brāhmi in south India by the Mauryas is well known; it was the north Indian agency which brought it to the peninsula.[6] The traders and missionaries who came to south India used a script which they had already known for documenting what they wanted in the language of the area which they were dealing with. In short, what is called the Tamil Brāhmi script did not evolve in south India to meet a locally felt need of storing and retrieving information in the local language, Tamil;[7] it was clearly the adaptation of something which originated in north India to write Indo-Aryan language(s), and its use in south India was largely confined to the trading and religious groups that had strong bonds with north India.

Whatever the origin and course of development of Tamil Brāhmi script, it is a significant fact that not one inscription in that script has come down to us from the west coast in what is modern Kerala, in spite of this region having been an integral part of Tamiḻakam in the early centuries of the Christian era, and its arguable contacts with northern India and Sri Lanka where Brāhmi was known. Inscriptions from Kerala date from the ninth century and correspond with the Cēra Kingdom of Mahōdayapuram, the earliest of them being what is contained in the Vāḻappaḷḷi Copper Plate assigned to the early part of ninth century AD.[8] To be sure, there is a record of an earlier date from the Eḍakal cave in Vayanad and another from Eḻuttukal in the Nilambur forests;[9] but neither is of any significance so far as the history of writing in Kerala is concerned. The real beginning of writing in Kerala, therefore, is with the Vāḻappaḷḷi Copper Plate and records of its kind.

This means that this part of the country had no use for the Tamil Brahmi script and the kind of inscriptions in it. The inscriptions from the ninth century onwards, among other things, announce the presence of the state. These inscriptions, dated in the regnal years of the Cēra rulers, are seen throughout the length of Kerala from Kasaragod district in the north to Thiruvananthapuram district in the south. They are administrative records of sorts, although this need not be taken as if 'administration' meant any centralized structure reaching out uniformly to all the areas covered by the inscriptions. They had a symbolic value as well, the state being what was symbolized there.[10]

A recital of certain details about the inscriptions dating from the period of the Cēra kingdom, a little over 150 in number, may be in place here.[11] These records differ fundamentally from the Tamil Brāhmi cave labels found in other parts of Tamiḻakam in an earlier period, but compare with the inscriptions that begin to make their appearance in south india in a subsequent period, that is, in the monarchical states under the Pallavas and Pāṇḍyas. They are largely located in Brāhmaṇical temples and executed on stone, either on free-standing slabs or forming part of the structure on the plinth, door-frame, etc. A few of them are on copper plates. The usual distinction made in south India between records on copper plate and stone is not valid in Kerala all the way: elsewhere the former are documents recording grants generally of land and the latter, proceedings of bodies of a 'public' nature such as village assemblies, urban corporations, etc.[12] Most of the copper plates from Kerala are documents recording such proceedings, with only two records, the famous Syrian Christian Copper Plates (2 sets)[13] and the Jewish Copper Plates,[14] being 'grants' of any description. Another copper plate record, the Pāliyam Copper Plates,[15] recording a grant to a Buddhist vihara, and yet another of a later period, claiming to be a reissue of one dating from the eleventh century,[16] too, may be included in this list, although both of them are issued by chiefs of localities without any reference to the Cēra overlord whatsoever. Other records on copper, such as the Vāḻappalli Copper Plate, Tiruvāṟṟuvay Copper Plate,[17] Tirunelli Copper Plates (2 sets),[18] Tiruvalla Copper Plates,[19] mentioning the names and regnal years of kings are of the nature of stone inscriptions so far as their contents are concerned. There is one more copper plate record dated Kollam era 149 (AD 973) mentioning a locality chief,[20] which is also in the nature of the stone inscriptions. These similarities and variations have their own interest. The number of 'royal grants' is too limited to be of any significance; the information that the bulk of the documents seek to store is generally of a 'public' nature rather than that meant to be locked up in safe deposit vaults of institutions/private individuals as title deeds of landed properties or other claims. Although even the stone inscriptions had such a function,[21] the emphasis is more on public exhibition than on safe custody in private hands. The information stored was of a public nature and the clientele that it addressed also was the public, subject to the limitation that the expression 'public' had in the context of pre-modern societies.

The script of these records, except in the case of the Pāliyam Copper Plates where it is Nāgarī,[22] is Vaṭṭeḻuttu with an occasional use of Grantha characters to represent Sanskrit or Sanskritic words. This is very important considering that a majority of the inscriptions from Kerala in this period are from temples and are concerned with the Brāhmaṇical groups. They got established here by seventh to eighth centuries AD and are demonstrated to have formed part of a long chain of migration, the earlier links of which are to be seen further north on the west coast in the Tulu-Kannada-speaking regions. This would naturally raise the question as to why the Brāhmaṇical groups, familiar with the art of writing which was already known in the Kannada-speaking regions, did not use the script that had developed here by the time they had migrated here. The relevance of the question becomes all the greater when it is considered that it was these relatively exotic groups who had the necessity to record their decisions.

Literacy was, indeed, the means of storing information and retrieving it for any future reference; but its use was conditioned by contemporary political realities. The Cēra dynasty, which presided over the monarchical state that came to be established in Kerala in this period, had its connections more with the Tamil-speaking regions than with the other parts of the west coast. The rulers claimed a continuity from what is called the Sangam age; they had greater contacts with the Tamil culture heroes, such as the Bhakti saints; their world was still part of the old land of the *mūvaraśar* as Kulaśēkhara Āḻvār, who is identified with Cēra Sthāṇu Ravi (AD 844–83),[23] proudly proclaims in his *Perumāḷ Tirumoḻi*.[24] That is to say, if one takes script primarily as an instrument that the state wielded for purposes of administration, then the Vatteḻuttu script, the earlier forms of which are seen in the Tamil-speaking regions, particularly the neighbouring

Pāṇḍya territory, was the natural choice in the territories of the Cēra state. This is more so because a local evolution from Brāhmi either directly or through the Tamil-Brāhmi was not possible in Kerala for the simple reason that this part of the country had no antecedent of either. In other words, even though the 'power behind the throne' in the Cēra kingdom was indeed in the Brāhmaṇa groups, that *on* it still had a strong Tamil tradition, using a script borrowed from the Tamil-speaking regions with which it still had not cut the umbilical cord and not from the Kannada-speaking regions towards which the notables in society looked. This is clear also from the identity of the scribes. Where it is available from their signatures, we gather that it was professionals, mostly goldsmiths,[25] who performed this function. Literacy was a special skill, cultivated by professional groups. The inscriptions hardly communicated anything to the bulk of the local population, except through their semiotic means of being linked to state power.[26] There are, however, no instances recorded from Kerala where ceremonial receptions of records as in the case of the Cōḻa situation are mentioned. Things could not have been different, and there is no reason to assume universal literacy and to link literacy with 'development'.

Equally important is the question of language. The early epigraphists and historians who published and used these documents were working under the assumption that it was Tamil. Official publications such as *South Indian Inscriptions* and *Travancore Archaeological Series* transcribed these Vaṭṭeḻuttu records into the Tamil script. Wherever the text did not conform to the grammar and structure of the Tamil language, they explained away such 'inconsistencies' as a deviation, *malaināṭṭu vaḻakkam* ('the practice of the Hill Country'). Even later scholars carried this assumption forward and noticed stages through which Tamil passed. Rules were identified, observing which Tamil 'became' Malayalam. Rarely was it considered that languages are not really born, and certainly not in this way! They did not spare a thought to the fact that these are official records and that they would, therefore, contain a language different from what is used in day-to-day life and even literary expressions. Officialese being an instrument of power, the greater slant towards Tamil in these records has to be explained in the very terms in which we saw the use of the script. Even when the inscriptions were related to the Brāhmaṇical groups and their properties, the presence of the Cēra state with its affinities to the Tamil language is hard to miss. These records, therefore, should not be taken as an index to the language used by the 'people', most of whom were probably non-literate; not even by those whose interests are recorded there. As the script, so the language, too, has to be seen as an instrument of the state.

The way in which these records are dated assumes importance in this context. Most of them are dated in the regnal years of the ruling Cēra king. The usual *praśasti*s characterizing inscriptions from elsewhere in contemporary south India, or the kind of *meykkīrtti*s which Rājarāja I inaugurated in the Cōḻa kingdom, are absent in Kerala. A simple but elegant monosyllabic *kō* describes the king. This is followed by his name and the year. That is about all in speaking about the date, thereby pointing to the difference in the character of the state in the Cēra kingdom. Another means of dating the records is with reference to the position of heavenly bodies. Generally, the zodiacal position of *Vyāḻam* (Bṛhaspati: Jupiter) is mentioned; but in many cases more details such as the position of *Śani* (Saturn), *Ñāyar* (the solar month), *pakṣa* (the lunar fortnight), *tithi* (date) and week day, asterism, etc., are also provided. These details are very accurate and modern epigraphists and historians have used them to date these records and the kings mentioned in them with commendable precision. Another means adopted for dating the records is the use of different eras such as the Śaka era, Kali era and in just two cases, the Kollam era. Kali era is mentioned either in terms of years or elapsed days, expressed in so many words or in chronograms following the *bhūtasamkhyā* or *ka-ṭa-pa-yādi* system, assuming not only literacy but also a high level of proficiency in astronomy. What it all implies for us, at least in such cases, is the fact that the dating is addressed to a small section of society which could make sense of these astronomical details. In fact, to assume even widespread literacy in that context is very questionable, in spite of independent evidence of advances in knowledge in areas like astronomy. But this knowledge, like literacy itself, was confined to a limited section of society. As mentioned earlier, universal literacy was something which cannot be assumed in pre-print societies.

The contents of the records offer an equally interesting study. There are practically no 'royal orders' among these inscriptions with the sole exception of the Jewish Copper Plates. Most of the records document the resolutions of local bodies, particulary committees of

Brāhmaṇa landowners managing affairs of temples, much of which centred on landed property. This fact has serious implications for the nature of society and polity, a fact that has been recognized by scholars.[27] What interests us here are the contents of these records and the conventions used in them. The very first of these, namely, the Vāḻappaḷḷi Copper Plate, records the *kaccam* (proceedings) of a joint meeting of the committees of Vāḻappaḷḷi and Tiruvāṟṟuvāy, presided over by the Cēra king himself.[28] The term used, namely, *kaccam*, which is derived from Sanskrit *kārya*, is of importance. Another word used is *cavattai*, from Sanskrit *vyavasthā*. Many other documents of its nature speak of their contents as *kaccam* or *cavattai*. That even a trivial decision regarding the allotment of a gift of gold for a particular service here or the assignment of a piece of land on lease there should have been so meticulously recorded as a *kaccam* or *cavattai* points to the extraordinary nature of the situation where a relatively exotic people enjoyed superior rights, mostly created afresh, over the principal means of production. These *kaccams* authenticated and legitimized these rights and privileges in a convincing fashion.

There is considerable intertextuality exhibited by these documents, in the sense that they assume a whole world of prescriptive literature, valid all over India in the post-Gupta period. The Jewish Copper Plates describe the document as a *prasāda*, a term used in *Dharmaśāstras* to indicate grants of a non-religious nature.[29] Again, the expressions used such as *kaccam* or *cavattai* themselves invoke Brāhmaṇical ideas contained in Sanskrit *dharmaśāstras*, where we have detailed prescriptions regarding the conduct of the Brāhmaṇical corporations such as the *sabhā* and *pariṣad*. These details agree with what we gather from the inscriptions, almost to the last letter.[30] Even the terms used for decisions, *kārya* or *vyvasthā*, are exactly the same in both the texts and the inscriptions. Thus, the inscriptions invoke a whole world of Dharmaśāstraic conduct as well, particularly in the matter of safeguarding the corporate interests of the bodies. It is here that cross-references to the *kaccam* or *cavattai* adopted in one place acquire importance. For instance, inscriptions from all over Kerala make a mention of the *kaccam* of Mūḻikkaḷam, variously referred to as *cavattai, oḻukkam*, etc.[31] There are other *kaccams* which the inscriptions make a reference to, although not on the same scale as the Mūḻikkaḷa kaccam. Thus, we have references to the *kaccams* adopted at Kaṭaṅkāṭṭu, Tavaranūr, Kaitavāram, Kōṭṭuvāyiravēli,

Śankaramaṅgalam, etc., in inscriptions from this period.[32] Not only do the inscriptions have such an intertextual connection with one another, they are connected with the Dharmaśāstraic texts as well in a similar manner. The Vāḻppaḷḷi Copper Plate says that those who stand in the way of the day-to-day services will be equated with those that have married their mothers.[33] There are many more such imprecatory provisions in a large number of other records—this is an obvious invocation of the idea of *pañcamahāpātakas* of the *Dharmaśāstras* without using the expression as such.[34] We have such situations referring to the *Śāstra* texts directly and indirectly in the Tamil country[35] and the situation was not different in the case of Kerala. A world which obeyed, and demanded obedience of, the *Dharmaśāstra* rules is in evidence here. This involves storage of information and its retrieval when it was necessary for future references. Such storage and retrieval, as in the case of reference to Mūḻikkaḷa *kaccam*, also shows how the practice of setting up inscriptions in the temples constituted an important aspect of the 'information technology' of the period. This is important not only for the technical aspect of the information technology but also for its social and political implications.

It is important that much of what was recorded related to transactions in land. Such transactions interested a new class of intermediaries, placed between the state on the one side and the peasants on the other, with superior rights over land. This was the very class at the base of state formation. Not only were their rights and privileges new; but their position itself was precarious in a society where they were still a minority of relative strangers, albeit their substantial political clout and control of resources. As such, writing down what was central to their existence on materials of permanence, such as stone slabs and copper plates—the phrase used is 'for as long as the moon and stars endure'—becomes extremely important. It is significant that, of the several thousands of inscriptions from the neighbouring Cōḻa kingdom in the same period, only a handful are related to the non-Brāhmaṇa, *veḷḷānvagai*, villages.[36] Nevertheless, it has been shown that such villages constituted a vast majority of the agrarian settlements. In the absence of records relating to non-Brāhmaṇa peasant establishments from Kerala in this period, a relative absence of the non-Brāhmaṇa element is postulated.[37] As absence of evidence is not necessarily evidence of absence, an assumption of this kind is out of place. In fact, the sidelight that the records throw suggests that there was a major section of peasants with considerable power, even though there may not have been comparisons with the Tamil or Karnataka situations. In any case, they do not appear in records for the probable reason that they had nothing special to record, what they were doing being too routine a thing to merit such recording. That is, 'information', which demanded storage and retrieval, did not include that which was related to these sections, however influential they were in society. It was the minority of Brāhmaṇical groups for whom it was necessary to store information in this way, given the nature of society and polity and their own influential but precarious position in it. The difference between the non-Brāhmaṇa magnates and the Brāhmaṇical groups lay in this respect: the one found recording of information necessary while the other did not feel the need for it.

The scene gets significantly altered in the period after the disappearance of the Cēra kingdom in the twelfth century. The practice of setting up inscriptions tapers off, except in the southern regions of Kerala. Even there, the trend is downward. This tendency contrasts with what obtains in the neighbouring regions of Tamil Nadu and Karnataka, where the practice continues. In fact, the age of Vijayanagara, from the fourteenth to the sixteenth centuries, witnessed a spurt in the inscriptions in those regions, on the basis of which much of the history of that 'empire' has been reconstructed. In the case of Kerala in this period, on the other hand, there are very few inscriptions, and practically none from the kingdoms of Cochin, Calicut, or Kōlattunāḍu, when these kingdoms were on the ascendant following the disintegration of the Cēra kingdom of Mahōdayapuram. An alternative practice of storing information regarding governmental business and property transactions of a major nature begins in what is known as the *granthavari* or palm leaf documents. Thus, we see the fabulous archives of the Mahārāja of Travancore in the famous *Matilakam Granthavari*, that of the Zamorin of Calicut in the *Kōḻikkōṭan Granthavari*, etc.[38] In fact, nearly every visitor to the kingdoms of Kerala in the medieval period was impressed by the secretarial arrangement there as is apparant from what the Portuguese official, Duarte Barbosa, had to say in the sixteenth century:

> The King of Calicut continually keeps a multitude of writers in his palace who sit in a corner far from him; they write upon a raised platform, everything connected with the King's Exchequer and with the justice and governance of the realm. They write on long and stiff palm leaves, with an iron style

> without ink; they make their letters in incised strokes, like ours, and the straight lines as we do. Each of these men carries with him whithersoever he goes, a sheaf of these written leaves under his arm, and the iron style in his hand, and by this they may be recognised. And, there are seven or eight more, the King's private writers, men held in great esteem, who stand always before the King with their styles in their hands, and the bundle of leaves under their arms. Each one of them has a number of these leaves in blank, sealed by the King at the top. And, when the King desires to give or to do anything as to which he has to provide, he tells his wishes to each of these men and they write it down from the Royal seal to the bottom, and thus the order is given to whomsoever it concerns. These men are old and much respected and trusted.[39]

We have similar archives of big temples such as of Iriññālakkuṭa, Peruvanam, Kumāranallūr, etc. The practice of elaborate documents being prepared and maintained need not be taken as a sudden development: although we have no direct evidence of the existence of an elaborate secretariat in the Cēra kingdom, the parallel situation in the neighbouring Cōḻa state, with innumerable references to *varippottakam*, *varikkaṇakku*, *paṭṭōlai*, etc.,[40] may indicate a widespread practice of preparing and maintaining such elaborate documents in the king's government in these states, if on a much smaller scale.

This change from inscriptions exhibited in public to palm leaf records stored in the archives of palaces, temples and private families would call for an explanation. Nobody has addressed this problem. It would seem that the practice of setting up inscriptions died out as the groups who were responsible for these records gained in confidence. That is, it was no longer necessary for them to nervously put on record, permanently 'as long as the moon and the stars endure', whatever was happening to their property. They were now sufficiently established as the masters of their property and their rights were recognized unequivocally by the rest of society. The new landed magnates coming into prominence in the newly rising kingdoms, consisting of the royal functionaries and military personnel, did not require any such recording in inscriptions of a public nature. At the same time, as the institution of private property became more deeply entrenched, a need to have title deeds increased. So also, the greater preoccupation with a 'documented administration' in these kingdoms demanded the use of such records in a bigger way. In any case, the strategies of storing and retrieving information, as well as the nature of the information itself, underwent a major change, as the nature and need of society had changed.

NOTES AND REFERENCES

1. There is considerable discussion on the problems of orality and literacy and their interface. See, for instance, Jack Goody, *The Domestication of the Savage Mind* (Cambridge, 1977); *The Logic of Writing and the Organisation of Society* (Cambridge, 1986); *The Interface between the Written and the Oral* (Cambridge, 1987); Rosalind Thomas, *Oral Tradition and Written Record in Classical Athens* (Cambridge, 1989). For a discussion in the Indian context, Romila Thapar, *Cultural Pasts* (Delhi, 2003), pp. 195–212.
2. This is a matter of recent recognition, thanks to the work of Elamkulam P.N. Kunjan Pillai. Most of his writings are in Malayalam, a few important essays of which are available in summary form in English translation. Elamkulam P.N.K. Pillai, *Studies in Kerala History* (Kottayam, 1969).
3. For a most recent and authoritative study of these records, Iravatham Mahadevan, *Early Tamil Epigraphy: From the Earliest Times to Sixth Century* AD (Chennai, 2003). For a discussion of the uses of writing in that society, Rajan Gurukkal, 'Writing and its Uses in Ancient Tamil Society', *Studies in History*, vol. 12, no. 1, new series, 1996, pp. 67–81.
4. They speak of the donees of the caves as Jain or Buddhist monks, and their donors were largely traders. Gurukkal, 'Writing and its Uses', p. 70.
5. Some of them even claimed a north Indian origin. Others speak of their being *vāṇiyar* (from Sanskrit *vaṇij*) and being members of *negama* or *nigama*, both indicating a heavy north Indian bias.
6. The earliest written records from south India are the edicts of Aśoka. However, none has come down from the Tamil- and Malayalam-speaking regions, the inscriptions, engraved in Brāhmi, being found in the Kannada- and Telugu-speaking regions.
7. Gurukkal, 'Writing and its Uses', p. 71, has pointed out that the language of the inscriptions is considerably different from the Tamil of contemporary poetry.
8. *Travancore Archaeological Series* (hereafter *TAS*), vol. II, no. 2, pp. 8–14.
9. For the Eḍakkal Caves, F. Fawcett, 'Notes on the Rock Carvings in the Edakkal Cave, Wynad', *Indian Antiquary* (hereafter *IA*), vol. XXX, pp. 409–12. For the Eḻuttukal record, Rajan Gurukkal and Raghava Varier, *A Cultural History of Kerala* (Thiruvananthapuram, 1999), p. 198.
10. Romila Thapar observes that among the functions of the inscriptions of Aśōka was the symbolic one. She takes up the case of the Allahabad Pillar, which was 'almost a notebook of historical records'. Thapar,

Cultural Pasts, pp. 445–6. It is interesting that inscriptions in public places are looked upon with reverence in most places in India. The granite outcrop on which the Aśōkan inscriptions are engraved in Brahmagiri in Karnataka is locally called the *Akṣaraguṇḍu*, 'the hillock of letters'. Even when there is no indication whatever that these 'letters' made any sense to the local population, it is believed that the rock with writings on it has magical, healing powers. Men and cattle, afflicted with certain diseases, are administered water after washing the engravings on the rock. Inscriptions, even when they are not read, or more because of that reason, are thought to inspire awe elsewhere as well. Homage is paid to inscriptions in many temples in Karnataka and Kerala by both devotees and priests, for the wrong reason!

11. It was in the nineteenth century that a systematic attempt at surveying the inscriptions began by the Government of Madras, of which Presidency Malabar was part. Many records were noticed in the *Annual Reports* of the Department of Epigraphy and a few texts were published in the *South Indian Inscriptions*, *Indian Antiquary* and *Epigraphia Indica*. In Travancore, *TAS* brought out more texts and translations. So also other inscriptions were available in print by the middle of the twentieth century. Elamkulam took up a reconstruction of the history of Kerala in this period with the help of these inscriptions. M.G.S. Narayanan's definitive and exhaustive study of the history of the Cēra kingdom of Mahōdayapuram improved upon it considerably. Narayanan re-read many of the inscriptions used by Elamkulam and discovered and deciphered many more. The result is that we have a dependable corpus of epigraphical material, although publication of these inscriptions is a crying need. The companion volume to Narayanan's PhD thesis submitted to the University of Kerala in 1972 gives essential details of these inscriptions. 'Index to Cera Inscriptions', a companion volume to the PhD thesis 'Political and Social Conditions of Kerala under the Kulasekhara Empire', University of Kerala (Trivandrum, 1972). The text of the thesis is available in print as *Perumals of Kerala* published by the author (Calicut, 1996); but this Index is not yet available in print.
12. Kesavan Veluthat, *The Political Structure of Early Medieval South India* (Delhi, 1993), p. 10.
13. *TAS*, vol. II, no. 9 (i & ii), pp. 62–70, 80–5.
14. *Epigraphia Indica* (hereafter *EI*), vol. III, pp. 68ff.
15. *TAS*, vol. I, no. 13, A, pp. 187–93.
16. *TAS*, vol. IV, no. 7, pp.22–65.
17. *TAS*, vol. II, no. 9 (iii), pp. 850–6.
18. *IA*, vol. XX, pp. 285–90; *EI*, vol. XVI, no. 27, pp. 339–45.
19. *TAS*, vol. II, no. 3, pp. 131–207. This is a fabulous document, or rather collection of documents. A single record, of which a few plates are lost, it summarizes a large number of different transactions made at

different points in time. This is a goldmine of information for the historian.

20. *TAS*, vol. IV, no. 1, pp. 1–11.
21. K.A. Nilakanta Sastri wrote in the context of Cōḻa inscriptions of a similar nature: 'Quite often, inscriptions on temple walls served the purpose of a public registration office by conserving a trustworthy record of sales, mortgages, and other forms of transfers of property-rights in village-lands', *The Cōḻas* (Madras, 1955), p. 6.
22. Even this exception, proverbially, proves the rule. This document of the Ay chief Vikramāditya Varaguṇa registers a grant to a Buddhist *vihāra*, namely, the famous Śrīmūlavāsa. It is reasonable to assume that the donees, for whom the record was a title-deed of the landed property granted with it, were more at home with the *Nāgari* script and the Sanskrit language (in which the bulk of the record is), except for the 'operational part' dealing with the details of the land, which is in Vaṭṭeḻuttu script and Tamil language.
23. Narayanan, *Perumals of Kerala*, pp. 25–6, 212–14.
24. Although Kulaśēkhara Āḻvār was more conscious of being the Cēra king, a consciousness expressed through his titles such as *Śēralarkōn*, *Kolli kāvalan*, *Villavar kōn*, etc. (*Perumāḷ Tirumoḻi*, opening stanza), he had greater contacts with temples such as Śrīraṅgam in the Tamil-speaking regions. He also claimed what might have delighted the *Mūvaraśar* in the early historical period, that is, a status of at once being the lord of the Pāṇḍya, Cōḻa and Cēra capitals. See his titles such as *Kolli kāvalan*, *Kūṭal nāyakan*, and *Kōḻi kōn*. Ibid.; 2.10. So also, his predecessor, identified with the Tamil Bhakti saint Cēramān Perumāḷ Nāyanār, had his friends from the Tamil country and looked towards temples such as Cidambaram.
25. An inscription from north Kerala, from the chiefly territory of Kolattunāḍu, speaks of its scribe as *Mūṣikēśvara-svarṇakāra*. A slightly later record identifies its scribe as *Cēramān Lōkapperuntaṭṭān*. Writing on copper plates naturally required skills in smithy. If this is extended, it will appear that engraving on stone was done by stone-cutters, which is not the case at least in the known instances. Will it mean that specialists were called for the purpose? That will suggest an exclusiveness for literacy, which is not entirely out of place in our context.
26. Sastri, *The Cōḻas*, p. 469, has drawn attention to the highly formal and deferential formula in which the receipt of royal orders in localities were mentioned in documents. In fact, the Anbil Plates, which Sastri quotes from, has the following statement: 'Seeing the *srimukham*, we rose to welcome it, saluted it and placed it on our heads before taking and reading it'. Of the reverence and ceremony there can be hardly any doubt; but how many did really 'read' it? The ceremony, in fact, is a function of the inability of the addressees to read it: for them it was a royal order which demanded veneration, whatever its content.

27. Narayanan, *Perumals of Kerala*; Kesavan Veluthat, *Brahman Settlements in Kerala: Historical Studies* (Calicut, 1978), passim; Rajan Gurukkal, *The Kerala Temple and the Medieval Agrarian System* (Sukapuram, 1992), pp. 9–10.
28. *TAS*, vol. II, no. 2, pp. 8–14, l.2.
29. *Cf.* R.S. Sharma, *Indian Feudalism* (Delhi, 1980) 2nd edn, pp. 9, 161–2.
30. Kesavan Veluthat, 'The *Sabha* and *Parishad* in Early Medieval South India: Correlation of Epigraphic and Dharmasastraic Evidence', *Tamil Civilisation*, vol. III, nos 2 and 3, June and September 1985.
31. The text of this *kaccam* has not come down to us. It was Elamkulam who noticed its importance. He took it for a decision, arrived at a grand assembly held at Mūḻikkaḷam, that had the force of law, the purpose of which was to protect the interests of the tenants. Elaṁkulam P.N. Kunjan Pillai, *Studies in Kerala History*, pp. 337–8. Narayanan, on the other hand, rejected this romantic idea and showed that it was one of the temple committee resolutions, which gained the status of a precedent all over Kerala, its aim being to protect the corporate character of the communitarian bodies against the selfish interests of individual members. Narayanan, *Perumals of Kerala*, pp. 114–16.
32. Narayanan, *Perumals of Kerala*, pp. 116–19.
33. *TAS*, vol. II, no. 2, pp. 8–14, ll.3–4.
34. Narayanan, *Perumals of Kerala*, p. 116, has drawn attention to this. See also his essay on 'The Socio-economic Implications of The Concept of Mahapatakas in The Feudal Society of South India', *Proceedings of Indian History Congress* (Calicut, 1976).
35. In an interesting article, J.D.M. Derrett draws attention to an interesting record where the decision of a *sabha* in a matter of *Dharmaśāstraic* question is recorded. Authorities in *Dharmaśāstra* are quoted and every detail of thc procedure related to the conduct of the *sabhā* as laid down in the texts is followed. 'Two inscriptions Concerning the Status of Kammalas and the Application of Dharmasastra', *Professor K.A. Nilakanta Sastri 80th Birthday Felicitation Volume* (Madras, 1971).
36. For the non-Brāhmaṇa groups, what was happening was too routine an event to be recorded, which was not the case in the case of the Brāhmaṇas! Veluthat, *Political Structure*, p. 169.
37. Much of the writing on the history of Kerala, excepting that of Elamkulam Kunjan Pillai, makes this assumption. Pillai had gone to the extreme of assuming that most of the land was controlled by the non-Brāhmaṇical group and this has been rightly rejected. In the process, however, an assumption in the other extreme, that all land belonged to the Brāhmaṇas seems to have struck roots. Even this has to be re-examined.
38. The *Matialakam Granthavari*, a treasure house of information for many matters in the history of southern Kerala, is languishing in the Kerala

State Archives. Unless something is done seriously, this huge corpus will decay. Much of the *Kōḻikkōṭan Granthavari* is already lost to us. What remains of it has been maintained by the Vallathol Vidyapitham, Edapal, on the basis of which the following PhD Thesis is written: V.V. Haridas, 'The King, Court and Culture in Medieval Kerala: The Zamorins of Calicut', unpublished, Mangalore University, 2003. There are similar archives of private families as well. A good example is the *Vaññēri Granthavari*, a collection of documents related to a rich Nampūtiri family and a temple it controlled in the Malappuram district. M.G.S. Narayanan, ed., *Vanneri Granthavari*, Calicut University Historical Series, vol. I (Calicut University, 1987). Another series of *granthavaris*, somewhat misleadingly called the *Tiruvalla Granthavari* (2 vols, ed., P. Unnikrishnan Nair, Mahatma Gandhi University [Kottayam, 1998 and 1999]), has been published. This is a collection of documents of two priestly families and relate to the temples with which they had relations, the kind of services their members performed in them and the incomes they received. There are many more such *granthavaris* which cry out for the attention of historians.

39. M.L. Dames, ed., *The Book of Duarte Barbosa*, vol. II, pp. 18–19.
40. Sastri, *The Cōḷas*, 1955, p. 467.

9

The King as Lord and Overlord*

'... of Śri Kulaśēkharavarman, the Supreme Lord of Mahōdayapura and the Crest Jewel of the Lineage of Keralas'.

Tapatīsamvaraṇam, Prologue.

'... of Kulaśēkharavarman, the Overlord of Kerala, [the Country] of Beautiful Paddy Fields'.

Subhadrādhanañjayam, Prologue. (See note 27 below).

The present essay embodies the results of an attempt to conceptualize the earliest form of state that came into existence in Kerala under the Cēramān Perumāḷs (ninth through eleventh centuries AD). The essay is provoked, on the one hand, by the rich and varied discussion that has taken place around the institution of state in recent decades both in India and abroad and, on the other, by a refusal of historiography in this part of the country to take such discussions into account. Analyses of the formation, transformation and ways of functioning of the state have enriched many branches of social sciences, of which history is one of the major beneficiaries. This has led to refreshing reappraisals of the empirical and theoretical aspects of that phenomenon in history. Even political systems that are thought to have been well researched, such as the ones in medieval France or ancient Egypt, have received the benefit of this re-examination.[1]

In the case of India, as a matter of fact, it is only recently that the nature of the state has been a subject of serious discussion among historians. Although this new interest is very lively and has been responsible for very rich debate throwing considerable light on the nature of the institution, the relatively late nature of the interest cannot

* Paper presented at a seminar on 'Interpreting Indian History', held at the University of Heidelberg, 20–22 July 2006.

be lost sight of. One of the reasons for this neglect or complacency seems to have been an abiding obsession with the construct of Oriental Despotism, with its variant in the notion of Asiatic Mode of Production. Accordingly, 'state' meant just the king. His powers were unlimited. The nature of kingship and of the 'state' did not undergo changes of any consequence and the scholarly disputes that historians engaged in were confined to details of the dynastic history and variations in the 'administrative systems' of the kingdoms/empires. Golden ages and dark ages alternated in this scheme. The ideological preoccupation of the historian did not matter much: both the so-called imperialists and nationalists shared the assumption of an unchanging east, often without being conscious of the implications of such an assumption.

The story in the case of Kerala is illustrative. When colonial writers began their attempts to recover the history of Kerala in the nineteenth century, what they confronted were timeless legends floating about apparently weightlessly. Most of these writers, such as William Logan, the collector of Malabar who wrote its District Manual, were inclined to reject the stories as so many legends and so much of nonsense.[2] This rejection also constituted the necessary first step in claiming authenticity for what they were themselves writing as *the* history of the region. Ironically, details of the very legends, which they sought to reject, were accepted for historical facts in the new histories they wrote! Thus a single, centralized polity was assumed in Kerala to begin with and it was shown to have got fractured following the flight of the [last] Cēramān Perumāl in the period beginning the Kollam Era (AD 825)—a picture that Kerala was stated to have presented of itself to the Portuguese when they arrived in the end of the fifteenth century. The political history of Kerala, thus, was of mutually bickering fragments. Interestingly, when 'nationalist' historians such as K.P. Padmanabha Menon wrote a history of Kerala in four volumes or earlier a history of Cochin in two volumes, this assumption was carried forward.[3] As a result, the notion of an assortment of changeless polities in the period following ninth century AD got strengthened. There was no place in this scheme, which did not allow for any changes, for questions related to the formation and transformation of the state. It was a small mercy that Kerala did not present itself as another case of Oriental Despotism, although many of its constituent elements, such as an immutable society and polity, unchanging village communities, etc., were identified there. All those who wrote histories of Kerala in the subsequent decades accepted this picture somewhat uncritically,[4] until a major historiographical shift came about in the second half of the twentieth century.

The availability of newer and richer sources, both literary and epigraphical, enabled this shift. A number of inscriptions had been discovered from different parts of Kerala towards the end of the nineteenth century and early in the next, which, however, did not immediately affect the historiography of Kerala.[5] Simultaneously, a huge body of literature in both Tamil and Sanskrit was discovered, the importance of which for the history of the deep south was recognized sufficiently early. The latter revolutionized the understanding of early south Indian history as a whole, recognizing a 'Sangam Period' there. The relevance of this body of Tamil literature for Kerala was not appreciated either, although a few texts were indeed about the Cēras and treated as useful for the history of Kerala. It was Elamkulam P.N. Kunjan Pillai who appreciated that the whole of what is called the Sangam literature is relevant to the history of Kerala as much as to Tamil Nadu. He wrote the history of the Cēra kingdom in the Sangam Period and identified nearly all aspects of a state society, although he did not discuss the question of state there. So also, piecing together information from the epigraphical records dating from about the ninth century, Kunjan Pillai came out with the bold statement that, instead of the inauguration of a phase of decentralization and fractures in the polity of Kerala, early ninth century witnessed the establishment of a unified and centralized polity in what he called the 'Second Cēra Empire' or 'Kulaśēkhara Empire'.[6] He drew the outlines of the political history of this second Cēra empire, which ruled over the whole of the territory of present-day Kerala, and presented the picture of its administrative system, social order and economic aspects. M.G.S. Narayanan corrected many of the details in the writings of Elamkulam, including the pretentious label of 'empire'.[7] He also brought out the way in which economy, society and polity were organically linked. However, neither Pillai nor Narayanan addressed the problem related to 'state' under the Cēras in these initial studies, particularly its origin, nature and dimensions of change. A few subsequent papers of Narayanan have raised some of these questions, describing the state under the Cēras as characterized by 'feudalism', 'ritual sovereignty', etc. differently on different occasions.[8] Contradictions between them and within each notwithstanding, this seems to be the only serious attempt to conceptualize state in medieval Kerala. The considerable work of Rajan Gurukkal and Raghava Varier, taken up jointly and separately, too has not raised and answered the question effectively.[9] We seek to raise questions regarding the nature of this state.

THE ANTECEDENTS

When we start getting historical evidence from the southern end of the peninsula, the region to the west of the Western Ghats covering the present-day state of Kerala was an integral part of a larger socio-cultural unit called Tamiḻakam.[10] Generalizations relevant to that larger unit are largely valid about Kerala as well. Thanks to recent researches, there is considerable clarity about the social formation which characterized that region in this period. References to different landscapes couched in the floral symbolism of the *tiṇai*, contained in the poetic conventions of early Tamil literature, demonstrate the uneven development of the macro-region. Among the various means of subsistence, agriculture occupied but a small place; hunting, gathering, fishing, pastoral activities and even plunder were the other chief means. Society was characterized by almost a hand-to-mouth existence, such labour as was necessary for the economic activities being available within the family itself. The units of social organization were the families, and the heads of the more important families in the settlements wielded power. It was a pre-state society, which had at best reached a chiefdom-level in its organization, with several major and minor chiefs wielding varying degrees of power. These chiefs lived on plunder and prestations, in a world of cattle-raids and hero-worship. Redistribution of the resources brought to the centre based itself on patronage and reciprocity. Bards and minstrels, singing the praise of these chiefs, provided the necessary legitimacy to them. Those on the west coast included the Cēras, the Āys, the Mūvas, and so on. The Cēras, who had several collateral lines with seats in different parts, seem to have been more important than the rest of these. One of their branches had their seat in Karūr near Tiruchchirappalli, and the river valleys on the west coast as well as the port towns at their mouths were under their control.

Historians in the past used to count these Cēras among the 'three crowned kings' of Tamiḻakam, assuming obviously that they presided over a state society.[11] In reality, however, most elements of a state, such as a political authority which functions within defined territorial limits and delegates its powers to functionaries, which acts as an instrument for integrating social segments not by rituals but by economic functions and which is financed by an income collected as regular contributions on an impersonal basis, are lacking there.[12] In the case of the west coast, it is also significant that one does not come across any evidence of urbanism, literacy and monuments of a political authority in this period. It is only in the period after the eighth century that we start getting evidence of a state society.

EMERGENCE OF THE STATE

Historians have not quite raised the question regarding the factors behind the formation of the state in Kerala. Earlier historians did not obviously think in terms of a transition from a pre-state to a state society; but they did see something of an epochal transformation in the period that lay between the close of the so-called Sangam period and the revival of the 'three crowned kings' in Tamiḻakam, that is to say, between the fourth and eighth centuries of the Christian era. The ghost of the Kaḷabhras, who were thought to have been 'ubiquitous enemies of civilization' and responsible for a 'long historical night' in the history of south India, kept haunting them.[13] It refuses to be exorcised even when the questions addressed have changed.[14] However, the evidence of a Kaḷabhra presence in south India is too slender to be the basis of an explanation for an epochal transformation, even if one accepts that an inconsequential invasion can bring about such major changes in all aspects of human life.[15] In the case of Kerala, there is absolutely no evidence, nor even a faint tradition, suggesting any Kaḷabhra connection. Therefore, one has to look for alternative explanations for changes in society which eventually led to the formation of state in Kerala.

Within the chiefdom-level societies of early historical south India, settled agriculture had registered its presence in the riparian plains, although it had not yet attained predominance in the economy of the day. So also, there is evidence of the knowledge of iron technology which that society had possessed, particularly the use of ploughshare in the archaeological record; but even that by itself was not sufficient to bring about any major change in economy or society. Things continued as they were for some time, apparently because there was no compelling factor to set the forces of change in motion. New elements in the relations of production and distribution were gradually introduced, which were capable of upsetting the comfortable balance in society. The unequal distribution of the social product and the creation of several sections with special privileges, but no participation in the processes of production in any manner, was the point from which this departure can be identified.

In early Tamil literature, which forms an important source of history for early historical Tamiḻakam including Kerala, there are songs celebrating generous gifts given to the fighters for their services, the bards for their songs and the Brāhmaṇa priests for the sacrifices they performed for and on behalf of the chief. Many of these gifts were in the form of land. The statements in the poems, like the one in the colophon to the fifth decad of the *Patiṟṟuppattu*, that Paraṇar, the Brāhmaṇa poet who not only sang the decad but also performed a sacrifice for Ceṅkuṭṭuvan, the Cēra hero of the poem, received a gift of 72000 villages along with Umparkāṭu, or the one in the colophon to the seventh decade that Kapilar, another Brāhmaṇa poet who composed the decade, was given all the land that can be seen from the top of the hill Naṉṟā, may be an exaggeration; but the practice of granting land to Brāhmaṇas for the performance of sacrifices and for composing songs praising a chief went on increasing. In fact, such references are far too many to be fictional. Non-Brāhmaṇa poet-singers, too, received munificent gifts. So also, there are references where fighters demand that they would settle for no less a gift from the chief than the best land in the most fertile district.[16] Such gifts had two effects. For one thing, they recognized the importance of agriculture and provided an initiative to its expansion. Second, and more important, they led to the creation of different shades of rights over land, over and above that of the actual tiller. That demanded a restructuring of the relations of production. In the earlier period, labour used for production was from within the family itself. That would not work any longer in the more labour-intensive field of agriculture, particularly where those who enjoyed the fruits of production did not do any labour at all. This meant induction of extra-kin labour for purposes of production; and it proved to be the thin end of the wedge which ultimately eroded the entire system and brought about a new formation.[17] It is here that the emergence of a class of non-cultivators enjoying superior rights over land becomes important. The ethic of Tamil poetry itself gets tuned to this formation, as the songs contained in the later texts, what is known as the *Kīḻkkaṇakku* literature, amply demonstrate. There is a definite sympathy to agriculture and a disapproval of plunder in this class of literature.[18]

Evidence from the near side is complementary. We start getting profuse epigraphic evidence from Kerala by the beginning of AD ninth century.[19] The documents are largely in the form of resolutions of Brāhmaṇical groups that formed committees to manage the affairs of the temple, the most important of which was related to land. There are a handful of records granting privileges to trading groups as well. A special feature of the Kerala inscriptions is the near-absence of 'royal' charters, which also precludes the typical *praśasti*s that form the 'historical introductions' in Indian epigraphy. What is available from the records, however, is useful to raise and answer questions regarding the nature of the state, the unmistakable presence of which these documents announce.

A close look at the very first of these documents is instructive.[20] This records the proceedings of a joint meeting of the committees managing the affairs of the temples of Vāḻappaḷḷi and Tiruvāṟṟuvāy, which were subsidiary settlements of one of the more prominent Brāhmaṇa *grāmas*, viz. Tiruvalla, in the south. It opens with an unusual invocation of Śiva and gives the date as the twelfth year of Rāja Rājādhirāja Paramēśvara Bhaṭṭāraka Rājaśēkharadēva (AD *c.* 820). Elsewhere the record styles him as the *Perumān Aṭikaḷ*, a term used in other parts of south India as well to describe the king. This shows that not only was there already a 'king' in Kerala by now but also that he conformed to the general pattern of kingship that had emerged in south India by that time. A closer look at his title, a translation of which in the local idiom as *kō kōnmai koṇṭān ko* is available in inscriptions of the later rulers of the dynasty, would also show that the pattern was of the model of the *cakravartin* that had developed in a still larger context. That the inscription is from, and related to, a couple of temples located far away from Mahōdayapuram, the capital of the kingdom, is important insofar as it shows that the authority of this king, such as it was, was not confined to the capital and its environs. In fact, the document stipulates that a fine levied on certain defaulters should go to the *Perumān Aṭikaḷ*. It points also to the ways in which land belonging to the temple had been assigned to tenants and the temple used to collect a rent.

If these are details available from a temple inscription, another record granting privileges to a Christian church by the lord of a locality has other interesting patterns to present.[21] The famous Syrian Christian Copper Plates are chronologically the second epigraphical record of the Cēras of Mahōdayapuram. Dated in the fifth regnal year of King Sthāṇu Ravi (AD 849), it was made by Ayyan Aṭikaṭiruvaṭikaḷ, who was the lord of the locality of Vēṇāṭu. A local lord in south Kerala, while making a grant, acknowledges the superior authority of the Cēra king far north. The grant shows the presence of many functionaries such as *adhikārar, prakṛti, Puṉṉaittalaippati, Pūḷaikkuṭippati, Kōyil Adhikārikaḷ, Tiyam āḻvān, Matil nāyakan,* and others to whom power was delegated. It also speaks, very elaborately, of the different kinds of dues collected on an impersonal basis. It makes a reference to crime and punishment; as well as assessment, collection and remission of various types of 'taxes'. The debt to texts like the *Arthaśāstra* is clear in this record. Political authority, wielded within a clearly defined territory, is unmistakable and its exercise went certainly beyond rituals. It speaks significantly about the transfer of many of these rights, which are thought to belong to the state, to the beneficiaries of the grant.

All this would mean that the phenomenon of state had already established itself in Kerala by the time of the very first inscriptions from that region, that is, AD ninth century. A consideration of the details in the records of that kingdom enables us to make generalizations about the emergence of that state. The picture of Kerala that we gather from these inscriptions is that of a land with certain areas forming clusters of agrarian settlements. These clusters were concentrated in the fertile valleys of rivers like Pērār, Periyār and Pampā and had very prosperous Brāhmaṇical temples at their centre.[22] The inscriptions show further that agricultural land in those areas were largely under the control of Brāhmaṇical groups, either as their own property called *brahmasvam* or as 'god's property' called *dēvasvam.* As a result, a vast section of population came under the control of these Brāhmaṇa landlords. This meant a stratified society with certain sections having greater claim over the surplus than others. References in the inscriptions to donations made by non-Brāhmaṇa magnates point to the other owning groups as well. All this was a far cry from the chiefdom-level societies of an earlier period, where there was no stratification in society in any visible manner, no political authority functioning within a more or less defined territory, no collection of revenue on an impersonal basis, and no monopoly of coercive power. That is to say, by the time we come to the ninth century, a monarchical state under the dynasty of the Cēras had come to be established in Kerala.

Conditions for the emergence of the state were, thus, mature by this time; but the actual take-off is not clear from the records. The picture that the documents present is of one where the state had already come into existence. However, the exact circumstances under which this happened is not known from the records. Fortunately, tradition contained in the *Keraḷōlpatti* acquires significance here.[23] It speaks of the creation, and donation to Brāhmaṇas, of the land by Paraśurāma. The Brāhmaṇas, who were settled in sixty-four villages, started ruling the land as *brahmakṣatra* with elected representatives running the government. But they grew corrupt, and realized that ruling is best done by Kṣatriyas. Thereupon they invited Kṣatriya rulers from outside. There is a chaotic list of the *Perumāḷ*s who ruled Kerala. In one place it says that a Kṣatriya brother and sister were brought, the brother was made the *Perumāḷ* and the sister given in marriage to a Brāhmaṇa with the express understanding that the children she bore him would succeed to the throne. There is no reason why this should not be taken as encapsulating the memory of the Cēras being established on the throne by the Brāhmaṇical elite what with the Tamil origins of the dynasty, its matrilineal character in Kerala and the heavy Brāhmaṇical support it got and so on. In this context, the *Periyapurāṇam* story[24] that Cēramān *Perumāḷ*, who was meditating in the temple, was persuaded by the ministers to take up the reins of the kingdom is parallel. In any case, that a state with a monarchical form with hereditary succession was established in Kerala by the beginning of the ninth century is not to be disputed.

What were its features?

THE SOVEREIGN

First and foremost, the king stands out. Usually he was styled by a simple but elegant monosyllabic *kō*, meaning, 'king'. He was also known as the *Perumāḷ*, or 'the Great One' and its variants such as *Perumān Aṭikaḷ*. As Cēra inscriptions do not have the typical *praśasti* which characterize the epigraphical records of other parts of south India, it is not as easy to reconstruct the image or self-image of the king.[25] However, it is possible to form some idea about him from available records. He was a member of the Cēra dynasty, expressed variously by the phrases *Cēramān*, *Cēran*, *Cērakulapradīpa*, *Kēraḷavamśakētu* and so on.[26] Although the pattern of succession is not clear, it has been suggested that they were matrilineal. This is not improbable, considering the matrilineal character of society in Kerala. The Kṣatriyas of Kerala in later period followed matriliny. The *Perumāḷs* claimed the status of a Kṣatriya as the suffix *varman* attached to their names indicates. He is presented as belonging to the *Sūryavamśa* of Purāṇic fame, which lent further support to the claim of Kṣatriya status. Kulaśēkharavarman, one of the early rulers of this kingdom and author of two major Sanskrit plays, was conscious that while he was *Mahōdayapuraparamēśvara* ('Supreme Lord of the City of Mahodaya'); he was also *Kēraḷādhinātha* ('Overlord of Kerala'), a statement with great factual and metaphorical significance.[27] Other titles of the rulers used in inscriptions, such as *Rājarājādhirājā*, *Kō kōnmai koṇṭān kō*, *Cakravarttikaḷ*, etc. indicate a claim to the status of *cakravartin* or universal emperor celebrated in the Brāhmaṇical literature.[28] The king continually shows an attitude of habitual obedience to Brāhmaṇas, once going to the extent of atoning for having offended them.[29] All this shows the nature and attitudes of the monarchy and its sacral character. At the same time, the sovereign character of the *Perumāḷ* cannot be doubted.[30]

The king was not alone at the capital or when on tour. He did not, to be sure, have a large entourage; but there was something of a council. This consisted of what the records call the *Nālu Taḷi* (lit., 'the four temples').[31] It has been shown that this council had eight members, two each coming from one of the four leading Brāhmaṇical settlements near the capital city, namely, Mūḻikkaḷam, Airāṇikkaḷam, Iruṅṅāṭikkūtal and Paṟavūr, and having their seats in the temples in the city such as Mēlttaḷi, Kīḻttaḷi, Ciṅṅapuram Taḷi and Neṭiya Taḷi respectively. They represented the Brāhmaṇical establishment in Kerala and had great influence on the king. Besides, there was a junior member of the royal house, *Kōyil Adhikārikaḷ*, about whose functions we do not have too many details.[32] At least in one case, he was a close kin of the sovereign and later succeeded to throne as the *Perumāḷ* himself.[33] In another case, the sovereign calls himself *Kōyil Adhikārikaḷ*,[34] perhaps in memory of his once having been one, or else to express the fact that he still retained that office. Then there was the chief of the royal bodyguards, known as the *Āyiram* ('the thousand').[35] A secretary, to write down royal orders, is present in the Jewish Copper Plates (AD 1000).[36] So also, a 'Commander of the Eastern Forces' shows his face there. In an inscription from Neṭumpuṟam Taḷi in Palakkad District, we come across a certain Pullūr Kumaran Kumarāticcan, who is described as the *Paṭanāyar* or 'the leader of the army'.[37] An inscription from Airāṇikkaḷam, which M.G.S. Narayanan and the present writer have deciphered, speaks about a *sēnāpati*.[38] This entourage seems to have accompanied the sovereign on his tours as well, as shown by records from Kollam and Perunna, situated far away from the capital city.

TERRITORY AND POPULATION

The documents give us a somewhat clear idea of the territory over which the Cēra Perumāḷs exercised their power. This is in sharp contrast with an earlier period, when the Cēras are known just as the name of a chiefly lineage, with no territory being associated with them. In fact, the practice of using the name Cēral/Cēra and its Prākṛt/Sanskrit variant, Kerala, to signify the lineage to which the ruler belonged continued. Gradually, the usage of the term Kerala gets shifted to signify a territory.[39] This territory is more or less coterminous with the present-day linguistic state of Kerala, although clearly demarcated boundaries can never be delineated in pre-cartographical situations.

The earliest definitive reference to Kerala as a separate geographical entity, and made by that name, is arguably in the *Avantisundarīkathā* of Daṇḍin.[40] The author, the eighth century Sanskrit poet from the Pallava capital in Kāñci, speaks of his friends including Mātṛdatta, 'the best of Brāhmaṇas from Kerala'. In the fashion characteristic of Sanskrit, Daṇḍin uses Kerala in the plural (*Kēraḷēṣu*), showing thereby that it was already familiar as the name of a country. Kulaśēkharavarman, a ninth century king of Kerala, and the author of *Subhadrādhanañjaya* and *Tapatīsaṃvaraṇa*, two Sanskrit plays and perhaps one more, *Vicchinnābhiṣēka*, as well as a work in prose, *Āścaryamañjarī*, is clearer. He has been identified with Sthāṇu Ravi Kulaśēkhara (AD 844–883) of the inscriptions, and with Kulaśēkhara Āḻvār of the Vaiṣṇava Bhakti traditions who wrote the *Perumāḷ Tirumoḻi* in Tamiḻ and *Mukundamālā* in Sanskrit. He uses the term Kerala in the sense of both a lineage and a territory.[41] As we have seen, he describes himself as both *Kēraḷakulacūḍāmaṇi* and

Kēraḷādhināṭha in the Sanskrit plays, the term Kerala in the former standing for the lineage and in the latter, for the dynasty.[42] A slightly later text clarifies that the king of Mahōdayapuram ruled *Kēraḷa-viṣaya*, 'the land of Kerala'.[43] So also, a contemporary of Kulaśēkhara describes his patron as 'ruling the earth', *vasudhām + avataḥ*, punning on which he also says that he possessed resources as well as his own city [of Mahōdayapuram] (*vasu+dhāma+vataḥ*).[44] The *Vyaṅgyavyākhyā*, a commentary on the plays composed during the playwright's lifetime, describes the author as *Kēraḷaviṣayādhipa* or the overlord of the *Keralaviṣaya*.[45] In short, Kerala gets identified as a geographical unit with more or less definite boundaries and that unit becomes the territory of the state by the time we come to AD ninth century. This consciousness of territory is not expressed just from within. We start getting references to Kerala as a separate political unit in the records of the Cāḷukyas, Pallavas and Pāṇḍyas a little earlier and of the Cōḻas by the time of these plays.[46] The Tiruvālaṅgāḍu Copper Plates of the Cōḻa (eleventh century), describes Kerala as 'the land created by Rāma who takes pleasure in exterminating the Kṣatriyas and where good people live with joy'.[47] Here, Kerala is not only the name of a land, but the enemy territory, which the Cōḻa king conquered.

This territory can be identified by the distribution of Cēra inscriptions. More than one hundred and fifty inscriptions have survived from the period of the Cēra kingdom between the beginning of the ninth and the end of the eleventh centuries. They are distributed fairly widely in present-day Kerala, from Kasaragod to Thiruvananthapuram, barring the High Ranges and some other regions. Most of them mention the name of a Cēra sovereign, in whose regnal year the document would be dated. A superordinate presence of the Cēras is in evidence in these inscriptions in other ways as well, as for example in the way in which the *kaccam* of Mūḻikkaḷam was honoured all over.[48] All this is evidence of a consciousness of territory that had emerged by the time the Cēra kingdom had come into existence, a feature absent in an earlier period.

There is less clarity in the matter of our understanding of the population. The inscriptions and literature of the Cēra period are not very useful to say anything about the people. However, the information that we have in *Kēraḷōlpatti* is interesting.[49] After narrating the story of the creation of the land of Kerala by Paraśurāma and its donation to Brāhmaṇas, it goes on to say how the new Brāhmaṇa settlers refused to stay. Upon this, Paraśurāma brought a fresh lot, gave them land, and enjoined a special hairstyle so that they would not be accepted if they went back. The narrative also speaks about the different castes which constitute the population of Kerala, each with its own characteristic features which later get defined in what is known as *Kēraḷācāra*. These are exclusive to Kerala. So also, at least from a slightly later period, there is a clear distinction made between the people of Kerala and those from outside such as the Tamils and the Tuḷuvas. Thus, a population, identifiable not just by residence and birth alone but by other clear markers, is evident.

THE LOCALITIES AND THEIR LORDS

Greater details concerning the functions of the state are available in relation to the localities. As we saw in the case of the Syrian Christian Copper Plates, there were the lords of the localities, described as *Nāṭu Uṭaiyavar* or *Nāṭu Vāḻumavar* or simple *Nāṭuvāḻi* in the records—the 'district governors' or 'feudatories' of an earlier historiography.[50] It was they who looked after the governance of the regions. Thus we have about thirteen such localities with their lords mentioned in the records of the period. Many of them continued into later periods and became the bases of the principalities of late medieval Kerala. The relationship in which these localities and their lords stood to the Cēra king was by no means uniform. At the northern extreme was Kōlattunāṭu enjoying near-autonomy, acknowledging nominally a weak suzerainty of the Cēra king; there were hereditary lords of localities such as Eṟāḷanāṭu while the names of three lords of Neṭumpuṟayūrnāṭu are given as if they belonged each to a different house. It may be that they were nominated by the king, as we also get an instance where the same person, Paṉṟitturutti Pōḻan Kumaran was lord of both Kālkkaraināṭu and Neṭumpuṟayūrnāṭu.[51] Is it a case that the lord of Kālkkaraināṭu was placed in additional charge of Neṭumpuṟayūrnāṭu as well? This is not improbable, as the lords of Neṭumpuṟayūrnāṭu too were from different families. Another instance of lords being nominated is that of Naṉṟuḻaināṭu, where we see two lords of another locality, Vēṇāṭu, successively in charge of this locality as well.[52] This means that there were lords who owed their position to a direct appointment probably by the Cēra king himself. There were a *mūtta kūṟu* or *mutu kūṟu* ('senior') and an *iḷaya kūṟu* or *iḷam kūṟu* ('junior') in the houses of certain lords,[53] while such dignities are not heard about in certain others. While some, such as Vēṇāṭu or Kōlattunāṭu, had a hoary past perhaps going back to the days of early Tamil literature, a few were clearly cases of a more recent emergence. Some continued into modern times; some others perished with the Cēra kingdom. The whole point, therefore, is that the localities and their lords were of such varied character that they cannot be described as so many 'district governors' ruling over 'divisions' of the Cēra kingdom.[54] It will be more realistic to perceive them as lords who had evolved in the respective localities, and later incorporated within the Cēra state structure with varying degrees of effectiveness.[55]

The character of these lords as so many warlords is brought out most effectively by their military role. It is well known that the first half of tenth century had witnessed hostilities between the Cōḻas and the Rāṣṭrakūṭas during the period of the 'balance of two empires'.[56] Other political powers in south India had to define their position vis-à-vis one of the two, and we see the Cēras on the Cōḻa side. The Cēras, naturally, expected the lords of localities under their overlordship not to go to the other side. Thus, when the Mūṣika prince Īśāna married a Cēdi princess from the Rāṣṭrakūṭa camp, the Cēras undertook a punitive expedition against the Mūṣikas and forced them behave.[57] A more important situation is available in the famous Battle of Takkōḷam fought between the Cōḻas and the Rāṣṭrakūṭas. We see the Cēras fighting on the side of the Cōḻas; and it was the forces of the localities such as Vaḷḷuvanāṭu, Neṭuṅkālāynāṭu, etc. that did the actual fighting.[58] Thus, the expectation and practice of the locality lords to render military service for and on behalf of the Cēra sovereign becomes clear. In this context, the presence of many such lords to attest the Jewish Copper Plates acquires significance.[59] When Bhāskara Ravivarman, the Cēra king, made a grant to the Jewish merchant Joseph Rabban in AD 1000, six of the locality lords endorsed it as witnesses together with the 'Commander of the Eastern Forces'. On another occasion, when Rāmavarma Kulaśēkhara was residing at the Panaiṅkāvil Palace at Kollam to make amends for the violence he committed to the *āryas*, a number of such lords, significantly described as his *sāmantas*, were present.[60] A repeat performance of this comes, typically as a farce, in the Vīra Rāghava Copper Plates (AD 1225): issued about a century after the disintegration of the Cēra kingdom, it still invokes the localities to endorse the grant although one does not come across the signature of any lord in the document.[61]

One of the most important features of the locality lords in this period is an organization, counted in hundreds, attached to them. Thus we have the Six Hundred of Vēṇāṭu, the Three Hundred of Naṉṟuḻaināṭu, the Six Hundred of Kīḻmalaināṭu, the Six Hundred of Vaḷḷuvanāṭu, the Six Hundred of Ēṟāḷanāṭu with the Three Hundred of Eṭattaṟanāṭu which in all probability was the junior lineage of the lords of Ēṟāḷanāṭu, the Six Hundred of Rāmavaḷanāṭu, the Seven Hundred of the senior lord and the Three Hundred of the junior lord of Kuṟumpoṟaināṭu, the Five Hundred of Puṟakiḻānāṭu, etc. in the inscriptions.[62] Till recently there was no information about the 'Hundred Organizations' attached to the lord of Kōlattunāṭu; but an inscription which M.G.S. Narayanan and I have brought out talks about the Thousand of Kōlam,[63] in obvious confirmation of references to the *Kōlabaḷi Sāsiravaru* in the inscriptions of the neighbouring Tuḷu country.[64] There are a few *nāṭu* localities in relation to which the information regarding the Hundred Organizations is not forthcoming. Earlier historians had looked at these as representative bodies at the *nāṭu* level and even built fanciful theories around them;[65] but M.G.S. Narayanan has shown that these constituted the trusted bodyguards, the 'companions of honour', of the *nāṭu* lords.[66] They constituted the core of the military arm of the lords; they gave the eleemosynary grants protection and they formed the base of the beginning of the Nāyar militia in medieval Kerala. In fact, this consideration of the Hundred Organizations also brings out the character of these lords as so many warlords, once again in bold relief.

Coming to the civil aspects of government, these lords can be seen discharging many administrative functions as well. Some of them had their own governmental establishment of sorts as can be gathered from the titles of functionaries attached to them. Thus we have the offices of *atikāran*, *paṭaināyan*, *mēnāyan*, *peruntaṭṭān*, etc. from Kuṟumpoṟaināṭu,[67] Neṭumpuṟaiyūrnāṭṭu *Paṭaināyar* from Neṭumpuṟaiyūrnāṭu,[68] the *atikārar*, *prakṛti*, etc. of Vēṇāṭu[69] and so on. While it was these lords who virtually carried out all governmental functions, they were still subject to the sovereign authority of the Cēramān *Perumāḷ*s. This sovereign authority went far beyond a ritual hegemony as the many instances we have quoted amply show. We have seen that the lords were referred to as *sāmanta*s as in a Kollam Rāmēśvarasvāmin temple inscription, which indicates that they were subordinate to the Cēra ruler. Another way in which the superordinate status of the Cēra ruler was acknowledged was by dating the records, even when the documents are related to the locality lords, in the regnal year of the Cēra king. The relative positions of the king and the lords can be ascertained further by the instances of the sharing of certain proceeds among them. Inscriptions from temples speak about the imposition of fines on defaulters of certain stipulated obligations. The proceeds of such fines are apportioned in a fixed proportion: it forms a regular pattern which helps in defining the hierarchy in which to place the locality lords in the power structure.[70] Thus, in many cases the king or his representative got twice as much as the local *nāṭu* lord. This makes the hierarchy amply clear, with the lords of localities enjoying a position second only to the Cēra king. The fact of the sovereignty transcending ritual is brought out by the military aspect of the relations discussed above. However, the exact mechanism by which this superordinate authority of the sovereign was enforced is not clear from the records.

UNEVENNESS IN SPACE AND TIME

One thing that stands out clear and unmistakable is the uneven character of development at all levels in the whole territory covered by the Cēra state. The different *nāṭu* units showed highly dissimilar character. While *nāṭus* such as Kīḻmalaināṭu, Muññināṭu, Kuṟumpoṟaiyūrnāṭu and Puṟakiḻānāṭu were well into the hilly tracts, those such as Vēṇāṭu, Veṇpolināṭu, Naṉṟuḻaināṭu, Kālkkaraināṭu, Vaḷḷuvanāṭu, Neṭuṅkālāynāṭu, Neṭumpuṟaiyūrnāṭu and Ēṟāḷanāṭu had their agrarian hinterlands. Kōlattunāṭu was integrated with the system only incompletely. The resource base of each was different. While the ones in the agrarian tracts produced rice and had the surplus from that production as a surplus, the ones on the hilly areas depended on wild products. Some, such as Vēṇāṭu, were also endowed with the resources of trade. This unevenness has serious implications for understanding the level of development in each. As the control of each region would depend upon the resources that it had to offer, differential control of the different *nāṭus* could be expected. It is interesting that in cases where we have evidence of the *nāṭu* lords attending court with the Cēra king, the hilly tracts are not represented. Will this mean that such lords and their territories were more loosely integrated with the state than those with agrarian and trading resources?

It is also interesting that we see changes over time as well. Scanning the three centuries (ninth through eleventh) covered by the rule of the Cēras, one sees that the Cēra inscriptions are distributed unevenly even in time. The ninth century, which saw the establishment of the kingdom, has only a few unmistakable Cēra inscriptions. They are, to begin with, generally seen in the southern half of the kingdom. The only inscription of Rājaśēkhara is from the vicinity of Tiruvalla, the few records of Sthāṇu Ravi are from Kollam, Tiruvalla and Iriññālakuḍa. Of the inscriptions known from the ninth century, there is one from Cōkkūr near Calicut, mentioning the fifteenth year of Kōtai Iravi (AD 898). If the statements in the *Mūṣikavamśakāvya* mentioned above relating to the imposition of Cēra overlordship in the region are accepted and if the Jayarāga mentioned there is indeed Vijayarāga identified with Kōtai Iravi, then Cēra authority may be said to have reached the northernmost tip by the end of ninth century. It is in the tenth century that Cēra inscriptions get widely distributed all over Kerala. By the eleventh century, again, we see that there is a thinning out of the distribution, indicating a decline in the power of the Cēra state, with the locality lords assuming greater power. All this would suggest that the Cēra state was not quite a finished product at any given point in time; it was in a state of flux, an ongoing process.

LOCAL GOVERNMENT

Local bodies carried out many of the governmental functions. Two kinds of them are mentioned in the records: the rural corporations with an agrarian bias and the urban corporations with their interest in trade. A majority of our records are of the former variety. Even as the *nāṭu* localities were described as so many 'divisions of the kingdom', these corporations are also thought to have derived their authority from a royal concession from above. 'The Cēra kings', writes M.G.S. Narayanan, '*allowed* the village assemblies and temple committees of Aryan settlements, which were rural agrarian corporations in character, *to enjoy* partial autonomy *and take part* in local administration as the urban guilds and corporations' (emphases added).[71] However, this position does not stand a close scrutiny of the evidence. Charters founding these corporations, comparable to the ones in the neighbouring Pāṇḍyan or Cōḻa cases, have not come down to us. In all likelihood, these groups had a local evolution and emerged powerful in their own right, upon which they were incorporated and made use of by the Cēra state. Acknowledging the authority of the *Perumāḷ* was perhaps in the interest of these bodies as well. The superordinate authority of the *Perumāḷ* and the locality lords is, in any case, hard to miss.

The constitution, procedures and functioning of these bodies are fairly well known, thanks to recent researches.[72] Historians have looked upon these bodies, known variously as the *ūr, ūrār, ūralār, sabhā,* etc. as so many units of the 'local administration' of the Cēra kingdom; but an examination of the business they transacted shows that their concern was largely with the management of their land, owned as either *dēvasvam* ('god's property') or *brahmasvam* ('Brāhmaṇa's property'). The bodies, with their membership ranging between ten and twenty-five, comprised heads of those Brāhmaṇa households which owned property of the *dēvasvam* and *brahmasvam* variety. The proceedings of these bodies followed the Brāhmaṇical *dharmaśāstras* almost to the last letter. They were described as *kaccam, kāryam, uṭampātu, oḻukkam, karumam, cavattai,* etc. and recorded in inscriptions. These, in fact, constitute the chief source of the history of this period. The bodies met in full attendance, and took their decisions unanimously. One such *kaccam,* accepted at Mūḻikkaḷam, was followed all over Kerala as a precedent, which nearly acquired the force of law. Members of these bodies were prevented from being tenants of the land; they were not to borrow gold from the temple; they were expressly forbidden from taking bribes while appointing various functionaries of the temple; they could not take up any employment of the temple; and, conversely, priests and other employees of temples could not be considered for membership of the bodies. There are many records which show that those who violated the decisions were punished ruthlessly. They would lose their properties, which earned them membership in the bodies, and even caste—dreadful things to happen in that society. Historians in the past had taken these as either senseless imprecations or attempts to protect the interests of the tenants; but M.G.S. Narayanan has shown that their purpose was to protect the corporate interests of the bodies against selfish interests of the members.

However, their command over the local population was comprehensive and their presence in the countryside, overwhelming. The Cēra state made use of these in a consummate manner. It identified and enlisted these bodies as its agents for the administration of revenue and justice.[73] A large number of the inscriptions recording the proceedings of these temple-centred bodies show the presence of the king himself or an officer of the state in the meeting, either presiding over the meeting or in other influential capacities.[74] There are many instances where these bodies collected the share of the king or the lord, as the case may be, called *rakṣābhōga* ('fee for protection') or *āṭṭaikkōḷ* ('the annual due') from the cultivators.[75] There are several cases where the king himself, or the locality lord, gave remission to the bodies from payment of the dues. Thus an inscription from Tṛkkaṭittānam says that the *kōyil adhikārikaḷ*, obviously representing the *Perumāḷ*, fixed the *āṭṭaikkōḷ* payable to locality lord of Nanṟuḻaināṭu at twelve *kalams* of paddy and permitted the use of the remaining twenty-four *kalams* for feeding Brāhmaṇas in the temple.[76] Another record from Perunna speaks of the agreement arrived at by the temple-committee to pay eighty *kalams* of paddy to the locality lord and a later representation to the latter that it be allowed to pay nothing more than this amount.[77] An important record, also from the same temple of Perunna, says that while King Kulaśēkhara, sitting in council with *Nālu Taḷi* and Tṛkkunnappoḻa at the Neṭiya Taḷi temple in the capital city, set apart forty kalams of paddy from out of the *āṭṭaikkōḷ* due from that village for instituting *namskāram* and *māpāratam* in the temple.[78] He also exempted the village from paying another due, the *arantai*, a 'war tax'. An inscription from Pullūr-Koṭavalam speaks of the *āṭṭaikkōḷ* collected in gold and to be paid to the *Perumāḷ*, an extremely important reference for reasons more than one.[79] Non-payment of tax invited punishment, as the Tiruvalla Copper Plates say: the *kōyilmanuccar* ('agents of the king') would obstruct the cultivation of the land.[80] We have the statement elsewhere that the agents of the lord of the locality of Veṇpolināṭu were free to 'do good and bad things' in the village of Kumāranallūr and that the *ūrāḷar* could not stand in the way of collecting fines.[81]

The village councils looked after administration of justice as well. The resolutions of these bodies prescribe severe punishment for those who violate the decisions: these punishments included confiscation of their property, loss of membership in the body, forfeiture of certain privileges such as free food in the temple, and ostracism in extreme cases. A usual stipulation is that one who violated the decisions of the bodies would be equated with those who had been guilty of sins such as killing one's father, sleeping with one's mother, killing one's teacher, etc.—the *pañcamahāpātakas*.[82] This provision has a significance going beyond mere curses of a formulaic nature: they were punishments by which one lost one's caste and all the entailing privileges including properties and membership in important bodies. In fact, the Mūḻikkaḷa *kaccam* mentioned above was a code followed in the enforcement of the discipline of the bodies and the punishments meted out in cases of failure to conform. Besides, there are many cases of the *ūrāḷar* collecting fine from different sections for various offences. There is a record stating that the temple confiscated all the properties of a certain Teñcēri Cēnnan Tāyan as he was caught stealing from the temple's treasury, a decision to this effect being taken probably by all [Brāhmaṇa] residents of the village.[83] A Kumāranallūr inscription is an extremely important record in this respect.[84] A meeting of the *ūr* laid down certain rules for themselves and others. No argument or violence was to take place on the premises of the temple. The residents of the village were to report to the *ūrāḷar* about the harvest from time to time. The *ūrāḷar* were neither to obstruct cultivation nor to exercise their authority within the enclosures mentioned. They were to attend personally to the individual grievances of the residents. Those who entered the houses and molested the people or obstructed their cultivation would forfeit their membership in the *sabhā*, any executive powers in it, a share in the property and so on. If the *śūdras* residing within the village abused the Brāhmaṇas, they would pay a fine of twelve *kāṇam* [of gold] as fine. If they injured them by using weapons, the fine would be double. In case it is one *śūdra* abusing another, the fine is six *kaḻañcu* of gold and if it resulted in death, the fine would be double. All these proceeds went into the temple. It also allows the agents of the lord of the locality of Veṇpolināṭu to 'do good and bad things' in the village of Kumāranallūr. The *ūrāḷar* could not stand in the way of their collecting fines. Finally, it is also stipulated that those who went against these decisions should pay a fine of 100 *kaḻañcu* of gold to the *Perumān Aṭikaḷ*. All such provisions go to show the administrative functions of the body of *ūrāḷar*, which went beyond simple management of property of an agrarian corporation, as well as the superordinate authority that the local lord and the Cēra *Perumāḷ* exercised in the process. These bodies functioned as veritable agents of the state, being so identified and made use of by the state itself.

So also the trading corporations in the urban centres. The details of the organization of such corporations are available to us mainly from two sets of copper plates related to the church of Tarsa at Kurakkēṇi Kollam, what are known as the Syrian Christian Copper Plates.[85] Mār Sapīr Īśō, who built the church, was also the founder of the town or the trading centre, the *nagaram*. He, in fact, not only founded it but also received it with 'libation of water', which certainly implies that there was some authority behind the relative autonomy that the *nagaram* enjoyed. Two trading organizations called *añcuvaṇṇam* and *maṇigrāmam* are described as the *kārāḷar* ('tenants') of the town. They managed the affairs of the *nagaram*. Functionaries of the state such as the *tīyam āḷvān* and *matil nāyakan* are prevented from exercising their authority within the town limits—a clear indication of the autonomy of the corporations. In the event of offences, the *paḷḷiyār* ('men of the church') were themselves to enquire into it—that is, judicial rights too were delegated to the body. The *paḷḷiyār* collected the different dues from within the settlement. The *añcuvaṇṇam* and *maṇigrāmam* were exempted from paying several taxes and were also required to be associated in the work of fixing the duties and prices of commodities entering the market place. They were the custodians of the dues collected every day. This shows that they functioned as agents of the state—a point stressed by the statement that the *patippatavāram* ('one-tenth share of the *pati*'), usually collected by the locality lord, should go to them while the *kōppatavāram* ('the one-tenth share of the king') went to the king himself. There are a few other references in the records to the functioning of such *nagarams* in relation to other places as well, although they are not as detailed as in the case of Kollam. All these go to show how the autonomous urban corporations were identified by the state and made use of in its business of government.

REVENUE AND COERCIVE POWER

Although the details of the revenue system available from the documents from Kerala are far less copious than what is available from the Cōḻa country, it is clear that the fiscal foundations of the Cēra state went beyond prestations, plunder or other arbitrary exactions. There are references to the payment of several dues on an impersonal basis, which were collected with a regular periodicity and at fixed rates. We do not intend to take up an elaborate survey and analysis of the revenue system here:[86] what is necessary is to look at its character and bearing for an understanding of the nature of the Cēra state. Much of the information regarding these dues is available from references to exemptions rather than actual collection. Thus the Syrian Christian Copper Plates and the Jewish Copper Plates speak of a large number of dues, the incidence of which may have fallen on the urban population. References to, for example, a toll on vehicles and boats coming into and going out of the market place, cesses on weighing and measurement, fees on taking goods into and out of the town, dues for roofing and building houses with more than one storey, and so on go to suggest that quibbling over whether the revenue was characterized by tax or rent is not relevant here. Again, it is significant that the dues belonged to the locality lord or the king and it is the right to collect them that are alienated to the bodies such as a merchant or a church or a trading organization. State based on such revenue is, in any case, not in doubt.

The story of revenue from the agrarian villages is comparable. As noted earlier, the most important collection made from the agrarian villages was the *āṭṭaikkōḷ* ('annual tax') or *rakṣābhōga* ('protection fee'). That both signified the same is brought out by a statement in a Tirunelli Copper Plate inscription, where *āṭṭaittiṟai* is described as due to the *niḻal* or the police force.[87] Both the expressions, namely, *āṭṭaikkōḷ* and *rakṣābhōga*, are very meaningful: the former shows the periodicity and the latter, the purpose for which it was paid. That this tax went to the state, represented either by the king himself or the locality lord, is clear from the records: it is one of them who received it or else assigned it fully or in part for some eleemosynary purpose. An instance of the payment of *āṭṭaikkōḷ* in gold from Pūllur-Koṭavalam is interesting: that place in the extreme north being distant from the capital by about 300 km, it is possible that this was to facilitate its transfer to the capital.[88] That the *āṭṭaikkōḷ* was collected from the actual cultivator is brought out by the statement that the tenants were to pay their *kaṭamai* to the temple authorities, which was part of the conditions of tenancy.[89] *Kaṭamai*, it is well known, was the name for the actual tax charged on land in other parts of south India as well in this period. A short record from Pantalāyini Kollam says that the *āṭṭaikkōḷ* was fixed at the rate of one-sixth of the total produce—an indication that the *Dharmaśāstra* rule was followed in this regard.[90]

Although much of the information on the *rakṣābhōga* or *āṭṭaikkōḷ* from the Brāhmaṇical temple inscriptions is related to the remissions given and thus likely to give an impression of dwindling resources of the state, it may be remembered that these references are few and far between. What was normal was not recorded as it was not worth recording. There is a reference to another due called *arantai* collected from agrarian villages.[91] This term means literally 'misery', and historians have taken this demand to mean a 'war tax'. Although details regarding this collection are fewer, it is clear that it was collected from places far away from the capital and also that it went to the king. All this would show that a dependable base of fiscal resources, constituted by a periodic assessment and collection of surplus at an impersonal level, supported the Cēra state.

Another item of revenue seems to have been what was collected as fine. There are a large number of instances in the records imposing fines on defaulters. It is not as exemptions that we have information on these; but as instances of actual demand and collections. In most cases such demands are expressed as *muṭṭukil muṭṭiraṭṭi* ('twice as much in the event of default'); and the proceeds of such fines went to the temple. But there are instances when other kinds of offences were punished with fine. In a few cases the proceeds were shared by a number of authorities including the temple, the locality lord and the king. The Vāḻappaḷḷi Copper Plate mentioned above says that those who stood in the way of the daily services in the temple should pay a fine of 100 *dīnāras* to the *Perumān Aṭikaḷ*, another instance of a large sum paid in gold from a village far away from the capital, probably to facilitate the transfer of the proceeds to the capital. There are many more instances of such payments of fine in gold, where it was the king who received them.[92] This shows that these fines constituted a source of state revenue, although there was no regularity about it. It, however, was impersonal and not arbitrary.

The nature of coercive power is indicative of the character of state. In the Cēra kingdom of Mahōdayapuram, there is evidence of the monopoly that state had over the use of violence. The 'Hundred Groups' whom we saw in connection with the military functions of the locality lords are seen more frequently in the records in their role of carrying out the work of policing. They are entrusted with the duty of 'protecting' pieces of land granted to temples. They are called upon, on occasions, to enforce certain decisions of the local bodies.[93] Chiefs of these groups represented the political authority in the meetings of local bodies in certain cases. There is at least one express statement which shows that the due called *āṭṭaitiṟai* or *āṭṭaikkōḷ* was realized in return for the protection offered by these groups. The very fact that the Nāyar militia of the later periods in the history of Kerala was drawn from these groups itself is evidence of their being part of the coercive power of the Cēra state.

URBANISM, LITERACY AND MONUMENTAL ARCHITECTURE

Details about the level of urbanism in a society are crucial in a discussion of the nature of the state. We have seen that the trading corporations in certain centres such as Kurakkēṇi Kollam and Muyirikkōṭu were relatively autonomous. There is no way to know the size of the settlement or the demographic composition of these 'urban' centres. However, it is clear that they emerged and drew their sustenance as trading centres. How they were related to the formation of the state is a moot question. Although the famous Syrian Christian Copper Plates related to Kollam do not offer any direct answer to this, it is reasonable to assume that the rise of that town and the development of the lords of Vēṇāṭu were not unrelated. The lords of Vēṇāṭu were known as Kōḷambanāthas ('the Lords of Kollam') much into the later period, even after Kollam had long ceased to be the capital of that territory, thereby showing the organic relation between the town of Kollam and the lordly unit of Vēṇāṭu. The same connection is seen, in later periods, between the kingdom of the Zamorins and the city of Calicut. In the same manner, the rise and functioning of the state under the Cēramān *Perumāḷs* can be shown to have had a strong link with the city of Mahōdayapuram.

In the first place, the Cēra king called himself *Mahōdayapuraparamēśvara*, the 'Supreme Lord of the City of Mahōdaya'. The rise of the city of Mahōdayapuram appears in the records as coeval with the rise of the kingdom; but its environs had a history of trade, transport and urbanism going back to several centuries earlier.[94] As the celebrated Muziris, 'the first emporium of India' of the classical authors, is identified as situated on the mouth of the Periyār and in the neighbourhood of Mahōdayapuram, a major factor behind the rise of the urban centre was the westerly trade that the port facilitated, particularly in spices such as pepper. Even in the centuries after Roman trade dried out, the town continued to exist and even prosper thanks to the continued West Asian clientele, particularly Syrian and Arab. The considerable Jewish, Christian and Muslim elements in the population of Kerala are attributed to this. In any case, urbanization of Mahōdayapuram did not get stymied. The newly rising agrarian settlements on the fertile river valleys must have only contributed to the process. A significant feature of these settlements, represented by the Brāhmaṇa corporations, is their concentration on the fertile river valleys.[95] Even there, the thickest cluster is on the Periyār, at the mouth of which was the complex of Muziris-Mahōdayapuram. With the antecedents of the earlier trading activities, it was easy for the new urban centre to take off, as it were, in the new formation dominated by agrarian activities. The city of Mahōdayapuram had arrived.

Situated in the middle of prosperous agrarian settlements controlled by the Brāhmaṇical groups, the new town had essentially a Brāhmaṇical character about it, as the new monarchy amply shows. Unfortunately, not too many details are available about the urban complex of Mahōdayapuram. Śaṅkaranārāyaṇa, the court astronomer and author of the commentary to *Laghubhāskarīya*, calls the town a *sēnāmukha*, which is a type of town defined by textbooks of architecture such as *Mayamata* and *Kamikāgama*.[96] Śaṅkaranārāyaṇa makes an explicit reference to the *prāsāda* in the town, showing that it was fortified. The town had an observatory and there was an arrangement for the regular announcement of time. There were several temples in the town, each of which had a definite role to play in the affairs of the state.[97] All these show the close linkage between the urban agglomeration on the one side and the state on the other. Thus, urbanism, which is a primary feature of state societies, was not only present in Kerala but it also had unmistakable connections with the state presided over by the Cēras of Mahōdayapuram.

The role of literacy as a means of storing and retrieving information is equally crucial in considering the nature of state in a society. It is well known that state societies were literate and that the state made heavy use of literacy. It is in this context that one has to look at the inscriptions from Kerala. The earliest inscriptions from Kerala date from the period of the Cēra kingdom.[98] To be sure, there are two earlier records from the forests of Nilambur and Wynad, neither being of any consequence. The Vāḻappaḷḷi Copper Plate is virtually the earliest inscription, and it announces the presence of the state in a manner that is loud and clear. Not only this record, but all the 150 or more records of this period, are such statements, symbolically and in terms of their contents. It has also been shown that the script of these records and their language, namely, Vaṭṭeḻuttu and a heavily Tamiḻized Malayalam respectively, eminently suited this purpose. Literacy was the means through which records were maintained—something that the agents of the state could use as both an expression and a prop of the state. In short, the script and the language have been shown as instruments of state in the context of Kerala under the Cēra kingdom of Mahōdayapuram.[99] Looked at from the point of view of the state, therefore, the importance of the particular kind of literacy and the special use to which it was put cannot be exaggerated. At the same time, it may not be entirely out of place to remember that the elaborate *praśasti*s, which form the introductory portions of the inscriptions in the rest of south India and a rhetorical device to legitimize the ruler, is conspicuously absent in the case of Kerala. Historians have tried to explain this absence by putting it down to the probable matrilineal system of inheritance followed by the house of the Cēramāns. However, it will be more meaningful to link it with the nature of the resource-base and the power structure obtaining in the state system. Unlike the Cōḻa situation, Kerala had too slender a base to have produced a megalomaniac ruler.

Monumental architecture is a definite sign of a state society. Kerala had not known any durable and substantial architecture before the rise of the Cēra kingdom, the only specimens of pre-Cēra architecture being the paltry megaliths. In contrast, by the time we come to the ninth century, big temples come into existence. Royal residences, or 'palaces', have not come down to us in south India until much later times, although in what is called the *Cēramān Paṟambu* in the town of Mahōdayapuram we have the site where the royal palace of the Cēramāns is believed to have stood. It is also true that 'royal temples', such as the Bṛhadīśvara Temple at Tañjāvur or the Hoysḷēśvara Temple at Haḷebīḍu, are wanting in Kerala. This has to be linked with the total resource-base of the Cēra state, which had no comparison with the Cōḻa or Hoysaḷa situations. In any case, from the ninth century onwards there are several temples of a relatively decent size, some of them really big such as the ones described as the *grāmakṣētras*.

M.G.S. Narayanan, who has also studied the temple architecture of Kerala under the Cēra Perumāḷs,[100] has rejected Stella Kramrisch and observed that there is no separate 'Kerala style' of architecture. Kerala saw the adoption of the same style in the rest of the south, with the roofing added for additional protection from the heavy monsoon. What is more important, from our point of view here, is a fleeting observation that Narayanan makes: 'The typical Cēra temple was not a royal monument but a common centre of the Aryan Brahmin village'.[101]

Most temples were indeed the centres of agrarian corporations managed by the Brāhmaṇical groups. The inscriptions in these temples, found on the plinth of the *sanctum sanctorum*, the door-jambs, the pillars of the several halls, etc., point to the Cēra dates from which they had existed. So also, they show a *presence* of the Cēra state. As we have seen in an earlier section, much of the real power in the state was wielded by the local groups, of which the Brāhmaṇical ones stand out most prominently. They had considerable resources and also functioned as veritable agents of the state in the localities. As such, it was they that represented the state. Thus, a monumental statement of the power of the state, as it were, had to be made through the temples in the localities. At the same time, the presence of the Cēra state, through the inscriptions and the state control that they register, should not be lost sight of. There are the clearly identifiable royal temples in the capital city. The Tiruvañjaikkaḷam temple, identifiable with the *Neṭiya Taḷi* of the *Nālu Taḷi*, the Tṛkkulaśēkharapuram temple, identified with the *Mēlttaḷi*, the Ciṅgapuram *Taḷi* and probably the Kīḻttaḷi were founded by one or the other *Perumāḷ*. Their political character is hard to miss.

SOCIAL PARAMETERS

The state, which is thus clearly visible in the records, has to be seen as a function of the differentiation and stratification that society had experienced. Wetland agriculture in paddy had spread widely with the opening up of river valleys and the use of iron technology. This had started even before we start getting records of the Cēra kings. No valid generalization can be made about the process of agrarian expansion. It involved the clearing of forests in certain areas, the levelling of undulating terrain in certain others and the draining of waterlogged fields in yet others. In any case, the records show that temples possessed huge estates of land producing rice.[102] It is safe to assume the existence of non-Brāhmaṇa magnates as well, if not on a scale comparable with the rest of south India, for we see them making assignment of land to temples and other institutions. The records bear testimony to their influential presence. With agricultural production involving labour outside kinship, it was but normal that surplus was expropriated from the primary producer. There was also considerable diversification of production, since we come across evidence of artisanal activities of different kinds.

The most important field of production being agriculture, a discussion of social differentiation has to begin from there.[103] The primary producers were the labourers. There are references in the documents to labourers being tied to the piece of land which they worked. When ownership or other superior rights over a piece of land changed hands, the title over the labourers was also transferred along with it. We have references to bonded labourers such as *āḷ*, *āḷ aṭiyār*, etc. Although there is no reference to the term *viṣṭi* as such or its Tamil form *veṭṭi* in the records from Kerala, the practice of *corvée* was widely prevalent. Grants or other transactions of land mentioned the transfer of the *āḷ* labourers, both male and female, along with such transactions, clear instances of the character of labour as not only bonded but also attached to the piece of land which they worked. The sections of society so described are often identified by the names of the ethnic groups to which they belonged, names such as Pulayar which denoted the castes of agrestic labourers in later times. The surplus labour at their disposal was expropriated mostly in the form of a labour rent. Other details regarding these groups are not available to us from Kerala. If experience in Kerala in the later periods and contemporary accounts in Tamil literature are any indication, theirs was a miserable life.

The most visible section of population in the records consisted of those who occupied the middle rungs in the hierarchy of economic and social status. They included both the landlords of different descriptions and the numerous tenants of the vast land including what was owned by the temples. The records mention various shades of right in land; and the existence of a graded hierarchy in land relations is a safe guess. Ranging from simple occupancy rights, we see that tenancy with some title, possession taken for some consideration, superior rights of a stronger nature, proprietary and beneficial rights bordering on the allodial, etc., were present there. Those who enjoyed these rights, naturally, occupied a corresponding position in the social hierarchy immediately above the primary producers. So also, those who provided various services in the temple, such as garland-making, musical services, cleaning, etc. were placed slightly above the rest on the scale on account of their doing what were considered as 'clean' jobs and their proximity to the temple and the Brāhmaṇas. Those who were engaged in artisanal activities, such as the different varieties of smiths, carpenters, washermen, etc., were lower on the scale. Native traders are rarely met with in the documents of this period. The identification of these groups, placed in a hierarchical order based on economic and social status, with so many *jāti*s of corresponding ritual status followed. On the whole, a highly stratified society with a graded hierarchy emerges with great clarity in the records of the period. Strangely, even the West Asian settlers of Judaic, Christian and Islamic persuasions fitted snugly into the pattern of *jāti* society. It is interesting that at least in the case of Christians, even patterns of worship followed those of the natives as the Syrian Christian Plates show.

CULTURE, IDEOLOGY, LEGITIMACY

Jāti was also a handy tool for the Brāhmaṇical owning groups to assert their superiority. Invoking the principle of *varṇāśramadharma*, which guaranteed the right kind of legitimacy to the differentiation in society and the position of the Brāhmaṇical owning groups within it, the Brāhmaṇical world view was imposed, and accepted, with great ease. The result was also the acceptance of the Āgamaic religion. As mentioned earlier, temples dedicated to Brāhmaṇical deities such as Śiva and Viṣṇu had come up with command over fabulous amount of wealth. Nearly every section of society stood in a subordinate relationship to the temple in one way or the other on the secular plane; it was not difficult to translate this loyalty into the religious world. Perhaps the earlier cults and practices continued but what is visible in the most striking way is the religion of the temples with its ideology of the *bhakti*. The Tamil Bhakti Movement has been shown as essentially a temple movement, which reflected and legitimized the emerging social political formation in south India.[104] The Bhakti Movement of this period boasted of two of its leaders from among the Cēra rulers themselves and a locality lord from one of the *nāṭus*.[105]

Many of the sacred centres of the movement are on the West Coast. At the higher levels of metaphysics and ethics, this was the period of the great Śaṅkara.

This heavy Brāhmaṇical content of the cultural expressions explains the choice of Sanskrit and the Sanskritic idiom. The impact of the Tamil Bhakti Movement on Kerala was marginal; but the Sanskrit compositions had a greater influence on the culture of Kerala. The plays of Kulaśēkharavarman, the Cēra king, such as *Tapatīsaṃvaraṇam* and *Subhadrādhanañjayam*, were not only the mostly widely used for theatrical presentations, they also served to promote royalty itself. So also, it was *Mukundamālā*, the Sanskrit hymn of Kulaśēkhara, that became more popular on the west coast than his Tamil compositions. The strong claims made by Brāhmaṇical groups about a role in the establishment and the sustenance of the Cēra monarchy are to be seen in this context. The claim as contained in *Kēraḷōlpatti*, the historical narrative of the Brāhmaṇa groups of Kerala in Malayalam, is that it was the Brāhmaṇas who ruled the country to begin with after Paraśurāma created the land and gifted it to them; but as they realized that a Kṣatriya has to be there as the king, they went out to *paradēśa* and brought *Perumāḷs* for successive terms of twelve years. This statement has to be seen as the Brāhmaṇas' way of remembering the past, in an attempt to project their position in the political structure.[106] So also, the role of the *Nālu Taḷi* in the administration, revealed by a couple of documents, supports the kind of information in the same narrative as well as literary texts, underlining the importance of that body. In short, the documents, which have an admittedly Brāhmaṇical character, give the impression that they were responsible for the Cēra kingdom and its sustenance. However, the historian has to go beyond what the sources say, for they conceal more than what they reveal. In such an exercise, it would be clear that these were attempts by which the state, and the king who presided over it, claimed legitimacy in a society where Brāhmaṇical groups had an important place due to the control of land they had.

The above survey shows that by the beginning of the ninth century the state had well and truly arrived in Kerala. Among the characteristic features of this period were a stratified society and the extraction of the surplus produced by one section by another on an impersonal basis. These enabled, and necessitated, a political authority that exercised actual political power going beyond rituals over a more or less defined territory. Features such as urbanism, literacy and monumental architecture are further pointers to the character of that society as a state society. The ideological apparatus was ostensibly Brāhmaṇical, and the image of royalty presented was one that would suit those groups.

However, this should not be taken to mean that it was a case of 'a bold and visible brāhmaṇ oligarchy thinly disguised as a monarchy to satisfy the sentiments of the lawgivers of India'.[107] In presenting the state under the *Perumāḷs* in this way, the Brāhmaṇical groups are taken as ubiquitous and all pervasive. In reality, however, their settlements can be seen as distributed in only certain clusters in the river valleys. Many *nāṭus*, such as Kīḻmalaināṭu, Muññināṭu, Ēṟāḷanāṭu, Kuṟumpoṟaiyūrnāṭu and Puṟakiḻānāṭu did not have even one Brāhmaṇical settlement in them. On the other hand, we see that the locality lords in them were relatively powerful and subject to the superordinate authority of the *Perumāḷ*. Most of the political activities are carried out by these *nāṭus* and their lords. There were, as we saw, wide variations in the level of their development, character, and composition of these *nāṭus*. The Brāhmaṇical groups, which are presented as haughty and even having forced the *Perumāḷ* to atone for offending them, were clearly subject to the authority of these *nāṭus*. The affairs of the temple are 'talked into agreement' by the military commander of a *nāṭu* in one place;[108] the lord and the king get the tax from the Brāhmaṇical settlements almost everywhere; transfers of revenue, both in the form of tax/rent and in the form of fines go to lords and the king; and the coercive power of the king and the lords was indispensable for the functioning of the Brāhmaṇical groups themselves. In the case of the symbolic and actual message conveyed through the inscriptions, too, the heavy hand of the state is to be seen even in the Brāhmaṇa villages. There were also what could be described as royal temples in the capital city, although not to be compared with the Cōḻa or Hoysaḷa institutions. The city itself was a ceremonial centre of the Perumāḷs[109] who had heavily used the Brāhmaṇical groups for purposes of legitimation. If one does not allow oneself to be misled by appearances, the Cēra monarchy had all political character about it and was presiding over a state that had emerged by the ninth century. The detailed information we have from the trading centres, on their part, shows clearly that the state had concerns going beyond the interests of the Brāhmaṇical groups. It was political all the way.

How do we characterize this state? In a study made about two decades ago, I had proposed that the political structure of early medieval south India could be explained within the framework of feudalism, of course with the necessary qualifications.[110] The bulk of evidence considered there was from Cōḻa country. While the analytical potential of that category is not denied, one has to recognize major differences in the situation obtaining in Kerala. One of them is that the resources available on the west coast were much less than what they were on the Kāvēri Delta, thereby making stratification less pronounced. In the field of agriculture, the huge non-Brāhmaṇa corporations of *ūr* and *nāṭu*, which characterize the Cōḻa country, are absent in Kerala. Relations of production differed considerably for these reasons, and comparability gets limited on that account. In any case, the subject character of peasantry, the widespread use of service tenements in lieu of a salary, the presence, bordering on supremacy, of a class of specialized warriors, ties of obedience and protection assuming the distinctive form of vassalage, and the survival of earlier forms of associations such as family and kinship—these features are hard to miss there.[111] But there are several aspects which are open to question, particularly in relation to the Kerala experience. In any case, repeating the expression 'feudalism' as a formula does not lead us very far.

It may be useful to recapitulate the essential features of the state before trying to build models to explain it. We have the king at the centre, whose power, certainly not very heavy, was nonetheless exercised all over the territory of Kerala. The population of this territory had its own identity. The king had an establishment of his own with functionaries used in the governance of the realm; but it is significant that most of them, such as the *Kōyil Adhikārikaḷ*, the *Nālu Taḷi*, the *Āyiram*, etc., derived their position on the principle of heredity. The real power seems to have been enjoyed by the locality lords, known as the *nāṭuvāḻis*. They were not uniform in their character. They had a local evolution; some of them inherited their position while some others owed it to an appointment by the *Perumāḷ*; their functionaries, including the extremely important bodyguards, were hereditary in nature. Although they had evolved spontaneously in their own right, they were, however, subject to the superordinate authority of the king at the centre, this authority being expressed and exercised in various ways. The armed forces of the *nāṭuvāḻis* were available to fight for the king where necessary; the *nāṭuvāḻis* generally took the king's endorsement over the grants they made; a larger share of the revenue—both tax/rent and fine—which they collected went to the king and they attended the court of the king as shown by at least two important instances. Perhaps the best attestation to the authority of the *Perumāḷ* is the later claim that all later principalities in Kerala made about their origin as a gift from the last *Perumāḷ* himself as a sanction behind their power. At levels lower than the *nāṭuvāḻis* were the local bodies at the rural and urban centres looking after their own affairs. The Brāhmaṇical bodies were in charge of temples who owned vast estates of land in the fertile river valleys. Urban corporations, sometimes of the Syrian Christians or the Jews, managed the port towns and their affairs. In the case of the regions which had forest produce as their source of income, much information is not available, although *nāṭus* such as Kīḻmalaināṭu or Muññināṭu seem to have belonged to this category. Where we have information, corporations whose membership was decided by the principle of heredity managed governmental functions in the rural and urban areas. Little is known about their origin, but they most certainly had a relatively autonomous existence. In the end, however, they too were identified by the state and co-opted into the system in its service.

Can we call it an 'early state' after Claessen and Skalnik? Before launching the case studies, they give a working definition of the early state as 'the organization for the regulation of social relations in a society that is divided into two emergent social classes, the rulers and the ruled'.[112] After considering the twenty-one cases presented by an authority in each case, Claessen has made a structural analysis of the features obtaining in them and identified fifty-one of them,[113] most of which obtain in the case of Kerala under the Cēramān *Perumāḷs*. Following this, he returns to the hypotheses put forward along with the working definition mentioned above. He sees that the seven criteria of early state, evolved at a hypothetical level there, stand fully supported by the case studies and the different features isolated from them. These criteria are:

1. There is a sufficient population to make possible social categorization, stratification and specialization.
2. Citizenship of the state is determined by residence or birth in the territory.

3. The government is centralized and has the necessary power for the maintenance of law and order through the use of both authority and force, or threat of force.
4. The state is independent, at least de facto, and the government has sufficient power to prevent separation, as well as the capacity to defend its external threats.
5. The population shows a sufficient degree of stratification for emergent social classes (rulers and ruled) to be distinguishable.
6. Productivity is high enough to enable a regular surplus, which is used for the maintenance of the state organization.
7. A common ideology on which the legitimacy of the ruling stratum is based.

In the examination of evidence from Kerala that we have taken above, *all the seven* criteria prescribed and tested by the cases are satisfied by the state under the Cēramān *Perumāḷ*s. The 'early state' has been further classified as the 'inchoate', the 'typical', and the 'transitional' early states. The features of each of them are given; but those of the Cēra state show an overlap. It may not be possible to pigeonhole the 'early state' in Kerala as one of these three. Again, it has been argued that the category of 'early state' is too general to be of any explanatory value. It tries to generalize a vast variety of systems ranging from Pharaonic Egypt (third millennium BC) to the Jimma and Kachari formations (AD twentieth century). Such a model can at best describe and not explain the situation. A specific issue which fails to be explained is the differential character of the regions which get incorporated into the system. For instance, how does one fit the *nāṭu* divisions in the scheme of the 'early state'? Moreover, the uneven character of these divisions and the slow process of their being incorporated into the system, that too with varying degrees of completion, are factors which are crucial for the understanding of the Cēra state.

Any simple generalization covering the long period of more than three centuries of the existence of the Cēra state will be too risky, as things were changing too fast. In the case of the evidence that we examined, what was applicable for the early stages of the history of the kingdom may have well undergone changes and new features may as well have emerged. So also, variations over space are to be reckoned with. The kind of control that the state exercised over the urban centres with trade as its chief source of revenue was certainly different from what it was in the agrarian districts. In a similar manner, variations in the level of development among the different regions that the state controlled are also significant. For instance, the *nāṭu* divisions in the hilly tracts and the plains may have required a different kind of control each. Thus, it is important to bear in mind that what we are dealing with is not a finished product, uniform in structure and immutable. On the other hand, if the processual character of the state is recognized, that will add greater clarity to our understanding. It will also relieve us from the burden of looking for rigid categories to explain it.[114] What is proposed is that, given the striking correspondence between the details available from Kerala on the one hand with the theoretical perspectives and empirical data contained in this model, it may be tested as a starting point, but bearing in mind the difficulties mentioned above.

Alternatively, some other model, which accommodates the incorporative character of the polity and the integrative role of the sovereign, may be tested. In this context, the now celebrated 'integrative model' proposed by Hermann Kulke should yield some result. Kulke's own summary gives the following details of the process:

> The three special parameters are (1) a nuclear area in the centre (usually a fertile riverine area), (2) its fringes or peripheral zones (usually mountainous or jungle areas) and (3) beyond them neighbouring core areas (usually also located in fertile areas). The variants of the time factor are determined by the historical process of a stepwise expansion of political authority radiating from the nuclear area into the peripheral zones and the neighbouring areas. The major political and structural differences between these three stages of state formation may be summarised as follows:
>
> The pristine *tribal/Hindu* chieftaincy consisted of a rather small nuclear area which had only limited relations with its peripheral zones.
>
> Under the *early kingdom* the political authority expanded from the nuclear area to its hinterland. Some of the formerly independent neighbours became tributary chiefs or 'kings' (*sāmanta*). A major characteristic of the early kingdoms was their 'circle of tributary neighbours' (*sāmantacakra*) who remained outside the central administration and enjoyed a high degree of autonomy. The *imperial regional kingdom* originated from a forcible unification of at least two major nuclear areas...[115]

Most of the data from Kerala would conform to this. The core area around Mahōdayapuram, in the present-day districts of Trichur and Ernakulam, have been shown to be among the most developed areas in terms of the expansion of agriculture symbolized by the presence of the Brāhmaṇical establishments. The thickest cluster of Brāhmaṇa settlements obtains in this region.[116] It is also significant that the earliest urban centre of Kerala, identifiable in both literature and archaeology, was Muziris, either Mahōdayapuram itself or in its vicinity. It is therefore least surprising that this constituted the nuclear area of the first state in Kerala. This state, coming in an area where the Brāhmaṇical establishment had taken deep roots, looked for the kind of legitimacy that those groups would have demanded; the official expressions of the state as well as the Brāhmaṇical groups give an impression that the state was Brāhmaṇical in character. Going beyond these sources, however, one has to see the elements of the locality lords in the *nāṭu* divisions, integrated into the system at varying levels. The significance of these nodes becomes clear when it is remembered that there was no force which cemented them together in the post-Cēra condition and that, curiously, most of them turned to a donation of the Cēramān *Perumāḷ* for sanction. This shows that the Cēra kingdom was successful, for some time, in integrating the different *nāṭu* units of varying levels of social and economic development and that this integration was lost for a long time to come on its disappearance.

Each one of these formulations—looking at the Cēra state of Mahōdayapuram as a feudal polity, an early state and as something of an integrative polity—has its own relevance and use for our understanding. It may sound as if to use all the three is eclectic and even self-contradictory. In the matter of looking at state as part of the larger whole with society and economy given their place, the feudal model will have greater validity, as no other formulation explains these aspects as fully. If descriptive richness is what one is looking for, then the categorization of the situation in early medieval Kerala as an 'early state' may be accepted. The category that accommodates the wide variations within the units of the state still remains the one which looks at it as integrative. Generalizations being tools for understanding phenomena with clarity and not matters of dogma, it may be proposed that our attempt to make sense of the Cēra state of Mahōdayapuram does not find it difficult to use the explanatory abilities of these three models.

NOTES AND REFERENCES

1. Henri J.M. Claessen and Peter Skalnik, eds, *The Early State* (The Hague, 1978).
2. William Logan, *Malabar*, vol. I (Madras, 1887, rpt, Trivandrum, 2000), p. 244.

3. K.P. Padmanabha Menon, *Koccirājyacaritram*, 2 vols (in Malayalam, Trichur, 1912; rpt, Calicut, 1989); *History of Kerala*, 4 vols (Ernakulam, 1924–35).
4. Even books published in later periods, after the historiographical scenario changed considerably, are good examples. K.V. Krishna Ayyar, *The Zamorins of Calicut* (Calicut, 1938); P.K.S. Raja, *Medieval Kerala* (Annamalainagar, 1957). The state-sponsored two-volume *History of Kerala* (in Malayalam), ed. and published by Kerala History Association in 1972, does not take things much beyond.
5. This project was begun in the Madras Presidency, of which Malabar had been a district, in the nineteenth century. *The Annual Reports of Epigraphy*, inaugurated by E. Hultzsch in 1886, had noticed a number of inscriptions from the district, the texts of many of which were published in the V and VII volumes of the *South Indian Inscriptions.* The state of Travancore began a Department of Archaeology early in the twentieth century and the *Travancore Archaeological Series* (hereafter *TAS*) published by that department brought out many inscriptions from that state. Cochin followed suit, and the *Bulletin of the Ramavarma Research Institute* published the text of several epigraphical records from the territory of Cochin. Again, a large number of literary texts in Sanskrit and *Maṇipravāḷam* (a union of Malayalam and Sanskrit) were discovered and published in the first half of the twentieth century. In the Tamil-speaking region, a corpus of literature that came to be known as 'Sangam literature' was discovered and published, the relevance of which for the history of Kerala was appreciated gradually. Thus, it was a veritable twin revolution at a heuristic level.
6. Pillai wrote mostly in Malayalam. *Kēraḷacaritrattiṉṟe Iruḷatañña Ēṭukaḷ* (Kottayam, 1953); *Cila Kēraḷacaritrapraśnaṅṅaḷ* (Kottayam, 1955); *Cērasāmrājyam Ompatum Pattum Nūṟṟāṇṭukaḷiḷ* (Kottayam, 1963); *Samskārattiṉṟe Nāḻikakkallukaḷ* (Kottayam, 1966), etc. A few of the important articles are translated into English: Elamkulam P.N. Kunjan Pillai, *Studies in Kerala History* (Kottayam, 1970).
7. M.G.S. Narayanan, 'Political and Social Conditions of Kerala under the Kulaśēkhara Empire (c. 800–1124 AD)' PhD Thesis, University of Kerala (Trivandrum, 1972). This is an exhaustive study of the history of this kingdom and a companion volume to this thesis, *Index to Cēra Inscriptions*, is an extremely useful aid to researchers. The author has published the text of the thesis for private circulation: *The Perumals of Kerala: Political and Social Conditions of Kerala Under the Cera Perumals of Makotai (c. AD 800–1124)*, (Calicut, 1996). References to this work below are to this edition.
8. There are many publications of Narayanan which argue in favour of a 'feudal' description of this state. See, for instance, M.G.S. Narayanan, 'Feudal Pattern of Society in Early Medieval Kerala', paper presented at the *Proceedings of the Indian History Congress* (*PIHC*) (Amritsar,

1985). Recently, however, he seems to have abandoned that position. M.G.S. Narayanan, 'The State in the Era of the Cēramān Perumāḷs of Kerala' in R. Champakalakshmi, Kesavan Veluthat and T.R. Venugopalan, eds, *State and Society in Pre-modern South India* (Thrissur, 2002), pp. 111–19. He summarizes his argument thus: 'The picture that emerges from the above discussion is that of a strong, well organized and self-conscious brahman community, ruling over the territory of Kerala and using the Perumāḷ, a member of the ancient Cēra dynasty, as a ritual sovereign to ensure legitimacy and unity among the nāṭuvāḻis who were powerful in their own right. Such a form of state is unique in the annals of post-Mauryan India'. Needless to say, many of these arguments are ridden with problems, some of which we shall take up below in this paper.

9. Raghava Varier and Rajan Gurukkal, *Kēraḷacaritram* (in Malayalam, Sukapuram, 1991); Raghava Varier, *Kēraḷīyata: Caritrmānaṅṅaḷ* (in Malayalam, Sukapuram, 1989); Rajan Gurukkal, *The Kerala Temple and the Medieval Agrarian System* (Sukapuram, 1992).
10. This was recognized by Elamkulam P.N.K. Pillai in the 1950s. Historians have worked on this assumption. A most recent and competent study of the history of Kerala by Gurukkal and Varier has presented a definitive and exhaustive picture of Kerala's historical evolution till the rise of the kingdom of Mahōdayapuram in the beginning of the ninth century. Rajan Gurukkal and Raghava Varier, eds, *Cultural History of Kerala*, vol. I (Thiruvananthapuram, 1999). We have largely followed this presentation below.
11. See, for instance, V. Kanakasabhai, *The Tamils Eighteen Hundred Years Ago* (Madras, 1904); K.G. Sesha Aiyar, *Chera Kings of the Sangam Age* (London, 1937); S. Krishnaswami Aiyangar, *Śēran Vañji* (Ernakulam, 1940); K.A. Nilakanta Sastri, *A History of South India* (Madras, 1955; 1971), pp. 115–45, esp. p. 118; T.V. Mahalingam, *South Indian Polity* (Madras, 1955); N. Subramanian, *Sangam Polity* (Madurai, 1966); etc. The idea that what is called the 'Sangam literature' related to a pre-state society is a matter of recent recognition. See next note.
12. Champakalakshmi, 'Introduction', *Studies in History*, vol. IV, no. 2, July–December 1982, pp. 161–7 suggested this for the first time in a fleeting manner. An alternative argument can be seen in the recent works of Rajan Gurukkal. See, for instance, his 'Antecedents of State Formation in South India' in R. Champakalakshmi, Kesavan Veluthat, and T.R. Venugopalan, eds, *State and Society in Pre-modern South India* (Thrissur, 2002), pp. 39–59 and 'Did State Exist in Pre-Pallavan Tamil Region?', *PIHC* (Amritsar, 2002), pp. 138–50. For a different pattern, Kesavan Veluthat, 'Into the "Medieval" and Out of It—Early South India in Transition', Presidential Address, *PIHC*, Section II, Medieval Indian History (Bangalore, 1997), Chapter 1 above.
13. Sastri, *History of South India*, p. 144. The story must actually begin from P.T. Srinivasa Aiyangar, *Tamil Studies; or Essays in the History of*

the Tamil People, Language, Religion and Literature (Madras, 1914), pp. 435–7.

14. Thus, Burton Stein, whose concerns are entirely different, accepts the notion of a Kaḷabhra interlude opposed to peasant agriculture in his analysis of the rise of peasantry in the Tamil country. *Peasant State and Society in Medieval South India* (Delhi, 1980), p. 65; so also Gurukkal, who speaks about a non-Brāhmaṇa resistance against the expansion of Brahmadēyas, uses the Kaḷabhras. Gurukkal, 'Non-Brāhmaṇa Resistance to the Expansion of Brahmadēyas: The Early Pāṇḍya Experience', *PIHC* (Annamalainagar, 1984), pp. 181–4. He later extended the argument to show that the presence of the Kaḷabhras represented a veritable social crisis of the type suggested by R.S. Sharma and B.N.S. Yadava in the Purāṇic descriptions of the Kali age: Gurukkal, *The Kerala Temple and the Medieval Agrarian System* (Sukapuram, 1992), p. 27. Historians like D.N. Jha and B.P. Sahu have been lured by this: D.N. Jha, ed., *Feudal Social Formation in Early India* (Delhi, 1987), 'Introduction', p. 92; B.P. Sahu, 'Conception of Kali Age in Early India: A Regional Perspective', *Trends in Social Science Research*, vol. 4, no.1, June, 1997, pp. 31–2.
15. Veluthat, 'Into the "Medieval"'.
16. See, for instance, M.G.S. Narayanan, 'The Peasants in Early Tamilakam', in H.V. Sreenivasa Murthy, B. Surendra Rao, Kesavan Veluthat and S.A. Bari, eds, *Essays on Indian History and Culture: Felicitation Volume in Honour of Professor B. Sheik Ali* (New Delhi, 1990), pp. 25–48; Narayanan, 'The Warrior Settlements of the Sangam Age', *PIHC* (Kurukshetra, 1982).
17. Veluthat, 'Into the "Medieval"'.
18. Rajan Gurukkal, 'Towards a New Discourse: Discursive Processes in Early South India', in R. Champakalakshmi and S. Gopal, eds, *Tradition, Dissent and Ideology: Essays in Honour of Romila Thapar* (Delhi, 1996).
19. There are a little more than 150 inscriptions of this period from Kerala, a majority of which are dated in the regnal years of Cēra kings. Even in relation to the rest, there is reason to assume their Cēra identity. For a comprehensive list and summary of the Cēra inscriptions, M.G.S. Narayanan, 'Index to Cēra Inscriptions' (A Companion Volume to his unpublished PhD Thesis (Trivandrum, 1972).
20. *TAS*, vol. II, no. 2, pp. 8–14.
21. *TAS*, vol. II, no. 9, (i & ii), pp. 62–70; 80–5.
22. Kesavan Veluthat, *Brahman Settlements in Kerala: Historical Studies* (Calicut, 1978), pp. 21–38 contains an identification of the early Brāhmaṇa settlements of Kerala, which are seen distributed thus.
23. This narrative was variously accepted and rejected by historians as a *source* of history; but never considered as a *form* of history. For an analysis of the *Kēralōlpatti* as expressing a particular kind of historical tradition and its social function, Kesavan Veluthat, 'The *Keralolpatti* as History: A Note on Pre-colonial Traditions of Historical Writing in India',

Chapter 6 above. A Malayalam version of this article is published in *Star Newsweek*, Book 1, nos 9 and 10, 11–17 and 18–25 February 2002.

24. *Periyapurāṇam, Kaḻariṟṟaṟivār Nāyanār Purāṇam.*
25. For a discussion of the self-image of royalty in early medieval south India, Kesavan Veluthat, *Political Structure of Early Medieval South India* (New Delhi, 1993), pp. 29–69.
26. Narayanan, *Perumals of Kerala*, pp. 74–5.
27. *'Kēraḷakulacūdāmaṇēḥ mahōdayapuraparamēśvarasya śrīkulaśēkharavarmaṇaḥ ...'*, *Tapatīsamvaraṇam*, prologue. '*Kaḷamarāśipēśalakaidārika kēraḷādhināthasya kulaśēkharavarmaṇo ...*' *Subadrādhanañjayam*, prologue.
28. Veluthat, *Political Structure*, pp. 29–69.
29. *TAS*, vol. V, no. 13, pp. 40–6.
30. Varier and Gurukkal, *Kēraḷacaritram*, p. 150, think that the power of the Perumāḷs was limited to coordinating the power of the various landowning groups and not an absolutely independent sovereign power. This is open to question.
31. This is an institution, whose importance in history was not sufficiently recognized by earlier historians. The narrative called *Kēraḷōlpatti*, giving an account of the past of Kerala as remembered by the Brāhmaṇical groups, has it that an oligarchy that was established following the gift of the land to them by Paraśurāma functioned through a council where the entire Brāhmaṇical establishment in Kerala was represented by four of their settlements. In course of time there were changes in the identity of these villages but the number of villages remained at four. The representatives of these four newly designated villages had their seats in the four temples, the *Nālu Taḷi*, in the capital city of Koṭuṅṅallūr or Mahōdayapuram after they had established the *Perumāḷ* rule there. For a discussion bringing out the historical importance of the *Nālu Taḷi*, Narayanan, *Perumals of Kerala*, pp. 76–7, 85–7.
32. Ibid., pp. 85–9.
33. Thus, Vijayarāga, who is described as the *Kōil Adhikārikaḷ* in the Syrian Christain Copper Plates, can be seen as a kin of the Cēramān. A certain Kiḻān Aṭikaḷ is mentioned as the daughter of Kulaśēkharadēva and wife of Vijayarāgadēva, Kulaśēkharadēva being Sthāṇu Ravi himself of the Syrian Christian Plates. Vijayarāga himself appears as the Cēramān in another record, and the Cēra king Jayarāga in the *Mūṣikavamśakāvya* is arguably the same person. A son-in-law succeeding to the throne is explained by the matrilineal system, where cross-cousin marriage is usual. Narayanan, *Perumals of Kerala*, p. 26.
34. *TAS*, vol. V, no. 13, pp. 40–6.
35. The significance of the *Āyiram*, too, is a matter of recent recognition. Narayanan, *Perumals of Kerala*, pp.122–4.
36. *Epigraphia Indica* (hereafter *EI*), vol. III, p. 68 ff.
37. *TAS*, vol. VIII, no. 33 (vii), p. 42.

38. For the text which Narayanan and I prepared *in situ*, Naduvattam Gopalakrishnan, *Kēraḷacaritradhārakaḷ* (in Malayalam, Thiruvananthapuram, 2003), pp. 63–8. Unfortunately, the estampage and eye-copy prepared and kept in the University of Calicut are reportedly missing. A critical edition of the text was not published.
39. Veluthat, 'Evolution of a Regional identity: Kerala in India', in Irfan Habib, ed., *India: Studies in the History of an Idea* (New Delhi, 2005), pp. 82–97, Chapter 13 below.
40. '*Mitrāṇi mātṛdattādyāḥ kēraḷēṣu dvijōttamāḥ,*' Daṇḍin, *Avantisundarīkathāsāra*, quoted in Ulloor S. Parameswara Iyer, *Kēraḷasāhityacaritram*, vol. I (Trivandrum, 1967), pp. 103–4. Kālidāsa, in his *Raghuvamśa*, has an obscure reference to Kerala, and so have others. They are, however, inconsequential.
41. Narayanan, *Perumals of Kerala*, p. 213.
42. Above, n. 27.
43. '*Kēraḷaviṣayam pālikkānāy mahitamahōdayanilayē maruvum nṛpasimhasya...*', *Anantapuravarṇanam*.
44. K. Kunjunni Raja, *The Contribution of Kerala to Sanskrit Literature* (Madras, 1980), p. 20. nn. 95–6.
45. '*Kulaśēkharanāmnā kēraḷādhipēna...*' *Vyaṅgyavyākhya*, quoted by N.P. Unni, *Sanskrit Dramas of Kulaśēkhara: A Study* (Trivandrum, 1977), p. 24.
46. Kerala starts figuring in the lists of conquests made by the Cāḷukyas, Pallavas and Pāṇḍyas from this period on. Narayanan, *Perumals*, chapter on 'Early Wars and Alliances'. Much of this is conventional rhetoric typical of Sanskrit *praśasti* poetry where long lists of conquests are given. It is not very clear whether Kerala, included in such lists, stands for the lineage or the country. Other references are indiscriminate.
47. '*Sarvakṣatravadhavratapraṇayinā rāmēṇa yannirmitam rāṣṭram śiṣṭajanābhirāmam atulam...*' *South Indian Inscriptions*, vol. III, p. 398.
48. For the Mūḻikkaḷa kaccam and its importance, see Narayanan, *Perumals of Kerala*, pp. 114–16.
49. Veluthat, 'The *Keralolpatti* as History',
50. Narayanan, *Perumals of Kerala*, pp. 90–105. However, Narayanan looks at them as so many 'divisions of the kingdom', under a 'governor' each.
51. *TAS*, vol. II, no.7 (H), pp. 42–4, ll.3–4; *TAS*, vol. VIII, no. 33 (vii), p. 42, ll.3–4. It is interesting that houses such as Paṉṟitturutti, Manalmaṉṟattu, etc. to which the lords of Neṭumpuṟaiyūrnāṭu belonged are from the territory of Kālkkaraināṭu.
52. Narayanan, *Perumals of Kerala*, p. 102 and references.
53. *Nāṭus* such as Puṟakiḻānāṭu, Kuṟumpoṟaiyūrnatu, Vēṇāṭu and perhaps Ēṟānāṭu had these distinct dignities, which indicates hereditary succession. Narayanan, *Perumals of Kerala*, pp. 94, 95, 96–7, 102–4.

54. Above, n. 50.
55. The origin and growth of these localities have not been the subject of any serious study. Given the variations in the base of each of these, no generalization can be made on present showing.
56. Narayanan, *Perumals of Kerala*, chapter on 'Early Wars and Alliances', pp. 37–49.
57. C. Girija, 'The Mūṣikavamśakāvya: A Study', unpublished MPhil Dissertation, Mangalore University, 1989.
58 Narayanan, *Perumals of Kerala*, chapter on 'Early Wars and Alliances', pp. 37–49, and Narayanan, 'The Anatomy of a Political Alliance from the Temple Records of Tirunāvalūr and Tiruvoṟṟiuyūr', *Journal of the Epigraphical Society of India (Bhāratīya Purābhilekha Patrikā)*, vol. V, *Studies in Epigraphy*, 1978, pp. 26–31.
59 *EI*, vol. III, p. 68 ff. In fact, historians have described this assemblage as a veritable 'war council'.
60. *TAS*, vol. V, no. 13, pp. 40–6. Narayanan has a slightly variant reading of this, which I have used here. *Index to Cēra Inscriptions*, A. 71.
61. *EI*, vol. IV, pp. 290–7.
62. For details, Narayanan, *Perumals of Kerala*, under 'Divisions of the Kingdom', pp. 90–105.
63. The text of this inscription has not been critically edited. For an *in situ* reading made by Narayanan and the present writer (and a photograph inserted upside down), Balakrishnan, 'Kēraḷaparyaṭanam' in *Dēśābhimāni* (Malayalam Weekly), no. 17, Book 35, 28 September 2003, pp. 42–5.
64. B.A. Saletore, *Ancient Karnataka*, vol. I, *History of Tuluva* (Poona, 1936), pp. 178–9; K.V. Ramesh, *A History of South Kanara* (Dharwar, 1970), pp. 252–3.
65. This body had raised questions of identification even from the time when historians like Logan started the study of the history of Kerala. Logan, *Malabar*, II, app. ccxi; Menon, *History of Kerala*, vol. I, p. 252. They were taken for representative bodies of the localities, on the basis of which R.C. Majumdar built fanciful theories such as that they were a continuation of the Vedic *sabhā* and *samiti*! R.C. Majumdar, *Corporate Life in Ancient India* (Calcutta, 1944), p. 132.
66. Narayanan, *Perumals of Kerala*, pp. 121–9; M.G.S. Narayanan, 'Companions of Honour', in M.G.S. Narayanan, *Aspects of Aryanisation in Kerala* (Trivandrum, 1973). See also Narayanan, 'The Hundred Groups and the Rise of Nāyar Militia in Medieval Kerala', *PIHC* (Burdwan, 1983).
67. *EI*, vol. XVI, no. 27, pp. 339–45, n. 21–5.
68. *TAS*, vol. VIII, no. 33 (v), p. 41; *TAS*, vol. VIII, no. 33 (vii), p. 42.
69. *TAS*, vol. II, no. 9, (i & ii), pp. 62–70; 80–5.
70. Narayanan has given a tabulated list of such fines mentioned in the inscriptions. *Perumals of Kerala*, pp. 136–7.

71. Ibid., p. 109.
72. Ibid., pp. 109–20; Veluthat, *Brahman Settlements*, pp. 52–67.
73. This is in the larger pattern obtaining all over south India in this period. Veluthat, *Political Structure*, pp. 80–98; Kesavan Veluthat, 'Landed Magnates as State Agents: the Gāvuḍas under the Hoysaḷas in Karnataka', in B.P. Sahu, ed., *Land System and Rural Society in Early India* (Delhi, 1997), pp. 322–8, Chapter 15 above.
74. I have counted fifty-five Cēra inscriptions showing this presence. *Brahman Settlements*, p. 57 and n. 29 on p. 65.
75. For a discussion of the revenue system under the Cēra kingdom, Narayanan, *Perumals of Kerala*, pp. 129–39.
76. *TAS*, vol. II, no. 7, (A), p. 33. This too brings out the 1:2 proportion in which the revenue was shared between the locality lord and the Perumāḷ.
77. *TAS*, vol. II, no. 7, (I), pp. 44–5.
78. *TAS*, vol. V, no. 12, pp. 37–40.
79. *Annual Report of Epigraphy*, no. 125 of 1963–4. I have used the text as deciphered by Narayanan, *Kēraḷacaritrattinṟe Aṭisthānaśilakaḷ* (in Malayalam, Calicut, 1972), pp. 69–78.
80. *TAS*, vol. II, (iii), p. 46, ll.331–3.
81. *TAS*, vol. III, no. 49, pp. 191–6.
82. Narayanan, 'Socio-economic Implications of the concept of Mahapataka in the Feudal Society of South India', *PIHC* (Calicut, 1976).
83. *TAS*, vol. V, no. 55, pp. 172–6. Narayanan, after inspecting the original stone *in situ*, has emended the reading a little whereby what the official epigraphist had read as *paṇṭāram kēṭṭa*, which does not make sense, is corrected as *paṇṭāram kaṭṭa*, meaning 'one who stole from the [temple] treasury', Narayanan, *Index*, no. A 64.
84. Above, n. 81.
85. *TAS*, vol. II, no. 9, (i & ii), pp. 62–70; 80–5.
86. For a competent analysis of the revenue system, Narayanan, *Perumals of Kerala*, pp. 129–39.
87. *Indian Antiquary*, vol. XX, pp. 285–90, ll.19–22.
88. Above, n. 79.
89. *TAS*, vol. III, no. 40, pp. 176–7.
90. *South Indian Inscriptions*, vol. VII, no. 165.
91. *TAS*, vol. V, no. 12, pp. 37–40.
92. Above, n. 70.
93. Many documents show that these 'Hundred Organizations' were placed in charge of the protection (*kāval*) of eleemosynary grants.
94. For a detailed study of Mahōdayapuram, Kesavan Veluthat, 'Mahōdayapuram-Koṭuṅṅallūr: A Capital City as a Sacred Centre', in Jean-Luc Chevillard and Eva Wilden, eds, *South Indian Horizons: Felicitation Volume for François Gros on the Occasion of His 70th Birthday* (Pondicherry, 2004), pp. 471–85, Chapter 10 below.

95. Veluthat, *Brahman Settlements*, pp. 21–38.
96. Narayanan, *Perumals of Kerala*, pp. 75–6. According to *Mayamata*, '*sarvajanasaṅkīrṇam nṛpabhavanasamyuktam ... bahurathyōpētam yad sēnamukham ucyatē tajñaiḥ*'. The *Kamikāgama* defines it thus: '*rājavēśmasamyuktam sarvajātēḥ samanvitam guhyapradēśa-samyuktam sēnāmukhamivōcyate*'. In both cases, the fact of a *sēnāmukha* being a town with the royal residence is underlined.
97. Veluthat, 'Mahōdayapuram-Koṭuṅṅallūr'.
98. Kesavan Veluthat, 'Storage and Retrieval of Information: Literacy and Communication in Pre-modern Kerala', in Amiya Kumar Bagchi, Dipankar Sinha and Barnita Bagchi, eds, *Webs of History: Information, Communication and Technology from Early to Post-Colonial India*, pp. 67–82, Chapter 8 above.
99. Ibid.
100. Narayanan, *Perumals of Kerala*, pp. 201–4.
101. Ibid., p. 204.
102. The case of just one temple, Tiruvalla, is illustrative: Veluthat, *Brahman Settlements*, pp. 39–52. The experience of other temples was not different.
103. Narayanan and Kesavan, 'The Traditional Land System of Kerala', Logan Centenary Seminar (Calicut, 1981) (unpublished).
104. Narayanan and Veluthat. 'The Bhakti Movement in South India' in S.C. Malik, ed., *Indian Movements: Some Aspects of Dissent and Protest* (Simla, 1978), pp. 33–66.
105. Cēramān Perumāḷ Nāyanār, the Śaiva saint and Kulaśēkhara Āḻvār, the Vaiṣṇsava saint were both rulers of this kingdom. In fact, they were the first two rulers, according the chronology proposed by Narayanan, *Perumāḷs*. There is another Śaiva saint mentioned in the hagiology of that sect, Vēnāṭṭaṭikaḷ, who was in all probability a lord of Vēṇāṭu in this period.
106. Veluthat, 'The *Keraḷōlpatti* as History',
107. Narayanan, 'The State in the Era' p. 116. See also n. 8 above.
108. *TAS*, vol. VIII, no. 33 (vii), p. 42.
109. Veluthat, 'Mahōdayapuram-Koṭuṅṅallūr'.
110. Veluthat, *Political Structure*.
111. This draws on the classic definition of the 'fundamental features of European feudalism' as given by Marc Bloch, *Feudal Society* (translated from the French by L.A. Manyon, London, 1961) vol. II, p. 446.
112. Claessen and Skalník, eds, *The Early State*, p. 21.
113. Ibid., pp. 533–96. They are as follows:
    1. A definite territory, divided into territorial divisions, whose residents are the subjects or citizens of this state.
    2. Independence.
    3. A single governmental centre.
    4. Practice of trade.
    5. Presence of markets.

6. Existence of long-distance trade.
7. Trade and markets as a source of income for the ruling hierarchy.
8. Presence of clearly defined division of labour and full-time specialists.
9. Agriculture as the most prevalent means of subsistence.
10. The production of a surplus.
11. Presence of a sovereign and an aristocracy.
12. Presence of smallholders.
13. Presence of tenants.
14. Social stratification at least into two strata.
15. Direct participation in food production limited to lower sections of society.
16. The obligation to perform services for the state.
17. Existence of the obligation to pay taxes, including for the aristocracy in most cases.
18. Unequal access to basic means of production, in the case of land.
19. Tribute as the main source of income of the sovereign and aristocracy.
20. Primary production as the source of income of smallholders and tenants.
21. The relationship between the sovereign and his subjects based on a mythical character.
22. The sacral status of the sovereign.
23. Genealogical status explaining the sovereign's exalted position. The aristocracy often bases its privileged position on its connection with the sovereign's lineage.
24. The sovereign performs rites.
25. The sovereign as the formal lawgiver.
26. The sovereign as the supreme judge.
27. The existence of informal influences on lawgiving.
28. The sovereign as supreme commander.
29. The sovereign generally has a bodyguard.
30. The sovereigns present gifts to their people.
31. The sovereign remunerates his people for services rendered.
32. The sovereign generally pays offerings.
33. The payment of salaries and remunerations and the presentation of offerings or gifts are found to be general, also on the lower levels of the government hierarchy.
34. Presence of a royal court.
35. The sovereign's kin belong to the aristocracy.
36. Tenure of high office renders one eligible for classification with the aristocracy.
37. The heads of certain clans belong to the aristocracy.
38. Internal stratification of aristocracy according to rank, order of birth and function occupied.
39. The priesthood supports the ideological basis.

40. Commoners' obligation to pay taxes, tribute, or comparable levies.
41. Commoners' obligation to perform military service.
42. Commoners' obligation to perform menial services for the state, the aristocracy, or functionaries.
43. The absence of kinship relations between the sovereign and the commoners.
44. Delegation of tasks and power as a principle of political organization.
45. The presence of a three-tier administrative apparatus.
46. The greater presence of general functionaries on the regional level, and less frequently at the national and local levels.
47. Specialist functionaries at the top level of the administrative apparatus.
48. Influence of courtiers on political affairs.
49. Influence on political decisions by members of the sovereign's family.
50. Influence of priests on decision-making.
51. The travel of sovereign through his realm in order to exact allegiance and tribute.

It is interesting to examine the features of the Cēra kingdom against this checklist. Significantly, most of them are present there.

114. It is accepted that the early state has to be looked at as a process is contained in the study. Peter Skalnīk, 'The Early State as a Process', in Claessen and Skalník, eds, *The Early State*, pp. 597–618. The case studies and the structural analysis mentioned above do not recognize this, though.

115. I have no access to his paper in German 'Die frühmittelalterlischen Regionalreiche: Ihre Struktur und Rolle im Proze Bstaatlischer Indien' ('Early Medieval Regional States: Their Structure and Role in the Process of State Formation'), in H. Kulke and D. Rothermund, eds, *Regionale Tradition in Südasien*, Wiesbaden, 1985. I depend on an extended quotation given by the author himself in Hermann Kulke, 'The Integrative Model of State Formation in Early Medieval India', in Masaaki Kimura and Akio Tanabe, eds, *The State in India: Past and Present*, New Delhi, 2006, pp. 64–5.

116. Veluthat, *Brahman Settlements*, above, n. 95.

10

A Capital City as a Sacred Centre*

Mahōdayapuram or Makōtai, identified with the coastal town of modern Koṭuṅṅallūr in the Trichur (Tṛśśūr) district in Kerala, India, was the capital city of the Cēramān *Perumāḷs* who ruled over much of the present-day state of Kerala for a little over three centuries from *c.* AD 800.[1] Even after the last of the Cēramān *Perumāḷs* had long disappeared from the scene, the town was still nostalgically remembered in literature and popular tradition as a political centre from where Kerala was ruled.[2] But the town is known today more as a sacred centre. In fact, Koṭuṅṅallūr is so much a sacred centre that the Dravidian place name, Koṭuṅṅallūr, is fancifully derived from Sanskrit *Kōṭiliṅgapura,* 'the town of ten million *liṅgas*'. To this day, it attracts pilgrims from all over Kerala to the temple of Kāḷi who, in her fierce form, is supposed to be the custodian of the 'seeds' of smallpox. The temple is famous or notorious for the *Bharaṇi* festival in the solar month of *Mīnam* (March–April) every year, when people from all over Kerala throng there chanting 'prayers' that are less than acceptable to a decent audience. The celebrated Śiva temple of Tiruvañcikkuḷam or Tiruvañcaikkaḷam, which forms part of the pilgrimage circuit of Śaiva devotees because of its association with the Tamil Bhakti saints such as Cēramān Perumāḷ Nāyanār and Sundaramūrtti Nāyanār, makes it sacred for the Śaivas. So do other Śiva temples in the town such as Śṛṅgapuram and Kiḻttaḷi. Mahōdayapuram-Koṭuṅṅallūr is equally holy for the Vaiṣṇavas for the Tṛkkulaśēkharapuram temple, possibly built by Kulaśēkhara Āḻvār, one of the twelve Āḻvārs of the Tamil Bhakti

* First published as 'Mahōdayapuram-Koṭuṅṅalūr: A Capital City as a Sacred Centre', in Jean-Luc Chevillard and Eva Wilden, eds, *South Indian Horizons: Felicitation Volume for François Gros on the Occasion of His 70th Birhtday* (Pondicherry, 2004) pp. 471–85.

tradition. The Muslims, too, hail the town as sacred, as it is claimed that Muslim scholars won the last Cēramān *Perumāḷ* in disputations and not only got him converted to Islam but also had the first mosque in India built there during the lifetime of the Prophet himself.[3] The Christians, in their turn, believe that it was there that St Thomas, the apostle, landed and began his missionary activities.[4] The Jews had a considerable settlement there; but, following the atrocities of the Portuguese in the sixteenth century, they left the place swearing never again to spend another night in the vicinity of the towns.[5] They have, however, left behind the place name *Jūtakkaḷam* (Jewish Settlement) as the relic of their having been in that town. There are also unsupported claims linking the place with Jainism and even Buddhism.[6] In any case, Koṭuṅṅallūr has been a sacred centre for the followers of nearly every religious persuasion. It is our primary purpose in this paper to bring out the linkages between this sacredness on the one hand and the political and economic importance of the centre on the other and show how the one factor was as much the cause, as it was the effect, of the other in the complex development of the town and the locality of which it is part. Both the sacred character and the economic and political importance can be seen as a function of the geographical situation of the town and the locality of which it is part.

In fact, a study of the development of Koṭuṅṅallūr as a sacred centre can clarify several issues related to the transformation of an ordinary place into a sacred centre. The complex processes leading to any centre becoming sanctified would show how a certain place, on account of a combination of circumstances, becomes more central than others in a region and how this centrality is sought to be retained by attaching a religious aura to it. This is not, to be sure, to say that behind the process of a place acquiring sacredness was a deliberate action with sinister motives calculated to achieve secular ends through invoking religion. Nor may there be any agency that consciously does this. A second purpose of this paper, thus, is to demonstrate the process of the sanctification of a place, transforming its character from the secular to the sacred. We examine the historical evidence regarding the centre as a sacred place first and then look at the importance of the place from the social and political points of view. This procedure may bring out causal connections between the two with clarity.

The earliest clear indication of Koṭuṅṅallūr being a sacred centre is in the Tamil Śaiva tradition. Sundaramūrtti Nāyanār, one of the sixty-three celebrated Śaiva saints of the Tamil Bhakti Movement, has an exquisite hymn devoted to the deity of Tiruvañcaikkaḷam in Koḍuṅkōḷur.[7] The Nāyanār does not fail to mention the location of the town, on the walls of which the ocean breaks its waves. *Periyapurāṇam,* a slightly later text cherishing the tradition continuing from an earlier period, says that Sundaramūrtti had stayed in the town on two occasions as a guest of his fellow-devotee, Cēramān Perumāḷ Nāyanār, the royal Śaiva saint.[8] In fact, both Sundaramūrtti and Cēramān *Perumāḷ* were so closely associated with the temple that both are stated to have ascended to Kailāsa, the abode of Śiva, from there. The works of Cēramān *Perumāḷ*, namely, the *Ādiyulā, Ponvaṇṇattantādi* and *Tiruvārūr Mummaṇikkōvai* are, however, curiously silent about Tiruvañcaikkaḷam. But the *Periyapurāṇam,* a twelfth century hagiographic work, does refer to the temple as the place where the Nāyanār was sitting in meditation when the Cēra ministers persuaded him to shoulder the responsibilities of the kingdom.[9] There are two bronze statues in the temple, believed to be of Cēramān *Perumāḷ* and Sundaramūrtti Nāyanār.

That Tiruvañcaikkaḷam was the royal temple of the Cēras is attested by evidence from epigraphy and literature.[10] It is located close to the royal residence, the site of which is identified with what is known today as *Cēramān Paṟambu* ('the Compound of the Cēramān'), immediately to the south of the temple. Local tradition describes this temple as *Cēramān Kōvil* ('the Temple of the Cēramān').[11] *Kēraḷōlpatti,* the traditional historical narrative of Kerala, states that one of the *Perumāḷ*s, Kulaśēkhara, built the temple of Tiruvañcaikkaḷam.[12] The idol is taken out in a ritual procession which forms part of the annual festival of the temple to the site of the old palace in *Cēramān Paṟambu.*[13] On the whole, the associations of the temple with the house of the Cēramāns are unquestionable.

Cēramān Perumāḷ Nāyanār is identified with Rājaśēkhara (AD *c.* 800–844), who was probably the first ruler of the Cēra kingdom of Mahōdayapuram.[14] Rājaśēkhara presided over a joint meeting of the representatives of the temple-centred Brāhmaṇa settlements of Vāḻappaḷḷi and Tiruvāṟṟuvāy in Tiruvalla, which was one of the more prominent Brāhmaṇa colonies in Kerala. An inscription on copper plate recording the proceedings of this meeting, dated in his thirteenth year and datable to the first quarter of the ninth century, starts curiously with the invocation *namaśśivāya* ('obeisance to Śiva'), a solitary exception to the inscriptions from Kerala which begin usually with the invocation *svasti śrī* ('Hail! Prosperity!').[15] It is pointed out that this may indicate the Śaivite bias of the founder of the kingdom. In any case, the big way in which the Bhakti Movement acted as props to the newly established monarchies in early medieval south India is well known.[16] It is hardly surprising that the founder of the Cēra kingdom too recognized its immense possibilities and promoted it personally.

The sacred associations of the city of Mahōdayapuram in the middle of the ninth century, immediately following the period of Rājaśēkhara or Cēramān Perumāḷ Nāyanār, are brought out by an astronomical treatise composed in AD 869. This is a detailed commentary on the astronomical work called *Laghubhāskarīya* of the famous Bhāskarācārya by Śaṅkaranārāyaṇa.[17] Śaṅkaranārāyaṇa lived in the court of the Cēra king Sthāṇu Ravi Kulaśēkhara (AD 844–883). He describes the city of Mahōdayapura significantly as a *sēnāmukha*.[18] He refers to the royal residence situated in a quarter of the city known as Gōtramallēśvara where there was a shrine of Gaṇapati called Bālakrīḍēśvara. However, the work does not mention any other temple in the town. Perhaps the references to temples there, such as they are, are only incidental to the work as its central concern is with problems of astronomy. Bālakrīḍēśvara, the shrine of Gaṇapati, is identified on the basis of a fourteenth century *Maṇipravāḷam* text, *Kōkasandēśam*.[19] It gives a detailed description of the town of Mahōdayapuram-Koṭuṅṅallūr, the details of which we shall turn to later in this paper. In the course of the description, there is a reference to the shrine of infant Gaṇapati in Bālakrīḍēśvara. This shrine is in the vicinity of the Tiruvañcaikkaḷam temple complex. Gōtramallēśvara, too, survives, arguably in its slightly altered form, Lōkamallēśvaram, which is where the *Cēramān Paṟambu* is located immediately to the south of the Tiruvañcaikkaḷam temple. Excavations at the site, conducted by the Department of Archaeology of the erstwhile Cochin State and later by the Archaeological Survey of India, have brought out pottery and other interesting details.

Śaṅkaranārāyaṇa was patronized by Sthāṇu Ravi Kulaśēkhara.[20] This ruler, who in all probability was the immediate successor to Cēramān Perumāḷ Nāyanār or Rājaśēkhara, was himself an interesting figure if we go by a couple of identifications. In the first place, it is suggested that he was identical with Kulaśēkhara Āḻvār, the royal

Vaiṣṇava saint who is stated to have belonged to the dynasty of the Cēras of the West Coast.[21] There is no reason why the author of the *Perumāḷ Tirumoḻi,* evidence of the recitation of which at Śrīraṅgam is available at least from AD 1088,[22] should not be identified with this *Perumāḷ* who ruled in the ninth century as we will have to wait till the end of the eleventh century for another Cēra *Perumāḷ* with a name or title of Kulaśēkhara. Apart from *Perumāḷ Tirumoḻi* in Tamil, he is also described to have composed *Mukundamālā,* a hymn in Sanskrit. In the colophon to certain editions of this work, it is stated that a pilgrimage to Śrīraṅgam is celebrated every day in the town of king Kulaśēkhara.[23] There is also the tradition that this Cēra ruler dedicated his daughter to that temple as a dancing girl, and the shrine of Cērakulanācciyār within the temple complex is believed to commemorate her. It may be noteworthy in this connection that an inscription from Pagan in Myanmar, referring to a merchant from Mahōdayapuram, quotes a whole verse from the *Mukundamālā.*[24]

It is interesting that the successor to the royal Śaiva saint of the dynasty of the Cēra *Perumāḷs* of Mahōdayapuram was a Vaiṣṇava saint. Obviously, this points to the realization of the vast potentials of the Bhakti Movement in both the streams as an ideology of the newly emerging order over which the Cēra *Perumāḷs* were called upon to preside.[25] It is in this connection that another identity of Kulaśēkhara acquires significance: he is also thought to be the royal playwright called Kulaśēkharavarman, the author of the Sanskrit plays *Subhadrādhanañjayam* and *Tapatīsamvaraṇam* and the *campūkāvya, Āścaryamañjarī.*[26] The author calls himself *Mahōdayapuraparameśvara*, 'supreme lord of Mahōdayapura'[27] and *Keraḷādhinatha*, 'the overlord of Kerala',[28] terms that are very meaningful in ways more than one. His Vaiṣṇavite leanings are unmistakable in the plays; the somewhat unwarranted inclusion of the Vāmana story in the *Tapatīsamvaraṇam* is not without significance either.

This royal playwright is also believed to have been responsible for the inauguration of the Sanskrit theatre in Kerala through patronizing the *Kūṭiyāṭṭam* form of presenting Sanskrit plays. Commentaries on his plays known as *Vyaṅgya Vyākhyā* are stated to be prepared under instructions of the author himself and for easy enactment of the plays on the stage.[29] So also, there is the story of a legendary court jester, Tōlan, stated to be a contemporary of the royal playwright, who is believed to have contributed much towards choreographing the plays.[30] Even to this day, Cākyārs who stage Sanskrit dramas in the form of *Kūṭiyāṭṭam* use Kulaśēkharavarman's plays in a big way in spite of their being not exactly the best of dramatic compositions available in Sanskrit. This has significance going beyond being one more jewel on the monarch's crown; as theatre was one of the important means of communication, useful in propagating the ideology of bhakti through the popularization of the *Mahābhārata* and other stories, its patronage by a ruler meant patronage of the movement in a considerable manner. This argument gets added emphasis when it is recognized that Kulaśēkhara was not only a *patron* of the Bhakti Movement but he was its great *leader*. Incidentally, it may also be mentioned that the *Cākyār*s of Kerala believe that when their art has no longer any takers, they are to abandon their profession by leaving their costumes on the branch of a banyan tree in front of the Tiruvañcaikkaḷam temple.

Neither the Tamil hymns of Kulaśēkhara Āḻvār nor the Sanskrit plays of Kulaśēkharavarman refer to a temple in the capital city, Mahōdayapuram, much less one built by him. But there does exist a temple in the town of Koṭuṅṅallūr with the name Tṛkkulaśēkharapuram. An inscription in the temple dated in the 195th year of the construction of the temple has been assigned palaeographically to the eleventh or twelfth century.[31] Reckoning backwards, then, the date of its construction would fall well within the regnal period of Sthāṇu Ravi Kulaśēkhara, identified with both Kulaśēkhara Āḻvār and Kulaśēkharavarman, and the name of the temple may point to his hand in its construction and consecration. That the Tamil and the Sanskrit works of the monarch do not mention the temple may be because the temple was built after their composition. In any case, it forms part of the pilgrimage circuit of Vaiṣṇava devotees in south India.

Apart from the Tiruvañcaikkaḷam temple associated with Cēramān Perumāḷ Nāyanār and the Tṛkkulaśēkharapuram temple founded by Kulaśēkhara Āḻvār, the city of Mahōdayapuram in the age of the Perumāḷs boasted of two other temples both in close proximity to the former—the Kīḻttaḷi and the Ciṅṅapuram or Sṛṅgapuram Taḷi. Both are dedicated to Śiva. These four temples were together known as the *Nālu Taḷi* or 'The Four Temples' and they had a major role to play in the government of the Cēra kingdom.[32] In fact, a discussion of the role of the *Nālu Taḷi* in the polity of Kerala in this period can be useful in bringing out a major aspect of the sacred geography of Mahōdayapuram as well as the sacral character of Cēra kingship.

The role of *Nālu Taḷi* in the government of the Perumāḷs of Mahōdayapuram is a matter of recent recognition by historians. When research into the history of Kerala was initiated on 'modern' lines in the twentieth century, statements about the Nālu Taḷi in the narrative called *Kēraḷōlpatti* were dismissed, together with other details there, as 'legendary nonsense'. The story goes that after Paraśurāma created the land of Kerala and gifted it to Brāhmaṇas who were settled in 64 *grāmas* or 'villages', he invested the donees with the right to carry on the governance of the land as *brahmakṣatra,* 'Brāhmaṇas in the role of kṣatriyas'. The sixty-four *grāmas* elected four from among themselves, namely, Peruñcellūr, Panniyūr, Paṟavūr and Ceṅṅannūr as *kaḻakams* to represent them. Each of them sent an agent known as *rakṣāpuruṣa*. They together carried out the work of governance. But they promptly got corrupted in course of time and it was realized by the community that the work of governance was not their cup of tea, it being the function of kṣatriyas. Thereupon they decided to have a ruler of the kṣatriya caste elected for a period of twelve years, to be succeeded by another similarly elected kṣatriya ruler. These rulers were known as *Perumāḷs* and were established at Mahōdayapuram. The Brāhmaṇa representatives of the four *grāmas* continued to be the advisors of the *Perumāḷs*. However, as the *grāmas* from which they hailed were too far away from the capital city, four new *grāmas* were elected, superseding the earlier four, to represent the Brāhmaṇa community. The newly elected ones were Mūḻikkaḷam, Airāṇikkaḷam, Paṟavūr and Iruṅṅāṭikkūṭal, all within close proximity to the capital. Each of these was also accorded a seat in the capital city in a temple, namely, Mēlttaḷi, Kiḻttaḷi, Neṭiya Taḷi and Ciṅṅapuram Taḷi, respectively. The narrative also mentions the names of Nampūtiri houses, younger members of which were officiating as the *Taḷi Adhikārikaḷ* or *Taḷiyātiris*.[33] At least two of these houses which used to enjoy considerable aristocratic privileges, namely Kariṅṅampaḷḷi and Eḷamprakkōṭ, survive to this day.

The narration in *Kēraḷōlpatti* is necessarily confused and devoid of a chronological order. Different layers of memory collapse and are mixed up. There is no trace of evidence in other sources to help us say anything about the four *kaḻakams* in the pre-*Perumāḷ* era. But the statements about the *Perumāḷ* era in relation to the *Nālu Taḷi* are interestingly supported by other sources from the period and immediately thereafter.[34] There are inscriptions which suggest that the *Perumāḷ* had a council called *Nālu Taḷi.* At least a couple of them speak of the *Perumāḷ* having taken important decisions in consultation with it. In one case, the meeting is described as being held in Neṭiya Taḷi. The affiliation of Neṭiya Taḷi to Paṟavūr is brought out by literature[35] and that of Kīḻttaḷi to Airāṇikkaḷam by an inscription from Kīḻttaḷi.[36] The affiliation of the other two temples to their respective *grāmas*, namely Ciṅṅapuram Taḷi to Iruṅṅāṭikkūṭal and Mēlttaḷi to Mūḻikkaḷam may be assumed safely. A record of the immediate post-Cēra period, granting trade privileges to the Syrian Christians in Mahōdayapuram, speaks of '*Nālu Taḷi* and the *grāmas* attached to them' as situated within the limits of the town.[37] Literary texts of the fourteenth and fifteenth centuries, too, refer to *Nālu Taḷi* and the *grāmas* which they represented. A verse in the *Śukasandēśa,* a Sanskrit text of the fifteenth century, is worth quoting for various reasons:[38]

> This [capital city] shines forth on account of the great Brāhmaṇas who live in rows of *maṭhas* in the *sthalīs* here. These leaders of the sixty-four *grāmas* are equal to Bhṛgu in their command of the weapons and the sciences and are paragons of acceptable manners, upon whose bidding the king is verily the lord of the earth.

An understanding of the *Nālu Taḷi* is crucial in trying to look at the sacred character of the city of Koṭuṅṅallūr; it is equally crucial for the sacral nature of the Cēra kingship as well. The *Nālu Taḷi* and the *maṭhas* attached to the temples are known to have been the seats of the representatives of the four *grāmas* of Mūḻikkaḷam, Airāṇikkaḷam, Iruṅṅāṭikkūṭal and Paṟavūr. These grāmas are situated in the southern parts of the Trichur and the northern parts of Ernakulam districts, where there is a concentration of Brāhmaṇa settlements. It may be remembered that the Brāhmaṇa settlements in Kerala had come up in the immediate pre-Cēra period, forming clusters around the lower reaches of the Pērār, Periyār and Pampā rivers, in the tract which is most hospitable to rice cultivation.[39] Even there, it is the Periyār Valley which can boast of the greatest density. It is but natural that four Brāhmaṇa settlements from this cluster should be representing the establishment in Kerala, particularly when the seat of government was in that locality. Thus, when the Brāhmaṇas of the *Nālu Taḷi* are described in the verse quoted above as 'paragons of acceptable manners leading the sixty-four *grāmas*'—'*grāmān ṣaṣtim catura iha yē grāhyaceṣṭā nayanti*'—our author was stating something which was well known. The *Nālu Taḷi* was the symbol of the Brāhmaṇical world of Kerala in the Cēra capital.

What is more important is the political role which the *Nālu Taḷi* played. Epigraphic evidence tells us that this body functioned as the king's council. It seems that it influenced the decisions of the monarch considerably in administrative and fiscal matters. An inscription from the Rāmēśvaraswāmin temple at Kollam speaks of the amends that king Rāmavarma Kulaśēkhara had made for the wrong he had done the '*āryas*'—an expression used to indicate the Brāhmaṇas.[40] This shows the extent of power that the Brāhmaṇas had whereby they could force such an act of atonement on the ruler himself. That the document makes a specific reference to the presence of the *Nālu Taḷi* on the occasion is significant. In fact, accounts in the *Kēraḷōlpatti* say that the *Nālu Taḷi* had extracted an oath of habitual allegiance from the ruler and that it was the *Nālu Taḷi* that was responsible for establishing the king on the throne. *Nālu Taḷi*, and the Brāhmaṇa power it represented, have been demonstrated as the real power behind the Cēra throne. It is this fact that is underlined by the verse quoted above: 'upon whose bidding the king is verily the lord of the earth'—'*vācā yēṣām bhavati nṛpatir nāyako rājyalakṣmyāḥ*'.

It was not for nothing that Kerala was described as *brahmakṣatra*—a land where Brāhmaṇas played the role of Kṣatriyas. Paraśurāma himself, who created the land, had combined these two in him! The story goes that Paṛaśurāma created the land of Kerala and donated it to Brāhmaṇas as *brahmakṣatra* with the right to rule and protect the land which they so got.[41] Several Brāhmaṇa families of Kerala were even given training in the use of arms for this purpose, a tradition which is again attested by epigraphy and literature.[42] Thus, when our author says that the Brāhmaṇas of Kerala were 'equal to Bhṛgu in their command of the weapons and the sciences'—'*śastrē sāstrē pi ca bhṛgunibhaiḥ*'—we have to see this historical allusion.

This heavy Brāhmaṇical influence and a certain sacredness claimed on account of it was a characteristic feature of the Mahōdayapura monarchy. The *double entendre* employed in the opening verse of the commentary on *Laghubhāskariya* brings this out clearly. It praises the ruler, Sthāṇu Ravi, who was the patron of the astronomer, although all the terms used to describe the object of the praise are also equally applicable to Śiva.[43] In fact, one of the characteristic features of the image of royalty in the whole of south India in this period is this divinization through various means.[44] This is seen in the case of the Cēra kings of Mahōdayapuram as well. The rulers of this dynasty are described as *deva* (god) as witness the titles Rājaśēkharadeva, Kulaśēkharadeva, Rāmadeva, Manukulādiccadeva, etc., in the epigraphic records.[45] Kulaśēkharavarman, the royal playwright, liked to call himself Mahodayapura-Parameśvara. This divine claim or attribute is a pointer to the sacral character of kingship and, naturally, the seat of that king becomes a sacred centre. Even this, at least in the case of Mahōdayapuram, was probably because of the role of the Brāhmaṇas in the polity. It may be remembered that the largest number of inscriptions of this period in Kerala are from the Brāhmaṇa settlements centred on temples and that the majority of them are concerned with land and its use for rice cultivation. What is peculiar there, in contrast to the rest of south India, is the general absence of a powerful class of non-Brāhmaṇa landowners. Therefore, it was easier and more appropriate to use the Brāhmaṇical idioms in politics and its legitimacy in Kerala: Mahōdayapuram, the capital, naturally represented and projected this sacredness through the large number of temples and other symbols of Brāhmaṇical religion.

At the same time, Mahōdayapuram-Koṭuṅṅallūr was equally sacred for those who practised the non-Brāhmaṇa cults as well. This is brought out by the importance of the Kāḷi temple there, although even Kāḷi has been co-opted to the pantheon of the Brāhmaṇas. Interestingly, there is no reference to this temple in the sources of the Cēra kingdom of Mahōdayapuram, although the possibility of the temple having been there cannot be ruled out. By the time the temple finds mention in the post-Cēra records, it was already a Brāhmaṇical temple, with centrality given to Śiva in a technical sense but Kāḷi herself remaining more important for the worshipping devotees.[46]

Three *sandēśakāvyas* from the post-Cēra period, all modelled on the *Mēghasandēśa* with the separated and pining hero sending a message to the heroine through an unlikely messenger, are interesting in this context. In all the three, like in other similar *sandēśakāvyas*, the hero gives detailed descriptions of the route to be taken by the messenger. Of these fourteenth to fifteenth century texts, the *Kōkasandēśam* is a *Maṇipravāḷam* (a mixture of Malayalam and Sanskrit) work of anonymous authorship while the *Kōkilasandēśa* of

Uddaṇḍa and *Śukasandēśa* of Lakṣmīdāsa are in Sanskrit. The destination of the messenger is different in each case; but each has to go *via* Mahōdayapuram-Koṭuṅṅallūr.

Kōkasandēśam has about twenty-five verses to describe the complex.[47] Kāḷi of the Kuṟumpakkāvu shrine takes more than three verses.[48] She is the dark, tall and fierce goddess, who drinks the blood of the demons, and is surrounded by goblins dancing in the blood of the demons so fallen. But she is also the benevolent mother of the entire world. For the author of *Śukasandēśa,* the fierce goddess in the sacred grove is the deity of destruction for whom the entire cosmos is not enough for one gulp at the time of the ultimate flood.[49] Uddaṇḍa in his *Kōkilasandēśa* describes her as enshrined in a grove and as very fierce. Even Death is scared of her and thus she is helpful to Life. Her attendants are described as trying to sacrifice the buffalo which Yama, the god of death, rides on![50]

The way in which this shrine in the grove is described in these three important *kāvya*s is significant. This place of worship, just outside the city of Mahōdayapuram, is where animal sacrifices were offered. The deity there presides over the final dissolution of the universe. She is herself bloodthirsty and is surrounded by goblins who play in blood. In fact, this is a faithful picture of the goddess in the Kāḷi temple of Koṭuṅṅallūr, who is a non-Brāhmaṇical deity in a fierce form, pleased by animal sacrifice. At the same time, attempts to link her with Purāṇic mythology and cosmology are made in these texts, which are of great significance.

The Kāḷi temple at Koṭuṅṅallūr became a centre of pilgrimage for non-Brāhmaṇa devotees in the period after the decline of the Cēra kingdom. Pilgrims from all over Kerala, after fasting and observing several other month-long austerities in March-April, go there in groups for the *Bharaṇi* festival, shouting obscene songs as part of their worship. They offer turmeric and pepper to Kāḷi. Till recently, cocks and goats were also sacrificed at the festival. How and why this festival began and took shape is hard to say; but it is interesting that people from different parts of Kerala, which were recognized as separate political units under the Cēras of Mahōdayapuram, participate in this festival. It is significant that members of the Nāyar and Īḻava castes who had military pretensions formed the largest number of pilgrims. There are a large number of Kāḷi shrines in different parts of Kerala where it is claimed that the deity is a close kin, mostly an elder or a younger sister, of the goddess of this temple. A number of Teyyams, the folk deities worshipped by the non-Brāhmaṇas in north Malabar, cherish this tradition.[51] The special rights that members of the Taccōḷi house from north Malabar, famed for their military achievements in the post-Cēra period, had in this festival are particularly noteworthy.[52] It is tempting to ask if this annual pilgrimage was a vestige of the movement of soldiers from the chiefly territories to the capital of the overlord. One is reminded of the important statement made by Śaṅkaranārāyaṇa, the commentator of *Laghubhāskarīya*, that the city of Mahōdayapura had a separate *senāmukha* ('Cantonment').[53] The role that a Nāyar body of Koṭuṅṅallūr known as the *Onnu Kuṟe Āyiram* ('The Thousand Less One') had in this festival would support this surmise, although nothing can be said definitely about this.

The *Onnu Kuṟe Āyiram Yōgam* continues to have considerable rights and privileges in the Kāḷi temple. M.G.S. Narayanan has proposed that this body may represent a continuation, in altered form, of the *Āyiram* ('The Thousand') identified as the bodyguards or Companions of Honour of the Cēra *Perumāḷ*s of Mahōdayapuram.[54] That a body with military and police functions got transformed largely as a body managing the affairs of a temple with rights and privileges there during a major festival where non-Brāhmaṇas had a greater participation is significant for our understanding of the sacred character of a political centre. If the process of the former can be known in greater detail, the latter could be brought out with greater clarity.

As stated earlier, Koṭuṅṅallūr is sacred also for the Jews, Christians and Muslims. There are no Jews there any more, but that there used to be a considerable Jewish settlement is attested by the place-name Jūtakkaḷam. The Jewish Copper Plates of Bhāskara Ravi Varman (AD 1000) were not only issued from this town but also gave Joseph Rabban, the Jewish merchant chief, considerable aristocratic privileges.[55] Jewish tradition believes that the first permanent settlement of the Jews in this town, known to them as Shingly, dates from AD 370, following the destruction of the second temple at Jerusalem by Titus Vespasian. There is rich folklore among the Jews of Cochin, which preserve the memories of the Synagogue at Kōtai or Makōtai, another name by which the town of Koṭuṅṅallūr was known. It was in AD 1567 that the Portuguese razed this settlement and the Synagogue to the ground.[56]. So also, a strong Christian settlement exists there. In fact, Christians believe that it was there that St Thomas, the apostle, began his missionary activities. They boasted of a Christian royal house known as the Villārvaṭṭam *svarūpam,* which is believed to have had its seat in the vicinity of Koṭuṅṅallūr.[57] So also, there is a mosque that is presented as dating from the beginning of the Kollam era (AD ninth century), that being the date on which the legendary Cēramān *Perumāḷ* was believed to have been converted to Islam and gone to Mecca.[58] Even if this early date is an exaggeration, it is possible that there was a strong Islamic presence in the port town which had trade contacts with West Asia in a big way. Whether or not the last *Perumāḷ* was converted to Islam and had one of first mosques established there, a medieval Sanskrit text, the *Viṭanidrābhāṇam,* makes a reference to the '*paḷḷi* of the shaven heads' (*muṇḍadhāriṇaḥ paḷḷi*) to the south of the Tiruvañcaikkaḷam temple.[59] There are also unsupported claims linking the town with Buddhists and Jains.

We have seen that Mahōdayapuram-Koṭuṅṅallūr was a sacred centre as much as it was a capital city. The factors responsible for the one were themselves working towards the other. It may be necessary to go a little backward in time in order to realize this. It is well known that Mahōdayapuram-Koṭuṅṅallūr was a continuation of the ancient port town, known to Tamil sources as Muciri and to Greco-Roman records as Muziris.[60] Muziris was 'the first emporium of India' for the Romans, where the ships of the Yavanas arrived in large numbers and took back pepper and other products in exchange of gold. *The Periplus of the Erythraean Sea* tells us that Muziris abounded in ships sent there with cargoes from Arabia and Greek ships from Egypt. Pliny, however, has reservations about the desirability of the port because of pirates from Nitrias and also because ships had to anchor at some distance with the result that boats had to be employed for taking the cargoes to the coast. It was the land of Coelobotros. The pepper came there from Cottonara. The Greco-Roman accounts speak of the variety of goods exported from and imported through Muziris. Evidence from a papyrus in the Vienna Museum, published recently, speaks of trade in bulk goods between Muziris and Alexandria.[61] This record is a trade agreement between a *vaṇikar* (trader) from Muziris and a trader from Alexandria. The fabulous amount of trade which this single document testifies to underlines the substantial scale of the Indian trade with the Greco-Roman world in the second century that passed through Muziris. It did continue, as suggested by statements about considerable Roman settlements in Muziris. In fact, the *Peutingerian Tables* even speak of a temple of Augustus in the town.[62] However, this temple has not come down to us in archaeology or in memory. In any case, the fact of Muziris having been a port of considerable importance for Roman trade cannot be disputed. So also, records dating from later times as well attest its continuity as a centre of trade, particularly with the western world. Into this latter category would fall documents like the Jewish Copper Plates of Bhāskara Ravi (AD 1000) and even the so-called Syrian Christian Copper Plates of Vīra Rāghava *Cakravarttikaḷ* (AD 1225).[63]

This extensive trade with West Asia from the early centuries of the Christian era brought Muziris into contact with Judaism and Christianity early on. It is only natural that this *entrepot* of West Asian trade, 'the first emporium of India', was also the place where the earliest settlements of Semitic communities sprang up. One need not accept the tradition of St Thomas as a precondition to imagine that Syrian Christians arrived on the Indian coast in ships that came to Muziris. The presence of Jews in Muyirikkōṭu, the way in which Muciri or Muziris came to be known in later Malayalam, gets an explanation in the same way. Again, whether or not Muslim scholars had won one of the Perumāḷs in disputations and converted him to Islam, it is not hard to believe that Islam disembarked on the west coast in Kerala at the port of Koṭuṅṅallūr. The centre also became sacred for the followers of these Semitic religions.

Mahōdayapuram-Koṭuṅṅallūr was acquiring importance at another level as well. Early Tamil literature known as the 'Sangam Literature' and Greco-Roman accounts are clear in linking this port town with the early Cēras, who had their seat in Karūr (in the modern Tiruchirappalli district of Tamil Nadu). One does not know what happened to the Cēras in the period between the close of the early historical period ('the Sangam Period') and AD ninth century when evidence of the later Cēras is available from Mahōdayapuram. It has been suggested that a collateral line of the Cēras may have been residing in Muciri even in the early historical period and that, following the 'decline and fall' of the Roman empire and the drying up of Roman trade, this line as well as the port town suffered an eclipse. It may have been this line which got revived in the period after the eighth century under totally different conditions.

It is these conditions that are important in this context. One of the major developments that took place in the intervening period was the phenomenal expansion of agriculture, particularly in the major river valleys. It is seen from the records that this agrarian expansion was also linked with the rise of Brāhmaṇa settlements. In fact, the Brāhmaṇa settlements formed clusters in the more fertile regions of the river valleys.[64] The thickest of such clusters was on the lower Periyār basin, in the southern parts of the Trichur and the northern parts of the Ernakulam districts of modern Kerala, in the centre of which was the town of Koṭuṅṅallūr. The causal connection between the expansion of agriculture, the rise of the Brāhmaṇa settlements as corporations of a class of intermediaries placed above the cultivating peasantry and the development of the Āgamaic temples which were also the nuclei of the Brāhmaṇa settlements on the one side and the rise of the Cēra monarchy of Mahōdayapuram on the other has been brought out in a convincing manner.[65] Thus, even in an entirely different socio-economic and political formation, Mahōdayapuram-Koṭuṅṅallūr remained a centre with considerable sacred character. The sacredness in the changed context eminently suited the elements that had acquired importance in the new formation. That it was a seat of a sacral monarchy is brought out by the fact that temples sacred to the Bhakti tradition of both the Śaiva and Vaiṣṇava persuasions exist there. These temples enjoyed considerable patronage from the royalty; the royal patrons were themselves Bhakti saints of the respective canons. The mutual support that the Bhakti Movement and the new monarchies in south India had is a point that has been brought out by historical studies.[66] So also, the institution of *Nālu Taḷi* brings out the Brāhmaṇical character of this sacredness. Incidentally, it is significant that two of these 'four temples' are royal temples, associated with Bhakti saints.

In the period following the break-up of the Cēra kingdom, Koṭuṅṅallūr retained its sacred character. While the Brāhmaṇical temples continued to be important, the Kāḷi temple, with its non-Brāhmaṇa forms of worship and animal sacrifice, came into prominence and got Brāhmaṇized to a great extent. The martial character of the body of Nāyars who managed the temple and its Bharaṇi festival as well as the pilgrims who went there is interesting. The post-Cēra period of the history of Kerala, it is suggested, was a period of continual bickering among the principalities that formed a heterogeneous assortment in the political geography of Kerala. The Semitic religions, too, continued to hold the town as important and sacred, for there was a revival of trade by the second millennium. Mahōdayapuram's standing as a centre of trade in the post-Cēra period is brought out by epigraphic evidence from South-east Asia and also from Mahōdayapuram itself. It continued its brisk trade with West Asia, until a cataclysmic flood filled the port with silt in AD 1341 and rendered it literally high and dry.[67]

Thus, Mahōdayapuram-Koṭuṅṅallūr offers a good case study in sacred geography. Endowed with geographical peculiarities such as location on the estuary of a river and potentials as a port, it attracted traders from different parts of the world who brought with them religions of different descriptions. It is well known that pepper dominated the merchandise of that trade. That pepper should also be an offering dear to the deity of the Kāḷi shrine is of its own significance. Even after that early trade dried up, the religions which came with it thrived. At a later point in time, again on account of the location of the centre in the midst of rich rice-producing plains, it becomes the centre of a sacral monarchy and the sacred institutions attached to it. In fact, the sacral character of the monarchy of the Perumāḷs of Mahōdayapuram and the sacredness of the institutions attached to it were themselves factors which contributed to the sacredness of the town. The fall of that monarchy did not, however, lead to the loss of its sacredness. On the contrary, the urban centre became a centre of pilgrimage. Even in the period following the fall of that monarchy, the memory of the town as a capital city lingered. Even this memory was sacred in character. The sacredness of royalty and the relics of royal institutions made the town sacred in the period that followed. The way in which the Kāḷi temple rose to prominence in the post-Perumāḷ era, commanding allegiance from all over Kerala, is suggestive of this. The military character of the pilgrims to this shrine in the Bharaṇi festival is of particular interest in this connection. The Semitic religions, in their turn, continued with renewed vigour in the context of the revived trade that the port facilitated. The flood of AD 1341 and the consequent deposit of silt rendered the port literally high and dry; but the town continued as, and remains, a sacred centre.

NOTES AND REFERENCES

1. The history of Kerala, written on 'modern' lines, had not recognized that Mahōdayapuram or Koṭuṅṅallūr was the capital of Kerala in historical times, despite the strong tradition to this effect. When epigraphists discovered and published a large number of inscriptions

in the twentieth century, this recognition came about gradually. It was Elamkulam Kunjan Pillai who hit the nail on the forehead by both identifying the existence of a kingdom of Kerala in the three centuries after *c.* AD 800 and locating its capital at Mahōdayapuram. He also 'identified' it with Koṭuṅṅallūr and wrote a somewhat defensible history of that kingdom. Most of his writings are in Malayalam; but the more important ones are available in English translation. Elamkulam P.N. Kunjan Pillai, *Studies in Kerala History* (Kottayam, 1970). M.G.S. Narayanan continued the good work of Elamkulam, offered many important corrections and placed the kingdom of the Cēras of Mahōdayapuram on secure foundations. For details, M.G.S. Narayanan, *Perumals of Kerala: Political and Social Conditions Under the Cera Perumals of Kerala (c. AD 800–1124)* (Calicut, 1996).

2. This Cēra kingdom had ceased to exist in the first quarter of AD twelfth century. However, literary texts produced in the subsequent periods continued to remember it as *the* capital city of the kingdom of the Cēramāns, *the* rulers of Kerala. This is true of creative literature of the classical variety contained in Sanskrit and *Maṇipravāḷam* (a union of Malayalam and Sanskrit) as well as folk memories of history as contained in the *Kēraḷōlpatti*. The literature is too extensive to be cited; but for samples, see *Kōkilasandēśa, Kōkasandēśa, Śukasandēśa, Anantapuravarṇana,* etc.
3. For an analysis of the tradition, see below.
4. There is considerable literature on the traditions of Christians in Kerala. A balanced discussion of the present problem is available in Narayanan, *Perumals of Kerala*, pp. 155–61, 186.
5. For a discussion of Jews in Mahōdayapuram, see below.
6. One of the fancy explanations of the Bharaṇi festival, where obscene songs are sung as 'prayers', is that it was to drive away the nuns from the Buddhist *vihāra* which stood there!
7. M. Raghava Aiyangar, ed., *Cēravēntar Ceyyuṭkōvai*, vol. II (Trivandrum, 1951), pp. 78–82. Is *Mahōdayapuram* (Mahā+udaya+pura) a Sanskrit translation of this Tamil word *Koṭuṅkōḷūr* (koṭum+kōḷ+ūr)?
8. *Periyapurāṇam, Kaḷarir̲r̲arivār Nāyanār Purāṇam.*
9. Ibid.
10. The *Kōkilasandēśa*, I, v. 88 describes the temple of Añjanakhaḷa (Tiruvañcaikkaḷam) as where the flags from roof-tops fan the horse of the Sun. An inscription of Rājasimha from Tiruvañcaikkaḷam, *c.* AD 1036, although not detailed, is significant. *South Indian Inscriptions* (hereafter *SII*), vol. V, no. 789, p. 340; *Travancore Archaeological Series* (hereafter *TAS*), vol. VI, II, no. 138, p. 1191. This temple was probably one of the constituents of the *Nālu Taḷi*. See below.
11. In his translation of the *Śukasandēśa*, Koṭuṅṅallūr Kuññikkuṭṭan Tampurān, a renowned scholar-poet of the late nineteenth/early twentieth century, who hailed from this town, uses the term *Cēramān Kōvil* for Tiruvāncaikkuḷam. Koṭuṅṅallūr Kuññikkuṭṭan Tampurān,

trans., *Raṇṭu Sandēśaṅṅal* (Thrissur, 1900), v. 70, p. 32. The Sanskrit original uses the word Jayarāteśvaram. There is one Cēra ruler called Vijayarāga known to epigraphy, who ruled after Sthāṇu Ravi. Sthāṇu Ravi is certainly known to have gone up to AD 870, perhaps even beyond. This Vijayarāga has been identical with the Jayarāga of *Mūṣikavaṃśakāvya*. Narayanan, *Perumals*, pp. 26–7. Is the temple of Jayarātēśvaram in any way associated with the name of this Perumāḷ?

12. Hermann Gundert, ed., *Kēraḷōlpatti* (*The Origin of Malabar*) (Mangalore, 1868). The references below are to the edition of eight works of Gundert brought together with a prefatory study by Scaria Zacharia, ed., *Keralolpathiyum Maṟṟum* (Kottayam, 1992), p. 172.
13. This compound is known by that name even to this day. The site was excavated in 1944–6 and the Archaeological Survey in 1969–70 recovered pottery, foundations of a big house and a temple, and other odd little things from there. *Administration Reports of the Archaeological Department of Cochin for* 1944–45 *and* 45–46 and *Annual Reports of the Archaeological Survey of India, Southern Circle for 1970–71*. Full reports are awaited.
14. Narayanan, *Perumals of Kerala*, pp. 24–5, 212.
15. *TAS*, vol. II, no. 2, pp. 8–14.
16. M.G.S. Narayanan and Kesavan Veluthat, 'The Bhakti Movement in South India', in S.C. Malik, ed., *Indian Movements: Aspects of Dissent and Protest* (Simla, 1978), pp. 33–66 esp. pp. 43–5.
17. P.K. Narayana Pillai, ed., *Laghubhāskarīya of Bhāskara* (Trivandrum, 1949). The commentary of this work called *Vivaraṇa*, by a certain Śaṅkaranārāyaṇa, is published along with it. Śaṅkaranārāyaṇa says clearly that he was patronized by Ravivarma, who had the title Kulaśēkhara, and alludes to him as a Sthāṇu in the opening verse.
18. P.K.N. Pillai, *Laghubhāskarīya*, chapter III, p. 42.
19. Elamkulam P.N.K. Pillai, ed., *Kōkasandēśam* (rpt, Kottayam, 1972), p. 76, v. 75.
20. Narayanan, *Perumals of Kerala*, pp. 25–6.
21. Ibid., pp. 213–14.
22. *SII*, vol. III, pp. 148–52.
23. '*ghuṣyatē yasya nagarē raṅgayātrā dinē dinē / tamaham śirasā vandē rājānam Kulaśēkharam* //'
24. *Epigraphia Indica*, (hereafter *EI*), vol. VII, no. 27, p.97.
25. Kesavan Veluthat, 'The Socio-Political Implications of Kulaśēkhara Āḻvār's Bhakti', *Proceedings of the India History Congress* (*PIHC*) (Bhubaneswar, 1977).
26. Narayanan, *Perumals of Kerala*, pp. 213–14.
27. *Tapatīsamvaraṇam*, prologue.
28. *Subhadrādhanañjayam*, prologue.
29. *Vyaṅgyavyākhyā*, quoted by N.P. Unni, *Sanskrit Dramas of Kulaśēkhara: A Study* (Trivandrum, 1977), p. 24.

30. K. Kunjunni Raja, *The Contribution of Kerala to Sanskrit Literature* (Madras, 1958, 1980), pp. 11, 18, 57. Raja accepts the identification, first proposed by Koṭuṅṅallūr Kuññikkuṭṭan Tampurān, of Tōlan with the author of *Vyaṅgyavyākhyā*.
31. *SII*, vol. V, no. 790, p. 340; *TAS*, vols VI, II, pp. 193–4.
32. Narayanan, *Perumals of Kerala*, pp. 85–6.
33. Zacharia, ed., *Keralolpathiyum*, pp. 161–2, 166.
34. Narayanan, *Perumals of Kerala*, pp. 85–6.
35. P.N.K. Pillai, ed., *Kōkasandēśam*, pp. 82–3, v. 84.
36. *Administration Reports of the Archaeological Department of Cochin*, 1100 ME (AD 1924–25), App. E., no. 36, p. 21; Ibid., 1103 ME (AD 1927–28), p. 4.
37. *EI*, vol. IV, pp. 290–7. Incidentally, this is an extremely important document giving many details of the town of Makōtaiyar paṭṭinam-Koṭuṅkōḷūr with its *aḻi*, *gōpura* and other details of the urban centre.
38. '*vācā yeṣām bhavati nṛpatirnāyako rājyalakṣmyāḥ / grāmān ṣaṣṭim catura iha ye grāhyaceṣṭā nayanti / śastre śāstre'pi ca bhṛgunibhaiśśaśvadudbhāsatē yā / viprēndraistairvipulamaṭha-varyāvalīṣu sthalīṣu*' // *Súkasandeśa*, I, v. 69, in Koṭuṅṅallūr Kuññikkuṭṭan Tampurān, trans., *Raṇṭu Sandēśaṅṅaḷ*, p. 32.
39. For the identification of the Brāhmaṇical *grāmas* in Kerala and their geographical location, Kesavan Veluthat, *Brahman Settlements in Kerala: Historical Studies* (Calicut University, 1978), pp. 21–38.
40. *TAS*, vol. V, no. 13, pp. 40–6.
41. Zacharia, *Keralolpathiyum*, p. 156.
42. For the arms-bearing Brāhmaṇas of Kerala, Veluthat, *Brahman Settlements*, pp. 101–15.
43. P.K.N. Pillai, ed., *Laghubhāskarīya of Bhāskara*, v. 1.
44. For a discussion, Kesavan Veluthat, 'Royalty and Divinity: Legitimisation of Monarchical Power in South India', *PIHC* (Hyderabad, 1978).
45. For references, Narayanan, *Perumals of Kerala*, chapter on 'Chronology of the Ceras'.
46. For a recent study of the temple of Kāḷi at Koṭuṅṅallūr and the worship there, Sarah Caldwell, *Oh Terrifying Mother: Violence, Sexuality and Worship of the Goddess Kali* (New Delhi, 1999).
47. P.N.K. Pillai, ed., *Kōkasandēśam*, pp. 63–79, vv. 55–79.
48. Ibid., vv. pp. 55–7.
49. *Śukasandēśa*, v. 71 in Koṭuṅṅallūr Kuññikkuṭṭan Tampurān, trans., *Raṇṭu Sandēśaṅṅaḷ*, p. 33.
50. *Kōkilasandēśa*, v. 86 in Koṭuṅṅallūr Kuññikkuṭṭan Tampurān, p. 43.
51. M.R. Raghava Varier, 'The Sacred Geography of Teyyams', an unpublished paper.
52. V.T. Induchudan, *The Secret Chamber* (Trichur, 1969), pp. 117, 118. Fantastic theories contained in it notwithstanding, this book documents many important details regarding Koṭuṅṅallūr.

53. P.K.N. Pillai, ed., *Laghubhāskarīya of Bhāskara*, chapter 3, p. 42.
54. Narayanan, *Perumals of Kerala*, pp. 122–4.
55. *EI*, vol. II, pp. 68 ff.
56. I owe these details to the articles contained in the 400th anniversary souvenir of the Jewish Synagogue of Cochin.
57. There are many claims, most of them of a glorifying variety, related to the history of Christianity in Kerala. Among the factors responsible for the arrival of Christianity in Kerala, the West Asian connections of Koṭuṅṅallūr was not the least.
58. What is known as the 'Cēramān Mosque' in Koṭuṅṅallūr exhibits a modern plaque showing the date of its construction as AD 828. This is not acceptable. However, historians are in a mood to accept the story that the last Perumāḷ got converted to Islam and left for Mecca. Narayanan, *Perumals of Kerala*, pp. 64–70.
59. '*ahō cūrnīsaritkallōlahstāliṅgitamēkhalāyāḥ kēraḷakularājadhānyaḥ śrirāmavarmaparipālitāyāḥ mahōdayapuryaḥ ... śaṭhakōpasya muṇḍadhāriṇaḥ paḷḷīmuttarēṇa*'. Cited in Narayanan, *Perumals*, Chapter V, n. 47. Narayanan, however, takes the *paḷḷi* for a Jain institution, with nothing to support the identification. Given the fact that there is a Muslim mosque to the south of the temple, that mosques in Malayalam are called *paḷḷi* and that Muslims in Kerala till recently used to shave their heads, I propose this identification.
60. For Muziris as a centre of Roman Trade in the early centuries AD and a most recent attempt at its identification within Koṭuṅṅallūr, Rajan Gurukkal and Dick Whittaker, 'In Search of Muziris', *Journal of Roman Archaeology*, vol. 14 (2001), pp. 333–50.
61. Cited in Romila Thapar, 'Black Gold: South Asia and the Roman Maritime Trade', *South Asia* (Journal of the South Asian Studies Association), Armidale, NSW, Australia, New Series, vol. xv, no. 2, December 1992. Thapar's study is useful in this context.
62. Gurukkal and Whittaker, 'In Search'.
63. *EI*, vol. IV, pp. 290–7.
64. Veluthat, *Brahman Settlements*, pp. 21–38.
65. Narayanan, *Perumals of Kerala*, passim.
66. Narayanan and Veluthat, 'The Bhakti Movement'.
67. Till recently, there was an era reckoned from this point onwards, which was known as the Puduvaippu Era. This commemorated the throwing up of the land mass known as *Puduvaippu* ('the New Deposit') to the south of Koṭuṅṅallūr. The closing down of the port of Koṭuṅṅallūr and the opening up of Cochin, together with the creation of the Puduvaippu, marked a new era in the history of Cochin. So, the Puduvaippu Era commemorates both a fact and a metaphor.

11

Medieval Kerala*

State and Society

Kerala, as an entity distinct from the rest of south India, came to acquire its socio-cultural identity at the beginning of the ninth century. Ideas and institutions typically Keralan started crystallizing themselves and a single state structure presided over most of present-day Kerala.[1] This political unity, however tenuous, got disrupted a little more than three centuries later;[2] but the economic, social and cultural processes set in motion in the earlier period continued to work, and new elements, brought in particularly by maritime trade, were introduced. Vasco da Gama's appearance in Calicut at the end of the fifteenth century did not immediately usher in a new period in the history of Kerala.[3] But the steady interference by European powers in affairs economic and political led to the gradual hooking of this part of the country too to the colonial state system. A prelude to this were the continual inroads of powers from Karnataka, starting with the Nāyaks of Ikkēri, and followed by Haider Ali and Tipu Sultan, in the northern parts of Kerala and the formation of a somewhat strong monarchical state in Travancore in the south. A clearly identifiable break in the history of Kerala is thus visible in these developments.[4] Hence, the period from the ninth to eighteenth centuries is both distinct and intelligible as a chronological unit for the study of Kerala's history.

Social formation and state formation were not among the problems that historians of Kerala were concerned with in an earlier period.[5] Researches in the past, meticulous though they were, addressed issues

* First published in J.S. Grewal, ed., *The State and Society in Medieval India*, vol. VII, pt I of *History of Science, Philosophy and Culture in Indian Civilization*, General Editor D.P. Chattopadhyaya (Delhi, 2005), pp. 177–94.

such as chronology and political history and at best aspects of economy, society and culture in isolation. To be sure, there is rich data and intelligent discussion available on the history of Kerala in relation to much of the period that we intend to take up. What is desired, however, is a perspective that views history as a process and not as a series of events. Therefore, we do not presume so much to undertake any fresh research here as arrange the already available pieces of information in a fashion that makes meaningful generalization possible. Such data, however, are not available uniformly for the whole millennium. There are areas where copious work is available; there are also areas where primary research, or even a search for data, remains a desideratum. For instance, the first three centuries of this period are relatively well lit thanks to the path-breaking researches of Elamkulam P.N. Kunjan Pillai and M.G.S. Narayanan.[6] For the next three centuries or so the studies are not as detailed and comprehensive, although some details are available here and there in the writings of Pillai, Raghava Varier, Rajan Gurukkal and the present writer.[7] In the researches concerning the period after the sixteenth century, there is a marked tendency to use European sources in a bigger way and therefore the picture there tends to be heavily one-sided.[8] Historians who wrote in the pre-Independence period, such as William Logan, K.P. Padmanabha Menon and K.V. Krishna Aiyar, showed a tendency to speculate on the basis of very sketchy information, particularly drawn from the foreign accounts.[9]

I

During the 'Dark Ages' from the fourth to the eighth century, there are references in literature to gifts of land to fighters and Brāhamaṇas. The fighters or the priest-scholars did not cultivate the land by themselves. This meant the use of labour from outside the kin groups. The introduction of such extra-kin labour proved to be the thin end of the wedge, which resulted in the final erosion of the old system. The recently discovered inscriptions from Pūlāṅkuṟichi in Tamil Nadu demonstrate various shades of rights that begin to emerge in land.[10] So also we see various shades of political rights and power emerging, as documented in the later hero stones known as the *Ceṅkam Naḍukaṟkaḷ*.[11] Following the differentiation in society that resulted from the opening up of the river valleys for cultivation, society with a graded hierarchy with innumerable shades in status came to be established and, with it, the state.

We come across a large number of Brāhmaṇa settlements on the lower reaches of the more fertile river valleys by the ninth century.[12] They constituted the last links in a long chain of migration along the west coast, starting probably from Gujarat or further north, and cherishing the tradition of Paraśurāma.[13] In fact, this is a tradition which the Nambūdiri Brāhmaṇas of Kerala share exclusively with other west coast Brāhmaṇas.[14] Brāhmaṇas do not participate in this tradition in other parts of the peninsula. This migration need not be taken as a wave or waves; it was rather a process of what could be called 'leapfrogging'. In any case, these Brāhmaṇa settlements that were established around temples in the river valleys came to be synonymous with so many agrarian corporations. The Brāhmaṇas possessed vast estates of land both as their individual property (*brahmasvam*) and as collective property in the name of the temple (*dēvasvam*). It is not possible to know how exactly these settlements were established, for the charters creating them, if they existed, have not come down to us. What is certain is that most of the settlements celebrated in the Brāhmaṇical tradition of Kerala were well established by the ninth century.

By the close of the eighth century, thus, vast areas of land had been brought under the plough for the cultivation of rice, and a huge chunk of the tribal population was transformed into peasants. This resulted in the production of unprecedented surplus and, through its unequal distribution, a crystallization of social stratification. As the whole process was under the initiative of the Brāhmaṇical corporations, their organizations around the temples came to have immense influence on the economy and society. For one thing, since much of the land was under the control of these corporations, the Brāhmaṇas came to enjoy considerable economic privileges. They were naturally able to command a large number of privileges over the rest of the society. Thus, Brāhmaṇical ideas and institutions, such as the Āgamaic religion, *jāti* and *varṇāśramadharma*, came to be accepted in society. Social stratification was sanctified through the ideology represented by these principles. Thus, we see that Kerala was marked by all the features necessary as a pre-condition for the formation of the state: the production of considerable agrarian surplus, stratification of society and acceptance of a hegemonic ideology.

The very first epigraphic record from the plains of Kerala is a copper plate related to a place called Vāḻappaḷḷi near Tiruvalla in the south.[15] Tiruvalla was one of the major Brāhmaṇical settlements and Vāḻappaḷḷi was its subsidiary.[16] The document, dated in the twelfth regnal year of Rājaśēkhara, '*Rājarājādhirāja Paramēśvara Bhaṭṭāraka*' (*c.* 820), opens with the invocation '*namaśśivāya*'. The ruler mentioned is identified as the founder of the Cēra kingdom of Mahōdayapuram. The very first record from Kerala announcing the presence of the state is thus heavily Brāhmaṇical in character. Not only is it concerned with the affairs of a Brāhmaṇical temple, regulating its services as well as landed properties, but the entire phraseology is permeated through and through with a Brāhmaṇical ideology. It goes without saying that the state was presided over by a Kṣatriya king who was supported in a big way by the Brāhmaṇical groups. The Cēra king, who was described as the *perumāḷ* ('the great one') or simply *kō* in Tamil or *rājā* in Sanskrit, claimed Kṣatriya status and was located in Mahōdayapuram identified with modern Koṭuṅṅallūr in Trichur district.[17] He was occasionally presented as *rāja-rājādhirāja* or *kō-kōṉmaikoṇḍān* ('king of kings'). He was styled as *Mahōdayapura-paramēśvara* ('the supreme lord of Mahodayapura') and *Keraḷādhinātha* ('the overlord of Kerala'), both descriptions representing important facts about the nature of polity in the state.[18]

The *perumāḷ* had a council of Brāhmaṇa advisers known as the *nālu taḷi*.[19] This council was present in important meetings of the king with other functionaries of the state during times of emergency and it was consulted in matters of importance such as the remission of tax. The importance of this council is not accidental. In fact, one of the major factors that brought about a transformation of Kerala in the second half of first millennium AD was the steady immigration of Brāhmaṇical groups and their settlement in the fertile river valleys. They emerged as the major owning groups when private property emerged in land. The Brāhmaṇical groups constituted a communitarian force with a strong sense of all-Kerala identity. Their own traditions testify to this sense.[20] According to them, the creator of the land itself, Paraśurāma, gave the entire land of Kerala as a donation to Brāhmaṇas from the north, who were settled in sixty-four villages between Gōkarṇa and Kanyākumāri. They carried out the governance of the land through a representative body of four villages. This body grew corrupt in course of time and the Brāhmaṇa community realized that to rule was the function of the Kṣatriyas. Accordingly, they invited a Kṣatriya from outside and made him king of Kerala for twelve years. A new sovereign was brought in this way at the end of every twelve years. Four *grāmas*, known as the *nālu taḷi*, continued to be the advisers of the king. To be sure, there is no support in other documents to the elective character of the Cēra monarchy; nor do the long regnal periods of kings mentioned in inscriptions support the idea of a twelve-year term for the rulers. However, the Brāhmaṇical prop that the throne had is not to be disputed. The king had a council called *nālu taḷi* at the capital with representatives from four important Brāhmaṇa villages in the neighbourhood, and this council was present when the 'war council' met or an important decision such as the remission of tax was taken. Decisions taken in one of these villages, Mūḻikkaḷam, regarding the nature of conduct for the Brāhmaṇa members of the village committees had the privilege of setting the standard code of conduct, which was followed throughout Kerala.[21] These Brāhmaṇa villages, big and small, show evidence of the presence of the Cēra perumāḷ directly or indirectly, and the *perumāḷ* himself readily acknowledged his obligation to the Brāhmaṇas.[22]

In all probability the temple of Kāḷi, for which the town is famous today, existed in the capital city apart from these four big Brāhmaṇical temples of the *nālu taḷi*. Members of the important Nāyar caste with their military pretensions managed the affairs of this temple through their body called the *onnu kuṟe āyiram* (The 'Thousand *minus* One'). The *āyiram* (the 'thousand') was, in fact, a body of the Cēra king's bodyguards, his 'Companions of Honour'.[23] Evidence of this body and its counterparts in the *nāṭu* divisions standing in close proximity with the ruler or the local chief is available in Cēra inscriptions. In the period after the *perumāḷs* the Nāyar militia or the 'Companions of Honour' attached to the local chiefs continued to worship in this temple. Epigraphs attest to the presence of these chiefs in an earlier period in important meetings with the king. Thus, we see that the Cēra king at Mahōdayapuram had in his establishment a council of Brāhmaṇas, the head of his trusted bodyguards, and the more important local chiefs apart from other members of the royal household on occasions. There is no evidence of anything that would approximate to a bureaucracy or a military arm; and the real power in the state appears to have been exercised by the chiefs at the local levels, the corporate bodies in the agrarian villages, and the trading groups in the urban enclaves.

The local chiefs who exercised considerable power in the localities were of two major varieties: those who continued from an earlier period such as the Āy-vēḷs or the Mūṣikas, and those who appeared along with the Cēra state. Among the latter were those who owed their position to an 'appointment' by the Cēra king and those who owed it to the principle of heredity. We come across about thirteen of them in the documents. They too had their 'Companions of Honour' in what are described as the 'Hundred' organizations.[24] In fact, the chiefs exercised a greater amount of real power than the Cēra sovereign himself. They fought wars with neighbours such as the Cōḻas and Pāṇḍyas. They made grants of land and gave away considerable privileges, for example, to groups of traders. They are shown as so many 'feudatories' under the *perumāḷ*. The political structure, in short, appears to be that of a Cēra monarch enjoying a vague hegemony over a congeries of such chiefs with real political power. When it came to the exercise of power at actual grassroots level, the local groups in the agrarian villages and trading centres did it in a consummate manner.

The inscriptions from Kerala of this period have a peculiar feature. Most of the documents are from or related to agrarian villages, centred on temples, and managed by Brāhmaṇa groups.[25] Evidence of a strong non-Brāhmaṇa peasantry, present ubiquitously in the rest of south India in this period, is missing here.[26] This results in a heavy bias in favour of Brāhmaṇical groups in a study of local groups and their organization. Nevertheless, it seems safe to imagine that these groups controlled most of the rice-producing land. The records speak about an uncompromising solidarity that they exhibited. They owned property as both *dēvasvam* and *brahmasvam*, and managed the affairs of the *ūr* (the village). These groups, also known as the *ūrār* (those of the village), met regularly in the temples and decided on important affairs such as the management of landed property, assignment of revenue, policing, law and order, etc. A lengthy record from Tiruvalla, a major Brāhmaṇa settlement in south Kerala, sheds considerable light on the fabulously vast landed properties that a temple owned and the efficient way in which a Brāhmaṇa village functioned as an important node of political power in the Cēra kingdom.[27] Each *ūr*, or *sabhā* as it was otherwise known, consisting of a handful of Brāhmaṇa landowners of the village, functioned as a corporate group and decided things in their meetings.[28] Members attended the meetings without fail and decisions were unanimous. Any abrogation of the decisions was punished ruthlessly invoking provisions in the *Dharmaśāstras*.[29] Defaulters were ostracized and banished from the territory of the village. Their properties were confiscated and added to the common pool of 'god's property'. This solidarity and sense of discipline, often bordering on the masochistic, helped in consolidating themselves and gaining dominance over the population over which they were originally a superimposed minority. They gained control over the majority of population, which was related to them in various subordinate ways. In the course of time this was also instrumental in dictating the shape of things in society and culture.

A similar pattern is observed in the way in which the trading centres functioned. Evidence of a few such centres is available to us,[30] with elaborate details about one of them, namely, Kurakkēṇi Kollam or modern Quilon.[31] A body called *nagaram* controlled such urban enclaves. They had the same kind of autonomy as the agrarian villages. These *nagarams* were often controlled by organizations ('guilds' in the fashion of an earlier historiography) called *añcuvaṇṇam*, *maṇigrāmam*, etc. These bodies enjoyed considerable privileges in matters administrative, fiscal and judicial. Traders of West Asian origin, such as Christians, Jews and perhaps Muslims, were members of these bodies and had much influence in the urban centres. These trading centres enjoyed nearly everything of the autonomy and self-rule that characterized the agrarian corporations of the Brāhmaṇas. Operating from port-towns such as Kollam or Koṭuṅṅallūr, these centres functioned as entrepots of international trade and, incidentally, gateways through which elements such as Judaism, Christianity and Islam entered this land. In the absence of quantifiable data, the role that such trade played in the economy is not easy to determine. However, given the geography and climate of the region where land is not exactly famous for its fertility, agriculture at best just sustained the population. The surplus produced was not sufficient to support an 'oriental' state with the attendant luxuries and monument building, which presents a sharp contrast with the situation obtaining elsewhere in contemporary south India. Naturally, there was absolute necessity and immense scope for the trading factor in the economy and polity of Kerala. The rulers welcomed these traders with open arms and, naturally again, Kerala witnessed the peaceful coexistence of all these religions. Kerala has been given unearned credit for religious toleration on this account, but as a modern historian has observed, 'charity began at the marketplace, for it will be difficult for us with our inhuman caste system to say that charity began at home'.[32]

The presence of the state, which is clearly visible in the records, points to the existence of differentiation and stratification in society. Wetland agriculture in paddy had spread widely with the opening up of river valleys and the widespread use of iron technology. No valid generalization can be made about the process of agrarian expansion. It involved the clearing of forests in certain areas, the levelling of undulating terrain in certain others, and the draining of waterlogged fields in yet others. Records show that temples possessed huge estates of land producing rice. It is safe to assume the existence of non-Brāhmaṇa magnates as well, if not on a scale comparable with the rest of south India, for we see them making assignments of land to temples and other institutions.[33] The records bear testimony to their influential presence.[34] Thus, with agricultural production involving labour outside kinship, it was but normal that surplus was expropriated from the primary producer. There was also considerable diversification of production, since we come across evidence of artisanal activities of different kinds.[35]

The primary producers were the labourers. There are references in the documents to labourers being tied to the land they worked. When ownership or other superior rights over a piece of land changed hands, the title over the labourers was also transferred along with it.[36] We have references to bonded labourers such as *āḷ*, *āḷ aṭiyār*, etc. Although there is no reference to *viṣṭi*, or its Tamil form *veṭṭi*, in the records from Kerala, the practice of *corvée* was widely prevalent. Grants or other transactions of land mention the transfer of *āḷ* labourers, both male and female, along with such transactions. The sections of society so described are often identified by the names of the ethnic groups to which they belonged, names such as *Pulayar*, which denoted the castes of agrestic labourers in later times.[37] The surplus labour at their disposal was expropriated mostly in the form of a labour rent.[38] No other detail regarding these groups is available to us from Kerala. If contemporary accounts in Tamil literature are any indication, theirs was a miserable life.[39]

The most visible section of population in the records consisted of those who occupied the middle rungs in the economic and social hierarchy. They included the numerous tenants of the vast land owned by the temples. The records mention various shades of rights in land. The existence of a graded hierarchy in land relations is a safe guess. Ranging from simple occupancy rights, we see that tenancy with some title, possession taken for some consideration, superior rights of a stronger nature, proprietary and beneficial rights bordering on the allodial, and so on were present. Those who enjoyed these rights naturally occupied a corresponding position in the social hierarchy immediately above the primary producers. So also those who provided various services in the temple, such as garland-making, musical services, cleaning, etc., were placed slightly above the rest on the scale on account of their doing what were considered as 'clean' jobs and their proximity to the temple and the Brāhmaṇas. Those who were engaged in the artisanal activities, such as the different varieties of smiths, carpenters, washermen, etc., were lower on the scale.[40] Native traders are rarely met with in the documents.[41]

From the identification of these groups, placed in hierarchical order based on economic and social status, so many *jāti*s of corresponding ritual status follow. *Jāti* was a handy tool for the Brāhmaṇical owning groups to assert their superiority. Invoking the principle of *varṇāśramadharma*, which provided the right kind of legitimacy to the differentiation in society and the position of the Brāhmaṇical owning groups within it, the Brāhmaṇical world view was imposed, and accepted, with great ease. This is one of the peculiar features of Kerala society where, unlike other parts of south India, Brahmanical dominance was accepted, and it went on without much of a challenge till recently. The result was also the acceptance of the Āgamaic religion. As mentioned earlier, temples dedicated to Brāhmaṇical deities such as Śiva and Viṣṇu had come up with command over fabulous amount of wealth. Nearly every section of society stood in a subordinate relationship to the temple in one way or the other on the secular plane; it was not difficult to translate this obligation into the religious world. Perhaps the earlier cults and practices continued, but what is visible in the most striking way is the religion of the temples with its ideology of Bhakti. The Tamil Bhakti movement[42] of this period boasted two of its leaders from among the Cēra rulers themselves. Many of the sacred centres of the movement are on the west coast. At the higher levels of metaphysics and ethics, this was the period of the great Śaṅkara, although the way in which he represented intellectual developments *in* Kerala is questionable.

Side by side with Brāhmaṇical 'Hinduism', religions of West Asian origin such as Judaism, Christianity and Islam thrived in Kerala, at least in the coastal towns. We have elaborate details of the rights and privileges that the church of Tarsā was given at Kurakkēṇi Kollam.[43] So also the Jewish Copper Plates of AD 1000 tell us of the aristocratic privileges granted to a Jewish merchant. The signatures in the Syrian Christian Plates testify to the presence of Islam.[44] The 'deity' consecrated in the Tarisāppaḷḷi, the church of Tarsā, was referred to as *tēvar* (*dēva*). An important offering to the *tēvar* was the sacred oil lamp as in the case of the Brāhmaṇical temples. The incorporation of the local idioms in Christian religious ideas and practices show how the local mainstream culture had influenced them. The fact that the patterns of worship in the temples had influenced Christian idioms does not show that the converse was also correct; these groups seem to have confined themselves to the coastal towns and remained traders for the most part. Much has been written based on the existence of these exotic creeds here, about the religious tolerance of the rulers of Kerala. In any case, their immense influence on society dates from a later period.

Far-reaching changes in the economy, society and polity of Kerala were taking place by the first quarter of the twelfth century due to further expansion of plough agriculture in the wetlands.[45] Consequently, more centres emerged as nodes of political power, rendering the superordinate authority of the *perumāḷ* irrelevant. The last Cēra *Perumāḷ* is said to have disappeared from the scene mysteriously, after partitioning his kingdom among his relatives and dependants, and without leaving anybody to succeed him on the throne.[46] What is important is not so much the historicity of this tale as the attempt it makes to legitimize a *fait accompli*.

The locality chiefs of an earlier period, who functioned as 'feudatories' under the Cēra *Perumāḷ*s, and the new ones that came up, established themselves as rulers of their territories. These included the more powerful ones like the rulers of Vēṇād in the south and those of Kōlattunāḍ in the north; there were also the upcoming ones such as those who were to become the Zamorins of Calicut or the rulers of Cochin. They exercised considerable power and had many features, including a mint, which are usually taken as indicating some sort of sovereignty. The lesser ones, such as Kuṟumpuṟaiyūrnāṭu, Puṟakiḻānāṭu, Kīḻmalaināṭu and Muññināṭu, had not registered as much development, nor as much differentiation, on the social and political scale. Hence, they just functioned under the umbrella of one of these more powerful rulers. All of them claimed a donation from the last *perumāḷ* as the sanction behind that piece of furniture which they called their throne.

The area around the old capital, Mahōdayapuram, was still under a weakling, perhaps of the same family of the *perumāḷ*s. He had no territory to boast of and nothing in the form of other sources of power and resources. Nostalgia for old glories, however, continued in medieval *Maṇipravāḷam* (a blend of Malayalam and Sanskrit) and Sanskrit literature[47] where the *rājā* of Mahōdayapuram was still the Cēramān *Perumāḷ*, described as *rājā* even by other *rājā*s and the sovereign of the whole of Kerala. His residence was the *rājadhāni* guarded by the fourfold army, and the streets of that town were graced by comely women and cultivated men. The meagre trade with West Asia continued for some more time, but a cataclysmic flood and severe tectonic movements led to the closure of the port of Koṭuṅṅallūr.[48] A whole new island, known as the *Puduvaippu* (the 'New Formation') was thrown up to the south, an event that is remembered to this day in the *Puduvaippu* Era reckoning from AD 1341. So also, a *koccaḻi* (small port) was opened a few miles to the south. We do not hear about the ruler of Mahōdayapuram any more; but a new base of power came up gradually around the newly opened *koccaḻi*, which was eventually to become Cochin, the 'Queen of the Arabian Sea'. It is not clear whether there is any historicity in the claim that the house of Cochin, known as the Perumpaḍappu *svarūpam*, is a direct continuation of the house of the Cēramāns. Such claims did legitimize the newly organized kingdom. The support that the old monarchy had from Brāhmaṇical orthodoxy continued, which was only a liability in the changed circumstances. The rulers of Cochin had also to contend with their overgrown vassals, which stood in the way of their own power. Strife among the different branches of the family too was a source of weakness. Nor did they have much to lean on as a resource base in land revenue; but Jewish, Syrian Christian and Arab traders considerably supported this port and brought in revenue enough for the kingdom to sustain itself.[49]

The different principalities, which came up on the ruins of the old kingdom, had already started competing among themselves for larger territory, greater prestige and even in a bid to step into the shoes of the *perumāḷ*. The newly formed kingdom of Veṇāḍ, with Kollam or Quilon as its capital, had old political traditions dating back to several centuries.[50] Kollam also had the definite advantage of sea-borne trade in an age of flourishing commerce with the Arabs and the Chinese. Veṇāḍ took out expeditions eastward across the Āruvāymoḻi and Shengottah passes to the other side of the Western Ghats to claim territories that were earlier under the Pāṇḍyas. The control that was established was feeble; but this brought in a heavy Tamil influence in the culture of Veṇāḍ. The expansion southward was of greater political and economic significance. The rice bowl of the Nāñcil region, in the present-day Kanyākumāri district of Tamil Nadu, was certainly a prize catch, which supplemented the otherwise slender resource base of the kingdom.[51] The control of the Ananta Padmanābha temple of Thiruvananthapuram which this conquest fetched for the ruler of Veṇāḍ too, was crucial. It went a long way in the legitimization of the new monarchy. All this meant that among the 'successor states' of the Cēra kingdom, Veṇāḍ was destined to be one of the most significant.

II

In the northern half of Kerala, the kingdom of Kozhikode rose into prominence in the period following the *perumāḷ* era. The chiefs of Ēṟānatu, who were among the 'feudatories' of the Cēra perumāḷs, now became independent rulers styling themselves as the *kunnalakkōn* or *śailābdhīśvara* ('Lord of Hill and Sea'), and claiming a donation of the last *perumāḷ* as the authority behind their power.[52] They were to become the future Zamorins. They engaged themselves in a policy of 'die and kill to annex', a leave that they claimed to have had from the last *perumāḷ* himself.[53] Starting from a small landlocked territory, they first expanded to the north to include the region of the coast of Calicut. Calicut offered immense possibilities of Arab trade, to which the kingdom owed nearly everything. In fact, *'Calicut'* is the Europeanized form of the Arabic variant *'kaalikuut'* for the Malayalam place name, *'kōḻikkōṭŭ'*. A hereditary Muslim noble, *Shah Bandar*, was in charge of the port of Kozhikode. He came to be known as *ṣābandra kōya* or simply *kōḻikkōṭṭu kōya*.[54] It was he who is stated to have advised the Zamorin to acquire the right to preside over *māmākam* at the temple of Tirunāvāya and assisted him in the venture.[55] This was one of the major festivals in medieval Kerala,[56] which offered considerable legitimacy to the Zamorin. The *kōya* came to have many privileges in the court and the rituals of the state, including the *māmākam*, which is also indication of the heavy influence that Arab trade and Muslims had in the life of Calicut. In the wake of his annexations, the Zamorin came to be the overlord of a large number of petty chieftains to the south of Calicut. He even knocked at the doors of Mahōdayapuram, which, however, did not open before him. Eventually, the Zamorin emerged as the most powerful ruler in Kerala in the period between the disappearance of the last *perumāḷ* and the arrival of the Portuguese.

Kōlattunāḍ, operating from Ē̱limalai in the north, was the next powerful political entity in the northernmost limits of Kerala in this period. Closer to the Tulu-speaking regions of South Canara, this unit was somewhat special among the *nāṭus* under the *perumāḷs*. Its tradition dated from the early historical period.[57] The *Mūṣikavamśakāvya*, an eleventh century Sanskrit *kāvya* with claims to be historical, pertains to this *nāṭu* unit.[58] The submission of this *nāṭu* to the hegemony of the *perumāḷs* never being complete, it had a special position even in that period. While other *nāṭu* units had their 'Hundred Organizations', this one had its 'Thousand', a privilege which the *perumāḷ* had reserved for himself. Inscriptions from the region as well as from the neighbouring Āḷupa kingdom further north refer to the 'Thousand' of Kōlam.[59] In the post-Cēra period, Kōlattuṇāḍ retained much of its old position. Even here, the resource base was trade rather than agriculture. Ē̱limalai, the Mount d'Eli of European writers, was the first landfall for voyagers in the Arabian Sea. There were ports such as Mā̱rāhi (modern Māḍāyi), Valabhapaṭṭaṇam (modern Valapattanam), Dharmapaṭṭaṇam (modern Dharmadam), etc., which were all built by the Mūṣika rulers and frequented in a later period by Arab and Chinese traders. The region was also blessed with a hinterland rich in hill products such as pepper, cardamom and other spices, which these traders were here to collect.

There were a large number of other chieftaincies with varying sizes of territories and power. Some accepted the overlordship of bigger powers in the neighbourhood; others stood obstinate. In any case, none of them had a strong monarchy. The structure of power in these and even the lesser political units shows that it was a continuation and a development from the time of the *perumāḷs*. On the face of it, there was a setback in matters political as there was a loss of the unity of the whole of Kerala, and the central authority that ostensibly presided over it gave way to what looked like anarchy characterized by a heterogeneous assortment of bickering fragments. If, however, one frees oneself from the obsession that a larger political unit represents a more developed political form, it can be seen that this involved, in reality, a maturing of the political forces at work in an earlier period. In the case of the newly emerged 'kingdoms' and the lesser units of power, it was a fulfilment of what had begun earlier.

A complex institution called the *svarūpam* gets defined in this period. This expression is used in the general sense of a ruling house; but its significance went beyond this narrow dynastic sense.[60] An important feature about the *nāṭus* under the *perumāḷs* was the existence of the senior and the junior positions of the chief: what is described in the sources as *mūtta kūṟu* and *iḷaya kūṟu*. This obtained in almost every new political entity in the post-*perumāḷ* era. Since these positions were clearly defined, there was little scope for disputed succession and wars on that account. In fact, in the house of Neḍiyiruppu, the family of the Zamorins of Calicut, positions to the sixth prince, each with clearly defined rights and duties, were recognized. However, there was another source of trouble: the existence of disputes among competing branches of the chiefly houses. In fact, in the dynastic histories of Cochin or Travancore, or any other major or minor ruling family of pre-modern Kerala, such disputes were far too many. There have even been cases of friction in which neighbouring chiefs took part on one side or the other, leading to occasions that historians have, incongruously, described as 'the War of Veṭṭam Succession'.[61]

These chiefly houses in the principalities, or *svarūpams*, did not enjoy any absolute political power. There were numerous local nodes of power. There were, for instance, the numerous magnates that had come up. They functioned as petty chiefs in their own rights. This category included potentates that came to be known as *nāṭuvāḻis* and *dēsavāḻis*. They had a few villages under their control. Many of them had military pretensions. They were the products of a further expansion of agriculture in the plains. The 'Companions of Honour' of an earlier period had become more localized by now with these lesser heroes wielding the military arm. Several groups of militia known as *caṅṅātam* (literally, 'camaraderie' or 'companionship'), which took up *kāval* ('watch and ward'), came up during this period. Professional classes/castes of fighters in the Nāyars and mercenaries in the Īḻava or Tīya were also something that crystallized in this period.

There were also the local groups such as the Brāhmaṇical village. These units, controlled by the village assembly of the Brāhmaṇa landowners in the past, continued that way in this period, but the corporate solidarity characterizing such units was no longer visible. Dominance of individual houses took its place. The insistence on full attendance and unanimity is not seen any more. Attendance by proxy as well as majority decisions take their place. The slow process of a prosperous Brāhmaṇa settlement coming under the control of a single Brāhmaṇa house is demonstrated by the documents of the Tṛkkaṇḍiyūr temple.[62] Such temples, whether under the control of a single house or a few houses, came to be the virtual masters of the territory around them in course of time. These units came to be known as *saṅkētams* with immunity against the political lords in most matters.[63] This too was the continuation, and fulfilment, of the process of agrarian expansion that had started in an earlier period.

The growth of the Brāhmaṇa bodies into such strength had its implications for both the structure of polity and the process of political evolution. The place that the *nālu taḷi* had in an earlier period appears to have been completely lost. Surely there was no role for the king's council in the absence of the king. The body survived for some more time as a matter of ritual, but individual Brāhmaṇa *grāmas* emerged as more consequential in the localities. A very important case is that of Panniyūr and Cōkiram, two villages on the left bank of Bhāratappuḻa. They were sufficiently influential early on and, naturally, fell out with each other. Their importance is attested to by epigraphy, while the quarrels between the two are the subject of literature.[64] Panniyūr, which was slightly lower in terms of ritual status, was patronized by the Zamorins seeking Brāhmaṇical support of any kind, while Cochin, with their claims to a higher status, espoused the cause of Cōkiram. It was a matter of social and ritual precedence to begin with, but it acquired political overtones in the years to come. Gradually, what began as a quarrel between two Brāhmaṇical villages acquired all-Kerala dimensions, the accounts of which left behind by foreign writers in and after the period of Vasco da Gama are as copious as they are interesting.

Such organizations with their autonomous realm were not confined to Brāhmaṇas alone. We come across units called *kaḻakam* among the non-Brāhmaṇa groups, particularly in the northern extremities of Kerala. There were similar units in the *taṟa*, *kara*, etc. in the southern parts. Each was dominated by a particular caste and had jurisdiction over a defined geographical territory. Such bodies are usually seen as constituted and controlled by castes with command over land or other means of production and some military pretensions. They also looked after the shrines of the 'folk' deities of the particular locality and the periodical festivals in them, which brought to them some social significance. Groups that were engaged in the actual process of production are not, however, visible in the records except marginally. Where they do appear, they are unlettered, quarrelsome and despicable, apt to be exploited in every way.[65]

As mentioned earlier, these developments resulted from an all-round expansion of agriculture. One feature of agricultural expansion in this period was that it did not just mean a simple growth of the area of land brought under the plough. There was a certain amount of diversification of agricultural production as well. References in literature, both indigenous and foreign, testify to the existence of 'cash crops' such as coconut, betel-nut, pepper, cardamom, etc.[66] Side by side, there was also an expansion of artisanal activities, most of which were related to agriculture in one way or another. Smithy in various metals, carpentry, masonry, textile production, etc., are in evidence. The list of articles imported from South-east Asia and West Asia includes copper, zinc and mercury, items necessary in the craft of braziers.[67] All this also meant further refinements in the graded hierarchy of caste society to which more and more castes and sub-castes were added as more and more professional groups came into being as so many endogamous kinship groups. Even here, the point of reference in fixing the ritual status was contact with Brāhmaṇical groups. This hegemony got strengthened in the matter of religion. The non-Brāhmaṇical cults and practices continued, but got increasingly subjected to a process of acculturation by which the innumerable folk deities were identified as a son or a daughter or some other relative of one of the deities of the Āgamaic pantheon. Some kind of a network of temples and deities also emerged through this kinship and through stories about the peregrinations of deities.[68] Religions of a West Asian origin, such as Judaism, Christianity and Islam, continued to flourish in the coastal region. Some of them had even been identified as so many *jātis* and accepted many of the typical 'Hindu' ways in social practices and rituals.

Elaborate accounts of trade are available, particularly overseas trade with West Asia and South-east Asia. In fact, Kerala functioned, from very early on, as an important point on what could be described as a trade arc connecting Southeast Asia and West Asia. This had come to be institutionalized in the age of the *perumāḷs*, to which documents such as the Syrian Christian Copper Plates and the Jewish Copper Plates testify. In the period that followed this was taken further. We start getting evidence of the continued prosperity and further expansion of trade with the West from numerous accounts of Arab and European travellers in this period. Recent studies have brought to light the magnitude and direction of trade with China as well.[69] A major factor that this new understanding of trade brings out is the relative poverty of the land where even rice, the staple food of the population, had to be imported. It is also recognized that the participation of traders from the Indian side was marginal. We do come across Malayāḷi merchants in Karnataka and Tamil Nadu in this period,[70] but much of the overseas trade appears to have been carried on by foreigners.

This trade brought the Europeans to Calicut. Historians in the past have waxed eloquent about the momentous change that the arrival of Vasco da Gama brought about in the history not only of Kerala but of the whole world. This picture is overdrawn at least in the case of Kerala.[71] There was brisk trade with the Western world in Calicut even before his arrival. The Arab Muslims were the middlemen in this trade. Portuguese entry had only marginal impact on it. To begin with, they were here as healthy competitors in the trade going on in the port towns. When the Portuguese did not play the game according to its rules, Calicut no longer offered them hospitality, whereupon they turned to Cochin. The latter received the Portuguese with open arms for two reasons. For one, any opportunity for trade was welcome for the newly developed *koccaḻi*. Second, following the old law of politics that an enemy of the enemy is a friend, Cochin saw in the Portuguese prospective allies in their not-so-happy relations with Calicut.[72] This gave the Portuguese entry into the world of political squabbles in Kerala, on which they capitalized in both trade and politics. In the political structure of Kerala, however, this hardly had any effect. Life went on in the same old way of petty feuds among the principalities. Society and economy in the sixteenth century hardly bore any stamp of the presence of the Portuguese. Indeed, previously unknown fruits and vegetables such as cashew, pineapple, breadfruit, papaya, chilli, potato, etc. from other tropical climes were added to the list of agricultural products and to the table. Portuguese pretensions of an overseas empire did not have any effect on the people of Kerala as it did not involve any colonial features comparable to the experience under the British in a later period.

The fortunes of the old Christian community in Kerala, however, were affected. As mentioned earlier, the Syrian Christian community in Kerala was well established with a strong tradition of many centuries. They had their affiliations to the Patriarch of Babylon, who used to appoint the bishop and the archdeacon as their spiritual head. The Christians were nearly completely nativized, to the extent of being identified as one of the *jātis*.[73] Their archdeacon, known as the *jātikku kartavyan* ('responsible for the caste') was very independent. The hegemony of Brāhmaṇical Hinduism in Kerala was so pervasive that it had considerably influenced the rituals and rules of conduct of the Christians. This ensemble was known as 'the law and patterns of worship of St Thomas' ('*Mārthōmayuṭe mārgavum vaḻipāṭum*'). The Portuguese, coming here 'in search of spices and Christians', were mortified to see the kind of heresies that were going on in the community. Brought up in the atmosphere of Counter-reformation and armed with engines of coercion such as the Inquisition, they could hardly look on when a community calling themselves Christians went a way diametrically opposed to their own. Hence, a grand synod of all Christians was held in 1599 at Diamper (Udayampērūr in Malayalam) under Dom Menezes, governor and bishop of Goa.[74] The purpose of this synod was to make the Christians reject their affiliations to Babylon. It was insisted that 'the Nestorian Bishops who came to Kerala from Babylonia [*sic*] were thieves [and] murderers of the folk'.[75] The Malabar Christians were forced to conform to the idea of 'one shepherd and one flock upon earth'. They also had to submit to the Roman Catholic church and papal authority—the 'Law of St Peter'. It was also demanded with characteristic arrogance that they reject all that they had held dear for centuries. Supreme among the losses was the solidarity they had and the feeling that they were an integral part of the society of Kerala. Political pressure and a certain amount of helplessness dictated that they acquiesce, and the very foundations of a whole community were dismantled. However, a major section reacted sharply, as the somewhat violent 'Oath of the Coonen Cross' (1653) testifies to.[76] The Christian community in Kerala was never the same again; communal indifference too became a thing of the past.

Along with the loss of this communal harmony, there were also symptoms of communal hatred. As early as the end of the sixteenth century, we hear Shaikh Zainuddin Makhdum giving a call for a jihad in his famous book *Tuhfat ul-Mujahidin*.[77] To be sure, that call was for struggle against the Portuguese and their ungodly ways. But the way in which the Makhdum sought to identify Muslims as one community and organize them in the name of religion against a common political danger should not be lost sight of. There is nothing on record to show any unpleasant relationship between the Hindus on the one side and the Muslims on the other. The *Paṟaṅki* (the Portuguese) was the object of hatred in the beginning. Gradually, however, communal identity got consolidated. Political ambitions of the newly formed community started looking at those who had political influence with suspicion. What was a haven of communal harmony gradually got transformed into a hotbed of communal distrust and even suspicion. In any case, no major communal violence or outrage is recorded in this period, which surfaced only in the nineteenth century under the English East India Company.

The Dutch did not quite meddle with social matters; they were happy with trade and interference in politics was necessary for furthering their commercial interests.[78] They dealt with the kingdoms of Calicut, Cochin and Veṇāḍ variously. It did not, however, alter the political structure substantially except that it gave the necessary push for the kingdom of Veṇāḍ to emerge as Travancore, one of the most powerful kingdoms in south India in the eighteenth century. The French power was too marginal to have any political consequence and so was that of the English in the seventeenth century. The English factories at Tellicherry and Anjengo did not have any major political consequence in that context.[79]

Despite the increasing involvement of European powers and some inflow of cash, the economy continued to be largely agrarian during this period. The increased production of cash crops did bring about some changes in the structure of agrarian economy although the rise of huge estates as, for example, in coconuts had to wait for another century and those in rubber, coffee, etc., yet another. With the economy rooted in traditional agriculture, social and economic structures did not witness changes of any significance. The old hierarchy continued in the relations of production and was reflected and legitimized in *jāti* in a most comprehensive manner. The same hierarchy expressed itself in the political relations as well. Landed magnates, whether institutions like the temples or individuals like the putative lords, wielded great power and authority. *Saṅkētam*s around temples developed into virtually independent territorial units. More important than that was the growth of those 'lords' with both land control and military pretensions. A whole corpus of folk literature related to such 'heroes' is available in what is known as the *Vaṭakkan Pāṭṭukaḷ* (the 'Northern Ballads'), in which a class of such military heroes is represented and a section of mercenaries who had made war a means of livelihood are depicted.[80] In Travancore in the south the combination of military power with landed wealth in some of the Nayar magnates appeared deadly for the monarchy, at least for a while.

However, promptly assisted by commercial prosperity and the Dutch readiness to make hay while the sun shone, the monarchy in Travancore succeeded in putting down such elements and establish itself convincingly.[81] As a fitting finale to the entire episode, the Dutch in their turn were defeated by the same monarchy of Travancore in the famous battle of Colachel.[82] The northern regions did not share this fate, although there were bleak prospects under Śaktan Tampurān of Cochin for the establishment of a strong monarchical state there.[83] Given the resource base of that 'kingdom', it is not surprising that his efforts did not meet with success. Further north, barring the Zamorin of Calicut, there was no political power strong enough to try such an experiment.[84] The entire region lay fragmented without the wherewithal to attempt any such 'unification'. In the northern extremities continual incursions from the ambitious Nayaks of Ikkēri, one of the 'successors' of the once mighty Vijayanagar empire, had made times very hard for people and politics alike.[85] They established actual political control over the whole of the present-day Kasaragod district as half a dozen Ikkēri forts bear testimony to.[86] The hated memory of Ikkēri rule continues to this day. An inscription from a temple near Taliparamba in Kannur district speaks about the vandalism that the Ikkēri depredations had caused.[87] As far as the northern parts of Kerala were concerned, when Haider Ali led his raids across the land after defeating the Nayaks of Ikkēri and Chitradurga, it was only a repeat performance. The native accounts do not mention the *nabhāvu* (nawab) with any particular hatred.[88] Even when he descended on Kerala for a second time, this time across the Palghat Gap, there was no major demurring. It is only the raids of Tipu that are remembered with some bitterness.[89] In any case, what father and son had acquired in Kerala passed on smoothly to the English East India Company in 1792.

The reports of the early representatives of the Company in Kerala give a somewhat clear picture of state and society in Kerala on the eve of the nineteenth century. The entire land was more or less settled. Land was held mostly as agricultural land, although patches of waste, including forest land, were known. A graded hierarchy of rights obtained in land, which was defined clearly under the colonial masters for purposes of revenue administration. The hierarchy in the relations of production was reflected in society as well, which found expression in *jāti*. There was no superordinate political authority with command over the whole of Kerala. A large number of chiefs with varying degrees of power and authority obtained with territories of varying size also. The elaborate treaties and engagements, which the Company entered into, give evidence of the kind of polity it replaced: an assortment with 'kingdoms' as big as Travancore or Calicut or as small as a couple of villages. Each of the petty ones paid allegiance to one of the bigger kings. The power of major rulers themselves was not very effective.

There, however, were a few features that had an all-Kerala appeal. One of them was closely linked with religion. The large number of cults and practices of the 'folk' variety was getting affiliated to the Brāhmaṇical, Āgamaic, religion, a phenomenon that had been taking place through the centuries. This was obviously accepting, under whatever circumstances, the 'greatness' of the 'great tradition'. Consequently, the Brāhmaṇa high priest became an inevitable feature in society, now even for the lowest sections of society. He had access to the 'courts' of the rulers as well. He was a respected guest and had his free meal anywhere. In the households of the Nāyar, *sāmanta* and Kṣatriya aristocrats, he was welcomed also as a 'visiting husband' of the womenfolk. This kept the property of the Nambudiri Brāhmaṇas undivided, because junior Nambudiris who courted such alliances were not required to look after their 'wives' or children. On their side, this fetched prestige for the chiefly houses. The result was the increased influence that the Nambudiris came to wield in economy and society, which the Tamil or Tulu Brāhmaṇas, who had become a considerable force, did not have. This also made the Nambudiris complacent, with no ability to read the graffiti of time. They became a laughing stock.

In any case, the Kerala that the colonial masters saw was one characterized by extreme differentiation on account of caste, so much so that Swami Vivekananda chose to describe the region as a 'madhouse'. Mad or not, it certainly represented a cross-section of Indian society, ready to be part of the emerging reality in India, that is, the reality of colonial modernity.

NOTES AND REFERENCES

1. It was under the Cēra *Perumāḷs* of Mahōdayapuram that Kerala was united under the umbrella of one political system for the first time. Malayalam emerged recognizably as a separate language in this period and so did other features that lent Kerala a personality of its own. For a comprehensive and definitive study of Kerala under the *Perumāḷs*, see M.G.S. Narayanan, *The Perumals of Kerala: Political and Social Conditions of Kerala Under the Cera Perumals of Makotai (c. AD 800–1124)* (Calicut, 1996).
2. Some scholars place the end of the *Perumāḷ* rule in AD 1102 while Narayanan does it in AD 1124. More important than that, there is an argument that the clear definition of the personality of Kerala can be identified only in the post-*Perumāḷ* period: M.R. Raghava Varier, *Kēraḷīyata: Caritrmānaṅṅal* (Sukapuram, 1989). A more acceptable position would be to see the latter period as representing an unbroken continuation from the former.
3. In spite of the insistence of Sardar K.M. Panikkar that the arrival inaugurated what he called the 'Vasco da Gama epoch', historians are now nearly unanimous that major breaks did not follow the non-event. This becomes one of those 'turnings points' where history refused to turn!
4. It is in the eighteenth century that Kerala becomes subjected to a colonial system. P.K. Michael Tharakan, 'Factors in the Penetration and Consolidation of Colonial Power in Kerala (1721–1819)'; in P.J. Cherian, ed., *Perspectives on Kerala History: The Second Millennium. Kerala State Gazetteer*, vol. II, part 2 (Trivandrum, 1999), pp. 327–59.
5. Historiography in Kerala can be said to have crossed its infancy. For an interesting historiographical critique of the situation in the early 1970s, see Narayanan, *Perumals of Kerala*, Chapter on 'Historiography and Sources'. For the giant strides that historical writing has taken in

Kerala, see K.N. Ganesh, *Kēraḷattinṟe Innalekaḷ* (Trivandrum, 1990); Raghava Varier and Rajan Gurukkal, *Kēraḷacaritram* (Sukapuram, 1991). In spite of these brilliant attempts at interpretation and integration, there is scope for more interpretative exercises, particularly in relation to the pre-colonial periods of Kerala history.

One of the pioneers in the historiography of Kerala, Professor Elankulam P.N. Kunjan Pillai, was a teacher of Malayalam by profession. His articles published in Malayalam revolutionized historical writing in Kerala. A selection of his more important articles, in English translation, is available—*Studies in Kerala History* (Kottayam, 1971).

6. Narayanan has undertaken a thorough revision of the formulation of Kunjan Pillai. In fact, Narayanan's work is a landmark in the historiography of Kerala. To him goes also the credit of bringing up a number of students who have carried the tradition forward.

7. Varier, *Keraliyata*; Varier, 'Jainism in Kerala', MPhil Dissertation, Jawaharlal Nehru University (New Delhi, 1979). Varier has published a number of articles in learned journals as well as popular magazines, which have a bearing on the history of Kerala. Besides, he was also responsible for the discovery and decipherment of a number of inscriptions.

   Rajan Gurukkal, *The Kerala Temple and the Medieval Agrarian System* (Sukapuram, 1992). Gurukkal has since done considerable work on the early and 'early medieval' periods of Kerala history, including a good survey with Varier, *Keraliyata*. There is a recent volume brought out by the Department of Cultural Publications, Government of Kerala, which Rajan Gurukkal and M.R Raghava Varier have edited, *Cultural History of Kerala*, vol. I (Trivandrum, 1999).

   Kesavan Veluthat, *Brahman Settlements in Kerala: Historical Studies* (Calicut, 1978). There are a few other articles on Kerala history by Veluthat.

8. Most of the studies in relation to the period after the fifteenth century were till recently under the spell cast by Sardar K.M. Panikkar, *History of Kerala* (Annamalainagar, 1964). He was guided by the work of Whiteway and Danvers. Panikkar's book itself is a concatenation of his two earlier books *Malabar and the Portuguese* (Bombay, 1929) and *Malabar and the Dutch* (Bombay, 1931). When later scholars such as Poonnen, Mathew, Koshy and others wrote on the history of Kerala in the sixteenth and eighteenth centuries, they relied heavily on Portuguese, Dutch and French sources. More recent work of scholars such as Ashin Dasgupta, Tapan Raychaudhuri, Pamela Nightingale, Om Prakash, Sinnappa Arasaratnam and Sanjay Subrahmanyam are naturally concerned with the problem from the European side and therefore necessarily use the sources in European languages. The history of Kerala in this period from the Kerala perspective is yet to be written.

9. William Logan, *Malabar* (2 vols), (Madras, 1887); K.P. Padmanabha Menon, *Koccirājyacharitram* (Malayalam) (2 vols) (Trichur, 1912); K.P. Padmanabha Menon, *History of Kerala* (4 vols) (Ernakulam, 1924–35); K.V. Krishna Ayyar, *The Zamorins of Calicut* (Calicut, 1938). Ayyar's deservedly obscure *History of Kerala* does not do credit to his scholarship.
10. Y. Subbarayalu, 'A Note on the Socio-economic Milieu of the Pulankuricci Rock Inscription', *Avanam*, vol. III, 1993.
11. M.D. Sampath, 'Hero Stone Inscriptions from the Dharmapuri District', an unpublished paper, 1976. I thank Sampath for a copy of it.
12. Veluthat, *Brahman Settlements.*
13. This was first suggested by B.A. Saletore, *Ancient Karnataka* (vol. I, *History of the Tuluva*) (Poona, 1936). Narayanan developed it in the context of Kerala. Veluthat added further evidence in support of it. A recent study has corroborated it further: Nagendra E. Rao, 'The Historical Tradition of South Canara and the Brahmanical Groups: A Study of Gramapaddhati and Sahyadrikhanda', MPhil Dissertation, Mangalore University (Mangalore, 1996).
14. Kesavan Veluthat, 'The Brahmanical Traditions of Kerala and Coastal Karnataka: Points of Contact', *Proceeding of Karnataka History Congress*, Second Session (Mysore, 1979).
15. *Travancore Archaeological Series* (hereafter *TAS*) vol. II, pp. 8–14.
16. Veluthat, *Brahman Settlements*, pp. 39–51.
17. Narayanan, *Perumals of Kerala*, chapter on 'Chronology'.
18. *Epigraphia Indica* (hereafter *EI*) vol. III, p. 68; *Tapatīsamvaraṇam*, prologue, and *Subhadrādhanañjayam*, prologue, quoted in Narayanan, *Perumals of Kerala*, chapter VI, 'Nature of Monarchy', n. 10.
19. Narayanan, ibid., chapter on 'Nature of Monarchy', pp. 76–7, 85–7.
20. The historical tradition of the Brāhmaṇa community in Kerala is contained in a narrative called *Kēraḷōlpatti*, Hermann Gundert, ed., *Keraḷōlpatti* (Mangalore, 1886).
21. Narayanan, *Perumals of Kerala*, chapters VIII and IX, 'Local Bodies' and 'Police and Revenue'.
22. Most of the Cēra inscriptions are proceedings of the Brāhmaṇical agrarian corporations centred on temples. Many of them say explicitly that the decisions were taken in meetings where the Cēra king himself or one of his representatives was present. The king always acknowledged his subordination to the Brāhmaṇas as witness the report of the amends the last ruler made for the wrath he incurred from the *Āryas*: *TAS*, vol V, no. 13, pp. 40–6. This sentiment runs through other royalist expressions as well.
23. M.G.S. Narayanan, 'Companions of Honour', in *Aspects of Aryanisation in Kerala* (Trivandrum, 1973).
24. Narayanan, *Perumals of Kerala*, chapter on 'Divisions of the Kingdom'.
25. Ibid.; Veluthat, *Brahman Settlements.*

26. Kesavan Veluthat, *The Political Structure of Early Medieval South India* (Delhi, 1993), p. 176.
27. *TAS*, vol. III, Part ii, pp. 131–207.
28. Veluthat, *Brahman Settlements*, chapter on 'Organisation and Administration'.
29. Kesavan Veluthat, 'The *Sabha* and *Parishad* in Medieval South India: Correlation of Epigraphic and Dharmasastraic Evidence', *Tamil Civilization*, vol. III, nos 2, 3, 1985, pp. 75–82.
30. Narayanan, *Perumals of Kerala*, pp. 106–9, 171–3, 186–7; M.G.S. Narayanan, *Cultural Symbiosis in Kerala* (Trivandrum, 1972).
31. *TAS*, vol. II, no. 9, pp. i, ii.
32. Narayanan, *Cultural Symbiosis*, 'Introduction'.
33. The Tiruvalla Copper Plates refer to a large number of such donations.
34. There are many cases where a military representative of the *perumāḷ* presided over, or was at least present in, the meetings of the sabha. Veluthat, *Brahman Settlements*, chapter on 'Organisation and Administration'.
35. The Syrian Christian Copper Plates refer to different artisanal groups.
36. Several examples of such transfer are available in the Tiruvalla Copper Plates: *TAS*, vol. V, no. 1, pp. 63–85.
37. C.H. Jayasree, 'Slavery and Serfdom in Malabar', unpublished PhD Thesis, Mangalore University (Mangalore, 1994).
38. For an analysis of the contemporary situation in the Cōḻa country, see Kesavan Veluthat, 'Labour Rent and Produce Rent: Reflections on the Nature of Revenue under the Cōḻas', *Proceedings of the Indian History Congress* (Dharwad, 1987), Chapter 4 above.
39. The story of the Śaiva saint Nantanār, who was a paṟaiya by caste, as contained in the *Periyapurāṇam*, tells us how miserable the plight of the hamlets of paṟaiyas were: *Periyapurāṇam*, verses 2–9.
40. For the percolation of *jāti* and other details of social stratification, Narayanan, *Perumals of Kerala*, chapter on 'Social System'.
41. For details of trade, ibid., pp.171–3.
42. For a study of the Bhakti movement, M.G.S. Narayanan and Kesavan Veluthat, 'The Bhakti Movement in South India', S.C. Malik, ed., *Indian Movements: Some Aspects of Dissent, Protest and Reform* (Simla, 1978), reproduced in D.N. Jha (ed.), *The Feudal Order* (Delhi, 2000).
43. *TAS*, vol. II, no. 9, pp. i, ii.
44. C.P.T. Winkworth, 'Notes on the Pahlavi Signatures to Quilon-Plates', with notes by T.K. Joseph and F.C. Burkitt, *Kerala Society Papers*, vol. I, series 6, pp. 320–3.
45. M.R. Raghava Varier, 'Further Expansion of Agrarian Society: B. Socio-Economic Structure', in Cherian ed., *Perspectives on Kerala History*, pp. 79–122.
46. For a discussion of the legend and its various possibilities, Narayanan, *Perumals of Kerala*, pp. 64–70.

47. Veluthat, 'Further Expansion of Agrarian Society', pp. 62–3.
48. Ibid., p. 70.
49. No comprehensive study of the history of Cochin in the period between AD 1100 and 1500 is available. Conventional accounts contained in C. Achyutha Menon, *Cochin State Manual* (Ernakulam, 1911) and K.P. Padmanabha Menon, *Koccirajyacaritram* are inadequate.
50 For the antecedents of Veṇāḍ, see Narayanan, *Perumals of Kerala*, pp. 102–5.
51. P.L. Chackochan, 'Historical and Cultural Geography of Vēṇāṭu, Travancore, *c.* AD 1124 to 1729', unpublished PhD Thesis, Deccan College, Pune, 1980; K.N. Ganesh, 'Agrarian Expansion and Consolidation in Vēṇāṭu in the Post-Cēra Period', unpublished PhD Thesis, Jawaharlal Nehru University (New Delhi, 1986).
52. Narayanan, *Perumals of Kerala*, pp. 68, 96–7; V.V. Haridas, 'The Emergence of a Medieval South Indian Kingdom: Calicut under the Zamorins', *Proceedings of the Indian History Congress* (Patiala, 1998).
53. Aiyar, *Zamorins of Calicut*, pp. 60–2.
54. Ibid., pp. 87–8.
55. Ibid., pp. 93–7.
56. Ibid., pp. 91–120.
57. Narayanan, *Perumals of Kerala*, pp. 91–4.
58. C. Girija, 'The Mūṣikavamśakavya: A Study', unpublished MPhil Dissertation, Mangalore University (Mangalore, 1990).
59. An inscription from the Kōvūr temple, Kannur district, deciphered by Narayanan and the present writer, speaks of *Kōlattāyiravar* (the 'Thousand of Kōlam'). Inscriptions from South Canara make references to *Kōlabāḷi Sāsiravaru*, again, the 'Thousand of Kōlam': K.V. Ramesh, *A History of South Kanara* (Dharwad, 1970), pp. 251, 262.
60. There is considerable new discussion on the *svarūpam* in recent years. For a most recent analysis, M.R. Raghava Varier, 'Svarupam as a Political Unit in Medieval Kerala', in R. Champakalakshmi, Kesavan Veluthat and T.R. Venugopalan, eds., *State and Society in Pre-modern South India*, Trichur, 2003.
61. A. Sreedhara Menon, *A Survey of Kerala History* (Kottayam, 1971).
62. Narayanan (ed.), *Vanjeri Granthavari*, Calicut University (Calicut, 1987). For the developments in a Brāhmaṇa settlement leading to its transformation into a *saṅkētam*, see Veluthat, 'The Temple and the State', in Champakalakshmi *et al.*, eds, *State and Society*.
63. Veluthat, *Brahman Settlements*, pp. 88–95.
64. For epigraphic reference, *EI* vol. IV, pp. 290–9. For references to literature, Veluthat, *Brahman Settlements*, pp. 72–5 and nn. 30, 31. See also Aiyar, *Zamorins of Calicut*, pp. 97–102.
65. M.R. Raghava Varier, 'Further Expansion of Agrarian Society', in Cherian, ed., *Perspectives on Kerala History*, pp. 94–5.

66. Ibid., pp. 84–91.
67. Ibid., pp. 100–18.
68. M.R. Raghava Varier, 'Perigrinations of Folk Deities and the Making of a Sacred Geography', paper presented to a seminar on Sacred Geography in Honour of Professor R. Champakalakshmi, Jawaharlal Nehru University, New Delhi, November, 1997.
69. Varier, 'Further Expansion of Agrarian Society', pp. 100–18.
70. Ibid., pp. 99–103; Hanuma Nayaka, 'Malayali Merchants in Medieval Karnataka', *Proceedings of the Indian History Congress* (Calicut, 1999).
71. Narayanan, *Perumals of Kerala*, pp. 64–70.
72. M. Gangadharan, 'Is there a Portuguese Period in Kerala History?' *Samvāda*, (Souvenir of the International Conference on Europe and South Asia) (New Delhi, Institute of Social Sciences, 1998). The debate has a long pedigree, dating from Sardar K.M. Panikkar's famous pronouncements on the 'da Gama Epoch'. For some refreshing discussion, C.J. van Leur, *Indonesian Trade and Society* (Bandung, 1960); Neils Steensgaard, *The Asian Trade Revolution of the Seventeenth Century: The East India Companies and the Decline of Caravan Trade* (Chicago, 1975). For a note of dissent, K.S. Mathew, 'Trade and Commerce', in Cherian, ed., *Perspectives*, pp. 181–227.
73. Kesavan Veluthat, 'Community and Religious Identity', *Communalism Combat* (special millennium issue), vol. 7, no. 54, 1999, pp. 54–6. For details of the way in which Christians in Kerala were identified as a *jāti* comprehensively. Scaria Zacharia ed., *The Acts and Decrees of the Synod of Diamper* (Edamattam, 1994), pp. 7–59. The bibliography given in the book is extremely valuable.
74. Ibid., p. 42. Zacharia translates it as 'Law of Thomas'.
75. Quoted, K.J. John, *The Road to Diamper* (Cochin, 1999), p. 130.
76. Zacharia, *The Acts and Decrees*, p. 17.
77. Muhammed Hussain Nainar ed., *Tuhfat ul-Mujahidin* (Madras, 1946).
78. T.I. Poonen, *The Dutch Hegemony in Malabar and Its Collapse* (Trivandrum, 1978); M.O. Koshy, *The Dutch Power in Kerala (1729–1758)* (New Delhi, 1989).
79. K.K.N. Kurup, *History of the Tellicherry Factory* (Calicut, 1981).
80. M.R. Raghava Varier, *Vaṭakkan Pāṭṭukaḷute Paṇiyāla* (Sukapuram, 1980).
81. For a recent analysis from the Dutch perspective, Mark de Lannoy, *The Kulasekhara Perumāḷs of Travancore: History and State Formation in Travancore from 1671 to 1758* (Leiden, 1997).
82. A.P. Ibrahim Kunju, *Marthanda Varma and His Times* (Trivandrum, 1975); Koshy, *Dutch Power in Kerala*.
83. The figure Śaktan Tampurān, though very much historical, has become legendary in the folklore of Kerala. For details of his rule, see Menon, *Cochin State Manual*, pp. 159–77.

84. For a picture of the fragmented political condition of the northern parts of Kerala, William Logan ed., *A Collection of Treaties, Engagements and Other Papers of Importance Relating to British Affairs in Malabar: Malabar Manual*, vol. III (Trivandrum, 1998 [rpt]).
85. K.N. Chitnis, *Keladi Polity* (Dharwar, 1974).
86. For details of the Ikkēri forts in the Kasaragod district, A. Sreedhara Menon, *Kerala State Gazetteers: Kannur District* (Trivandrum, 1968).
87. I owe this information to Raghava Varier.
88. N.M. Nampoothiri, *Veḷḷayuṭe Caritram* (Sukapuram, 1998). This is an accuunt of a Nambudiri Brāhmaṇa in the form of some sort of a diary which gives details aboul Haider's raids. He records an interview he had with the *nabhāvu* (nawab).
89. Memories of Tipu's raids are not exactly sweet. For a representation, A.R. Rajarajavarma, *Āṅgalasāmrājya* (Trivandrum, 1997 [rpt]), pp. 295–415. This is an interesting historical *kāvya* written in Sanskrit in the early twentieth century. The poet is influenced through and through by the dominant historiographical tradition. Perhaps that explains his harsh judgement of the sultan.

12

Landlordism in Medieval Kerala*

Time was when the south Indian epigraphist would lament that 'the great bulk of the inscriptions consists of grants to tanks and temples which are of no interest whatever... [O]f the condition of the country and the people [they tell] us nothing'.[1] After a century of epigraphical studies in India since Butterworth and Chetty wrote these words, such complaints are not likely to arise: giant strides have been taken towards laying bare the economic and social aspects of our past with the help of the same kind of inscriptions recording 'grants to tanks and temples', particularly in south India. A whole new world of relationships is exposed by a study of the land-grants—the working of local groups and its implications for society and polity have been worked out systematically with the help of these records. More recently, the computer has accorded greater precision to the analysis of the epigraphist's data.[2] This achievement, and similar efforts undertaken manually in an earlier period, helped in replacing the speculative and the impressionistic by the scientific and the systematic. When this approach is supplemented by a greater concern with the contexts in which the terms so analysed appear, the results are bound to be more meaningful. Epigraphical expressions and terms are no doubt important; but their significance can be better appreciated if they are understood in the right context. Context here means not only the context of the expression in the record but also the context of the record itself within the space and time in which it occurs.

The present essay makes an attempt to study the rise of landlordism in medieval Kerala with the help of a contextual analysis of inscriptional terms in the light of the author's earlier study of the inscriptions of

* Paper presented at the D.C. Sircar Centenary Seminar, Asiatic Society, Calcutta, November 2007.

Kerala during the period AD. 800–1200.[3] Most inscriptions dating from this period, with a few exceptions, were discovered, deciphered and published in the last century. The absence of the typical *dānaśāsanas*, prefaced with the usual *praśastis* found in the records of other parts of the country, made it difficult for the early epigraphists to tie these records around a dynasty and work out the details of political history.[4] It was only in the latter half of this century, thanks to the labours of Elamkulam P.N. Kunjan Pillai,[5] that these records were assigned incontrovertibly to the Cēra Perumāḷs who ruled from Mahōdayapuram. In the light of the evidence provided by these records, Pillai reconstructed the outlines of the political history of that dynasty and also presented a picture of social and economic evolution.[6] However, the failure to place the names of a large number of individuals figuring in the records in the proper context misled the great pioneer. If only the learned professor had appreciated the context of the records as well as placed the names within the right context in the records, the picture of socio-economic evolution he presented would have been different and, consequently, he would have been spared, at least in part, of the casteist accusations levelled against him.[7]

Epigraphical records of this period from Kerala are generally resolutions of temple committees. The temples owned vast areas of land and commanded the allegiance of large sections of people. Pillai rightly appreciated the significance of this crucial character of the temples and realized that the key to understanding the pattern of socio-economic evolution in Kerala lay in these records which he studied, for all practical purposes, for the first time. According to him, these temples were managed by committees known as the *ūrāḷar* or *sabhā* which was a body elected from among the entire population of the village (*ūr* or *ūrār*), and subject to its ultimate authority. A larger body at a higher level, namely of the *nāṭu* which he called the *nāṭṭukūṭṭam* and identified with the 'Hundred' organizations attached to the various *nāṭu* divisions under the Cēras of Mahōdayapuram, subjected the *sabhā* of the *ūrāḷar* further. These elected committees of the *ūrāḷar* and the *nāṭṭukkūṭṭam* consisted of both Brāhmaṇas and non-Brāhmaṇas to begin with, when things were going on smoothly in a democratic and egalitarian way. During the period of most of the eleventh century, described by Pillai as of the 'Hundred Years' War' between the Cēras and the Cōḻas, however, Brāhmaṇas came to dominate these bodies. This led to the loss of their democratic and egalitarian character. This, in turn, led to a concentration of the huge landed properties in the hands of a few Brāhmaṇa landlords, giving rise to the peculiar pattern of land tenure in Kerala known as the *janmi* system, translated as 'landlordism'.[8]

This presentation of the evolution of Brāhmaṇa landlordism in Kerala is based on three major premises:

1. the elective, democratic, character of the *sabhā* or the *ūrāḷar* which functioned within a larger unit of the *ūr*, *ūrār* or *ūrkūṭṭam*,
2. the existence of a still larger body known as the *nāṭṭukūṭṭam* identified with the 'Hundred Organizations' and its superordinate authority over both the *ūrkūṭṭam* and the *sabhā* of the *ūrāḷar* within it, and
3. the changes in the character and organization of these bodies brought about by the so-called 'Hundred Years' War' and the resultant domination of the Nambūdiri Brāhmaṇas.

The first two assumptions flow from an inadequate consideration of the context of the names in the inscriptions and the third, from a faulty understanding of the political process, which itself is conditioned in part by the first two. We shall consider the first two assumptions in greater detail now.

The inscriptions, most of which are from temples, contain names of a large number of individuals figuring as witnesses to transactions, donees and also members of the managing committees of the temples. The names generally consist of three segments: the names of the family, the father and the ego in that order, for example Vaṉṟalaiccēri-Kōtai Iravi.[9] In a few cases there would be one more segment before such three-segmented names, for example, Mūḻikkaḷattu-Kūṟṟampaḷḷic-Cuvākaran-Tāmōtaran[10] where the first segment signifies the village from which the individual hailed. There are, however, cases where one or more of these segments are omitted.

In studying these names, Pillai failed to distinguish the members of the temple-committees from the donors and witnesses to the transactions. There are certainly names of non-Brāhmaṇas, but they figure mostly as donors or tenants and functionaries of the temple or the state. In other cases it can be clearly demonstrated that the names are of Brāhmaṇas. However, the absence of the Brāhmaṇical suffix *śarman*, the total absence of references to *gōtra* and the corruption of personal names into unrecognizable Dravidian forms (such as Cāttan for Śāstṛśarman, Kaṇṭan for Nīlakaṇṭha, Tuppan for Subrahmaṇya, Uruttiran for Rudra, etc.), led Pillai to assume that these members of the bodies were not Brāhmaṇas.[11] Thus, for instance, even where Pillai conceded Brāhmaṇa status to six out of the ten donees in a Kiḷimānūr record, who constituted the *sabhā* of the *ūrāḷar* there, the unmistakable Brāhmaṇa identity of the remaining four was lost sight of.[12] On account of this failure to appreciate the exclusively Brāhmaṇical character of the *sabhā* and *ūrāḷar*, he was driven to assume that they were popular bodies, organized on an elective and democratic basis, with a heavy representation of non-Brāhmaṇas in them.

Apart from the absence of *gōtra* names or the *śarman* suffix, what stood in the way of Pillai's appreciating the Brāhmaṇical character was an inadequate consideration of the context in which the records appear. His lack of familiarity with conditions in central and northern Kerala, from which regions most of these records come, may have prevented him from appreciating this. In fact, many of these records are from temples which are reputed as *grāmakṣetra*s of Brāhmaṇas, a tradition which Pillai ignored. Nor did he know that many of the houses mentioned in them survive as so many Brāhmaṇa houses to this day with their traditional *grāma* affiliations.[13] This knowledge is essential to realize that those who figure in the records in the capacity of members of the sabhā and witnesses are Brāhmaṇas. But then, Pillai mixed up all names figuring in records and argued, somewhat theatrically, that a large number of them were non-Brāhmaṇas.[14] He did not realize that such non-Brāhmaṇas as are present are in the capacity of donors or tenants and not as those who controlled the land of temples. It was this misunderstanding which vitiated his findings in relation to the character of the temple-centred agrarian corporations in Kerala.

A closer examination of the spatio-temporal contexts in which these records occur, or the context within the records themselves where the names figure, would dispel such misunderstandings. As stated earlier, there are practically no *dānaśāsana*s recording the creation of a new Brāhmaṇa settlement. In the absence of such founding charters, we have to depend on the records registering the proceedings of the temple committees for understanding the nature of their organization. However, there are at least three records registering the consecration of new temples and the accompanying endowment of lands and creation of settlements around them. This would serve as an index to the character of the settlements. The Kollūr Maṭham Plates,[15] dated AD 1189, purports to be the renewal of an earlier charter said to be granted in late tenth century AD. The record lists names of twenty-three Brāhmaṇa families which constituted the settlement around the Dēvīdēvēśvaram temple. An unpublished stone inscription of early eleventh century from Tiruvaṭūr[16] in the Kannur district gives further details about the composition of the newly created settlement. Twenty-four Brāhmaṇas from well-known, pre-existing, Brāhmaṇa *grāmas*—five from Vaikkam,[17] two from Paṟavūr, six from Āvaṭṭiputtūr, four from Iruṅgāṭikkūṭāl and seven from Perumanam (all from central and south Kerala)—were invited and settled around this newly endowed temple in north Kerala with land and other privileges. Details in the record show in an unmistakable way the Brāhmaṇical character of the temple committee which was charged with the management of the landed properties in the village. Another record of AD 1168 from Kiḷimānur in south Kerala,[18] describes the creation of a Brāhmaṇa settlement around the newly consecrated temple of Tiruppālkkaḍal. The record names ten Brāhmaṇas drawn from eight well-known Brāhmaṇa *grāmas* in central and south Kerala as the *ūrāḷar* of the temple in so many words.[19] These records demonstrate the Brāhmaṇical character of the temple-centred agrarian corporations in early medieval Kerala. Although the above instances form a very small fraction of the extant records, that the pattern suggested by them is applicable to the various regions of Kerala is clear from a study of the working of such committees there.[20] In a few cases the decisions recorded are endorsed by individuals who obviously formed members of the temple-committees; and they too were Brāhmaṇas as shown by the names of their houses.[21]

In certain other cases, the follow-up of the decisions was achieved by invoking imprecatory clauses which include loss of caste as if involved in one of the five heinous sins (*pañcamahāpātaka*).[22] Sometimes, such decisions in Kerala are stated to be modelled on the lines of well-known precedents such as the one at Mūḻikkaḷam, known variously as Mūḻikkaḷa-k-*kaccam*, Mūḻikkaḷa-c-*cavattai*, Mūḻikkaḷa-tt-*oḻukkam*, etc. This was followed in all the temple-centred Brāhmaṇical corporations of Kerala with the force of law. Mūḻikkaḷak-*kaccam* was a typical *vyavasthā* following the prescriptions in the *Dharmaśāstras*; and so was the invocation of the *mahāpātakas*. In fact, it has been shown that the rules of the *Dharmaśāstras* governing the constitution and conduct of the *sabhā* of Brāhmaṇas were followed in such *sabhās* in south India, Kerala not excluded.[23]

Pillai, however, missed this exclusively Brāhmaṇa character of the *sabhā* of the *ūrāḷar* and assumed that it was a body elected from among the entire population of the village, attributing an elective, democratic character to the body. His political and social commitments too may have prompted him in this direction. There was one more factor behind this assumption: he thought that above the *sabhā* was a larger body of the *ūrār* at the village level, consisting perhaps of the entire population of the village.[24] The basis of this argument is a faulty interpretation of slender evidence, taken out of context. In a solitary record, detailing the arrangements for leasing out a piece of land owned by the temple, it is stated that the *ūrāḷar* should not obstruct cultivation.[25] Elsewhere in the same document, it is stated that even a unanimous decision of the *ūrār* could not alter these decisions.[26] These two terms, *ūrār* and *ūrāḷar*, in the same document and in a few other documents in relation to bodies at the village level, led Pillai to assume that these were two different bodies. However, if the terms *ūr*, *ūrār* and *ūrāḷar* figuring in inscriptions from Kerala from this period are analysed in their proper context, it can be seen that they are used as synonyms.[27] The honorific plural, *ūrāḷar*, was also used to refer to an individual member of the body.

The second premise that the *ūr* and the *sabhā* within it was subject to the superordinate authority at the *nāṭu* level is, in a similar way, the result of a scant consideration of evidence in context. This body, which Pillai called *nāṭṭukūṭṭam* without any support in the sources, was identified in the 'Hundred Organizations' figuring in the inscriptions.[28] In many cases, the protection of land and other properties endowed to temples were placed under these 'Hundreds'—'The Three Hundred', 'The Five Hundred', 'The Six Hundred', 'The Seven Hundred', etc. Taking all such records where the 'Hundred Organizations' figure and analysing them in context, M.G.S. Narayanan has demonstrated that they constituted the prototype of the Nāyar militia in Kerala who formed the 'Companions of Honour' to the local chieftains and the Cēra king.[29] In fact, a fragmentary inscription from Tiruvanvaṇḍūr[30] shows that the expression 'Three Hundred' stood there for a single individual, thereby ruling out the idea that it was a larger body with superordinate powers over the bodies at the village level. It is possible that Pillai took in this case the analogy of the Cōḻa country where a body at the *nāṭu* level, known as the *nāṭṭār,* existed, which had superordinate powers over the bodies at the village level.[31] The crucial difference between *nāḍus* in the two situations, namely that while it was a political unit under the chieftaincy of a *nāṭuvāḻi* (local ruler) in Kerala, it was a peasant locality, a socio-political sub-region, in the Cōḻa country[32] was not considered by Pillai.

A contextual examination of these terms makes it clear that the first two premises of Pillai are unwarranted. The third one, which seeks to explain changes in the character and organization of the temple-centred agrarian corporation with a predominance of Brāhmaṇas there and leading to the rise of Brāhmaṇa landlordism, is actually necessitated by the first two, wrong, premises from which Pillai started. Recent research has shown that a 'Hundred Years' War' between the Cēras and the Cōḻas had indeed not taken place.[33] The two powers in south India—unequal in all respects—stood in different kinds of relationship over the period and there was no situation of war for any continuous period. Moreover, the supposition that political events like a war could bring about basic changes in the relations of production is unacceptable.

The fact appears to be that there was no dramatic change in the tenurial pattern in Kerala in the eleventh century, as imagined by Pillai. The rise of the Cēra kingdom in the beginning of the ninth century itself was a function of a major economic transformation, the most important aspect of which was in relation to the opening up of river valleys and clearing of land in other ways for purposes of agriculture. Inscriptions start making their appearance in Kerala from this period, and a vast majority of them are from or related to temples and dealing with the arrangement of landed property. A somewhat clear pattern of the land tenures is available from these records.

As suggested above, the temples in relation to which the inscriptions are available owned huge estates of land. The case of the Tiruvalla temple alone is sufficient to show the magnitude of the possessions.[34] There are other temples as well which commanded similar landed properties. These temples were the nuclei of Brāhmaṇa settlements. All their affairs were managed by the committee of Brāhmaṇas who controlled both the ritual and the properties of the temple. Unfortunately, royal charters 'creating' such big settlements and endowing them with land have not come down to us. In all probability, they did not exist, as we see that most of the influential settlements were already in place by the time state had emerged and royalty had established itself in Kerala. In fact, this has been shown as causative to the emergence of state there.[35] Therefore, to believe that these settlements, with the command of vast tracts of agrarian land, owed their existence to a donation by the Cēra king or his 'governors' does not fit in with evidence.[36] There are, to be sure, instances of land-grants to groups of Brāhmaṇas in the later period; but all these are made by the local chiefs—and in some cases such land was either purchased or exchanged from the previous owner. If the person who granted the land owned it 'in theory', the question of his having to acquire it by purchase or exchange would not arise. What is likely is that when the 'great transformation' which Rajan Gurukkal and Raghava Varier are talking about took place in Kerala,[37] the major Brāhmaṇa settlements with their control of land were already there, with their claims to a gift of Paraśurāma seeking to legitimize it.

In discussing the structure of land-relations in Kerala, what the *Kēraḷōlpatti,* a traditional narrative of the history of Kerala, has to say about it is often ignored, primarily because the authenticity of the text as history was always in doubt.[38] According to this tradition, Paraśurāma created the land and donated it to Brāhmaṇas. Even here, it is not to be taken that it was Paraśurāma who was responsible for structuring the land-relations as they obtained in the pre-colonial period; but the somewhat detailed exposition of the structure is too important to be dismissed summarily. According to the *Kēraḷōlpatti,* Paraśurāma created the land of Kerala and settled it with Brāhmaṇas in sixty-four *grāma*s, thirty-two in Tuḷunāṭu and thirty-two in Kerala proper. He also ordained that 36000 of them belonging to 16 *grāma*s take to the profession of arms. They were exempted from studying the *Vēda*s and were described as *ardhabrāhmaṇa*s to distinguish them from the *Vēdabrāhmaṇa*s. Such arms-bearing Brāhmaṇas were given land with libation of water, such land being *rājāmśam*. It was worthy of being described as *janmam,* no other tenure being entitled to that description. Subsequently, he made all arrangements so that the inhabitants of Kerala would live like the residents of heaven. The text continues to say that the *Vēdabrāhmaṇa*s got land donated from the *ardhabrāhmaṇa*s. Śūdra cultivators were brought from different places and settled there and were given several rights and prerogatives. They were enjoined to be the servants and tenants. The tenants were allowed a lower share (*kīḻāykkuṟŭ*) while [the Brāhmaṇas] themselves retained the upper share (*mēlāykkūṟŭ*). The tenants were bestowed with the *kāṇam* right while [the Brāhmaṇas] granted themselves the *janmam* right. The system of *kāṇam* and *janmam* (*kāṇa-janma-maryādā*) was defined in this way.[39]

It is not our argument here that this account in the *Kēralōlpatti* in relation to the origin of the *janmisampradāyam* or landlordism is to be taken as *the* way in which the land tenurial patterns had their origin in Kerala. A two-tier arrangement, with the *janmam*, a superior right vested in the Brāhmaṇa lords and the *kāṇam*, in the hands of the tenant-cultivators immediately below them, is clear here. It is exactly this pattern with further elaborations in detail that obtained in Kerala in the pre-colonial days, where *janmam* was defined as the absolute proprietorship and *kāṇam*, an intermediary tenure placed between *janmam* and tenancy-at-will. In practice, the latter was some kind of a usufructuary mortgage, where land was held by the tenant after a certain amount of money was paid to the landlord as security. The interest accrued on such moneys was deducted from the returns of the land, which was to be paid to the landlord as rent.

The picture that emerges from the epigraphical records of the later Cēra kingdom conforms to this. As mentioned above, most of the inscriptions are concerned with the way in which temple-centred Brāhmaṇa settlements managed their landed property. They give a fairly clear picture of the land tenures obtaining in Kerala during those days. Accordingly, we see that a major chunk of land where rice was cultivated was controlled by the temple-centred Brāhmaṇa settlements, which included both *dēvasvam* or the 'property of god', which was collectively held by the corporate group of Brāhmaṇas, and *brahmasvam* or 'the property of Brāhmaṇa', which was individually held by the Brāhmaṇa households. The title they had over such land is described as *aṭṭippēṟŭ*. There are other instances where institutions and individuals received land and other privileges as *viṭupēṟŭ*. The crucial term in both these expressions is *pēṟŭ,* which means, literally, 'birth'. In all likelihood, *janmam* is a Sanskrit translation of this term. In certain other cases, members of the ruling family or other private individuals kept land under the control of temples. Such tenure is described as *kīḻīṭŭ,* amounting to some kind of subordinate lease-hold. There is another kind of tenure called *iṭaiyīṭŭ,* an intermediary lease-hold. In these cases, the crucial term, *īṭŭ,* means 'security'. Was some security taken from the lessee and charged on the land leased out to him, where the transaction had clear features of a usufructuary mortgage? If it is so, was the security paid in terms of gold in the absence of coined money? In this context, it may be remembered that the unit of exchange in gold was a weight, *kāṇam. Kāṇam* was used as a standard unit of transactions, and stood for 'money' in a general sense.[40] It may, therefore, be suggested that the *īṭaiyīṭŭ* and *kīlīṭŭ* tenures in the records of the Cēra kingdom answer to the *kāṇam* tenure of later days.[41] Lower in hierarchy, there were the tenants-at-will, who were described as *kārāḷar,* their right being called *kārāṇma.* At a still lower level were occupants called *kuṭi* with the *kuṭimai* rights. It was much more nuanced than a three-tier hierarchy.[42] Thus, it may be proposed that the essential aspects of the landlordism of Kerala, which included what is called the *kāṇa-janma-maryādā,* were already in existence in the period of the Cēra kingdom of Mahōdayapuram.

The post-Cēra period witnessed its elaboration and the addition of further nuances in the graded hierarchy, what with greater land-use and the diversification of crops in that period. Inscriptions on stone and copper thin out during this period.[43] A large number of records on palm leaves called *granthavaris*, many of them registering transaction of land, take their place. A few of them have been published; many more await publication. Even those that have been published are not subjected to systematic analysis. But what little has been done is useful. In an excellent study of legal practices and jurisprudence in medieval Kerala[44], Donald R. Davis, Jr., has obliquely touched upon the land tenures in medieval Kerala. In the large number of documents transferring *aṭṭippēṟŭ* rights, Davis sees the equivalent of the transfer of *janmam* rights. He shows a brilliant flash of insight in taking the terms *aṭṭippēṟŭ* and *janmam* as 'technically synonymous'.[45] He takes up samples of the transfer of such rights in relation to Brāhmaṇical temples, Brāhmaṇa houses, Nāyar houses and temples under their control. Each of these transfers of *aṭṭippēṟŭ* rights is done with libation of water and for a consideration, a 'price fixed at the current rate determined by four people' or, more simply, 'price at the current rate' (*annu nālar kaṇṭu peṟum vila artham* or *annu peṟum artham,* respectively). It is interesting that the way in which price, *vila* or *artham,* is linked to the property is by the verb *peṟum,* lit., 'bearing'. *Pēṟŭ,* meaning 'birth', is its noun and translates into

Sanskrit as *janmam*. Although Davis takes up only a few sample documents of such transfers, the validity of his generalization is borne out by the large number of records transferring *aṭṭippēṟŭ* rights. It turns out that this right answered, in every detail, to the *janmam* right of later days. In fact, a couple of documents, which Davis has not mentioned, use the two terms as synonymous.[46] One document calls itself a *janmakkaraṇam*, '*janmam* document' while other documents of a similar nature are *aṭṭippēṟṟōlakkaraṇam* '[palm] leaf document of *aṭṭippēṟŭ*. In the context in which other documents speak about the transfer of *aṭṭippēṟŭ* rights, the term used here is *janmam*. In a similar case, an *aṭṭippēṟṟōla* dated AD 1608, included in the *Vanjeri Grandhavari*, transfers typically the *aṭṭippēṟŭ* rights for the 'current' price.[47] At the end of the document, it is stated that a letter each was taken from the senior prince and junior prince of Veṭṭam (the local chieftaincy) on the day on which this *janmam* was purchased. Unequivocally, thus, *janmam* and *aṭṭippēṟŭ* are synonymous. In this connection, another term used in medieval Malayalam to denote such rights over cultivated land is '*ulpatti*', a *tadbhava* of Sanskrit *utpatti*, 'origin'[48]. It can be seen that this term is close to *janmam* and *pēṟŭ*, both semantically and contextually. However, *ulpatti* is also used in the more general sense of 'landed property'.

Other shades of right over land, which are adumbrated in the Cēra records, are more clearly visible in the records of the post-Cēra period. Of these the most important is one that went between the *aṭṭippēṟŭ* or *janmam* and the actual cultivation—that is to say, the *iṭaiyīṭŭ* and *kīḻīṭŭ* of the Cēra records. This was created and given to intermediaries often in return for a loan or security, the interest of which was adjusted against the proceeds of the land, something of a usufructuary mortgage. The terms used most frequently in the post-Cēra documents are *veppŭ*, *oṟṟi* and *paṇayam*. The relationship in this case was somewhat complex, combining in it those of a debtor and a creditor as well as a landlord and a tenant. The *granthavari*s contain a large number of documents called *veppōlakkaraṇam* and *oṟṟiyōlakkaraṇam* creating and transferring such rights.[49] In a few documents, the money taken as loan/security is described as *kāṇam* in so many words.[50] Although different terms are used, the details in the documents show that there was no difference whatever among the *kāṇam, veppŭ, oṟṟi* or *paṇayam* tenures, where the tenancy is on the condition of a deposit of loan/security.[51] This tenure obtains immediately below the *janmam* or *aṭṭippēṟŭ* tenure. The holder of the *aṭṭippēṟŭ* tenure, which was the closest to absolute property rights, reserved a superior right over the *kāṇam, veppŭ, oṟṟi* or *paṇayam* tenures as indicated by his right to levy an upper share called *mēlāyma* or *mēlāma*, as brought out by the Koodali Granthavari.[52] In this context, the statement in the *Kēraḷōlpatti,* that shares of the landlords and tenants were the upper share (*mēlāykkūṟŭ*) and lower share (*kīḻāykkūṟŭ*) respectively, particularly the terminology used, acquires significance.

Further down, at the extreme bottom of the hierarchy, records of the Cēra kingdom show that there were the labourers who worked the land and were transferred along with land when transactions of land took place. In fact, historians have equated this with similar practices in medieval Europe and called it answering to serfdom. Whatever the validity of that description, such labourers are described variously as *āḷ, aṭiyār,* etc. The former term means 'man' and the latter, 'the lowly, subservient, one'. So also, the occupants of the land called *kuṭi*s, who had only the right of possession of land, are mentioned in the records of the Cēra kingdom. In fact, the ubiquitous Malayalam word for tenant, *kuṭiyān*, is derived from this. An inscription from Kumāranallūr speaks about those Śūdra cultivators of the settlement (*matilakattu kuṭiyirikkum śūdrar*).[53] It may be recalled that the *Kēraḷōlpatti,* too, describes the cultivators as Śūdras.[54] This pattern continues in the later records as well. It is these two shades at the lowermost rungs of the hierarchy that can be seen by the terms *aṭima* and *kuṭima* in the later records and the *Kēraḷōlpatti*.[55] Donald Davis, although his central concern is not with the structure or evolution of land-rights, has shown how there were other shades of rights vested in the *aṭiyār* and *kuṭiyār,* rights to perform labour services and to cultivate the land respectively, which consolidated themselves in this period.[56] What emerges, therefore, is that the peculiar kind of land tenures obtaining in Kerala had their origin in the Cēra kingdom. There were no cataclysmic changes taking place towards end of that kingdom or in the period immediately following it. What is seen is the congealing of a tradition which was already under way in the Cēra kingdom.

Another feature of the post-Cēra period was a loss of the corporate character of the bodies of Brāhmaṇas at the level of the villages. In the age of the Cēras, the Brāhmaṇical bodies in the *sabhā* of the *ūr* functioned as corporate entities with great solidarity. The remarkably jealous way in which the corporate interests of this body were guarded is brought out by the documents.[57] In the subsequent period, however, they lost this well-knit corporate character. This can be seen from a large number of features such as the non-insistence of full attendance, lack of unanimity in decisions, the practice of attendance by proxy, decrease in the numerical strength of the *sabhā*, the domination of certain individuals in it and their exercise of greater powers, and so on.[58] The result of it all was that individual families came to acquire prominence and in the process started controlling all the properties of the temple, that is *dēvasvam,* apart from their own *brahmasvam* properties. There are also instances where *dēvasvam* properties were appropriated as *brahmasvam.*[59] Elamkulam Kunjan Pillai had argued that this appropriation happened through the intermediate stage of *brahmasvamāṉa dēvasvam*, that is, '*dēvasvam* that is *brahmasvam*'[60]. This may very well have been so; but the process was more complex than what could be explained in terms of the cruelty and caprice of individual families in the wake of the uncertainties during a war. Factors such as the expansion of agriculture, changes in the cropping patterns, introduction of new crops, and so on, as well as the increase of the new landowning sections of service professionals who were remunerated in terms of land as service tenure are to be considered as causative to the process of the growth of landlordism in the post-Cēra period. The entry of the Portuguese and Dutch players into the political and economic arena also contributed to the process after the fifteenth century. The radical changes in the administration of revenue after the colonial take-over demanded redefinition of tenurial rights and the nineteenth century witnessed solidification of the relations.

NOTES AND REFERENCES

1. Alan Butterworth and V.Venugopaul Chetty, *A Collection of Inscriptions on Copper Plates and Stones in the Nellore District* (Madras, 1905), p. v.
2. The excellent work done by Noboru Karashima, B.Sitaraman, Y.Subbarayalu, Toru Matsui, P. Shanmugham, *et.al.* in the case of south Indian epigraphy is relevant here. Karashima, *History and Society in South India* (Delhi, 2001); N. Karashima, Y. Subbarayalu and Toru Matsui, *A Concordance of Personal Names in Chola Inscriptions* (Madurai, 1978); P. Shanmugam, *The Revenue System Under the Cholas* (Madras, 1987); N. Karashima, Y. Subbarayalu and P. Shanmugham, *Vijayanagar Rule in Tamil Country as Revealed through a Statistical*

Study of Revenue Terms in Inscriptions (Tokyo, 1988), etc. are good examples.

3. The present paper is based on the author's earlier research for his two dissertations: Veluthat Kesavan, 'Aryan Brahman Settlements of Ancient Kerala', unpublished MA Dissertation, University of Calicut (Calicut, 1974 and 'Brahman Settlements in Kerala, AD 1100–1500', unpublished MPhil Dissertation, Jawaharlal Nehru University (New Delhi, 1978). Some of the results are available in Kesavan Veluthat, *Brahman Settlements in Kerala: Historical Studies* (Calicut, 1978).
4. For a brief survey of the progress of epigraphical studies in Kerala, M.R. Raghava Varier, 'Epigraphical Studies in Kerala', *Tamil Civilization*, vol. 5, nos 1 and 2, March, June 1987; Veluthat, 'Epigraphy in the Historiography of Kerala', Chapter 7 above.
5. Most of Professor Elamkulam P.N. Kunjan Pillai's writings pertaining to this period are in Malayalam. Some of the crucial articles, however, are available in English translation. Pillai, *Studies in Kerala History* (Kottayam, 1971).
6. His studies on the matrilineal system or *marumakkattāyam* and landlordism or *janmisampradāyam,* both appearing in his *Studies in Kerala History,* are of particular interest in this respect.
7. Kanippayyur Sankaran Nambudiripad, *Eḷamkuḷattiṉṟe Nampūriśśakāram* (Kunnamkulam, 1968). This and some other Nambudiri tirades against Pillai are silly casteist outbursts.
8. Elamkulam P.N. Kunjan Pillai, *Janmisampradāyam Kēraḷattil* (Kottayam, 1959), pp. 8–44.
9. Pillai takes him for a non-Brāhmaṇa. Ibid., p. 19. This house figures in later Malayalam poems as a famous Nambudiri house. For a list of 200 Brāhmaṇa houses in Cēra inscriptions, Veluthat, Aryan Brahman Settlements, Appendix II, pp. 92–102. Pillai mistakes many as non-Brāhmaṇas.
10. *Travancore Archaeological Series* (hereafter *TAS*), vol. V, part I, no. 24, pp. 63–86. 1–4. Kūṟṟampaḷḷi of Mūḻikkaḷam survives as a Brāhmaṇa house.
11. It was M.G.S. Narayanan who first challenged this. 'Political and Social Conditions of Kerala under the Kulasekhara Empire c. AD. 800–1124', unpublished PhD Thesis, University of Kerala, 1972. This dissertation, a definitive and exhaustive study of the history of Kerala in this period, is not formally published although the author has circulated a few printed copies. Narayanan, *Perumals of Kerala: Political and Social Conditions of Kerala Under the Cera Perumals of Makotai (c. AD 800–1124)* (Calicut, 1996). The present writer has largely followed his line: see n. 3 above.
12. Pillai, *Janmisampradāyam Kēraḷattil,* pp. 22–3. The four non-*Brāhamaṇas* whom he identifies in the record, *TAS,* V, I, no. 24, are from the houses of Vaññippuḻa, Vilakkilimaṅgalam, Kamukañcēri and Makiḻañcēri. Vaññippuḻa is an influential Brāhmaṇa house to this day.

A *bhaṭṭasōmayājin* of Vilakkilimaṅgalam figures in an eleventh century record from Tiruvalla. *TAS*, vol. II, iii, pp. 131–207, ll.584–5. Elsewhere in the record under reference (ll.11–12), land assigned to these ten families is described as *paṭakāram*, an exclusively Brāhmaṇa privilege. And the names such as Nārāyaṇa and Trivikrama are apparently of Brāhmaṇas.

13. I have made an examination of the inscriptions and shown that many Brāhmaṇa families mentioned in them survive to this day. Veluthat, 'Aryan Brahman Settlements', Appendix 2. There are other scholars who continue to mistake them for non-Brāhmaṇas. R.N. Nandi, in *Indian Historical Review*, vol. VIII, nos 1–2, pp. 126–8.
14. Pillai, *Janmisampradāyam*, pp. 19–20.
15. *TAS*, vol. IV, no.7, pp. 22–65.
16. Nos 477 and 478 of 1926.
17. There is a traditional list of 32 original Brāhmaṇa settlements in Kerala. The present writer has identified them: *Brahman Settlements*. Vaikkam, however, is not one of them.
18. *TAS*, vol. V, i, no. 24.
19. Ibid. See also *supra*, n. 12.
20. For a comprehensive study of the organization and administration of the temple-centred agrarian corporations in early medieval Kerala, Veluthat, *Brahman Settlements*, pp. 52–67.
21. See above, note 13.
22. For a discussion and interpretation, Narayanan, 'Socio-economic Implications of the Concept of Mahapataka in the Feudal Society of South India', *Journal of Kerala Studies*, vol. VI, 1979, pp. 453–60.
23. Kesavan Veluthat, 'The *Sabha* and *Parisad* in Early Medieval South India: Correlation of Epigraphic and Dharmasastraic Evidences', *Tamil Civilization*, vol. 3, nos 2 and 3, June–September 1985, pp. 75–82.
24. Pillai, *Janmisampradāyam*, p. 21.
25. *TAS*, vol. V, no. 2, p. 6.
26. Ibid.
27. Above, n. 20.
28. Pillai, *Janmisampradāyam*, p. 38. The expression *nāṭṭukūṭṭam* which Pillai uses does not occur in the records.
29. M.G.S. Narayanan, *Reinterpretations in South Indian History* (Trivandrum, 1977), pp. 99–112.
30. *TAS*, vol. V, no.10, p. 34.
31. This is the general picture on local government in south India under the Cōḻas. K.A. Nilakanta Sastri, *The Cōḻas*, 2nd edn (Madras, 1955, 1975), pp. 503—6; for a re-examination, Y. Subbarayalu, *Political Geography*.
32. For this distinction, see Kesavan Veluthat, *The Political Structure of Early Medieval South India*, Delhi, 1993, pp. 114, 177, et passim.
33. Narayanan, *Perumals of Kerala*, chapters on 'Early Wars and Alliances', and 'Cola Invasions and The Last Phase'.

34. Veluthat, *Brahman Settlements*, chapter on 'The Tiruvalla Settlement: a Case Study', pp. 39–51. There is an unpublished PhD dissertation on this temple and the copious epigraphical records from there: Alex Mathew, 'Political Identities in History', School of Social Sciences, Mahatma Gandhi University (Kottyam, 2006).
35. Narayanan, *Perumals of Kerala*, chapter on 'Early Wars and Alliances' under 'Rise of the Kingdom', 'Influx of Aryans', 'Governors from Outside', and 'Founder of the Kingdom'.
36. Ibid., chapter on 'Economic Conditions' under 'Land Tenures'. Narayanan makes the following important statement on p. 174:

> All land seems to have belonged to the Cēra king in theory. The governors were his feudatories and as such they enjoyed the lands in their districts in return for payment of tribute. These lands possessed by the king or his feudatories and inhabited and cultivated by the native population are known as Cērikkal in the records of the age. It is from such land that nagaras and grāmas were carved out and leased out to the foreign and native merchants or the Aryan Brahmin cultivators.

However, this position is not supported by evidence of any such 'theory' and of the 'leasing out' to the 'Aryan Brahmin Cultivators'. It also goes against his own position mentioned above, n. 35.
37. Rajan Gurukkal and Raghava Varier, eds, *Cultural History of Kerala*, vol. I (Thiruvananthapuram, 1999), pp. 235–74.
38. For a recent discussion of *Keraḷōlpatti* as history, Kesavan Veluthat 'The *Keraḷōlpatti* as History: A Note on the Pre-colonial Traditions of Historical Writing in India', in K.N. Ganesh, ed., *Culture and Modernity: Historical Explorations*, University of Calicut (Calicut, 2004), Chapter 6 above.
39. Skaria Zacharia, ed., *Kerlolpathiyum Maṟṟum* (Kottayam, 1992)., pp. 159–60. Translation by the present author.
40. Narayanan, *Perumals of Kerala*, p. 164. This was one-tenth of a *kaḻañcu*, which was accepted as a unit all over south India. Sastri, *The Cōḷas*, pp. 613–4. A *kaḻañcu* was equal to a *gadyāṇa* figuring in the documents from Karnataka.

The term *kāṇam* is used in the sense of 'money' in general in many post-Cēra records. There is at least one place where the term *kāṇam* is used in Malayalam literature in the sense of money. Describing the wedding of Śiva and Pārvati elaborately, an old song which Nampūtiri women recite calls the dowry that Śiva received as *kāṇam*. '...*kāṇavum nīrumāy vāṅṅikkoṇṭaṅṅane hōmam tuṭaṅṅī namaśśivāya*'. I quote this from memory as heard from my grandmother who used to recite it in the evenings.
41. Narayanan, however, believes that *kāṇam* is derived from the verb *kāṇuka*, 'to see' and used in the extended sense of 'to acquire' as used in the Syrian Christian Copper Plates. Narayanan, *Perumals of Kerala*, p. 174. He takes it to mean 'a kind of proprietorship prevalent

in Kerala in later times also' and defines it as a 'perpetual lease, "as long as the world, sun and moon endure...'". He continues to say that the right that the temple-centred Brāhmaṇa settlements had over land was such *kāṇam* right. None of these is borne out by evidence which he has himself competently marshalled.

42. For a three-tier hierarchy, Ibid., p. 174.
43. For a discussion of this pattern, Veluthat, 'Storage and Retrieval of Information: Literacy and Communication in Pre-modern Kerala' in Amiya Kumar Bagchi, Dipankar Sinha and Barnita Bagchi, eds, *Webs of History: Information, Communication and Technology from Early to Post-colonial India* (Delhi, 2005), pp. 67–82, Chapter 8 above.
44. Donald R. Davis, Jr, *The Boundaries of Hindu Law: Tradition, Custom and Politics in Medieval Kerala* (Torino, 2004).
45. Ibid., p. 52.
46. K.K.N. Kurup, ed., *Koodali Granthavari* (Calicut University, 1995), Document no. 157, p. 97.
47. Narayanan, ed., *Vanjeri Grandhavari* (Calicut University, 1987), pp. 29–30.
48. Hermann Gundert, *A Malayalam and English Dictionary* (Mangalore, 1872), s.v., *ulpatti*. The documents contained in Kurup, ed., *Koodali Grandhavari*, use the expression in the same sense. When the *aṭṭippēṟu* rights in a piece of land are sold, such land is described as *ulpatti*.
49. Narayanan, ed., *Vanjeri*, passim; Kurup, ed., *Koodali*, passim.
50. E.g., Kurup, ed., *Koodali*, Document no. 51, p. 53,
51. Davis, *The Boundaries*, p. 67 believes that *kāṇam* was 'still a relatively higher tenure [than the other two] in which the holder of the *kāṇam* right receives much of the produce from the land of his (or his family's) supervision'. The documents he has used, or the others in the *granthavaris* he has consulted, do not, however, warrant this conclusion.
52. Kurup, ed., *Koodali*, passim.
53. *TAS*, vol. III, no. 49, pp. 191–6.
54. Above, n. 39.
55. Zacharia, ed., *Kerlolpattiyum*. It is interesting that the *Kēraḷōlpatti*, like the Kumāranallūr inscription mentioned above (n. 53), assigns a Śūdra status to those who belong to this category.
56. Davis, *The Boundaries*, p. 67.
57. Narayanan, *Perumals of Kerala*, pp. 109–20. This is by far the most elaborate and systematic treatment of the problem. For other discussions, Veluthat, *Brahman Settlements*, chapter on 'Organization and Administration during the later Cēra Period, AD 800–1100', pp. 52–67; Gurukkal, *The Kerala Temple and Early Medieval Agrarian System* (Sukapuram, 1992). Neither of these takes it beyond what Narayanan had written.
58. For an elaborate treatment, Veluthat, *Brahman Settlements*, chapter on 'Changes in the Organization and Administration', pp. 86–95.

59. A clear instance of this can be seen in the Peruñcellūr Copper Plate. Kesavan Veluthat, 'Peruñcellūr Ceppēṭū, Kollam 321 Kanni 21 (1145 September 22)', *AdhAram: A Journal of Kerala Archaeology and History,* vol. 1, 2006, pp. 75–82. This record speaks of how the temple committee of Peruñcellūr and the ruler of the local *nāṭu* together lent a sum of 707 *ānaiyaccŭ* to a private Brāhmaṇa individual, taking from him landed properties and the labourers who worked them as mortgage. An additional sum of 300 *ānaiyaccŭ* was lent three years later and charged on the same properties. The whole transaction is described as *paṇayam* and the second instalment of money charged on it is called *brahmasvam*.
60. Pillai, *Janmisampradāyam*.

13

Evolution of a Regional Identity*

One basic requirement of history as knowledge is that its practitioners, located in the present, must try to understand and explain the past. This may sound like a truism; but historians often tend to forget this simple nature of their business. They are sometimes given to think that they are studying the past in its own terms; some would make a plea to spurn the 'Euro-centric' approach to Indian history and adopt an 'indigenous' view. But, the reality is that the historian cannot escape familiar categories and patterns in his attempts to come to grips with the past. These categories and patterns, it must be noted, are artefacts of the present, the ones through which the present looks at itself. They are not from the past which is the historian's subject matter; on the contrary, they belong to the present, with the help of which the historian seeks to understand, and occasionally to manipulate, the past.

Units of historical study are typical examples of the choice made under these pressures. Ranging from vast entities such as the whole world itself or more romantic ones such as civilizations, they include smaller and smaller units such as regions, localities, villages, or even households. It is not as if these units offer themselves as so many 'natural' objects of historical study. It is the historian, with his own agenda, who identifies his units. The constituent-constituted relationship among them is often lost sight of as also the changing nature of both. In the present chapter we seek to substantiate this argument by presenting a report on the attempt to look for the idea of India in sources from the Malayalam-speaking region and to examine how the two categories (the 'local' and the 'global') were constituted,

* First published as 'Evolution of a Regional Identity: Kerala in India', in Irfan Habib, ed., *India: Studies in the History of an Idea* (Aligarh, 2004), pp. 82–97.

and interacted with each other, from the time that evidence expressing these ideas is available in literature. We shall also see how these two changed at a particular point in time, which change was dictated by the changing socio-economic and political circumstances.

Of these units, some are larger in extent than the others and, in a geographical sense, include these others within them. The combination often makes the smaller of the two look as if it is part of the larger one. Sometimes it is as if the number of boxes within boxes goes on increasing, as in the case of Kerala in India in the early historical period. It did exist in its own way; it was included in a larger socio-cultural unit called 'Tamiḻakam'; and it was located within the geographical limits of the subcontinent that goes by the name 'India'. It can be seen, however, that these identities and affiliations were not fixed at any point in time; they underwent transformations over long or short periods. An examination of these aspects in some detail will demonstrate the essentially historical character of the process of the emergence of such identities. It was not a 'natural' process: there were forces behind such 'emergences'. This chapter will also seek to explain these forces, placing the process within the social and economic context in which the processes were taking place.

To be sure, early sources do not use the term 'Kerala' to denote the land that now goes by that name. The term Cēra/Cēramān occurs in early Tamil literature in the sense of a lineage of chiefs.[1] The Prakrit/Sanskrit translation of the term Cēramān, namely Kētalaputa/Kēraḷaputra, figures in the edicts of Aśōka. The Greco-Roman accounts of the early centuries of the Christian era use a Greek variant, Kerobotros/Kaelobotros.[2] Many places in the Malayalam-speaking region of today figure in the copious literature in Tamil produced in this period; and many lineages of that region are mentioned in this literature. But there is no notion of Kerala as a geographical unit. Tamiḻakam is the land south of Vēnkaṭam, north of Kumari (Cape Comorin) and bounded by the seas on either side. This was the Tamil homeland, which subsumed present-day Kerala as its integral part. Nor does the Malayalam language or even its name figure in any of the sources of this period. There are occasional references to variations in linguistic usage described as features characteristic of Malaināṭu, a purely geographical name by which the land west of the Western Ghats was known. Even these references are of a much later date, occurring in the medieval commentaries to the early Tamil anthologies.

The earliest definitive reference to Kerala as a separate geographical entity, with the use of that name, is arguably in the *Avantisundarīkathā* of Daṇḍin.[3] The author, the eighth century Sanskrit poet from the Pallava capital in Kāñci, speaks of his friends including Mātṛdatta, 'the best of Brāhmaṇas from Kerala'. In the fashion characteristic of Sanskrit, Daṇḍin uses Kerala in the plural (*Kēraḷēṣu*), showing thereby that it was already familiar as the name of a country. In the same century or early in the next, Śaktibhadra, a dramatist from Kerala, composed *Āścaryacūḍāmaṇi*, a Sanskrit play where the author makes the director speak of the unlikelihood of it being a composition coming from the South, demonstrating not only its distinctiveness but also its affiliation to a larger whole of a Sanskrit literary world all over India.[4] He does not, to be sure, refer to Kerala by name. A junior contemporary of Śaktibhadra does it, almost with a vengeance. He was Kulaśēkharavarman, a ninth-century king of Kerala, and the author of *Subhadrādhanañjaya* and *Tapatīsaṃvaraṇa,* two Sanskrit plays and perhaps one more, *Vicchinnābhiṣēka,* as well as a work in prose, *Āścaryamañjarī*. He has been identified with Sthāṇu Ravi Kulaśēkhara (AD 844–883) of the inscriptions, and with the Vaiṣṇava Bhakti saint known as Kulaśēkhara Āḻvar, author of *Perumāḷ Tirumoḻi* in Tamil and *Mukundamālā* in Sanskrit.[5] Kulaśēkharavarman describes himself as *Kēraḷakulacūḍāmaṇi* and *Kēraḷādhinātha* in the Sanskrit plays.[6] While the former is a reference to the Kerala or Cēra lineage to which he belonged, the latter is an unmistakable reference to the Kerala country of which he was the ruler. In fact, he styles himself more authentically as *Mahōdayapuraparamēśvara*, 'Supreme Lord of the city of Mahōdayapura', than as *Kēraḷādhinātha*, the 'Overlord of Kerala', a statement with significant political implications. In any case, a slightly later text clarifies that the king of Mahōdayapurm protected *Kēraḷaviṣaya*, 'the land of Kerala'.[7] So also, a contemporary of Kulaśēkhara describes his patron as 'ruling the earth', *vasudhām+avataḥ,* punning on which he also says that he possessed resources as well as his own city [of Mahōdayapuram] (*vasu+dhāmavataḥ*).[8] *Vyaṅgyavyākhyā,* commentaries of the plays composed during the playwright's lifetime, describes the author as a *Kēraḷaviṣayādhipa* or the lord of the Kerala-*viṣaya.*[9] In short, Kerala gets defined as a geographical unit with definite boundaries, and that territory also becomes the territory of a political unit by the ninth century.

Interestingly, we start getting references to Kerala as a separate political unit in the records of the Cāḷukyas, Pallavas and Pāṇḍyas a little earlier and of the Cōḻas by the time of these plays.[10] Whether or not the early references are to the lineage of the Cēras or the country of Kerala, the later ones, found in Cōḻa records, are certainly to the Kerala country. It is significant that this coincides with the emergence of the state in what is now Kerala. The Cēra kingdom of Mahōdayapuram or Makōtai makes its appearance in the records at least from the beginning of the ninth century.[11] This kingdom is to be distinguished from the chiefdom of the Cēras found in an earlier period, evidence of which is available in ancient Tamil poetry, Aśōkan edicts and the Tamil Brāhmi cave label inscriptions.[12] The rise of this later Cēra kingdom of Mahōdayapuram was not just another 'event' in the political history of this region; it represented the culmination of a series of complex processes with far-reaching consequences for economy, society and polity. The entire area covered by the modern linguistic state of Kerala formed the territory of this newly formed state and a kind of uniformity, however loosely defined, is seen in this area.[13] Inscriptions from this period, discovered from the entire length of Kerala, bear the stamp of a single socio-political unit, which was presided over by the Cēra *Perumāḷ*. The same language and script are used in these records, [14] which are dated in the regnal years of the Cēra *Perumāḷ* or else follow some other means of dating such as the mention of the position of Jupiter, use of the Śaka or Kali era, etc., which were known all over the region. Conventions accepted all over the area emerged, and among these there was some kind of uniformity in the matter of the organization and functioning of the agrarian corporations of Brāhmaṇical groups.[15] It is also significant that this identity and uniformity were defined in contradistinction with what was obtaining in the Tulu-speaking regions to the north and the Tamil-speaking regions to the south and east.

The emergence of the Cēra kingdom of Mahōdayapuram marks the beginning of a new era in the history of Kerala, as indeed does the emergence of the new state under the Pallavas or Pāṇḍyas in relation to the respective regions in south India. An epochal transformation has been identified in this process, and a veritable 'transition debate' has grown around it.[16] The social formation of the early historical period, described somewhat wrongly by historians as the 'Sangam Period', was characterized by a subsistence economy maintained by family labour, reciprocity and patronage. A highly differentiated economy and society, with extra-kin labour, production of surplus and its distribution and notions of pricing and profit in exchange came to replace the older one by the time the new state, as for example the Cēra kingdom of Mahōdayapuram on the west coast, was established in south India.[17] A characteristic feature of the state that came into existence by this period, under the Pallavas, Pāṇḍyas, Cēras and Cōḻas, is the highly Kṣatriyaized monarchy which presided over them, answering in every detail to the model available in the *kāvya-śāstra-nāṭaka* literature in Sanskrit. In the case of Kerala, there were further differences from its counterparts elsewhere in south India.[18]

One of the factors responsible for the formation of the state and the peculiar character it had as distinct from the rest of south India was the rise of Brāhmaṇical settlements in the river valleys of Kerala. Although some Brāhmaṇical presence with the characteristic Paraśurāma tradition of the west coast and a Vedic sacrificial background is noticed in Kerala early in the age of the Tamil anthologies such as *Akanāṉūṟu,*[19] the majority of them took shape only in the period of the transition from the early historical to early medieval period.[20] These were somewhat unique in ways more than one. The Brāhmaṇas of Kerala cherished the Paraśurāma tradition, something which they shared with their counterparts in the rest of the west coast but distinct from other parts of the peninsula.[21] They developed a number of unusual practices, known as *anācāra*s, and these distinguished the Brāhmaṇas of Kerala from those in the rest of India.[22] There was difference in the pattern of settlements, which was a function of the physiography and ecology of the region.[23] In any case, the Brāhmaṇical settlements of Kerala developed certain features that were entirely different from their counterparts in other parts of the peninsula. This Brāhmaṇical character with the Paraśurāma stamp can be seen from the statement in an eleventh-century Cōḻa record, the Tiruvālaṅgāḍu Copper Plates, describing Kerala as 'the land created by Rāma who takes pleasure in exterminating the Kṣatriyas and where good people live with joy'.[24] At the same time, they also shared, with the rest of south India or perhaps the entire country, many common features of what was laid down in the *Dharmaśāstra* texts in the matter of their community organization, even when the *Dharmaśāstra*s were flouted with impunity in the matter of many of the *anācāras* as well as other practices.

The introduction of the Brāhmaṇical element with the Paraśurāma tradition seems to be the starting point of the distinctiveness of Kerala and its departure from the rest of Tamiḻakam. The Brāhmaṇical claim, that it was Paraśurāma who created *their* land and donated it to *them*, is seen all over the western seaboard in India. In the case of the south, it is the strip of land from Gōkarṇa to Kanyākumāri which is identified as the land retrieved by Paraśurāma. Gradually, even this unit disintegrates, as the land between Perumpuḻa (in Kasaragod district) and Kanyākumāri is defined as actually the Malanāṭu within the Paraśurāma-*kṣētra*. This newly defined unit was earlier a part of Tamiḻakam, but there is a conscious rejection of this affiliation in the changed context. The historical tradition of this new formation does not cherish details concerning the earlier Cēra rulers and their exploits contained in early Tamil songs such as the *Patiṟṟuppattu* any more. For instance, a Malayalam narrative called *Kēraḷōlpatti*, concerned with the history of Kerala, is totally silent about this aspect of the past. The contents of this narrative date from this period, although the date of its composition itself is problematic.[25]

This text is significant as an attempt to historicize Kerala as a separate unit, with its own defined territory and peculiar institutions. It opens by giving an account of Paraśurāma's creation of Kerala, the land between Gōkarṇa and Kanyākumāri, by claiming it from the Arabian Sea with a fling of his axe and settling it by Brāhmaṇas brought from the north in sixty-four *grāmas*, of which thirty-two are in Tuḷunāḍu and the remaining in present-day Kerala. Speaking about the way in which Paraśurāma peopled the land of Kerala after raising it from the sea, the *Kēraḷōlpatti* says that the Brāhmaṇas, who were brought and settled in the first instance, would not stay; they returned to their original home in Ahicchatra (a historical place and now also an archaeological site in northern India) for fear of serpents in the new land. Paraśurāma brought a second wave of Brāhmaṇas, again from Ahicchatra. In order that they would not be accepted back 'home' if they returned, he had their hair style and dress code changed. He also persuaded them to accept the mother right so that he could expiate for his own matricidal sin; but only those of one village, namely Payyannūr, obliged him by following matrilineal descent. Paraśurāma also established 108 temples each for Śiva, Śāstā, and Durgā. He chose

36,000 Brāhmaṇas from the different *grāmas* and conferred on them the right to arms (*śastrabhikṣā*), so that they could protect their land themselves.

There is the crucial difference between the situation in Kerala and the land immediately to its north, viz. South Canara. It is a significant indication of the difference in the role of the Brāhmaṇical groups in the two societies. The landed wealth in South Canara was not under the control of the Brāhmaṇical groups as much as it was in Kerala and, therefore, the importance that the Brāhmaṇas of Kerala had in polity and society was not matched by what their counterparts in South Canara had. As it was much greater in the case of Kerala, Paraśurāma is invoked as not only the creator of the land but also the donor to the Brāhmaṇa groups. So also the exceptional importance attached to the arms-bearing Brāhmaṇas called *śastra-Brāhmaṇas* or *cāttirar* and their group meetings is another instance of the use of the past in seeking validation of the Brāhmaṇical groups in Kerala society. Paraśurāma established a *Brahmakṣatra* in Kerala, where Brāhmaṇas looked after the work of the Kṣatriyas, with every arrangement for the welfare of the people, including religion, administration and law. The Brāhmaṇical authority in Kerala was so great that it took Viṣṇu as Paraśurāma, a Brāhmaṇical *avatāra* with sufficient Kṣatriya pretensions, to legitimize it. And, that underlined the distinctiveness of Kerala with reference to the Tuḷu country, too.

In the next period taken up in the narrative, the text shows that the Brāhmaṇical groups played a major role in society and politics. Representatives of the Brāhmaṇical establishment governed the land gifted to them by Paraśurāma as *Brahmakṣatra*. In course of time, however, they realized that the business of governance corrupted them, and they themselves decided to get a Kṣatriya as their ruler. Accordingly, a Kṣatriya and his sister were brought; the brother was anointed king and was made to swear habitual allegiance to them. A monarchical state was established in Kerala. The sister was married to a Brāhmaṇa and it was agreed that the progeny would belong to the Kṣatriya caste according to the matrilineal system of succession. The descendants of this sister would be the successors to the throne. The conviction that government was not the Brāhmaṇas' proper occupation and that it belonged to the Kṣatriya is very much in tune with the Brāhmaṇical principles and the theory of *varṇāśramadharma*. The upper caste, Brāhmaṇical character of it all is hard to miss, both in the narrative and in other contemporary records. At the same time, there is no attempt to latch the origin of the dynasty on either to one of the reputed Kṣatriya lineages of Purāṇic fame or to those celebrated in the Tamil tradition; nor is an origin myth in the tradition typical of the medieval court literature in Sanskrit invented or the heroic deeds of the ruler or his ancestors recited. All this would show that Kerala had arrived as a separate political entity and that the *Kēraḷōlpatti* was historicizing it.

One feature which distinguished the new formation was its 'religion'. The cults and practices of the earlier period, aimed at the propitiation of the deities of the *tiṇai*s, gave way to the worship of *Āgamaic* deities consecrated in temples. The Brāhmaṇical element had a not insignificant role to play in this, for all the Brāhmaṇical settlements, which functioned as agrarian corporations controlling vast estates of land, were centred on temples. The native population was brought within their magnetic field, and this provided the necessary claims for the hegemonic elements to command the acquiescence of the hegemonized. Taking place in the period of the celebrated 'Bhakti Movement' in south India, of which at least two leaders were Cēra *Perumāḷ*s themselves, this religious transformation was very crucial for the realignment of identities as well. Gods worshipped by the people were part of a larger pan-Indian tradition from now on, and all the traditions of the epics and Purāṇas in Sanskrit became part of the heritage of anybody who identified himself with this 'new' religion. Sanskrit was getting precedence over Tamil, the fact that literary productions of the early leaders of the 'Bhakti Movement' from Kerala were in Tamil notwithstanding. To be considered along with religion, if not as part of it, is caste. It is here that Kerala presents its distinctiveness in the clearest manner. Interestingly, the *Kēraḷōlpatti* has a whole section giving details about the innumerable castes and the relative status of each defining the norms of purity and pollution and attributing the entire system to the inevitable Śaṅkarācārya.

The heavy Sanskritic nature of the ideas and institutions obtaining in this newly emerged political-cultural unit is obvious. Prescriptions of the *dharmaśāstra*s are followed in matters of social conduct and statecraft. In fact, even in laying down the details of the organization of an urban centre under the Christian church at Kurakkēṇi Kollam, it is the model of the *Arthaśāstra* that is followed. In cultural matters, the repertoire of the Sanskrit epics, *Rāmayaṇa* and *Mahābhārata*, is used heavily as the earliest dramas such as the *Āścaryacūḍāmani, Subhadrādhanañjaya* and *Tapatīsaṃvaraṇa* would show. The temple theatre, which had its beginning in this period, used these and other Sanskrit plays with their epic contents. Sculpture and such painting as there was drew liberally on this repertoire. Arrangements for the propagation of the epics were made through specialists such as the *Mahābhārata bhaṭṭa*s who expounded the epic in temples. And, there is no evidence that the old Tamil tradition was patronized any more. A comparison of the popularity of the Sanskrit works of Kulaśekharavarman and the Tamil hymns of the same author in Kerala in this and later periods will eminently prove this point. So also, themes from the equally rich treasure available in Tamil are not used by authors in Kerala for their compositions in Sanskrit. Even the first literary works in Malayalam are *Rāmacarita* and a translation of the *Arthaśāstra,* both dated to about the twelfth century. When more works were composed, the themes were either taken from the storehouse of Sanskrit epics and other literary works or invented *de novo.* Thus, the identity of Kerala that was crafted in the age of the Cēramān *Perumāḷ*s (AD 800–1124) was clearly of an upper caste, Brāhmaṇical, Sanskritic nature.

At this point, it is interesting to note a major variation in the course of history in this part of the country. While the Sanskritic tradition in literature mentioned above was matched by the production of Sanskrit inscriptions elsewhere, Kerala used old Malayalam for inscriptions from the beginning of the ninth century.[26] Inscriptions of the Cēras of Mahōdayapuram, starting from the very first one, are in old Malayalam and not Sanskrit. In fact, there is only one inscription in Sanskrit from Kerala,[27] and that too from the southern extreme and not of a Cēra king—the proverbial exception which proves the rule. Thus Kerala presents a deviation from the pattern which Sheldon Pollock has seen.[28] The model that he constructs, of a 'Sanskrit Cosmopolis' affiliating regional cultures to it before the 'vernacular transformation' of regions, is not empirically valid for the situation obtaining in the extreme south of the west coast. Even while inscriptions used the 'vernacular' when a literate tradition emerged there, literature used the Sanskrit language, made use of its rich repertoire and followed the science of its prosody and poetics (*alaṅkāraśāstra*) that had developed at an all-India level. In fact, contemporary as well as modern scholars have shown how even the Sanskrit dramas of Kulaśēkhara are influenced by the *dhvani* theory of the Kashmiri writer Ānandavardhana, which was barely half a century old at the time of their composition.[29] So also, compositions from Kerala were lauded by poets and critics from other parts of the country not long after they were produced. Both these instances show how the 'Sanskrit Cosmopolis' did exert its influence here on written literature in Kerala from the period of the Cēramān *Perumāḷs*.

It is this historical baggage of unity and identity that Kerala carried with it in the subsequent periods, in spite of the heavy fragmentation which its polity experienced. Kerala was still referred to as *Cēramān nāḍu,* the 'Land of the Cēramāns' in the literature of the post-Cēra period. The ghost of the *Perumāḷ* haunted the land in many ways. Mahōdayapuram is still represented in the literature as the town from which the Land of the Cēramāns was still ruled—a town of cultivated gentlemen and comely ladies, an epitome of civilized life.[30] A copper plate record dated a century after the formal disintegration of the Cēra kingdom suggests a pan-Kerala appeal that the town had.[31] It speaks, perhaps wishfully, of the endorsement that the important political divisions and social units had made on the grant recorded in it. Each of the large number of principalities that came into existence on the ruins of the Cēra kingdom claimed to be not only a splinter of the old kingdom but also deriving its authority from the donation of the last Cēramān *Perumāḷ*. Thus Vēṇāḍ in the south and Kōlattunāḍ in the north, and all other 'kingdoms' in between, participated in the same historical tradition and the same identity. Many of these rulers also claimed to step into the shoes of the *Perumāḷ* in claiming to be the overlord of Kerala. Thus the ruler of Vēṇād or the Zamorin or the *rājā* of Cochin staked this claim in various ways. *Māmākam,* a festival in the temple of Tirunāvāya every twelve years, was the occasion where this claim was ritually made, and contested. So also, a local era, originating in Kollam in Vēṇād in the ninth century and used only locally for the next three centuries, gained acceptance as a standard for reckoning dates all over Kerala. The strong Brāhmaṇical character that the earlier power structure had is not seen in most of the 'successor states' any more; but the cultural identity of Kerala, which was forged in the earlier period of Brāhmaṇical hegemony, continued. Ōṇam, which began as a Vaiṣṇava sectarian festival with a strong Tamil background, gets entirely 'Malayalamized' in this period.

All this would show that the clearly defined identity that Kerala had acquired in the Perumāḷ era continued in nearly all its detail. In fact, this period looked upon itself as a continuation of the earlier period whereas the earlier one was conscious of the break that it represented. These differences, and the factors behind it, are a matter recognized by the authors of this period. For instance, a medieval *Maṇipravāḷam* text speaks of the speciality of the land on account of its fertility also as a gift of Paraśurāma: 'the rainy season, under orders of Paraśurāma, comes here with such frequency as if to breastfeed her children'.[32] The *Śukasandēśa,* a work in Sanskrit, puts the same thing slightly differently. The messenger of love, on his way from Ramēśvaram to Guṇakā in Kerala carrying the message to the separated heroine, is introduced to the land when he is to cross the Western Ghats: 'Now you can see the *brahmakṣatra* land which testifies to the might of Paraśurāma's arms. This country, rich in pepper and betel vines growing on tall coconut and areca palms, is celebrated as Kerala'.[33] The distinctiveness of Kerala, these texts imply, was a function of its geography and climate.

It is here that one sees a conscious attempt at defining Kerala and its language, creating a self-image, as it were. M.R. Raghava Varier has made a brilliant analysis of a medieval text, *Līlātilakam,*[34] a manual of the grammar, prosody and poetics of *Maṇipravāḷam,* a 'union of *bhāṣā* and Sanskrit', where *bhāṣā* stands for Malayalam.[35] The language of this text itself is Sanskrit, not Malayalam, although the author exhibits his deep knowledge of literary texts in Malayalam as well as the literary and grammatical theories in Sanskrit, Tamil and Kannada. This, or any other contemporary text from Kerala, does not call Malayalam by that name, it being used for the first time outside Kerala, as in the fifteenth century Telugu work, *Śrībhīmēśvarapurāṇamu* of Śrīnātha.[36] Curiously, another term that *Līlātilakam* uses to denote the language of Kerala is Tamil, but the anonymous author hastens to explain that this Tamil is different from the language used in 'the Cōḻa country, etc...' A very detailed discussion, bordering on the polemical, follows in an attempt to demonstrate the way in which '*Kēraḷa-bhāṣā*' was distinct from other languages of south India; so also, the same text shows that Kerala had acquired the necessary self-confidence to consider languages, people and institutions outside Kerala as inferior.

At the same time, the eagerness to participate in an all-India tradition was on the increase. Identifying Kerala as a *janapada* in *Bhāratavarṣa* can be seen from the period of the *Purāṇas* on;[37] but that is as vague as it is inconsequential. The attempt to achieve linkages to the larger unit from this side can be seen, again, in the *Kēraḷōlpatti*. One of its recensions from Kōlattunāḍ in the northern part of Kerala has a pretentious beginning, with a claim to narrate *Jambudvīpōlpatti* in *bhāṣā* (Malayalam).[38] Kerala is clearly situated within the geographical horizon familiar to the *Purāṇic* world; and its 'origin', naturally, is part of the origin of *Jambudvīpa*. This attempt in a narrative that seeks to constitute Kerala is extremely significant. But, it goes beyond such technical texts. One of the medieval *Maṇiparavāḷam* texts, the *Candrōtsavam,* has a verse which seeks to participate in this tradition and includes Kerala within this geographical locus. It says that there are eight other *khaṇḍa*s around and that the southern one of *Bhārata* is more charming than them; even in it, the Land of the Cēramāns [is] like the auspicious mark on the forehead of the Goddess of Prosperity and God of Love.[39] By the time we come to Pūntanam Nampūtiri, a poet who wrote in simple Malayalam in the seventeenth century, we see this Purāṇic geography accepted without even an attempt to bring in any distinction for Kerala within *Bhārata*. He is happy that he was just living in *Bhārata* and that it was in the present age that he was doing so.[40]

The idea of *Bhārata* or *Bhāratavarṣa*, which evolved through centuries in the expressions of high culture in India, particularly in the period of and after the Guptas, was something which Kerala came to know about in the age of the Cēramān *Perumāḷ*s. To begin with, Tamiḻakam, of which present-day Kerala was an inseparable part, did not have much consciousness of this idea. The copious literature in Tamil, although containing stray influences of the Vedic-Śastraic-Purāṇic elements,[41] does not participate in this tradition at all. It was only in the age of transition from the early historical to the early medieval that such an idea itself makes its appearance in south India, perhaps through what Pollock has described as the 'Sanskrit Cosmopolis'. However, in spite of the knowledge of this idea of Bhārata, there is nothing in the records to show that Kerala sought affiliation to it even at this stage. What it did at this stage was to wean itself away from the old affiliation to Tamiḻakam. Gradually, however, Kerala began to participate in the common traditions of this larger unit of Bhārata as an affiliate. The post-Perumāḷ era in Kerala thus found itself as an integral part of *Bhāratavarṣa*, and it was the Brāhmaṇical agency which achieved it. The land created by Paraśurāma was already part of the land of Bharata.

NOTES AND REFERENCES

1. N. Subramanian, *Pre-Pallavan Tamil Index* (Madras, 1990), s.v., Chērakulam, Chēramān, several individual Chēramāns (20 entries), Chēral, Chēralan, Chēralādan, Chēran, pp. 392–5.
2. R.C. Majumdar, ed., *Classical Accounts of India* (Calcutta, 1960), pp. 305, 312, 339, 365, 376 and 381.
3. *Mitrāṇi mātṛdattādyāḥ kēraḷeṣu dvijōttamāḥ.*' Daṇḍin, *Avantisundarīkathāsāra,* quoted in Ulloor S. Parameswara Iyer, *Kēraḷasāhityacaritram* vol. I (Trivandrum, 1967), pp. 103–4. Kalidāsa, in his *Raghuvamśa,* has an obscure reference to Kerala; so have others. They are, however, inconsequential.
4. There is the introduction of the play in the prologue of *Āścaryacūḍāmaṇi* where the actress says that a drama from the south is as much of an improbability as flowers from the sky or oil from sand!
5. M.G.S. Narayanan, *Perumals of Kerala: Political and Social Conditions of Kerala Under the Cera Perumals of Makotai (c.* AD *800–1124)* (Calicut, 1996), p. 213.
6. *Kēralakulacūḍāmaṇēḥ, mahōdayapuraparamēśvarasya śrīkulaśēkharavarmaṇaḥ...*', *Tapatīsamvaraṇam,* prologue. '*Kalamarāśipēśalakaidārika kēraḷādhināthasya kulaśēkharavarmaṇō...*' *Subadrādhanañjayam,* prologue.
7. *Kēraḷaviṣayam pālikkānāy mahitamahōdayanilayē maruvum nṛpasimhasya...*', *Anantapuravarṇanam.*
8. K. Kunjunni Raja, *The Contribution of Kerala to Sanskrit Literature* (Madras, 1980), p. 20, nn. 95–6.
9. '*kulaśēkharanāmnā kēraḷādhipēna*', *Vyaṅgyavyākhyā,* quoted by N.P. Unni, *Sanskrit Dramas of Kulaśēkhara: A Study* (Trivandrum, 1977), p. 24.
10. Kerala starts figuring in the lists of conquests made by the Cāḷukyas, Pallavas and Pāṇḍyas from this period on. Narayanan, *Perumals of Kerala,* chapter on 'Early Wars and Alliances'. Much of this is conventional and it is not very clear whether Kerala there stands for the lineage or the country. Other references are indefinite.
11. The history of the Cēra kingdom of Mahōdayapuram was reconstructed only in the second half of the twentieth century. The epigraphical sources were published in the late nineteenth and early twentieth centuries; but it was the work of Elamkulam P.N. Kunjan Pillai that was responsible for bringing out the outline of the history of that kingdom. Pillai wrote largely in Malayalam. For a summary of his more important articles in English, P.N.K. Pillai, *Studies in Kerala History* (Kottayam, 1969). Improving upon the work of Pillai, Narayanan wrote a somewhat exhaustive history of this kingdom, *Perumals of Kerala.*
12. This lineage of the Cēras is celebrated in several early Tamil songs, the *Patiṟṟuppattu* being devoted exclusively to them. A few 'cave label'

inscriptions from Pugaliyur near Karur mention the names of some of these chiefs. Works like K.G. Sesha Aiyar, *Chera Kings of the Sangam Period* (London, 1937), and S. Krishnaswami Aiyangar, *Sēran Vañji* (Madras, 1912), deal with the 'political history' of this early Tamil 'kingdom'. It had its 'capital' in the interior, in the Tirucchirappalli district and it may have covered also regions on the west coast. It is important to remember that the Cēra kingdom of Mahōdayapuram has to be distinguished from this earlier chiefdom.

13. This is not to suggest that the Cēra kingdom of Mahōdayapuram represented a uniform structure with complete political control over the entire territory of Kerala from Kasaragod to Thiruvananthapuram. An earlier fashion of historiography represented by P.N.K. Pillai, *Studies*, had believed that this 'Second Cēra Empire', or 'Kulaśēkhara Empire' was a highly centralized polity. However, Narayanan, *Perumals of Kerala*, offered a major corrective to this. In fact, Narayanan has recently taken a position on the other extreme that the Cēra Perumāḷ had only a ritual sovereignty and the actual political power rested with 'a bold and visible brahman oligarchy' which was only 'thinly disguised as a monarchy to satisfy the sentiments of the lawgivers of India'. Narayanan, 'The State in the Era of the Cēramān Perumāḷs of Kerala', in R. Champakalakshmi, Kesavan Veluthat, and T.R. Venugopalan, eds, *State and Society in Premodern South India* (Thrissur, 2002), pp. 111–19. While we cannot go all the way with this formulation, Pillai's model of a highly centralized empire is not acceptable either. For our own understanding, see Chapter 9 above.
14. The political importance of the use of a uniform script and language has not been adequately recognized at least in the context of the history of Kerala. Script, unless used for purposes of trade, can be one of those engines used by a political agency to impose its authority over vast areas in pre-modern contexts where the use of literacy for purposes of communication was limited.
15. The Brāhmaṇical corporations of Kerala had a pivotal role in the power structure of the Cēra kingdom. This was adequately appreciated only in the work of Narayanan, *Perumals of Kerala*. The present writer has elaborated on this. Kesavan Veluthat, *Brahman Settlements in Kerala: Historical Studies* (Calicut, 1978), particularly, pp. 52–67. For a slightly different perception, Raghava Varier and Rajan Gurukkal, *Kēraḷacaritram* (Sukapuram, 1989).
16. For a discussion, Veluthat, 'Into the 'Medieval'—and Out of It: Early South India in Transition', Presidential Address, Section II, Medieval Indian History, *Proceedings of Indian History Congress* (Bangalore, 1997), Chapter 1 above.
17. Ibid.
18. For the image of royalty in south India and how it was different from what obtained in an earlier period, Kesavan Veluthat, *The Political Structure of Early Medieval South India* (New Delhi, 1993), chapter

on the 'Image of Royalty'. The difference that the Cēra kingdom presented is discussed there. See also Narayanan, *Perumals of Kerala*, chapter on 'Nature of Monarchy'.

19. *Akanāṉūṟu*, 220. For an analysis, Veluthat, *Brahman Settlements*, pp. 12–20.
20. This transition could be located between the third–fourth and seventh–eighth centuries of the Christian era. Veluthat, 'Into the 'Medieval'.
21. For a study of the Paraśurāma tradition of the Brāhmaṇas of the west coast of India, B.A. Saletore, *Ancient Karnataka*, vol. I, *History of Tuluva* (Poona, 1936). For a recent study, Pradeep Kant Chaudhury, 'The Cult of Parashuram: A Study in the Making of an Avatara', unpublished PhD Thesis (Delhi University, 2001).
22. They are called *anācāras* not because they were 'forbidden practices'. *Anyatrācaraṇābhāvād anācāra itiritaḥ*. A list of sixty-four of them is given in the law-book of Kerala Brāhmaṇas attributed to Śaṅkarācārya. For the list, William Logan, *Malabar*, vol. I (Madras, 1886), pp. 156–7.
23. Joan P. Mencher, 'Kerala and Madras: A Comparative Study of Ecology and Social Structure', *Ethnology*, University of Pittsburg, Pennsylvania, vol. V, part II, pp. 135–71.
24. '*Sarvakṣatravadhavratapranayinā rāmēṇa yannirmitam rāṣṭram śiṣṭajanābhirāmam atulam...*, *South Indian Inscriptions* (*SII*), vol. III, p. 398.
25. The date of this text is a matter of debate among historians; nor is there agreement regarding its validity as a 'source' of history. For a discussion, and a plea to look at it as an expression of the historical consciousness rather than as a source of history, Kesavan Veluthat, 'The *Kēraḷōlpatti* as History: A Note on the Pre-Colonial Traditions of Historiography', Chapter 6 above.
26. Early epigraphists and scholars of language who read the inscriptions took them for Tamil records and edited them in the Tamil script in the pages of *SII*, *Travancore Archaeological Series* (*TAS*) and similar publications. Most of the early scholars who edited and took up a linguistic study of these records were Tamil Brāhmaṇas (K.V. Subrahmaya Aiyar, A.S. Ramanatha Aiyar, L.V. Ramaswami Aiyar, Ulloor S. Parameswara Aiyar and A.C. Sekhar). Even A.R. Rajarajavarma was under the heavy influence of this Tamil tradition. They, naturally, failed to appreciate the 'Malayalamness' of these inscriptions. Narayanan recognized it in his *Index to Cēra Inscriptions*, a companion volume to his PhD thesis on 'The Political and Social conditions of Kerala under the Kulaśēkhara Empire' submitted to the University of Kerala, Trivandrum, 1972. The text of the thesis is available in print, although this extremely useful *Index...* is not yet published. For an argument in favour of Malayalam, see Kesavan Veluthat, 'Epigraphy in the Historiography of Kerala in K.K.N. Kurup, ed., *New Dimensions in South Indian History: Essays in Honour of M.R. Raghava Varier* (Calicut, 1996), Chapter 7 above.

27. Pāliyam Plates of Vikramāditya Varaguna. *TAS*, vol. I. part XII, pp.187–93.
28. Sheldon Pollock, 'The Cosmopolitan Vernacular', *The Journal of Asian Studies*, vol. 57, no. I, February 1998, pp. 6–37.
29. The *Vyaṅgyavyākhyā* commentaries mentioned above acknowledge this. See also, Raja, *The Contribution*, p. 15; Unni, *Sanskrit Dramas*, pp. 33–8.
30. For a detailed discussion, Kesavan Veluthat, 'Further Expansion of Agrarian Society: A Political Forms', in P.J. Cherian, ed. *Perspectives on Kerala History: The Second Millennium* (Trivandrum, 1999), pp. 62–78; Veluthat, 'Medieval Kerala: State and Society', Chapter 11 above.
31. *Epigraphia Indica*, vol. IV. pp. 290–7.
32. '*Sakalaphalasamṛddhyai kēraḷānām pratāpam / periya paraśurāmasyājñayā yatra nityam // kanivoṭu maḻa kālam pārttupārttarbhakānām / janani mulakoṭuppānennapōlē varunnū*' // *Candrotsavam*, I, p. 51.
33. '*Brahmakṣatram janapadamatha sphītamadhyakṣayēthāh darpādarśam dṛḍhataramṛṣēr jāmadagnyasya bāhvōḥ / yam mēdinyām ruciramaricōttālatāmbūlavallī-vēllatkērakramukanikarān kēraḷānudgṛṇanti*' // *Śukasandēśa*, Part I, p. 34.
34. Varier, '*Līlātialakatthinṟe rāṣṭrīyam*', in *Mathrubhūmi Weekly*, vol. 71, no. 43, pp. 23–8 reproduced in Varier, *Vāyanayuṭe Vaḻikaḷ* (Thrissur, 1998), pp. 9–19. Varier takes the formation of the identity of Kerala to the post-*Perumāḷ* era after the twelfth century, which we do not accept here. So also he does not appreciate the heavily upper caste character of this identity. It is interesting to see how Varier's arguments are used by Rich Freeman, 'Rubies and Coral: The Lapidary Crafting of Language in Kerala', *The Journal of Asian Studies*, vol. 57, no. I, February 1998, pp. 38–65.
35. *Maṇipravāḷam* did exist in the Tamil country, too; but it has to be distinguished from what developed in the Malayalam-speaking region. For a discussion of the character of Maṇipravāḷam in Kerala, K. Ramachandran Nair, *Early Maṇipravāḷam: A Study* (Trivandrum, 1978). For a discussion of *Līlātilakam*, K.N. Ezhuthachan, *The History of Grammatical Theories in Malayalam*, vol. I (Trivandrum, 1975), pp. 61–129.
36. Śrinātha, *Śrībhīmēśvarapurāṇamu*, vol. I, 72, 73. Quoted in Velcheru Narayana Rao, David Shulman and Sanjay Subrahmanyam, *Textures of Time: Writing History in South India 1600–1800* (Delhi, 2001), p. 20.
37. Muzaffar Ali, *The Geography of the Puranas*, second edition (New Delhi, 1973), p. 153.
38. Varier, ed., *Kerlolpatti Granthavari: The Kolattunad Traditions* (Calicut University, 1984), pp. 54–5. The document describes itself as '*Jambudvīpōlpatti*'.

39. '*Parabhṛtamoḻi cuṟṟum maṟṟu khaṇḍaṅṅaḷeṭṭuṇṭatilumadhikahṛdyam dakṣiṇam bhāratākhyam / vaḷarnila malarmātinnaṅgajannum trilōkī ceṟutoṭukuṟipōle cēramānnāḍu yasmin //*', *Candrōtsavam*, I, 46.
40. '*Lavaṇāmbudhi madhyē viḷaṅṅunna / jambudvīporu yōjana lakṣavum // ēḻu dvīpukaḷiṅṅaneyuḷḷatil uttamam i sthalam ennu vāḻttunnu // ... itil onpatu khaṇḍaṅṅaḷ uṇṭallō / atil uttamam bhāratabhūtalam // ...*' Pūntānam, *Jñānappāna,* in Manoj Kurur, ed., *Añcaṭi, Jñānappāna, Ōṇappāṭṭu* (Changanasseri, 1996), p. 96.
41. M.G.S. Narayanan, 'The Vedic, Puranic, Sastric Elements in Tamil Sangam Society and Culture', *Proceedings of the Indian History Congress* (Aligarh, 1975).

Part III

In the Neighbourhood: Early Medieval Karnataka

14

Vēḷevāḷi in Karnataka*

Institutions typical of a particular socio-political formation in a country may take local expressions, which the student of regional history is likely to mistake for things unique to the region he studies. This would lead to a tendency to glorify the region, the historical character of the institution itself being the first casuality there. Again, the fact of the region being part of a larger whole, a greater civilization, is often lost sight of in such studies. On the other hand, analysis of evidence in relation to such institutions in a region, made in the light of comparable institutions obtaining in other parts of the larger unit, can provide insight into the nature and significance of the institutions in a better way. Moreover, such a study will clarify the situation on both the sides, for what is inadequately represented in the documents from the one region may be brought out with clarity in those from the other. In the end, such exercises will help in clarifying the total picture of the whole unit.

In the present essay, we propose to take up an analysis of the institution of *vēḷevāḷi* figuring in documents from Karnataka during the period after the eighth century AD. This institution involved individual soldiers attached to chiefs taking oath of unswerving loyalty to them even in death. Historians and scholars of literature have commented on this in detail. For them it represented the highest form of sacrifice fired by sentiments of altruism. In their enthusiasm to praise the 'heroes' who laid down their lives for their masters, not only did they miss the most important aspect of personal dependence pushed to extremes characteristic of the whole of south India in this period,

* First published as 'The Nature and Significance of the Institution of *Vēḷavāḷi* in Karnataka in Historical Prespective (AD 800–1300)', *Proceedings of the Indian History Congress* (Calcutta, 1989), pp. 151–9.

but they also failed to place this institution within the context of other aspects of the social formation, with the result that the whole thing looks like an incongruity, a monstrosity, defying explanation.

Chidanandamurthy has made a cultural study of Kannada inscriptions in a competent way.[1] Speaking about the institution of *Vēḷevāḷi*, significantly in the chapter on 'Different Forms of Self Sacrifice', he says: 'The institution of *Vēḷevāḷi* is the ultimate in gratitude....'[2] Similarly, another eminent Kannada scholar, M.M. Kalburgi, discusses it as a form of self-sacrifice, again, significantly, in his book on the 'Memorials of Self-mortification, Sacrifice and Hero's Death'.[3] R. Sesha Sastri discusses it in his book on the 'Hero Stones of Karnataka'.[4] Even professional historians such as M.V. Krishna Rao[5] and K.S. Shivanna are interested in the idealism involved in their self-sacrifice, the latter going to the extent of describing the suicide of the soldiers as an 'altruistic suicide' after Emile Durkheim.[6] All of them have, surprisingly, failed to appreciate the significance of the institution within the context of the emerging socio-economic formation and the form that state took within that formation. To be sure, both Krishna Rao and Shivanna use the expression 'feudal' in connection with this institution;[7] but in the absence of the methodological rigour with which the totality of the historical situation is analysed within a feudal framework, this adjective is rendered meaningless in their writings.

I

The institution of *vēḷevāḷi* occurs in Kannada inscriptions from the beginning of the ninth century in a big way. This involved loyal servants, generally soldiers, laying down their lives on the occasion of the death of their masters. These servants were known as *vēḷevaḍica*s. They took an oath of unswerving loyalty to their masters and, when the latter died, they followed them in death. This act is known as *vēḷe*. Many records speak of their dedication to their masters and their courage even at the face of death. In fact, most of the information we have on the institution is from records commemorating the death of such *vēḷevaḍica*s, sometimes also registering the grant of land for their or their dependents' maintenance. A damaged inscription of AD 864 celebrates a person who laid down his life, but it is not clear if the reference is actually to a *vēḷevāḷi*.[8] The Mevundi inscription of

AD 865 is the earliest record making a clear reference to the institution of *vēḷevāḷi*.[9] The record says that a *vēḷevaḍica*, Reṭṭeyaṇṇa by name, took the king for his real parents and that he took an oath to die if his master died. His master died while he was away and he could see only his master's body burning in the funeral pyre. He immediately cut his head off. A few inscriptions of about AD 900 reveal an interesting situation. A soldier by name Nagattara dies in war.[10] Another record speaks of the death of Pegura who is described as his *manemaga* ('son of the household').[11] Probably this is typical of the institution of *vēḷevāḷi*. In another record is the fact of Nagattara's daughter, Koṇḍabbe, dying taking the duty of *vēḷe*.[12] Yet another record speaks of Nagattara's daughter taking to *saṃnyāsa* (renunciation) and eventually to death.[13] Finally, there is also the statement that Nagattara's son is invested with Nagattara's titles by the king.

There is the eulogy of a person called Śambhu who took *vēḷe* to the Cāḷukyan king in a record of about AD 900.[14] He, who entered fire with a smiling face, is described as unequalled by the *vēḷevaḍicas* of the past, present and future. A record of about AD 915 speaks of *Babiamma* who threw himself into fire when Permānaḍigaḷ, the Ganga king, died.[15] Another record speaks of Rācceya who entered the fire taking *vēḷe* probably to the same ruler.[16] Among the records related to this institution, perhaps a Doddahundi inscription is the most famous. It speaks of Aragayya, who is described as the *manemaga* of the Ganga king Permānaḍigaḷ, becoming *kīḻguṇṭe* on the death of his master.[17] On the stone where the record is inscribed is represented the lord lying dead on his cot and Aragayya killing himself with a dagger. Another record of AD 930 speaks of a *vēḷevaḍica* who is also stated to have become *kīḻguṇṭe*.[18] In AD 988, Muydamma, a soldier, is said to have become *kīḻguṇṭe* on the death of Eraigangayya.[19] There are many more records which speak of similar instances.[20]

There is an interesting record of AD 1096 where it is stated that a soldier, Eraiyamma, died on the death of his master, Vīradēva, son of the Santara chief, after giving away to his own children the three *sivane* of land which the Santara chief had given him.[21] This is a clear instance of the service of the *vēḷevāḷis* being remunerated in terms of land. There are other indications which we shall take up below.

II

If the instances we saw so far are related to *vēḷevāḷi*s laying down their lives on the death of their patron kings, there are also instances where the patrons were queens or other aristocratic ladies. Two couples take *vēḷe* on the death of the queen Padmaladēvi in AD 1077.[22] In the record that follows, there is the statement of Uttamaśōḷa Seṭṭi cutting the head of a woman, perhaps his wife, and then his own head.[23] Perhaps this record is related to the former, one of the couples there. When Ēcaladēvi, the daughter of Udayādityarasa, died, Madeya became *vēḷevāḷi* and died.[24] A record of AD 1150 speaks of Cāka Gauḍa entering heaven as both a *jōḷavāḷi* and a *vēḷevāḷi* in favour of Padmaladēvi, the queen of Narasiṅgadēva.[25]

There is a very interesting record of AD 1185 where there is a reference to the oath of allegiance and also the representation of the ceremony of commendation.[26] It speaks of Boppaṇṇa who died on the death of Laccaladēvi, the 'queen' of Mahāmaṇḍalēśvara Sōhadēva 'following the earlier oath (*bhāṣe*)'. The hero stone on which the record is inscribed has, on the lower panel, Boppaṇṇa receiving a piece of cloth from Laccaladevi in great veneration. Behind him are four men with folded hands. In the panel above are celestial damsels escorting him to Kailāsa.[27]

It was usually either entering fire or cutting oneself that the *vēḷevāḷi*s died. But in a record of AD 1070 there is the statement of a strange kind of self-mortification. When Santaradēva went to heaven, a certain Puravaleya Gāvuṇḍa peeled off the skin from his back and, suffering the pain for three days, died.[28] This kind of self-torture is alluded to by Basavaṇṇa in one of his *vacana*s.[29]

Our records give us to believe that once the oath of *vēḷevāḷi* was taken, that was ruthlessly followed. A couple of records, however, point to the other direction. There is an indirect suggestion to this effect in a Haḷebīḍ Inscription.[30] An inscription from Poḷali speaks of the punishment that a certain Candaya had received for abrogating the oath of *vēḷevāḷi*.[31] Although recorded instances of this kind are few and far between, it is possible that many more such cases were there. In a conflict between the instinct of self-preservation and obligations of a socio-political nature, it is only natural that the former gets the upper hand. But the occasion to record such instances will be very rare. What is visible in the records may be the narrow tip of the submerged iceberg.

III

By the time we come to the age of the Hoysaḷas, such loyal servants who laid down their lives came to be known as *garuḍas*, which expression is used in Hoysaḷa records to denote the *vēḷevāḷis*. The implication is perhaps that the servant stood to his master in the same way that Garuḍa did to Viṣṇu. Garuḍa, it will be remembered, was renowned for his bravery as well as his dedication to his master Viṣṇu. Hence there could be no better ideal for loyalty and allegiance. To begin with, *garuḍa* signified these qualities. For instance, in a record of AD 1040, a certain Eraiyammarasa, described as the *sāmanta* of Jagadēkamalla, is referred to as '*siṅgana garuḍam*'.[32] Another record speaks of a certain Ghatiyammarasa as '*sāmanta garuḍam*',[33] and in yet another record, a certain *sāmanta* Laksmanarasa is spoken of as '*sangrāma garuḍam*'.[34] A record of AD 1083 describes Ācugidēva as a *garuḍa* to serpents that are his enemies.[35] *Mahāsāmanta* Udayāditya is described as No̱lamba's *garuḍa*.[36] Another record, dated AD 1125, clearly states that Ecana *Daṇḍanāyaka* stood to his master in loyalty in the same way as Garuḍa stood to Viṣṇu.[37] Thus, the expression *garuḍa* which, to begin with, denoted bravery, loyalty, etc., came, by the time of the Hoysaḷas, to stand for those who laid down their lives following the death of their masters.

The practice of *garuḍas* committing suicide on the death of their masters reached its zenith in the thirteenth century. A couple of records are significant in this context. One of them, referring to Kuvaralakṣma, is very famous and has been quoted too often by scholars[38]. It speaks of the oath (*bhāṣe*) taken by the *garuḍa*, his ritual investiture, the practice of the *garuḍa*'s wife also being bound by the *bhāṣe*, etc. What is more significant is the statement that the 'one thousand heroes' (*ondu sāvira vīraru*) too died with him when his master Vīra Ballāḷa died. These 'heroes' are known as *leṅkas*. In fact, there are a number of other records which speaks of *leṅkas*. A record of AD 1257[39] and another of AD 1292,[40] speak of several *leṅkas* and *leṅkis* redeeming their oath (*bāseyana puraisi*) by laying down their lives on the death of their masters, both Hoysaḷa kings. It is interesting that on top of the pillars on which these records are engraved, Garuḍa is represented in sculpture. In the former record, there is the explicit statement that the *leṅkas* had been hereditary (*anvayāgata leṅkavāḷi*). Since the record speaking about the suicide of Kuvaralakṣma uses the expression *vēḷe*, it is presumed that both *leṅkavāḷi* and *vēḷevāḷi* are in effect the same.

There is a Kannada proverb, which was popular in north Karnataka till recently and which is attested in a fourteenth-century inscription, showing that the *leṅka*s are not to be killed.[41] The thirteenth-century poet Janna speaks of *leṅka*s offering their heads as sacrifice.[42]

In fact, the *leṅka*s figure prominently as soldiers in Kannada inscriptions.[43] Chidanandamurthy takes them for mercenary soldiers. But he has himself presented formidable evidence of their being hereditary soldiers attached to chiefs and their being remunerated by means of land as service tenure. There is an inscription which speaks of one thousand *leṅka*s attached to Nanhi Noḻamba Pallava *Permānaḍigaḷ*, himself a 'feudatory' of Āhavamalla.[44] They had separate titles and separate standards. They are described as looking after six villages as *aṇugajīvita*. Scholars have explained this as land which the king or his feudatory was pleased to grant as a mark of his affection to the donee.[45] But, if one looks at contemporary Tamil records, this can be clearly seen as a military service tenure.[46] There, *aṇukkar* are the king's companions. In fact, another Kannada inscription of AD 973 speaks of Tailapa, a Rāṣṭrakūṭa feudatory, as enjoying Tardapāḍi one thousand as *aṇugajīvita*.[47] The association of both these records as well as that of Kuvaralakṣma with the number one thousand is significant, especially in view of the fact of a similar situation in contemporary Kerala. Another Rāṣṭrakūṭa feudatory, Mārasimha *Permānaḍigaḷ*, is described as enjoying several *nāḍu*s as *aṇugajīvita*.[48] There are other statements of the *leṅka*s receiving land as service tenure. A certain Benayya, a *leṅka*, is stated to be collecting tolls from different places.[49] Another record describes a *leṅka* as protecting boundaries.[50] There are several records which identify the *vēḷevāḷi*s, *garuḍa*s and, *leṅka*s as *gāvuḍa*s. The present writer has shown elsewhere that the *gāvuḍa*s were landed magnates, who were identified and co-opted by the state in early medieval Karnataka into its service.[51]

IV

The above examination brings out several important facts about the institution of *vēḷevāḷi*. They could be enumerated as follows:

(a) *Vēḷevaḍica*s, *garuḍa*s and *leṅka*s were different names for a band of trusted soldiers gathered around the person of the king or some other political chief and bound to him by an oath of allegiance to follow him even in death.

(b) They were generally organized in multiples of hundred.

(c) They hailed from landed aristocracy and their services were remunerated in land assigned as service tenure.

(d) They were assigned the duty of protection of boundaries.

Details available from a study of the institution of *tuḷilāḷgal* made by S. Settar[52] would suggest that they too could be identified with the *vēḷevaḍicas*, bringing out that this institution figured most prominently in the epigraphic and literary records of Karnataka from the ninth century onwards, up to the close of the thirteenth century.

V

Details of this institution strike us with its close resemblance with the institution of *vēḷaikkārar* in Tamil records. 'The *vēḷaikkārar* were personal bodyguards of a chieftain who banded themselves to protect their master both in the battlefield and outside it, and to die along with him in case of his death'.[53] Professor Mahalingam rightly surmised that to the same group belonged the *Tennavan Āpattudavigaḷ* figuring in Pāṇḍyan records, who were 'helpers of the Pāṇḍya (king) in times of distress'.[54] They are referred to in Cōḻa records as *tirumeykāppār*.[55] Abu Zaid describes such bodyguards gathered around the person of the king as his 'Companions of Honour'[56] and Macro Polo finds in these 'Barons' the 'King's Trusty lieges'.[57] The *balaudjers* referred to in the Arab *Book of Marvels of India*[58] correspond to them in every detail and one is tempted to identify the term *balaudjer* as the corruption of Kannada *vēḷevaḍicar*.

In a couple of papers on the history of Kerala, M.G.S. Narayanan has brought out the nature of certain 'Hundred' groups attached to the local chiefs and a 'Thousand' attached to the Cēra king of Mahōdayapuram.[59] He has demonstrated that they formed the trusted body-guards of the chiefs and the king respectively. They were also entrusted the duty of protecting boundaries of eleemosynary villages, as indeed were the *vēḷaikkārar* in the Tamil country and the *leṅkas* in Karnataka.

VI

All this would show an interesting pattern all over south India in the period after ninth century AD. Interestingly, every detail of this pattern bears resemblance to the description of what Marc Bloch calls 'the household warriors' in the context of feudal Europe.[60] One is tempted to quote him at some length:

> Amidst the troubles of the Merovingian epoch, the employment of such armed followings became more necessary than ever. The king had his guard ... His principal subjects, whether Frankish or Roman by origin, also had their armed followers ... No doubt such service admitted of varying degrees of prestige and reward. It is none the less significant that in the seventh century the same form of document could be used indifferently for the donation of 'a small property' in favour of a slave or of a *gasindus*.
>
> In the last-mentioned term, we recognize the old name of the German war-companion ... Progressively, it yielded place to the indigenous word 'vassal' (*vassus*, *vassallus*) which was to have a splendid future ... We must beware of deducing from its incorporation in the feudal vocabulary some sort of distant ancestry of military vassalage ... The history of this word ... faithfully reflects the rise of the institution itself ... The ties which bound these war-companions to their chief represented one of those contracts of fidelity ... The term which designated the royal guard is extremely significant: *trustis*, that is to say fealty. The new recruit enrolled in this body swore to be faithful; the king in return undertook to 'bear him succour'.[61]

In the end, we may conclude with another quotation from Marc Bloch himself:

> 'Feudalism' he [Voltaire] wrote, 'is not an event; it is a very old form which, with differences in working, subsists in three-quarters of our hemisphere'. Modern scholarship has in general rallied to the side of Voltaire ....[62] It is by no means impossible that societies different from our own have passed through a phase closely resembling that which has just been defined ... Have other societies also passed through it? It is for future works to provide the answers.[63]

Does our study provide an answer at least to one major aspect of Bloch's question?

NOTES AND REFERENCES

1. M. Chidanandamurthy, *Kannaḍa Śāsanagaḷa Sāṁskṛtika Adhyayana AD 450–1150* (Mysore, 1979).
2. Ibid., p. 305.
3. M.M. Kalburgi, *Samādhi-Balidāna-Vīramaraṇa Smārakagāḷu* (Bangalore, 1982).

4. R. Shesha Sastry, *Karṇātakada Vīragallugaḷu* (Bangalore, 1982).
5. M.V. Krishna Rao, *The Gangas of Talkad* (Madras, 1936), p. 170.
6. K.S. Shivanna, A *Critique of Hoysala Polity* (Mysore, 1988), pp. 107–16.
7. Krishna Rao, *The Gangas*, Shivanṇa, *loc. cit.*
8. *Bombay-Karnatak Inscriptions* (hereafter *BKI*), vol. I, no. 10.
9. Ibid.,vol. I, no. 11.
10. *Epigraphia Carnatica* (hereafter *EC*), vol. IX, fn. 91.
11. Ibid., fn. 87.
12. Ibid., fn. 88.
13. Ibid., fn. 94.
14. *Indian Antiquary* (hereafter *IA*), vol. XX, p. 69.
15. *EC*, Ag. vol. V, Ag. 27.
16. Ibid., Ag. 5.
17. *EC*, vol. III, TN. To become *Kīḷguṇṭe* means to die as a *vēḷevāḷi.* Chidanandamurthy, *Kannada Sasanagala*, p. 306.
18. *EC*, Dg. 119.
19. *South Indian Inscriptions* (hereafter *SII*) vol. IX, no. i, p. 40.
20. Ibid., no. 35; *Mysore Archaeological Reports* (hereafter *MAR*), *MAR* (1939), p. 176; *MAR* (1943), p. 60; *SII*, vol. VII, p. 258; *MAR*, (1932), p. 190; *EC*, vol. VII, HI, 47 etc. See also Chidanandamurthy, *Kannaḍa Śāsanagaḷa* and Kalburgi, *Samādhi-Balidāna.*
21. *EC*, vol. VIII Sa. 80.
22. *EC*, vol. IX, Cg. 43.
23. Ibid., Cg. 44.
24. Ibid., Vi, Cm. 70.
25. *MAR* (1936), p. 88.
26. *EC*, vol. VII, Sk. 249.
27. *EC*, vol. VII, Introduction and plate facing p. 9.
28. *EC*, vol. VII, Sk. 62.
29. *Sadsthaladavacanagalu*, p. 28.
30. *EC*, vol. V, Be. ur, 112.
31. *Tuḷunāḍina Śāsanagāḷu*, vol. I. no. 30, Polali Ammunje.
32. *IA*, vol. XIX, p. 164.
33. *SII*, vol. IX, part i, p. 115. AD 1054.
34. *BKI*, vol. I, part i, p. 113. AD 1074.
35. Ibid., vol. I, part ii, no. 129.
36. *EC*, xi, Cd., 34.
37. *EC*, vol. IV, Ng. 28.
38. *EC*, vol. V, Bl. 112. AD 1220.
39. *EC*, vol. IV, Kr. 9.
40. Ibid.
41. For the proverb, Chidanandamurthy, *Kannaḍa Śāsanagaḷa*, p. 268, n. 187(a). For the inscription, *SII*, vol. XV, no. 657.
42. *Anantanātha Purāṇa*, 11.74; 12.11.
43. Chidanandamurthy, *Kannaḍa Śāsanagaḷa*, p. 268.

44. *SII*, vol. IX, i, p. 101. AD 1045.
45. Chidanandamurthy, *Kannaḍa Śāsanagaḷa*, p. 340.
46. Kesavan Veluthat, *The Political Structure of Early Medieval South India* (Delhi, 1993), chapter on 'Aspects of Administration'.
47. *BKI*, vol. I, i, p. 40.
48. Ibid., p. 43, AD 970.
49. Ibid., p. 50, AD 1066.
50. *SII*, vol. IX, i, p. 130, AD c. 1005.
51. Veluthat, 'Landed Magnates as State Agents: The *Gavuda*s under the Hoysaḷas in Karnataka', *Proceedings of the Indian History Congress* (Gorakhpur, 1989), chapter 15 below.
52. S. Settar, 'Tulilalgal', *Sadhane*, vol. IX, no. 3, July–September, 1980 (Bangalore University).
53. T.V. Mahalingam, *South Indian Polity*, 2nd edn (Madras, 1967), p. 66 and fn. 210, pp. 266–7.
54. Ibid., p. 267.
55. Ibid., p. 65.
56. Quoted, Ibid.
57. Quoted, Ibid.
58. Quoted in M.G S. Narayanan, *Reinterpretations in South Indian History* (Trivandrum, 1977), pp. 103–4.
59. Ibid.; Narayanan, 'The Hundred Groups and the Rise of Nayar Militia in Kerala', *PIHC*. Burdwan, 1983. See also K.P. Ammukutty, 'The Military System of Kerala (1000 AD to c. 1600 AD)', unpublished MPhil Dissertation (Calicut University), 1990. An inscription from Kovur in the Cannanore district in Kerala, deciphered by M.G.S. Narayanan and the present writer, speaks of 'Kōlattu Āyiravar', that is, The Thousand of Kōlam under whose protection the land of the temple was placed.
60. Marc Bloch, *Feudal Society*, translated from the French by L.A. Manyon (London, 1982), vol. I, pp. 151–6. In fact, the expression *manemaga* found in the Kannada records is striking in the context of household warriors.
61. Ibid., pp. 155–6.
62. Ibid., vol. II, p. 41.
63. Ibid., p. 447.

15

Landed Magnates as State Agents*

The present article reports the results of a preliminary enquiry into certain aspects of the socio-political organization in early medieval Karnataka, taking up a few inscriptions of the Hoysaḷas as a case study. It underlines the need for taking a fresh look at the inscriptional material from Karnataka, placing the information within the context of the pattern of socio-political evolution in early medieval south India, and explaining it within the perspective of historical development in the Indian subcontinent in a general way. In spite of the greater success of conceptual exercises in other parts of India, historiography in Karnataka has largely remained at the same conventional level. The theoretical refinement that has been brought to bear upon historical understanding in other parts of south India has not affected it to any considerable extent; nor has any advanced tools of research been developed or made use of in this part of the country. The present study is only in the form of suggesting the need for a reorientation in the historical writing of ancient and early medieval Karnataka. For the purpose of this study we have taken up references to the *gāvuḍa*s or *gāvuṇḍa*s or *gāuḍa*s figuring in Kannada inscriptions, with special reference to the period of the Hoysaḷas.

The *gāvuḍa*s are met with in inscriptions dealing with affairs of a locality such as regulating the services in a temple, transacting landed property at the village level, construction and upkeep of irrigation works, assessment and collection or remission of taxes, etc. Epigraphists and historians, ever since these inscriptions were deciphered and subjected to historical study, have taken *gāvuḍa*s to

* First published as 'Landed Magnates as State Agents: The Gāvuḍas Under the Hoysaḷas in Karnataka', *Proceedings of the Indian History Congress* (Gorakhpur, 1990), pp. 322–8.

mean 'a village headman'.[1] He is identified always as 'an officer' of the state, functioning at the village level. He was the 'chief executive' of the village assembly.[2] However, there is some lack of clarity as to whether he was exclusively an officer of the 'central' government placed at the village level or whether he was an officer recruited and maintained by the villages themselves, where very vital and autonomous bodies looked after the 'administration'. It is also not clear in these writings as to what exactly the source of his authority was.

The problem becomes slightly more complex when we find more than one such 'headman' in the same village, the number going up to as many as 106 in one record.[3] Those figuring in fewer numbers have been sought to be explained away in the following ways:

(a) This was probably due to the necessity of accommodating the claims of the numerous branches of the original family. Usually, however, claims were adjusted by allotting the office to each branch by rotation,[4]
(b) Sometimes a number of hamlets were knit together into a single unit for administrative convenience, which was placed under a chief headman with headmen of the various hamlets of the group under him.[5]
(c) In a big town, they appear to have represented different parts of it. Thus in Liṅga (Lingusugur in Raichur district), there were separate headmen for its eastern and western parts.[6] In fact, historians have even gone to the extent of describing two of them, stated to be hailing from two separate streets or *kēris* as headmen of those streets.[7]

I

Unfortunately, these references to the *gāvuḍas* have not been examined within the context of their occurrence in the records; much less have the records themselves been placed in the geographical/ecological and chronological contexts of their provenance. We do not claim to have undertaken any such systematic examination either; but this is one way in which greater clarity can be achieved in interpreting inscriptional terms. Such limited enquiry as we have made, however, suggests an unmistakable connection between the *gāvuḍas* and agriculture. It is from records, mostly pertaining to transactions of land that we learn about them; they are almost exclusively holders of land known as *gāvuḍagoḍuge*,[8] and in inscriptions dealing with other sections such as the pastoral groups and artisanal and trading communities they are not generally met with. In fact, G.S. Dikshit has suggested that the expression is used also to mean 'farmers',[9] although he does not recognize, let alone reconcile, the contradiction involved in his positions.

The *gāvuḍas* are otherwise referred to as *ūroḍeya*.[10] In a Sanskrit inscription, there is the exact translation of this term.[11] In speaking about a certain Āditya, the record says that he was the lord (*Īśvara*) of the village of Catagrāma. The expressions *oḍeya* in Kannada and *īśvara* in Sanskrit indicate ownership, possession, etc., thereby suggesting that the *ūroḍeya* or *grāmēśvara* was the 'owner' or 'possessor' of the village. But when we come across too many 'owners' or 'possessors' in the same village, even this meaning would not be apt to describe the significance of the term and its implications. Moreover, absolute 'ownership' or proprietorship of whole villages by an individual would raise other problems for the nature of economy and society, violating the nature of our understanding of the history of India in this period.

In this connection, information available from the neighbouring region of the Tamil country, in the very period of our own study, comes in very useful as it illumines the dark areas and provides very clear insights. Such expressions as *ūr-uḍaiyān*, *ūr-kiḻavan*, and the like, figure in the inscriptions from the Tamil country in the period from the ninth-tenth century onwards. *Ūr-uḍaiyān* literally means, like *ūroḍeya* in Kannada, the 'owner' or 'possessor' of a village and *ūr-kiḻavan*, the village elder, which can be translated into Sanskrit as *grāmā-vṛddha*, the Prakrit form of which is *gāvuḍḍa* or *gāvuḍa*. It is possible, therefore, to derive *gāvuḍa* in Kannada inscriptions from Sanskrit *grāmā-vṛddha* although what has been suggested by earlier historians is derivation from *grāmakūṭa* on the basis of comparison with Marathi records.[12] *Grāmāvṛddhas* are frequently met with in Sanskrit records, literary and epigraphical.[13]

The comparability between the *ūroḍeya-gāvuḍa* and the *ūr-uḍaiyān-ūr-kiḻāvan* does not depend upon the derivation of a word which can be looked upon as dubious. It goes further to the similarity of their nature and functions in the two situations. Both of them figure as landowners; both of them are found prominently in connection with transactions related to landed property and other agricultural activities; both had a significant role in the matter of the assessment and collection of revenue in the locality. In fact, a closer comparative study of the two situations would clarify several of the obscure aspects on either side.

II

The information from the Tamil side is far richer and more systematic for the fabulously larger number of records from there and the rigorous computational analysis they have been subjected to. In a computerized concordance of personal names in the Cōḻa inscriptions, which takes up 9590 names, about 20 per cent of the population represented there bore names which a segment indicating possession of a place or a village, expressions such as *uḍaiyān*, *kiḻān*, *kiḻavan* etc., were preceded by the name of the village signifying possession.[14] Since there are more than one person who 'possesses' the same village, it has been shown that the expression should be taken to mean one who possessed some land in the village.[15] It cannot have been used to mean simply a resident of the village, for not all residents of the village bore such a segment in their names. A large number of instances support the inference that wherever such expressions indicating possession of a village occurs, it meant possession of land in a village.[16] To take just one case, a Kuḍumiyamalai inscription of AD 1232 records the sale of land by the *ūr* of Viśalūr, where the new owner was permitted to enjoy all privileges due to the holder of the title *kiḻavan*.[17] That the *uḍaiyān* title indicated landownership is proposed further by the fact that, of the 119 cases where names of the members of different *ūr* assemblies are known, more than 60 per cent bore a title indicating possession;[18] even in the case of the remaining 40 per cent, it is suggested that the *uḍaiyān* or related title is left out in order to avoid repetition when two or more *uḍaiyār* of the same village are mentioned in quick succession. That the assembly of *ūr* consisted of the chief landholders of the village is a fact accepted on all hands. The computational analysis of names with the *uḍaiyān* title has shown a tendency for this title to increase steadily as Chōḻa rule progresses in the Cōḻamaṇḍalam region.[19] This has been explained as pointing to a steady increase in the number of landowners, suggesting the deeper entrenchment of private property in land outside the brāhmaṇa settlements and also a greater utilization of land, a pattern which is brought out by independent evidence.

A similar title indicating ownership of land is *veḷān* which also points to the caste status of the bearer of the title. Closely related to this title was the significant title of *mūvēntavēḷān*. Another one of equal or slightly higher status was the pseudo-chiefly title of *araiyan*. The Cōḻa records show clearly that it was from among the holders of such titles indicating possession of land that functionaries of the state, known as 'bureaucracy' to an earlier generation of historians, were drawn.[20] The graded hierarchy among the landowners, going up along the scale of the *uḍaiyān-mūvēntavēḷān-araiyan* title holders in that order, is relevant for the offices also. For, the higher positions were held by those who were higher in this hierarchy. In fact, a couple of records state in so many words that petty officials could not take the titles of *veḷān* and *araiyan*.[21] When thus the close connection between these titles on the one side and state offices on the other is recognized, the fact of the landed magnates being identified and made use of by the state as its agents comes out with clarity.

There is no reason why the pattern was different in Karnataka. Nine representatives from five villages in Mysore Taluk, all of them *gāvuḍa*s, are stated to have met as the *Nāḍu* (*bandu-samartha-nāḍāgi*)[22] which clearly reminds us of five different *ūr*s meeting as the *nāḍu* of Vaḍa = ciṟavāyil = nāḍu as recorded in a Kīranūr inscription from the former Pudukottah State. In a similar way, wherever information on the functionaries is available, we see that many of them sported titles such as *gāvuḍa*, *āḷva*, etc., exactly in the same way as their counterparts in the neighbouring Tamil country did. The process of the identification of such a magnate, holding the title of *ūroḍeya* or *grāmēśvara*, by the Hoysaḷa ruler and his being enlisted as a functionary of the state, is clearly brought out in a recently published copper plate inscription.[23] The presence of a number of *gāvuḍa*s in the agrarian villages as members of the *ūr* assembly also would suggest the similarity of the pattern on either side. Dikshit has identified the functions of the village magistrate and the head of the village militia as among those of the *gāvuḍa* with the help of inscriptions.[24] In an agrarian society characterized by peasant communities of a relatively autonomous character, it is only natural that these functions should be arrogated by the more prominent landed magnates. This could be appreciated better if one looks at the process of socio-economic evolution which led to the formation of state in this part of the country.

The present essay, by no means exhaustive or complete, stresses the need for placing the evidence from the epigraphical material from Karnataka concerning ostensibly political institutions within their socio-economic context. A comparative study with similar situations elsewhere in south India can be of great value. Such exercises can go a long way in exposing the mechanism and implications of the formation of the state in different parts of the country under dissimilar provocations.

NOTES AND REFERENCES

1. Among the pioneers of Kannada epigraphy, J.F. Fleet, R.C. Temple and B.L. Rice had suggested this translation in the pages of *Indian Antiquary* and *Epigraphia Carnatica* (hereafter *IA* and *EC*). Later epigraphists and historians have largely followed them without question. In the case of the Hoysaḷas, the first full-length monograph on them by William Coelho, *The Hoysalvamsa* (Bombay, 1950) is a conventional dynastic history which has practically nothing to say about the *gāvuḍa*s. J.D.M. Derrett, *The Hoysalas: A Medieval Indian Royal Family* (Oxford, 1957) is very idealistic in dealing with administration. He consigns the *gāvuḍa* to the lowest rung of an administrative hierarchy, p. 187.
2. G.S. Dikshit, *Local Self-Government in Medieval Karnataka* (Dharwar, 1964), p. 64.
3. This is recognized earlier. Dikshit, *Local Self Government*, p. 63, n. 42–3.
4. A.S. Altekar, *State and Government in Ancient India* (rev. edn, Delhi, 1972), p. 226. n. 6; A.S. Altekar, *The Rashtrakutas and Their Times* (Poona, 1936), pp. 189–90.
5. *Journal of the Bombay Branch of the Royal Asiatic Society*, vol. 10, p. 270 quoted in Dikshit, *Local Self-Government*, p. 64, n. 45.
6. P.B. Desai, ed., *A Corpus of Inscriptions* in *the Kannada Districts of Hyderabad State* (Hyderabad, 1958), no. 16, ll.53–62.
7. Dikshit, *Local Self Government*, p. 64. For the text of the inscription, *SII*, vol. II, i, no. 50.
8. Dikshit, *Local Self Government*, p. 64.
9. Ibid., p. 6.
10. *Cf. EI.* vol. 19, p. 236. See also Dikshit, *Local Self-Government*, p. 62.
11. Anekannambadi Plates of Hoysaḷa Vīra Sōmeśvaradēva in M.S. Nagaraja Rao and K. V. Ramesh, eds, *Copper Plate Inscriptions from Karnataka—Recent Discoveries* (Mysore, 1985), p. 94. ll.9. 90–101.
12. Altekar, *State and Government*, p. 226.
13. *Arthaśāstra*, Bk III, ch. 12 quoted in ibid., p. 229, n. 6; Kalidāsa's *Raghuvaṁśa* I, refers to *grāmavṛddhas* which is but one example of the numerous other references in the romantic literature.

14. Noboru Karashima, Y. Subbarayalu and Toru Matsui, *A Concordance of the Names* in *the Cōḷa Inscriptions* (Madurai, 1978) under Title groups TA 020, 021, 022. Also Appendix III, pp. xiv–xvii. For an analysis, Kesavan Veluthat, *The Political Structure of Early Medieval South India* (Delhi, 1993), pp. 80–95.
15. Karashima *et al. A Concordance*, p. xvi.
16. Ibid., Y. Subbarayalu, 'The State in Medieval South India', unpublished PhD Thesis, Madurai Kamaraj University (Tamil Nadu, 1976), pp. 115–18.
17. *Inscriptions of the Pudukotta State* (Pudukotta, 1929), no. 301.
18. Karashima *et al. A Concordance*, p. 118.
19. Ibid., Appendix III, pp. xiv–xvii.
20. Veluthat, *The Political Structure.*
21. *Annual Reports of Epigraphy*, 1918, nos 429 and 538.
22. *Epigraphia Carnatica* (*EC* New Series), vol. V (Mysore, 1988 passim).
23. Nagaraja Rao and Ramesh, *Copper Plate.*
24. Dikshit, *Local Self-Government*, pp. 64–5.

Index

Abdul Rahiman Samiri 150
Abu Zaid 321
Achyuta Menon, C. 274–5
Ācugidēva 319
adhikārar 190
Adigamān(s) 38
Āditya 327
Āditya Cōḻa 151
Ādityēśvara temple 71
aḍiyār 67
Ādiyulā 231
advaita 139
Āgamaic 63, 68, 72
  deities/temples 5, 36, 48, 62, 243, 302
  ideas/practices/religion/Hinduism 5, 38, 61–3, 68, 72, 211, 251, 257, 269
  pantheon 36, 264
  tradition 48
Agastya 70
agrarian 34, 55, 57–8, 60, 87, 96–7, 108, 123, 166, 181, 190, 207, 220–1, 271–5, 291, 293, 310
  corporations 6, 22, 49, 62–3, 72, 159, 199, 202, 209, 251, 255, 280–1, 283, 298, 302
  economy 6, 63, 267
  expansion 3, 7, 9, 30–1, 39–40, 47–8, 66, 112, 188, 209, 217, 243, 256, 258, 262–4, 289
  hinterlands/districts 198, 216
  land/plains/sub-region/tracts/village 8–9, 44, 73, 121, 198, 204–5, 254–5, 284, 329
  order/relations/system/society 34, 49, 64–5, 85, 87, 89–91, 111, 113–14, 156, 161, 329
  resources 198
  revolution 24
  settlement(s)/village communities 13, 30, 48, 76, 111, 112, 175, 207
  surplus *see* surplus
agriculture 3, 5–9, 13–14, 24–5, 30–2, 34, 36, 40–1, 47, 62–3, 65–6, 89, 92, 94–5, 112, 116, 138, 140, 186, 187–90, 209, 210, 214, 217, 221, 227, 243, 255–6, 258, 261–2, 264, 266, 268–9, 283, 289, 326–7
Āhavamalla 320
Ahicchatra 135, 300
Airāṇikkaḷam 54, 192–3, 235–6
Akanānūru 299, 309
ākhyāna 29
Akṣaraguṇḍu 179
āḷ/āḷaṭiyār 210, 256, 288
āḷaḍaṅga 86, 91
alaṅkāraśāstra 303
Alayev, L.B. 84, 96
Alexandria 241
Ali, Muzaffar 310
Altekar, A.S. 330
āḷvān/āḷva 107, 329
Āḻvāñcēri Tamprākkaḷ 139
Āḻvār(s) 60, 66, 229
Ambasamudram 86
Ammukutty, K.P. 324
anācāras 299–300, 309
ānaiyaccu 294

Ānandavardhana 303
Anantanātha Purāṇa 323
Ananta Padmanābha temple 260
Anantapuravarṇanam 223, 245
Añcaṭi 311
ancient/Pharaonic Egypt 183, 216
Añcuvaṇṇam 35, 203, 255
Āndhras 47, 59
Anekannambadi Copper Plate 330
Aṅgiras 69
Añjanakhaḷa *see* Tiruvañcaikkaḷam
Anjengo 267
Anshouman, Ashok 55
antarāyam 103
aṇugajīvita 320
aṇukkar 320
Appadorai, A. 79, 96, 100, 106
Appadurai, Arjun 56
Appar 66
Arabian Sea 261
araiyan 41, 88, 107, 121, 329
arantai 201, 205
Arasaratnam, Sinnappa 271
Arcot, South 38, 120
Ardhabrāhmaṇa 284
Ariñjaya 71
Ariñjigai-īśvara 71
Arjuna 69
Arokiaswamy, M. 56
Aṟṟūr 71
artham 286
Arthaśāstra 22, 103, 107, 159, 190, 302–3, 330
Āruvāymoḻi 260
Āścaryacūḍāmaṇi 297, 303, 307
Asiatic Mode of Production 89, 92
Aśōka/Aśōkan edicts 22, 178–9, 298
Aśvatthāman 69
atikāran/atikārar 197
aṭima 288
aṭiyār/aṭiyāḷar 34, 87, 288
Atri 69
āṭṭaikkōḷ 42, 201, 204–6
āṭṭaittiṟai 204, 206
aṭṭippēṟṟōlakkaraṇam/aṭṭippēṟṟōla 287
aṭṭippēṟu 285–8, 293
Atula 143
Augustus, temple of 242
Avanisimha 59
Avantisundarīkathā 193, 297
avatāra 36, 137, 301
Āvaṭṭiputtūr 281
Āy(s)/Āy-vēḷs 38–9, 70, 155, 180, 186, 254
Āyiram *see* Hundred/Thousand organization
Ayyan Aṭikaṭiruvaṭikaḷ 190

Babiamma 317
Babylon, patriarch of 266
Badami 45, 59
Bagchi, Amiya Kumar 225, 293
Bagchi, Barnita 225, 293
Bālakrīḍēśvara 232
Balakrishnan 224
Balambal, V. 56
Balasubrahmanyam, S.R. 81
balaudjers 321
Bāṇas 47, 59
Barbosa, Duarte 176
bards/minstrels 23, 26–7, 29, 186, 188
Bari, S.A. 52, 221
Basavaṇṇa 318
Begley, Vimala 53
Benayya 320
Berlin revolution 148
Bhakti Movement/religion/saints 4, 6, 22, 48–9, 60–1, 64, 66–8, 72–3, 79, 99, 171, 180, 211–12, 225, 231–4, 243, 246, 248, 257, 273, 302
Bharadvāja 69
Bharaṇi festival 229, 239, 243–5
Bharata 306
Bhārata/Bhāratavarṣa 305–6
Bharatappuḻa 263 *see also* Pērār
bhāṣā 11, 305–6
bhaṣe 318–19
Bhāskara 246, 248

Bhāskara Ravi 56, 154, 158, 196, 240, 242
bhaṭṭasōmayājin 291
Bhṛgu 69, 237
Bhūpati 71
bhūtasamkhya 173
Big Temple *see* Bṛhadīśvara temple
Bloch, Marc 98, 158, 322, 324
Boppaṇṇa 318
Brahma 69, 74
brahmadēya 31–2, 34, 45–7, 54, 58, 63, 65, 85–91, 113, 116, 119, 221
Brahmagiri 179
brahmakṣatra 11, 69, 137, 191, 235, 237, 301, 305
Brāhmaṇa(s)/Brāhmaṇical groups/ elites 5, 6, 9, 12–13, 28–9, 33–4, 36, 39, 41, 43–4, 46–7, 53, 58–60, 62–5, 67, 76, 84–5, 89, 92–5, 132–3, 135–42, 145, 152, 157, 159, 160–1, 171–2, 174, 176, 181, 188–91, 201–2, 207, 209, 210–14, 218, 220, 222, 235–8, 247–8, 251–7, 259, 263–4, 269–70, 276, 278–81, 283–5, 291, 294, 297–301, 306, 308–9
  ideology *see* ideology
  institutions/elements/norms/ order 6, 10, 22, 30, 36, 38, 43, 47–8, 60, 63, 64, 67, 94, 114–15, 138, 145, 147, 161, 170, 174, 190, 192, 200, 205, 211–12, 214–15, 217–18, 222, 237–8, 243, 251–3, 257–8, 263, 266, 269, 272, 280–2, 286, 288, 300–3, 308
  religion/rituals/texts/practices *see* - institutions/elements/ norms/order
  settlements/households/villages 5, 6, 9, 32–3, 46, 48–9, 55, 62–3, 72, 76, 81–2, 87, 93, 98, 133, 136, 140, 144, 161, 166, 181, 189, 191–4, 200, 207, 213, 217, 221, 225–6, 228, 231, 236, 238, 243, 247, 251–4, 263, 271–4, 280–1, 284–6, 290–3, 299, 302, 308–9, 328
brahmasvam 34, 65, 87, 190, 200, 251, 254, 285, 289, 294
Brāhmi 169, 178
Bṛhadīśvara temple/Big Temple 30, 44, 71, 73–4, 81, 90, 208
Bṛhaspati 173
British Malabar *see* Malabar
British rule in India 149, 153, 266, 276
Bronze Age *see* Copper/Bronze Age
Buddhism/Buddhist 8, 25, 28, 45–6, 131, 230, 241
Buddhist *vihāra* 180, 245
Budha 70
bureaucratic state *see* state
bureaucracy 28, 40, 70, 101, 107, 141, 253, 329
Burkitt, F.C. 273
Burnell, A.C. 149–50, 152, 163
Butterworth, Alan 277, 289
Byzantium 50

cakravartin/cakravarttikaḷ 37, 74, 189, 192
Cākyārs 234
Caldwell, Robert 152, 163
Caldwell, Sarah 247
Calicut 135, 140–2, 146, 153, 164, 176, 182, 199, 206, 219, 223, 249, 258, 260–2, 265, 267–9, 272, 274–5
Cāḷukya(s) 21, 45, 59, 70, 194, 223, 298, 307, 317
Cammiade, L.A. 151
Canarese coast 135
Candaya 317
Caṇḍēśvara 75
Candravamśa 69
Candrōtsavam 306, 310–11
Ceṅṅannūr 235
caṅṅātam 263
Capital 7
capitalism/capitalist 20, 50, 105

caravan 25, 28, 275
caste(s) 3, 6, 7, 12–14, 35–7, 39, 43, 56, 64, 67–8, 72, 78, 93–5, 134–5, 139, 157–8, 195, 200, 202, 210, 235, 239, 253, 256, 263–4, 266, 270, 273, 278, 281, 290, 301–3, 310, 329
-ization 14
society 6, 63, 76
Catagrāma 327
Cāttan 280
caṭṭas/caṭṭar/cāttirar 136–7, 161, 301
cattle 14, 26, 38, 44, 51–3, 94, 179, 186
Cāttu 25
cavattai 174, 200
Cēdi(s) 160, 196
Ceṅkam Naḍukaṟkaḷ 250
Ceṅkuṭṭuvan 188
centralized state *see* state
Cēra(s) 10, 12–13, 27, 34–5, 39–40, 43, 45–6, 55, 59, 63, 66, 68–71, 75–6, 78, 80, 82, 86–7, 93, 96, 98, 103, 110–11, 116, 132, 138, 140, 143, 145–6, 154–5, 158–61, 163, 166, 170–3, 176–7, 179–80, 185–6, 188, 190–2, 201, 203–9, 211–13, 216, 218–21, 224–5, 231–4, 236–40, 242–5, 252–4, 257–8, 260, 270, 278, 282–8, 290, 293, 296, 298–9, 300, 302–3, 308–9, 321
Cērakulanācciyār 233
Cērakulapradīpa 192
Cēral 9, 193
Cēramān 192, 208, 215–16, 222, 245, 296, 303, 306
Cēramān Kōvil 231, 245
Cēraman Lokaperuntaṭṭān 180
'Cēramān Mosque' 248
Cēramān nāḍu 303
Cēramān Paṟambu 208, 231
Cēramān Perumāḷ (Nāyanār) 49, 66, 79, 133, 150, 153, 161, 166, 180, 183–4, 191, 197, 206, 215–16, 218, 220, 226, 229–32, 234, 241, 259, 303–5, 308
Cērikkal 86–7, 292
Cēyōn 24, 36
Chackochan, P.L. 166, 274
Chalcolithic Age 22
Champakalakshmi, R. 23, 51–3, 55, 57–8, 60, 74, 76, 79, 81–2, 84, 96, 220–1, 274–5, 308
Champollion, François 4, 147
Chandra, Bipan 50
Chandrasekharan, T. 145
Chattopadhyaya, B.D. 2, 51, 143
Chayanov 92
Cherian, P.J. 142, 270, 273–5, 310
Chesnaux, Jean 50
Chetty, V. Venugopaul 277, 289
Chevillard, Jean-Luc 225
Chidanandamurthy, M. 316, 320, 322–4
chief/chiefdom/chieftaincies 27–9, 32, 34–5, 38–43, 47, 49, 60, 63, 65, 67, 70, 73–5, 77–8, 82, 86–7, 91, 95, 111–14, 118, 120–2, 132–4, 142, 146, 155, 159, 170, 180, 186–8, 190, 192–3, 200, 205, 216–17, 240, 253–4, 258, 261–2, 269–70, 282–4, 287, 296, 298, 308, 315, 317, 320–2, 326, 328–9
Chitnis, K.N. 276
Christians in Kerala *see* Syrian Christians in Kerala
Christopher Cellarius/Keller 50
Cidambaram 113, 180
Cikāruḍaiyan Tāyan Aḍigaḷ 119
Ciṅṅapuram taḷi/Śṛṅgapuram 192, 209, 229, 235–6
Claessen, Henri J.M. and Peter Skalnīk 215, 218, 225, 228
Cochin 152–3, 163, 176, 184, 219, 232, 240, 246–8, 258–9, 262–3, 265, 267–8, 274–5, 304
Coelho, William 330
Coelobotras *see* Kerobotras
Cōkiram 263
Cōkkūr 199
Cōḻa(s) 6, 8, 10, 13, 15, 21–2, 27, 32, 34, 36, 39–43, 45–9, 51, 54–9,

62–3, 66, 68–71, 73–5, 80–1, 83, 86–94, 96, 98, 100–8, 110–12, 114–16, 118, 120–3, 151, 155, 160, 162, 172–3, 175, 177, 180, 182, 194, 196, 199, 203, 208, 213–14, 254, 273, 278, 283, 291–2, 298–9, 305, 329
Colachel 268
Cōḻamaṇḍalam 103, 121
Cōḻaśikhāmaṇi Pallavaraiyan 117
colonial(ism) 20, 50, 129–30, 148, 266, 270, 289
  discourse/notions 109, 161
  historiography/writers 3, 184
  India 142
  masters/agents 129–30, 148, 153, 269–70
  modernity 270
  state 249
  anti- 157
colony/colonies 129–30, 148
Companions of Honour 14, 43, 75, 78, 82, 159, 161, 166, 197, 224, 240, 253–4, 262, 272, 282, 321
Coonen Cross, Oath of 267
Coorg 163
Copper/Bronze Age 22
corvée labour *see* labour
Cottonara 241
Counter reformation 266
court poetry/literature 4, 29, 37, 44, 70, 137, 143, 302
Cunaiyāikkuḍi 116
Curutimān 95

Dakṣiṇamēru 73
Dakṣiṇamēru-viṭaṅkar 74
Dames, M.L. 182
Damodaran, K. 158, 165
dānaśāsanas 279
daṇḍanāyakam 117
Daṇḍin 193, 297, 307
Danvers 271
dark ages 2, 184, 250
Dasgupta, Ashin 271
Davis, Donald R., Jr. 286–8, 293
Dayalan, D. 81
de Casparis, J.G. 80, 143
de Lannoy, Mark 275
de Puma, Richard Daniel 53
Deccan 111
Delhi Sultanate 50
Derrett, J.D.M. 51, 56, 181, 330
Desai, P.B. 330
dēśavāḻis 262
dēvadānam 34, 63, 65, 85–6, 91, 119
dēvadāsi 160
Dēva-rāja 71, 81
dēvasvam 34, 65, 87, 190, 200, 251, 254, 285, 289
Dēvīdēvēśvaram temple 281
dhanajanasahitā 86
dharma 37
Dharmadam/Dharmapaṭṭaṇam 261
Dharmapuri 38
Dharmaśāstra(s) 33, 55, 95, 174–5, 180, 200, 204, 255, 281–2, 299, 302
dhvani 303
Diamper *see* Udayampērūr
digvijaya 59
Dikshit, G.S. 327, 329–31
dīnāras 205
Doddahundi inscription 317
Dom Menezes 266
Dravidian 98, 156–7, 163, 169, 229
Drōṇa 69
Dumont, Louis 95, 122
Durgā 136, 300
Durkhiem, Emile 316
Dutch 149, 267–8, 271, 275, 289
dvārapālas 74–5, 82

Ēcaladēvi 318
Ēcana *Daṇḍanāyaka* 319
eccōṟu 103
Eḍakal caves 169, 178
Egypt 241
Eighteen Minor Works, the/ Kīḻkaṇakku 45, 189 *see also Patineṇkīḻkaṇakku*

Elamkulam P.N. Kunjan Pillai 12–13, 55, 93–4, 98, 144–5, 154–9, 163, 165, 178–9, 181, 185, 219–20, 245–8, 250, 271, 278, 280, 282–3, 289–91, 307–8
Eḷamprakkōṭ 235
Ē̱limala 261
Ellis, F.W. 151, 163
E̱luttaccan *see* Tuñcattu Rāmānujan E̱luttaccan
E̱luttukal 169, 178
English East India Company 148, 267, 269
English factories 267
Enlightenment 50, 130
Eraigangayya 317
Eraiyamma 317
Eraiyammarasa 319
Ērāḷanāṭu/Ērāḷanāḍu/Ēranāḍu 111, 195, 197–8, 213, 223, 260
Ērāṭi 140
Ernakulam 217, 243
Eṭattara̱nāṭu 197
Eṭṭutogai 23
Euro-centrism 295
European feudalism 226, 322, 324
European history 50
European powers in India 249, 267
exchange 3, 10, 14, 25–6, 34, 37, 241, 284, 286, 299
Ezhuttachan, K.N. 310

Feodium 50
feudal(ism)/society/system 2, 13, 15, 20, 43, 50–1, 56, 58, 67, 77, 82, 89, 92, 98, 117, 122, 159, 166, 181, 185, 214, 221, 225, 273, 291, 316, 322
feudal state *see* state
feudatory 38, 43, 56, 75, 77, 101, 121, 141, 195, 254, 258, 260, 292, 320
Fishcel, Walter J. 163
Fleet, J.F. 330
four temples *see Nālu Taḷi*
Frankish 322
French 267, 271
Freeman, Rich 310

gaṇa 145
Gaṇapati *see* Bālakrīḍēśvara
Ganesh, K.N. 161–2, 166, 271, 274, 292
Gaṅga(s) 21, 38–40, 59, 317, 323
Gaṅga Valley 28
Gangadharan, M. 275
Gaṅgaikkoṇḍacōḻapuram 31, 90
gāruḍa(s) 14, 319–20
gasindus 322
gāthā 29
Gatti, Satish 163
*gāvuḍa*s/*gāvuṇḍa*s/*gāuḍa*s 14, 97, 225, 324–5, 327, 329
gāvuḍagoḍuge 327
ghaṭikai 43
Ghatiyammarasa 319
Ghorian conquests 50
gift 10, 25, 27, 31, 46, 53, 59, 65, 137, 130–40, 174, 188, 212, 215, 222, 227, 235, 250, 284, 301, 305
Girija, C. 57, 143, 146, 224, 274
Goa 266
Gokarna 10, 135, 252, 300
golden ages 2, 155–7, 184
Goody, Jack 178
Gopal, S. 52, 60, 221
Gopinatha Rao, T.A. 80, 122, 146, 151–2
gōtra 279–80
Gōtramallēśvara 232
Gough, Kathleen 97
Govindaswamy, M.S. 56
Govinda Warrier, A. 153, 163
grāma 135–6, 189, 235, 247, 263, 280, 284, 300–1
grāmakṣētra 208, 280
grāmakūṭa 327
Grāmapaddhati 136, 144–5, 272
grāma-vṛddha 327, 330
grāmēśvara 327, 329
Grantha 147

granthavari 176, 182, 286–7
Greco-Roman accounts/tradition 22, 25, 130, 148, 241, 298
Gujarat 135
Guṇaka 10, 305
Gundert, Rev Hermann 133, 140, 144–5, 149–50, 163, 246, 272, 293
Gupta Empire 68, 131, 141, 306
Gupta, K.M. 87, 97
'Guptan', Sthāṇu Ravi 150–1
Gurukkal, Rajan 23, 46–7, 51–3, 55–6, 58–60, 84–6, 96–7, 111, 123, 162, 166, 178, 181, 186, 220–2, 248, 250, 271, 284, 292–3, 308
Gururaja Rao, B.K. 52

Habib, Irfan 50, 94–5, 98
Haider Ali 249, 269, 276
Haḷēbiḍ inscription 318
Haḷēbīḍu 208
Hall, Kenneth 56
Hanuma Nayaka 175
Haridas, V.V. 146, 182, 274
Harṣacarita 146
Hart, George L., III 23, 51
Heitzman, James 32, 54, 120, 125
Herodotus 129, 148
hero-stones 22, 26, 38, 250–72, 316, 318
Hindu 267
  chieftaincy/institutions/law 122, 217, 293
  -ism/religion 5, 9, 61–2, 64, 68, 258, 266
  period 20
  practices/rituals 265
Holla, Krishniah 145
Hosten, H. 163
Hoysaḷa(s) 21, 43, 51, 57, 97, 208, 213, 225, 319, 323–5, 329–30
Hoysaḷēśvara temple 208
Hultzsch, E. 151, 163, 219
Hundred/Thousand organization/group 43, 78, 159, 161, 182, 193, 197, 205, 214, 222, 224–5, 240, 253–4, 261, 274, 278–9, 282, 320–1, 324
Hundred Years' War in Kerala 13, 155–7, 160, 278–9, 283
Huzur office plates 70, 76

Ibrahim Kunju, A.P. 275
iḍaṅgai/left-hand caste 43, 56
ideology 3, 6, 19–20, 29, 37, 44, 48–53, 55, 58, 62, 64, 65, 67–8, 72, 81, 92, 96, 99, 137, 155–6, 184, 211, 213, 216, 221, 228, 233, 251–2, 257
Ikkēri 268 *see also* Nāyaks of Ikkēri
īḻaccēri 31
iḷam kūṟu 195
īḻava 31, 239, 263
iḷaya kūṟu 195, 262
Indian feudalism *see* feudalism
Indo-Aryan languages 169
Indra 70–1
Induchudan, V.T. 247
Indus Valley 167
in-nāḍ-uḍaiya 117
innāḍu-peṟṟa 117
irannūṇ 103
Iravi Cirikaṇṭan 77
iravu-cōṟu 103
Iriññālakkuṭa/Iruṅṅāṭikkūṭal/Irinjalakkuda 177, 192, 199, 235–6, 281
Iron Age 22, 51–2
Īśāna 196
Islam in Kerala 139, 161, 211, 230, 241–2, 248, 255, 258, 265
iṣṭadēvatā 75
Īśvara 327
iṭaiyīṭu 285–7
itihāsa 37
īṭu 285

Jagadēkamalla 319
Jain/Jainism 8, 27, 33, 45–6, 48, 66, 131, 230, 241, 248, 271
Jaiswal, Suvira 56
Jambūdvīpa 306
Jambūdvīpōlpatti 306
Jambukeśvaran temple 89

janapada 305
janmam/janmakkaraṇam 285–8
janmi/janmisampradāyam 156, 279
Janna 320
jāti 9, 36, 48, 92–5, 98, 211, 251, 257, 265–6, 268
jātikku kartavyan 266
Jaṭilavarman 70
Jayaṅgoṇḍacōḻamaṇḍalam 103, 111
Jayarātēśvaran temple 246
Jayasree, C.H. 273
Jayaswal, K.P. 155
Jerusalem 240
Jewish Copper Plates 56, 149–51, 154, 170, 173–4, 193, 196, 204, 240, 242, 258, 265
Jewish settlement/Jūtakkaḷam 230, 240
Jewish Synagogue of Cochin 248
Jews in Kerala 149, 196, 207, 211, 215, 230, 240, 242, 245, 255, 258–9, 265
Jha, D.N. 58, 84, 87, 92, 96–7, 119, 124, 221, 273
jihad 267
Jimma 216
Jñānappāna 311
jōḷavāḷi 318
Joseph Rabban 196, 240
Joseph, T.K. 163, 273
Joshi, S.D. 146
Judaeo-Christian tradition 130, 148–9, 211
Judaism *see* Jews in Kerala
Jupiter 173

kaalikuut 260
Kachari 216
kaḍaiyīḍu 119
kaḍamai/kaṭamai 42, 103–4, 204
Kadambas 21, 40, 47, 59
Kaelobotros *see* Kerobotros
kaikkōḷapperumbaḍai 43
Kailāsa 318
Kailasapathi, K. 23, 52
Kaitavāram kaccam 174
Kaḷabhra(s) 8, 45–6, 59, 187
  Kaḷavar- 45
  -interregnum 8, 21, 45, 60, 221
Kaḷabhra Accuta Vikkānta 46
kaḻakams 235, 264
kalam 201
kaḻañju 77–8, 201
Kaḻariṟṟaṟivār Nāyanār Purāṇam 222, 245
Kalburgi, M.M. 316, 322–3
Kali age *see kaliyuga*
kali arašan 59
kalibalamardana 59
Kālidāsa 223, 307, 330
Kali era 298
kalippagai 59
kaliśāsana 59
Kāḷi/Kāli temple of Koṭuṅṅallūr 229, 238–40, 243–4, 247, 253
Kalittokai 23, 48
kaliyuga/Kali age 2, 8, 46–7, 59, 133, 173
Kālkkaraināṭu 195, 198, 223
Kaḷḷar 95
Kamikāgama 207, 225
kammāḷas 56, 181
kammāṇaccēri 31
Kamukañcēri 290
Kanakasabhai, V. 22, 51, 220
kaṇakkar 93
kāṇam 145, 201, 285–8, 292–3
kāṇam-janmam-maryāda 285–6
Kāñci(puram) 48, 66, 68, 113, 193, 297
kaṇimuṟṟūṭṭu 34, 91, 115
Kanippayyur Sankaran Nambudiripad 290
kaṇiyuḍaiyār 31
kanmi 119
Kannada 14, 43, 136, 139, 171–2, 178, 305, 316, 320–5, 327, 330
Kannur/Cannanore 268, 274, 281, 324
Kāntaḷūr Śālai 159
Kaṇṭan 280
kāṇuka 292

Kanyakumari/Kumari/Cape Comorin 10, 135, 252, 260, 296, 300
Kanyakumari inscription 69
Kapilar 188
kār 98
kara 264
kāṟāḷa(r) 34, 47, 87, 90–1, 98, 203, 286
kārāṇmai/kārāṇma 33, 85–6, 90, 286
Karantai plates 44, 58
Karashima, Noboru 54, 57, 84, 87, 88–9, 96–8, 101, 103–4, 106–8, 110, 123–4, 167, 289, 331
Kariṅṅampaḷḷi 235
Karnataka 1, 5, 8, 13–14, 21, 43, 57–8, 97, 112, 136, 144, 176, 179, 224–5, 249, 265, 272, 275, 292, 309, 315–16, 320–1, 324–5, 329–30
karṣaka 98
karumam 200
Karunataṭakkan 70, 159
Karūr 186, 242, 308
kārya/kāryam 174, 200
Kasaragod 10, 170, 194, 268, 300, 308
Kashmir 303
kasu 35
Kaṭalōn 24
Kaṭaṅkāṭṭu kaccam 174
ka-ṭa-pa-yādi 173
Kāval 124, 225, 263
Kaveri Delta/Valley 1, 66, 73, 89, 110, 214
kāvya 10, 37, 68, 143, 146, 239, 276, 299
Keilhorn, F. 151
Keller *see* Christopher Cellarius
Kelu Nair, Kukkil 151
Kerala 1, 5, 9–14, 21, 40, 43, 55–9, 61, 65, 70, 76, 79–82, 86–7, 93, 96–8, 112, 123, 130–3, 134–51, 153–63, 165–6, 168–73, 175–6, 178–95, 199–200, 203, 206–10, 212, 214–26, 229, 231, 239, 242–86, 288, 290–4, 296–310, 320–1, 324
Kēraḷa(s) 47, 59
Kēraḷācāra 195
Kēraḷādhināṭha 192, 194, 222, 233, 252, 297, 307
Kēraḷa Kēsari 158
Kēraḷakṣmā 9
Kēraḷa-kula 9
Kēraḷakulacūḍāmaṇi 193, 222
Kēraḷaputra/Kētalaputa 296
Kēraḷa-vamśa 9
Kēraḷavamśakētu 192
Kēraḷa-viṣaya 9, 194, 297
Kēraḷaviṣayādhipa 194, 297
Kēraḷōlpatti 10–11, 129–30, 133–6, 138–42, 144–6, 148, 150, 160–1, 191, 194, 212, 221, 222–3, 226, 231, 235, 237, 245–6, 272, 284–5, 288, 292–3, 300, 302, 306, 309–10
kēris 326
Kerobotros/Kaelobotros/ Coelobotras 296
Kētalaputa *see* Kēraḷaputra
khaṇḍas 306
kiḻān/kiḻavan 41, 88, 107, 328
Kiḻān Aṭikaḷ 222
kīḻāykkūṟŭ 285, 288
kīḻguṇṭe 317, 323
Kiḷimānūr 280–1
kiḷippaṭṭu 133
kīḻīṭŭ 285–7
Kīḻmalaināṭu 78, 197–8, 213, 215, 259
kīḻpāti 86
Kīḻttaḷi 192, 209, 235–6, 229
kīḻvāram 86
Kimura, Masaaka 228
Kīranūr inscription 116
kō 173, 191, 252
koccaḻi 259, 265
Kōcceṅgaṇān 49, 66
Koḍumbāḷūr 38
Kodungallur/Koṭuṅṅallūr/ Koṭuṅkōḷūr 138, 222, 225, 229–30, 234, 236, 238–45, 247–8
kōil 67

Kōkasandēšam 232, 238, 245–6
Kokilasandēśa 238–9, 245
kō kōnmai koṇṭān kō 189, 192, 252
Kōlabaḷi Sāsirvaru 197, 274
Kōlam 132, 197, 261, 324
Kōḷambanāthas 206
Kōlattiri 146
Kōlattunāḍu 111, 135, 141–2, 146, 160, 176, 195–8, 258, 261, 303, 306, 310
Kōleḻuttu 147
Kōḻi kōn 180
Kōḻikkōṭan granthavari 176, 182
kōḻikkōṭṭu kōya 260
Kollam 193, 196, 199, 206, 255, 260, 303
Kollam era 139, 150, 154–5, 170, 173, 184, 241
Kollam Rāmēśvarasvāmin temple 165, 197, 237
Kolli Kāvalan 180
Kollūr Maḍham plates 144, 281
kōmaṟṟavar 117
Koṇḍabbe 317
Konkan/Koṅkaṇas 47, 59, 144
Koodali granthavari 288, 293
kōppatavāram 203
Koṟṟavai 24, 36
Kosambi, D.D. 95, 97–8, 123, 159
Koshy, M.O. 271, 275
Kōtai Iravi 199
Kōṭiliṅgapura 229
kōṭṭām 41, 110–11
Kōṭṭuvāyiravēli kaccam 174
Koṭuṅṅallūr Kuññikkuṭṭan Tampurān 245, 247
Kovur 274, 324
kōya 261
Kōyil Adhikārikaḷ/Kōil Adhikārikaḷ 190, 192, 201, 214, 222
kōyilmanuccar 201
Kozhikode/*kōḻikkōṭu* 260
Kramrisch, Stella 209
Krishna Aiyar, K.V. 12, 146, 153–4, 158, 164, 219, 250, 272, 274
Krishnan, K.G. 58
Krishna Rao, M.V. 316, 323
Krishna Sastri, H. 122
Krishnaswami Aiyangar, S. 56, 122, 220, 308
Kṛṣṇa 36, 69
Kṣatriya(s) 37, 39, 68, 94, 137–8, 143, 191–2, 194, 212, 235, 237, 252–3, 269
-ized monarchy/rulers 10, 69, 299, 301–2
Kuḍumiyamalai inscription 328
Kulaccirai Nāyanār 66
Kulacciṟaiyar Purāṇam 79
Kulaśēkhara 79–80, 154, 156–9, 165, 179, 183, 185, 192–3, 194, 201, 212, 219, 222–3, 229, 231, 233–4, 238, 246, 275, 290, 297, 303, 307–9
Kulaśēkhara (Aḻvār) 49, 60, 66, 171, 180, 193, 232, 246, 297
Kulke, Hermann 217, 228
Kuḷōttuṅga I 101, 104, 119, 121, 125
Kulōttuṅga II 101
Kulōttuṅga III 104
Kumāranallūr 177, 201, 288
Kumāranallūr inscription 293
Kumar, Dharma 87, 90, 92, 97
Kumbakonam 120
Kunjunni Raja, K. 223, 247, 307, 310
Kurakkēṇi Kollam 203, 206, 255, 258, 302
Kuṟiñci 24
Kūṟṟampaḷḷi 290
Kuṟumpakkāvu 239
Kuṟumpoṟaināṭu/Kuṟumpoṟaiyūrnāṭu 197–8, 213, 223, 259
kuṟunilamannar 27, 38
Kurup, K.K.N. 275, 293, 309
Kurur, Manoj 311
Kūṭal Nāyakan 180
Kuṭanāḍu 112
Kuṭavūr 77

kuṭi (s) 24, 34, 47, 85–6, 91, 288
kuṭima/kuṭimai/kuḍimai 34, 86, 103, 286, 288
kuṭi nīkki 84–5, 90
kuṭi nīṅṅā 90
kuṭiyāḷar/kuṭiyān/kuṭiyār 34, 86–7, 288
Kūṭiyāṭṭam 233–4
Kuṭṭanāḍu 112
Kuvaralakṣma 319

labour(ers) 7, 24, 31, 34, 86, 91–2, 95, 103, 105, 186, 188, 210, 227, 256, 288, 294
-rent 7, 42, 58, 100, 103–6, 210, 256, 273
agrestic- 90–1, 256
bonded- 86, 210, 256
extra-kin/non-kin- 10, 48, 60, 62, 188, 210, 250, 256, 299
family- 299
landless- 114
surplus- 7, 103, 105–6, 210, 256
Laghu Bhāskarīya vyākhyā 70, 80, 154, 209, 232, 237, 240, 246, 248
Lakṣmaṇarasa 319
Lakṣmīdāsa 239
landholders/landowners 31, 33, 43, 48, 54, 88–9, 93, 107, 113, 117–18, 121, 174, 238, 254, 263, 327–9
landlord(s)/landlordism/landed magnates 6, 13–14, 40–2, 57, 63–5, 67, 88–9, 91, 94, 97, 105, 118, 121, 124, 133, 141, 156–7, 159–60, 177, 190, 210, 225, 268, 277, 279, 283, 285–90, 320, 324–5, 329
Larger Leiden Plates 119
Larger Sinnamanur Plates 80
left-hand caste *see iḍaṅgai*
legitimacy/legitimation 6, 27, 29, 37, 44, 49, 64–5, 68, 72, 132, 138, 148, 186, 211–13, 216, 218, 220, 238, 257
leṅka 14, 319–21
leṅkavāḷi 319
Leshnik, L.S. 52
Līlātilakam 11, 305, 310
Liṅga (place name)/Lingusugur 326
Livy 148
Lockwood, Michael 80
Logan, William 12, 97, 130, 142, 144, 148, 150–1, 153, 157–8, 163–4, 184, 218, 224, 226, 250, 272, 276, 309
Lōkamallēśvaram 232

Mabbett, I.W. 81
Māḍāyi *see* Māṟāhi
Madeya 318
madhyasthan-karaṇattān 119
Madras Presidency 150, 179, 219
Madurai Aruvaivāṇikan Iḷavēṭṭanār 25
Mahābhārata/māpāratam 29, 69, 133, 201, 234, 302
*Mahābhārata bhaṭṭa*s 303
*mahādāna*s 59
Mahadevan, Iravatham 178
Mahalingam, T.V. 52, 54, 56, 83, 96, 100, 106, 122–3, 166, 220, 321, 324
Mahāmaṇḍalēśvara Sōhadēva 318
mahāpātakas/pañcamahāpātaka 81, 181, 201, 225, 281
Maharaja of Travancore 176
Maharashtra 135
mahāsabhā 33
Mahēndra 71
Mahēndravarman 49, 66, 71, 80
Mahōdayapuram 9–10, 12, 66, 82, 132, 138, 141, 146, 154, 158, 161, 169, 176, 179, 183, 189–90, 194, 205–8, 217–18, 220, 225–6, 229, 231–45, 252–3, 259, 261, 270, 278, 286, 297–9, 303–4, 307–8, 321 *see also* Makōtai and Makōtaiyār-paṭṭiṇam
Mahōdayapuraparamēśvara 192, 206, 222, 233, 238, 252, 297, 307

Maine, Henry 122
Majumdar, R.C. 155, 159, 224
Makilañcēri 290
Makōtai 55, 80, 96, 143, 165, 219, 229, 240, 270, 290, 298, 307 *see also* Mahōdayapuram and Makōtaiyār-paṭṭiṇam
Makōtaiyār-paṭṭiṇam 247 *see also* Mahōdayapuram and Makōtai
Malabar/British Malabar 144, 150–1, 153, 163–4, 179, 184, 219, 240, 246, 266, 271, 273, 275–6
Malabar Manual 130, 142, 151, 163, 184, 218, 224, 272, 276, 309
Malaināṭṭut-Tiruppatis 81
malaināṭṭu vaḻakkam 172
Malaiyamāns 120
Malaināṭu/Malanāṭu 10, 296, 300
Maḻavas 47, 59
Māḻava 59
Malayalam 10–13, 103, 107, 133, 147–8, 152–3, 156, 162, 164, 172, 178, 208, 212, 219–20, 222–5, 238, 242, 245, 259, 260, 266, 270–2, 287–8, 290, 292–3, 295–6, 300, 303–7, 309–10
Malik, S.C. 60, 79, 99, 225, 246, 263
Mallaimānagar 70
Mallāri 70
Maloney, Clarence 51
Māḷuvakkōn 78
māmākam 140–1, 261, 303
Manalmanṟattu 223
maṇḍalamudaligaḷ 119
manemaga 317, 324
Maṅgaiyākkaraśiyār Purāṇam 79
Maṇigrāmam 35, 203, 255
Maṇimēkalai 45
Maṇipravāḷam 10–11, 161, 219, 232, 238, 245, 259, 305–6, 310
Mannārguḍi 93, 116
manṟāḍi 94
Manu 69
Manukulāditya/Manukulādiccadēva 158, 238
Mānūr 54
māpāratam see Mahābhārata
Māṟāhi/Māḍayi 261
Mārasimha *Permānaḍigaḷ* 320
Marathi 327
Maṟavar 95
Māravarman 70–1
Marco Polo 321
Mārīca 69
maritime/transmarine/sea-borne trade 13, 27, 249, 260, 265 *see also* trade
Arab trade 141, 207, 258–61
Chinese trade 261, 265
Dutch trade 267
Roman trade 13, 23, 25–7, 207, 242, 248
Southeast Asian trade 265
West Asian trade 207, 241–2, 244, 259, 265
Marr, J.A. 52
Marumakkathayam Committee Report 156, 165
Marutam 24, 27
Maruvan Sapir Iso/Mār Sapīr Īśō 35, 203
Marwick, Arthur 50
Marx, Karl 7, 105–6, 108
Marxist historiography/ interpretation 8, 50
maṭhas 236
Mathen, Rev George 149
Mathew, Alex 292
Mathew, K.S. 271, 275
Matilakam granthavari 176, 181
Matil nāyakan 190, 203
Mātṛdatta 193, 297
matriliny/*marumakkattāyam* 132, 135, 137–8, 143, 156–7, 160, 165, 191–2, 208, 222, 290, 301–2
Matsui, Toru 57, 106–7, 124, 167, 289, 331
Mauryan Empire 27, 150, 169, 220
Mayamata 207, 225
Māyōn 24, 36
Mayūravarman 136
Mecca 139, 153, 241, 248
medieval Europe 15, 92

medieval France 183
Mēghasandēśa 238
Mekong Delta 167
mēlāma/mēlāyma/mēlāykkūṟū 288
Mēlpāḍi 71
Mēlttaḷi 192, 209, 235–6
mēlvāram 86
mēnāyan 197
Mencher, Joan P. 309
Menon, V.K.R. 153–4
Merovingian 322
mērpāti 86
Mēru 73
Mevundi inscription 316
meykkīrtis 58, 71, 159, 173
military 2, 4, 28, 37, 39, 40, 43, 44, 73, 75, 82, 136, 140, 141, 177, 196–8, 205, 213, 228, 239, 240, 244, 253, 262–4, 268, 273, 320, 322, 324
Minakshi, C. 83, 96, 123
Mīnam 229
mīyāṭci 34, 85–6, 90
monarchy/monarchical state 6, 9–10, 13, 21–2, 38–40, 43, 49, 62–9, 72, 75–6, 80, 121, 131–2, 137, 170–1, 191–2, 207, 212–13, 232, 234, 237, 243–4, 247, 249, 253–4, 259–61, 268, 272, 299, 301, 308, 309
Mookerjee, R.K. 155
Moore, R.J. 80, 143
Mound d'Eli *see* Ēlimala
Muciri 241–2
Mudaligaḷ 117, 124
Muḍigoṇḍacōḻa Viḻupparaiyar 119
mugaveṭṭi 101–2
Mukhia, Harbans 50
Mukundamāla 193, 212, 233, 297
mūlabhṛtya 75
Mūḻikkaḷam 55, 181, 192, 235–6, 253, 290
  kaccam/cavatai/oḻukkam 174–5, 195, 200–1, 223, 281
  Kūṟṟampaḷḷic-Cuvākaran-Tāmōtaran 279
Mullai 24
muṇḍadhāriṇaḥ paḷḷi 241
Muññināṭu 198, 213, 215, 259
mun-peṟṟārai maṟṟi 84
Munro, Thomas 122
Mūṣika(s) 39–40, 143, 160, 196, 254, 261
Mūṣikavaṃśakāvya 57, 132, 141, 143, 146, 148, 153, 199, 222, 224, 246, 261, 274
mūṣikēśvara-svarṇakāra 180
Muslim(s) 140, 207, 230, 240, 248, 255, 260–1, 267 *see also* Islam
  Arab- 265
  mosque at Koṭuṅṅallūr 248
  period 19–20
  scholars 230, 242
  vandalism 129
Mutal kuṭi nīṅṅā dēvadānam 86
muṭṭaiyāḷ 103
mūtta kūṟu 195, 262
Muttaraiyar 73
mutu kūṟu 195
Mūvas 186
mūvēndar/mūvaraśar 28, 171, 180
mūvēndavēḷān 41, 88, 102, 107, 121, 329
Muydamma 317
Muyirikkōṭu 206
Muziris 206–7, 218, 241–2, 248
Myanmar 233
Mysore 329

nabhāvu *see* nawab
nāḍāṭci 117
nāḍu *see nāṭu*
nāḍu kaṇkāṇi 119
nāḍu kaṇkāṇi nāyagam 118–19
nāḍu kaṇkāṭci 118
nāḍu kūṟu 119
nāḍu kūṟu ceyvār 118
nādu uḍaiya mudaligaḷ 117, 124
nāḍu vagai 119
nāḍu vagai ceyvār 118
Naduvattam Gopalakrishnan 223
Nagam Aiya, V. 144

Nagaraja Rao, M.S. 330–1
nagaram 35, 41, 76, 87, 115, 203, 255
Nāgari 171, 180
Nagaswami, R. 59, 80
Nagattara 317
Nainar, Muhammad Hussain 275
Nālu Taḷi 138, 166, 192, 201, 209, 212, 214, 222, 234–7, 243, 245, 252–3, 263
namaskāram 201
Namboodiripad, E.M.S. 158, 165
Nampoothiry, N.M. 146, 276
nampūtiri/nambūdiri brāhmaṇas 12, 139, 144, 156–7, 182, 235, 251, 269–70, 276, 279, 290, 292
Nāñcil/Nāñjil 260, 116
Nandi, R.N. 291
Nandivarman 59
Nanhi No̱lamba Pallava Permānaḍigaḷ 320
Na̱ṉra 188
Na̱ṉru̱lainātu 195, 197–8
Nantanār 68, 273
nāraśamsī 29
Narasimhavarman 59, 60
Narasiṅgadēva 318
Nārāyaṇa 291
Narayana Ayyar, C.V. 56
Narayanan, M.G.S. 5–6, 12–14, 23, 48, 51–60, 63, 79–80, 82, 84, 86, 93, 96–9, 103, 107, 123, 132, 134, 143–6, 158–61, 163, 165–6, 179–82, 185, 193, 197, 199–200, 209, 219–26, 240, 245–8, 250, 270–5, 282, 290–3, 307–9, 311, 321, 324
Narayana Pillai, P.K. 80, 144, 246
Narayana Rao, Velcheru 310
nāṭaka 10, 37, 68, 299
nationalist
 discourse 109, 184
 effusions/preoccupations 12, 157
 historians/historiography 155, 157, 184
 ideology 155
nāṭṭār 32, 113, 115–18, 120–2, 125, 283
nāṭṭavar 116
nāṭṭira̱iyili 117, 124
nāṭṭuk-kaṇakku 118
nāṭṭukkūṭṭam 155, 159, 278–9, 282
nāṭṭuppaḍais 43
nāṭṭup-pura̱vu 118
nāṭṭu-vari 118
nāṭṭu-viniyōgam 117
nāṭṭu-vyavasthai 117
nāṭu/nāḍu 8, 32, 34, 41, 77, 86, 109–23, 141, 197–8, 211, 213–14, 217–18, 223, 261–2, 278, 282–3, 294, 329
Nāṭu Uṭaiyavar 195
Nāṭuvāḷi/Nāṭu Vāḻumavar 195, 214–15, 220, 262, 283
nawab/*nabhāvu* 269, 276
Nayaks of Ikkēri 268–9
Nāyanār(s) 60, 66–7, 73, 81, 231
Ñāyar 173
Nāyar
 caste/houses 39, 286
 landlords/aristocrats 140, 268–9
 militia/soldiers 156, 197, 206, 224, 239, 240, 243, 253, 263, 282, 324
Neḍiyiruppu 262
Neḍumāran 49, 66
Neḍuñjaḍaiyan 59
negama 178
Nellore 289
Neolithic Age 24, 112
Neṭiya Taḷi temple 192, 201, 209, 235–6
Neṭumpura̱iyūrnāṭu 195, 198, 223
Neṭumpura̱m taḷi 193
Neṭuṅkālāynāṭu 196, 198
Neytal 24
nigama 25, 178
Nightingale, Pamela 271
Nīlakaṇṭa 280
Nilakanta Sastri, K.A. 4–5, 15, 42–3, 45, 51, 53–4, 56–9, 71,

79–81, 83, 87, 96, 100–1, 103, 106–7, 109, 122–4, 156, 180–2, 220, 291–2
nil̲al 204
Nilambur 169, 207
Nin̲r̲aśīr Neḍumārar Purāṇam 79
Nitrias 241
Niṣumbhasūdini temple 73
Nol̲amba 319
non-brāhmaṇa
  aristocracy/chiefs 133, 142
  bodies/corporations/establishment 41, 157, 175, 214, 278, 280
  castes 157
  corporation/groups/sections 88, 93, 142, 181, 188, 264, 279, 290–1
  cults/deities/devotees/religion 238–40, 243, 264
  landlords/landowners/magnates 88, 176, 190, 210, 238, 256 *see also* landlord(s)
  peasants 87–9, 254 *see also* peasants
  protest/resistance 58, 145, 221
  settlement/peasant localities/village 30, 32, 87–8, 111, 175
Northern Ballads *see Vaṭakkan Pāṭṭukaḷ*
Northern Black Polished Ware 22

Oḍuvūr 116
ol̲ukkam 174, 200
Om Prakash 271
Ōṇam 303
Ōṇappāṭṭu 311
Onnu Kur̲e Āyiram Yōgam 240, 253
Oriental Despotism 184
or̲r̲i/or̲r̲iyōlakkaraṇam 287–8
Ōṭanāṭu 77

Pachu Moothath, Vaikkathu 151, 157, 163
pāḍi 111
pāḍikāval 39
Padmaladēvi 318
Padmanabha Menon, K.P. 12, 153–4, 156, 158, 165, 184, 219, 224, 250, 272
pagan 233
Pahlavi 273
Paiyampalli 52, 112, 123
pakṣa 173
Pālai 24
Pal̲aiyār̲ai 113
Palakkad 193
Palghat Gap 269
Pāliyam Copper Plates 152, 163, 170–1, 310
Pallava 9–10, 22, 32–4, 38–9, 41, 45–6, 52–3, 55–6, 59, 63, 65–6, 68–71, 80, 83–5, 87, 91, 96, 110, 111, 116, 122, 124, 132, 170, 193–4, 220, 223, 297–9, 307
paḷḷi 95, 248
paḷḷiccandam 34, 85, 91, 115
paḷḷippaḍai 71–2
paḷḷiyār 203
palm leaf 13, 133, 149, 176–7, 286–7
Palyāga Muduguḍumi Peruval̲udi 47
Pampā 190, 236
pāṇas 27–8, 68
Panaiṅkāvil palace 196
paṇayam 287–8, 294
Pāṇḍya 9–10, 22, 27, 32–4, 43, 45–8, 54–6, 58–9, 63, 66, 68–71, 75, 80, 84–7, 90, 96, 98, 108, 110–11, 116, 122, 123, 155, 170, 172, 181, 194, 221, 223, 254, 260, 298–9, 307, 321
Pancakkanti 35
pañcamahāpātakas see mahāpātaka
Pañcavanmahādēvīśvara 71
Panikkar, Sardar K.M. 270–1
panmahēśvaras 117
Panniyūr 235, 263
Pan̲r̲itturutti 223
Pan̲r̲itturutti Pōl̲an Kumaran 195

Pantalāyini Kollam 204
paradēśa 212
paraiccēri 31, 91
paraiya 34, 68, 91
Paraṇar 188
paraṅki 267
Parāntaka Vīranārāyaṇa 70–1
Paraśupāṇi 82
Paraśurāma 10–11, 70, 133–8, 144–6, 160, 191, 194–5, 212, 222, 235, 237, 251–2, 284, 299–1, 305–6, 309–10
  -*kṣētra* 10, 300
Paravūr 192, 235–6, 281
Pargiter, F.E. 144
Paripāṭal 23, 48
pariṣad 33, 55, 89, 174, 291
Pārvati 292
pastoral(ism)/activities/agriculture/ groups 24, 36, 41, 60, 94, 115, 186, 327
paṭaināyan/paṭanāyar 193, 197
Paṭamēl Nāyar 133
Patikam Pāṭuvar 60
paṭakāram 291
Patineṇkīḻkaṇakku 23
patippatavāram 203
Patiṟṟuppattu 10, 148, 188, 300, 307
paṭṭam keṭṭina peyar 41
Pattattalmangalam plates 59
paṭṭattānam 141
paṭṭōlai 101–2, 177
Pattupāṭṭu 23
Payyannūr 136, 300
peasant(s)/peasantry 3, 6–8, 31–2, 36, 43, 45–6, 48, 51, 53–60, 63, 65, 76, 83–4, 87–90, 92, 948, 106, 113–14, 123–4, 175–6, 214, 221, 243, 251, 254
  community/society 83, 92, 121, 329
  establishment 175
  localities/settlements/villages 30, 34, 83, 91, 111–13, 116, 122, 283
  micro-region 54
Pegura 317
Pērār 190, 236
Periplus of the Erythraean Sea, the 241
Periyapurāṇam 79, 191, 222, 231, 245, 273
Periyār 190, 206–7, 236, 243
Permānaḍigaḷ 317
pēṟŭ/pēṟum 285–6
perumāḷ(s) 67, 71, 78, 134, 138–41, 146, 159, 191–2, 200–1, 212–16, 225, 235–6, 240–1, 246, 253, 259–62, 265, 270, 273, 278, 298, 308
Perumāḷ Tirumoḻi 171, 180, 193, 233, 297
Perumanam/Peruvanam 281, 177
Perumān Aṭikaḷ 189, 191, 201, 205
Perumpuḻa 10, 330
Peruñcellūr 235
Peruñcellūr Copper Plates 294
Peruñcēvar 116
Perunna (temple) 193, 201
peruntaṭṭān 197
Peter, St 266
Peutingerian Tables 241
Pliny 241
Plumb, J.H. 143–4
plunder 7, 26–8, 42, 47, 53, 186, 189, 203
Poḷali inscription 318
Pollock, Sheldon 303, 306, 310
Pondicherry 21, 66
Ponvaṇṇattantādi 231
Poonen, T.I. 271, 275
Portuguese 149, 176, 240, 261, 265–7, 271, 275, 289
potlatch 27
Pousin of Friege 50
Pradyumna 70
Prakrit 9, 193, 296
prakṛti 190, 197
praṇaya 107
prasāda 174
prāsāda 207

praśasti 37–8, 58–9, 131–3, 144, 173, 189, 191, 208, 223, 278
Prinsep, James 4, 147
produce rent 7, 42, 58, 100, 104–6, 273
Prophet (Muhammad) 230
Pudukkottai/Pudukotta/Pudukottah 120, 123, 331, 329
Puduvaippu/Puduvaippu Era 163, 248, 259
Pugaliyur 308
Pūḷaikkuṭippati 190
Pūlānkuṟichi/Pulankuricci 250, 272
Pulayars 210, 256
Pūlināḍu 112
Pullūr-Koṭavalam 204
Pullūr Kumaran Kumarāticcan 193
Puṉṉaittalaippati 190
Pūntānam Nampūtiri 306
pura 74
Puṟakiḻānāṭu 197–8, 213, 223, 259
purāṇa(s) 37, 69, 143, 302, 305
Purāṇic
  accounts 8
  characters/fame/figures/heroes/lore 69–72, 133, 137, 192, 302
  culture/elements/world 51, 79, 306, 311
  geography/world 306, 239
  Hinduism/religion 9, 63, 68, 72
  ideas/ideology 29, 62 *see also* ideology
  literature/texts 47, 69, 221
  mythology/cosmology *see* -geography/world
Puravalaya Gāvuṇḍa 318
puṟavuvari 101
puṟavuvari-tiṇaikkaḷam 101, 105
puṟavuvari-tiṇaikkaḷa-nāgayam 102
puṟavuvariyār/*puṟavuvariyilār* 102, 119
Pusalkar, A.D. 144
Quilon 255, 260, 273

Rācceya 317
Raghava Aiyangar, M. 245
Raghavan Pillai, K. 143
Raghava Varier, M.R. 11, 60, 144–5, 161–2, 166, 178, 186, 220, 247, 250, 270–1, 273–6, 284, 290, 292, 305, 308–9
Raghuvaṃśa 223, 307, 330
Raichur 326
rāja 259
Raja, P.K.S. 153, 158, 163, 219
rājadhāni 259
rājāṃśam 284
Rājarāja I 42, 73, 75–6, 81, 89–90, 101, 104, 110–11, 119–21, 125, 159
Rāja Rājādhirāja Paramēśvara Bhaṭṭāraka 189, 252 *see also* Rājaśēkhara
Rajarajavarma, A.R. 152, 163–4, 276, 309
Rājarājēśvaram Uḍaiyar 44, 71, 74
Rājaśēkhara 71, 158, 189, 199, 231–2, 238, 252
Rājasimha 158, 245
Rājēndra Cōḻa 44, 58, 70, 89
Rājēndra II 101
Rājēndra III 104
rakṣābhōga 42, 77, 201, 204–5
rakṣāpuruṣa 235
Rāma 69, 299
Rāmacarita 303
Ramachandran Nair, K. 310
Rāmadēva 238
Ramakrishna Pillai, T. 163
Ramanatha Aiyar, A.S. 80, 152, 154, 309
Rāmanāthankōil 71–2
Ramaswami Iyer, L.V. 163, 309
Ramaswamy, Vijaya 119, 124
Rāmavaḷanāṭu 197
Ramavarma Kulaśēkhara 154, 196, 237, 248
Rama Varma Research Institute 152

Rāmāyaṇa 133, 302
Ramesh, K.V. 224, 274, 330–1
Ramesvaram 10, 305
Raṇāditya 158
Rankaen tradition 129, 138, 149
Rao, Nagendra E. 144, 272
rāṣṭra 111
Rāṣṭrakūṭa(s) 21, 40, 43, 160, 196, 320, 330
Rāvaṇa 69
Rāvaṇānugrahamūrtti 75
Ravindran, V. 163
Ravivarma 246
Raychaudhuri, Tapan 271
Renaissance 50
reciprocity 3, 25–6, 28, 34, 48, 61, 63, 65, 186, 299
Reṭṭeyaṇṇa 317
Rice, B.L. 330
right-hand caste *see valangai*
ritual 44, 58, 60, 75, 93–5, 114, 129, 141, 145, 185, 187, 190, 197–8, 211–12, 220, 231, 257, 261, 263–6, 283, 304, 308, 319
Roman Catholic Church 266
Roman coins/presence/trade 13, 22, 25–6
Roman Empire/origin 50, 242, 322
Rothermund, D. 228

ṣābandra kōya 260
sabhā 33, 41, 55, 77–8, 89, 93, 145, 159, 174, 181, 200–1, 224, 254, 273, 278–80, 282, 288–9, 291
Sahlins, Marshall 92
Sahu, Bhairabi Prasad 57, 221, 225
Sahyādrikāṇḍa 145, 272
Said, Edward 153, 163
Saindhavas 47, 59
Śaiva/Śaivism 48, 56, 62, 66, 73–4, 81, 226, 229–31, 233, 243, 273
Śaka era 173, 298
Śaktibhadra 297
śālābhōgam 34, 91
śālai 43, 136
Saletore, B.A. 144, 224, 272, 309
sāmanta 77, 141, 196–7, 217, 269, 319
sāmantacakra 217
Śambhu 317
samiti 159, 224
saṃnyāsa 317
Sampath, M.D. 272
Śamyu 69
sandēśakāvyas 238
Sangam
  literature 5, 23, 51, 53, 62, 69, 78, 79, 112, 131, 169, 185, 219–20, 242
  period/age 8, 22, 45, 47–8, 51, 53, 58, 79, 113, 171, 185, 187, 220–1, 242, 299, 308, 311
saṅgrāma garuḍam 319
Śani 173
Śankara/Śaṅkarācārya 133, 139, 145, 155, 258, 302
Śaṅkaramangalam kaccam 175
Śankaranārāyaṇa 154, 207, 232, 240, 246
saṅkētam 263, 268
saṅkīrṇajāti 36, 95, 138
Sanskrit 9–11, 25, 37, 51, 68, 85–6, 98, 100, 103, 133, 137, 143, 145, 147–8, 155–6, 161, 164, 171, 174, 178, 180, 185, 192–4, 212, 219, 223, 229, 233–4, 236, 238–9, 241, 245–7, 252, 259, 261, 276, 285, 287, 296–7, 299, 302–7, 310, 327
Sanskrit cosmopolis 303–4, 306
Santaradēva 317–18
Sapta-koṅkaṇas 135
śarman 157, 279
Sārtha 25
Śāstā 300
Śāstra/Śāstraic 33, 37, 68, 138–9, 175, 299
  culture/elements 51, 53, 79, 306, 311
  ideas/ideology 29, 62 *see also* ideology
  texts/literature 47

śastrabhikṣā 136, 301
*śastrabrāhmaṇa*s 137, 301
Śāstṛśarman 280
satśūdra 94
Saturn 173
Schwindler, Gary J. 74, 81–2
segmentary state *see* state
Sekhar, A.C. 152, 163, 309
Semitic religions 243–4
sēnāmukha 207, 225, 232, 240
*sēnāpati*s 43, 119, 193
Śēralarkōn 180
Sesha Aiyar, K.G. 308
Sesha Sastri, R. 316, 323
Settar, S. 321, 324
*seṭṭi*s 36
Sewell, Robert 151
Shah Bandar 260
Shanin, Theodore 92
Shanmugham, P. 57, 101, 106
Sharma, R.S. 46, 80, 92, 98, 159, 181, 221
Shengottah 260
Shivanna, K.S. 316, 323
Shulman, David 310
Shungoonny Menon 151, 157, 163
Śibi 69
Śilappadikāram 45
Simhaḷas 47, 59
Sinnamanur plates 70–1
siṅgana garuḍam 319
Sinha, Dipankar 225, 293
Sircar, D.C. 97
Sitaraman, B. 101, 103–4, 289
Śiva 5, 36, 66, 70, 74–5, 81–2, 136, 189, 211, 229, 231, 234, 238, 257, 292, 300
Śiva-Brāhmaṇa 93
sivane 317
Sivaramamurthi, C. 74, 82
Sivathambi, K. 23, 52
Skanda-Kārtikēya 36
slavery 20, 273
Sopara 135
Soundararajan, K.V. 81
South Canara/Kanara 136–7, 144–5, 164, 224, 261, 272, 274, 301
Southeast Asia 81
sovereign(ty) 35, 37–9, 44, 58, 115, 140, 151, 157, 163, 185, 191–3, 194, 196–8, 218, 220, 222, 227–8, 253–4, 259, 308
Spencer, George W. 58, 73, 80–1
Sreedhara Menon, A. 158, 165, 174
Sreenivasamurthi, H.V. 52, 58, 221
Śrī 71
Śrībhīmēśvarapurāṇamu 11, 305, 310
Śrīkaraṇa 101
Sri Lanka 169
Śrimukham 180
Śrīmūlavāsa 180
Śrīnātha 11, 305, 310
Śrīnilaya 71
Śrīnivāsa 71
Srinivasa Aiyangar, P.T. 47, 59, 220
Srinivasan, K.R. 74, 81
Śrīpati 71
Śrīraṅgam temple 233
*śrīvaiṣṇava*s 117
Śrīvallabha 71
Śrīvānavan Mahādēvi 70
Śrīvaramaṅgalam plates 70, 80
Śṛṅgapuram *see* Ciṅṅapuram taḷi
state 2, 3, 6–10, 14, 21–2, 28, 30, 32–5, 37–42, 44, 49–50, 52–4, 56–8, 60–6, 68, 72–3, 75–8, 82–3, 85, 89, 91, 96–8, 100, 103, 105–7, 109, 116–18, 120–5, 131–2, 137, 140–1, 143–4, 155, 166, 170–3, 175, 177, 183, 189–91, 194–5, 198–9, 201–9, 212–21, 225–8, 231, 249, 251–3, 256, 260–1, 268–70, 274–6, 279, 284, 298–9, 301, 304, 308, 310, 316, 320, 324–6, 329–31
  society/system 1, 41, 49, 63, 118, 185, 187, 207–8, 213, 249
  pre-state society 186–7, 220

centralized- 73
early- 12, 215–16, 218, 226, 228
feudal polity 12, 15, 218, 219, 221, 225
integrative polity 12, 217, 228
oriental- 255
temple- 78
segmentary- 15, 113–15, 118–19, 121–2
statistical analysis/method 4, 93, 167, 289
Steensgaard, Neils 275
Stein, Burton 4, 32, 42–3, 54, 57–8, 56, 83–4, 90, 92, 96–7, 100, 106, 110–15, 118–19, 121, 123–5, 221
Sthalapurāṇa 73
sthalīs 236
Sthāṇu 71
Sthāṇu Ravi (Kulaśēkhara) 70, 150–1, 154, 158, 165, 171, 190, 193, 199, 222, 232, 234, 237, 246, 297
St Thomas Christians *see* Syrian Christians in Kerala
Subbarayalu, Y. 54, 57, 80, 84, 87–8, 93–4, 96–8, 101, 106–7, 110–12, 121–5, 167, 272, 289, 291, 331
Subhadrādhanañjaya 183, 193, 212, 233, 246, 272, 297, 303
Subrahmaṇya (god) 70
Subrahmaṇya 280
Subrahmanya Aiyar, K.V. 122, 152, 309
Subramaniam, K. 79
Subramanyan, N. 22, 52–3, 220, 307
Subrahmanyam, Sanjay 271, 310
Subramanyan, T.N. 55, 59, 80, 96
subsistence 7, 14, 24, 26, 95, 186, 227, 299
Sudhakaran, P.P. 146
Śūdras 56, 93–4, 98, 201, 288, 293
Śukasandēśa 10, 236, 239, 245, 247, 305
Sukthankar, V.S. 144
Śūlapāṇi 82
Sundara, A. 52
Sundaram Pillai, P. 151, 157, 163
Sundaramūrtti (Nāyanār) 67, 229–31
Surendra Rao, B. 52, 221
Suresh, B. 56, 93–4, 98
surplus 6–7, 10, 14, 24–6, 28, 30, 33, 37, 42, 48, 52, 63, 92, 95, 103–6, 113, 115, 190, 198, 205, 210, 212, 216, 227, 251, 255–6, 299 *see also* labour
Sūryavamśa 69, 192
svarūpam 262, 274
Swami Vivekananda 270
Synagogue of Kōṭai/Makōtai 240
Synod of Diamper *see* Udayampērūr
Syrian Christian Copper Plates 35, 149–51, 154, 170, 190, 195, 203–4, 206, 211, 222, 242, 258, 265, 273, 292
Syrian Christians in Kerala 149, 163, 190, 207, 211, 215, 230, 236, 240–2, 245, 248, 255, 258–9, 265–7, 275, 302

Taccōḷi 240
Tacitus 148
Tailapa 320
Takkōḷam 40, 75, 196
Talakad 323
Taḷi Adhikārikaḷ/Taḷiyātiris 235
Taliparamba 268
tambirān/tampurān 67, 134, 140, 142
Tamil 1, 4–5, 8, 10, 13, 215, 29, 36, 45–6, 51–5, 58–60, 63, 79, 85, 90, 100, 103, 109, 111–12, 115–16, 131, 133, 139, 145, 148, 152, 164, 167, 169, 171–3, 175–6, 178, 180–1, 185–6, 188, 191, 193, 195–6, 208, 210, 211, 212, 219–21, 230–1, 233–4, 241–2, 252, 256–7, 260, 270, 289–91, 296–300, 302–11, 320–1, 327–9

Tamiḻakam 9–10, 21, 45, 51, 53, 169, 170, 186–8, 221, 229, 296, 300, 306
Tamil Brāhmaṇa(s) 152, 309
Tamil Brāhmi 22, 25, 52, 169, 170, 172, 298
Tamil Nadu 21, 41, 54, 59, 61, 66, 97, 122, 155, 176, 185, 242, 250, 260, 265, 331
Tanabe, Akio 228
Taniyūr 116
Tanjavur 30, 44, 58, 71–2, 76, 81, 90, 120, 208
tannuṭaiya 77
Tapatīsamvaraṇa 183, 193, 212, 222, 233, 246, 272, 297, 303, 307
taṟa 264
Tardapāḍi 320
Tarsā/Tarisāppaḷḷi 203, 258
Tavaranūr kaccam 174
Tellicherry 267
Telugu 11, 178, 305
temple(s) 4–7, 9, 13, 22, 29–30, 32–4, 36, 48–9, 56, 58–68, 71–9, 81–2, 93–4, 116–19, 136, 141, 152, 156–7, 159–60, 162, 166, 170–1, 174–5, 177, 179–82, 189–92, 198–202, 204–5, 207–11, 213, 215, 220–2, 224–6, 229, 231–2, 234–6, 238, 240, 243–4, 246, 248, 251–4, 256–8, 263–4, 268, 271–2, 277–83, 285–6, 289, 291–4, 300, 302–4, 324–5
Temple, R.C. 330
Teñcēri Cēnnan Tāyan 201
Tennavan Āpattudavigal 43, 321
Teyyams 240, 247
Thakur, Vijay Kumar 51
Thapar, Romila 11, 49–53, 60, 95, 130, 143, 146, 178, 248
Tharakan, P.K. Michael 270
Thiruvananthapuram/Trivandrum 153, 170, 194, 260, 308
Thomas, Rosalind 178
Thomas, St 230, 240, 242, 266, 275
Thucydides 129, 148
Tillai 67
tiṇai(s) 23–5, 51, 186, 302
tiṇaimayakku 24, 52
Tipu Sultan 249, 269, 276
Tiruchchirapalli 120, 186, 242, 308
Tirukkoyilur 120
Tirumalai, R. 55, 57, 84, 87, 90, 96–7, 103, 108
tirumeykāppār 321
tirumugam 119
Tirunāvalūr 224
Tirunāvāya temple 261, 283, 303
Tirunāvukkaraśar Purāṇam 79
Tirunelli Copper Plates 151, 170, 204
Tiruppālkkaḍal temple 281
Tiruppāṇa Āḻvār 68
Tiruppatis 81
Tiruttoṇḍar Purāṇam 67
Tirutturaippundi 120
Tiruvālaṅgāḍu plates 80, 194, 299
Tiruvalla
  Copper Plates 76, 152, 201, 254, 273, 291
  granthavari 182
  temple 77–8, 189, 199, 225–6, 231, 252
Tiruvāmāttūr 117
Tiruvāmūr 113
Tiruvañcaikkaḷam temple/ Añjanakhaḷa 209, 229, 231–2, 234, 241, 245
Tiruvanmaṇḍūr 282
Tiruvāṟṟuvāy 189, 231
Tiruvāṟṟuvāy Copper Plates 170
Tiruvārūr Mummaṇikkōvai 231
Tiruvaṭūr 281
Tiruviḷaṅguḍi plates 116
Tiruvoṟṟiyūr 224
tithi 173
Titus Vespasian 240
Tīya 263
Tīyam āḻvān 190, 203
Tōlan 233, 247
Toṇḍamānāḍ 71
Toṇḍaimaṇḍalam 66, 111

trade 3, 14, 25, 28, 30, 34–5, 37, 41, 51–3, 55–6, 58, 65, 81–2, 95, 115, 141, 169, 178, 198–9, 206, 211, 216, 227, 236, 241–4, 254, 255, 257, 258, 273, 275, 308 *see also* maritime trade
transition debate 8, 298
Trautmann, Thomas 167
Travancore 70, 151–3, 157, 163, 166, 176, 179, 219, 249, 262, 267–9, 274–5
Travancore Archaeological Series/ TAS 55–7, 80, 82, 107, 144, 146, 151–2, 154, 163–6, 172, 178–81, 219, 221–6, 245–7, 272–3, 290–1, 293, 309–10
tribes/tribal 3, 7, 45, 65, 76, 95, 251
  areas 6, 63, 115
  chiefs/society/institutions 6, 42, 44, 60, 63, 217
  peasantation of- 14
  semi-tribal groups 36
Trichur/Tṛśśūr 217, 229, 243
Tripurāntaka 74–5, 81
Trivikrama 291
Tṛkkaṇḍiyūr temple 263
Tṛkkaṭittānam 201
Tṛkkulaśēkharapuram temple 209, 229, 234
Tṛkkunnappoḻa 201
Tuhfat-ul-Mujahidin 267
tuḻilāḷgaḷ 14, 321
Tuḷu(s)/Tuḷuva(s)/Tuḷu country/ Tuḷunāḍ 47, 59, 135, 144, 171, 195, 197, 224, 261, 272, 284, 298, 301, 309
Tuḷu Brāhmaṇas 270
Tuñcattu Rāmānujan Eḻuttaccan 133

uḍaiyān/uḍaiyār 41, 43, 67, 88, 102, 107, 121, 328
Uḍaiyār (Śrī) Rājarājadēvar 44, 71, 74
Uḍan Cenṟa Paḍai Vīrar 43
Udayāditya *Mahāsāmanta* 319
Udayādityarasa 318
Udayampērūr 266
Udayavarmacaritam 141
Udayēndiram plates 80
Uddaṇḍa 239
Ulloor S. Parameswara Iyer 152, 163, 223, 307, 309
ulpatti/utpatti 287, 293
ūḷvari 119
Umparkāṭu 188
Unni, N.P. 223, 246, 307, 310
Unnikrishnan Nair, P. 182
ūr(s) 24, 31–2, 34, 54, 77, 86, 118, 121, 145, 200–1, 214, 254, 278–9, 288, 328–9
ūrāḷar 155, 200–1, 278–82
ūrār 31, 155, 200, 254, 278–9, 282
Uṟaiyūr 113
Uṟaiyūr Iḷamponvāṇikanār 25
urbanization 34–5, 51–3, 55, 58, 81, 207
urban
  areas/centres/enclaves 26, 28, 30, 37, 203, 206–7, 215–17, 244, 247, 254–5, 302
  agglomeration/complex 207
  corporations 170, 199, 203, 215
  decay 2, 13
  growth 13
  guilds 199
  -ism 14, 187, 206–7, 213
  networks 37
  population 204
ūr-irukkai 31
ūr-kiḻavan 327
ūrkūṭṭam 279
ūr-nattam 31
ūroḍeya 327, 329
ūroḍeya-gāvuḍa 327
ūrōm 31, 116
ūr-uḍaiyān 327
uṭampāṭu 200
Uttama Cōḻa 101
Uttamaśōḷa Seṭṭi 318
Uttaramērūr 54, 93

Vaḍa-Ciṟuvayil-nāḍu 116
Vaigai 59
Vaikkam 281
Vaiṣṇava/Vaiṣṇavism 56, 58, 62, 66, 81, 193, 225, 233–4, 243, 297, 303
vaiśya(s) 35–6, 56, 94
Valabhapaṭṭaṇam/Valapattanam 261
vaḷanāḍu 110–11
valaṅgai/right-hand caste 43, 56
Vāḻappaḷḷi 189, 231
Vāḻappaḷḷi Copper Plates 169–70, 174–5, 205, 208, 252
vāḻkkai 77
Vallabha 59
Vaḷḷuvanāḍu 111, 196–8
Vāmana 233
vaṇik/vaṇij 25, 178
vaṇikan/vāṇiyar 25, 178, 241
van Leur, C.J. 275
Vaññēri/Vanjeri granthavari 182, 287, 293
Vaññippuḻa 290
Vaṉṟalaiccēri-Kōtai-Iravi 279
varakkal 35
vari 77
varikaṇakku 177
varippottagam 101–2, 177
varippottagakkaṇakku 101
vāriyam 33
variyilār 102
variyilārkaṇakku 118
variyil-iḍu 101–2
varman 192
varṇa 93–4
varnāśrama(dharma) 6, 36–7, 64, 68–9, 72, 137, 211, 251, 257, 301 *see also* ideology
Vasco da Gama 249, 264, 270
vassus/vassallus 322
Vāsu Bhaṭṭatiri 139, 145
Vaṭakkan Pāṭṭukaḷ/Northern Ballads 268
Vātāpi 70
Vaṭṭeḻuttu 147, 171–2, 180, 208
Vayanad/Wynad 169, 178, 207
Vēdabrāhmaṇa 284
Vēdas 33
Vedic 5, 29, 51, 79
culture/elements 51, 53, 79, 306, 311
ideas/ideology 29, 62 *see also* ideology
institutions/organizations 159, 224
literature/genres 29, 131
religion/Hindu religion 5, 62–3
sacrifices 5, 29, 62, 299
-*śāstraic-purāṇic* ideas/religion 29, 51, 62, 79
vēḷ(s) 27, 38, 98
vēḷaikkārar 43, 321
vēḷān 41, 88, 116, 329
veḷe 316–19
veḷevāḷi 14, 43, 58, 166, 315–20, 323
veḷevaḍicas 43, 316–17, 320–1
vēli (s) 31
vēḷīr 27
veḷḷāḷa 36, 90, 92–4, 116
veḷḷāmai 90
veḷḷānvagai villages 30–2, 110, 116, 175
Velu Pillai, T.K. 158
Veluthat, Kesavan 52, 54–5, 57–8, 60, 79–82, 97–9, 107, 124–5, 142–6, 166, 179, 181, 220–3, 225–6, 228, 246–8, 271–5, 290–4, 308–10, 324, 331
Vēḷvikuḍi plates 45, 59, 70, 80
Vēṇāḍ/Vēṇāḍu/Vēṇāṭu 35, 111, 161, 163, 190, 195–8, 206, 223, 258, 260, 274, 276, 303
Vēṅkaṭam 48, 66, 298
Venkayya, V. 122
Veṇpolināṭu 77, 198, 201
Vēntan 24
vēntar 27
Ventris, Michael 147
Venugopalan, T.R. 220, 274, 308
veppu/veppōlakkaraṇam 287–8
veṭṭāpēṟu 34, 91, 115

veṭṭi 91, 103–4, 210, 256
Vidhi 71
Vienna papyrus 241
Vijayālaya 66, 73, 104
Vijayanagara 5, 162, 167, 176, 268, 289
Vijayarāga(dēva)/Jayarāga 158, 199, 222, 246
Vikki Aṇṇan 40
Vikramāditya Varaguṇa 180, 310
vila 286
Vilakkilimaṅgalam 290–1
Villārvaṭṭam svarūpam 241
Villavar Kōn 180
vimāna 73
Vīra Ballāḷa 319
Vīradēva 317
Viraikkuḍi 116
Vīra Rāghava Copper Plates/ paṭṭayam 152, 154, 165, 196, 242
Vīrarājēndra 69, 90, 120
Vīra Sōmēśvaradēva 330
virutti 87
Viṣṇu 5, 36, 69–71, 137, 211, 257, 301, 319
viṣṭi *see veṭṭi*
Viṭanidrābhāṇam 241
viṭupēṟu 285
Voltaire 322
Vyāḻam 173
Vyaṅgyavyākhyā 194, 223, 233, 246–7, 297, 307, 310
vyavasthā 174, 281

War of Veṭṭam Succession 262
Western Ghats 11, 186, 296
Whiteway 271
Whittaker, Dick 248
Wilden, Eva 225
Winkworth, C.P.T. 273
Wolf, Eric 92
Wyatt, J.L. 163

Yadava, B.N.S. 46, 221
yamaka kāvya 145
Yavana 241

Zacharia, Scaria 144–6, 246–7, 275, 292
Zainuddin Makhdum, Shaikh 267
Zamorin 135, 140–1, 146, 153, 164, 176, 182, 206, 219, 258, 260–3, 268, 272, 274, 304
Zaphar 150
Zvelebil, Kamil 23, 52

റെഡ് ചില്ലീസ്
red chillies

മോനിഷ്
Mone
MONISH